The French Melting Pot

MW01053557

Contradictions of Modernity

The modern era has been uniquely productive of theory. Some theory claimed uniformity despite human differences or unilinear progress in the face of catastrophic changes. Other theory was informed more deeply by the complexities of history and recognition of cultural specificity. This series seeks to further the latter approach by publishing books that explore the problems of theorizing the modern in its manifold and sometimes contradictory forms and that examine the specific locations of theory within the modern.

Edited by Craig Calhoun
University of North Carolina at Chapel Hill

Volume 5 Gérard Noiriel, *The French Melting Pot: Immigration, Citizenship, and National Identity*

Volume 4 John C. Torpey, *Intellectuals, Socialism, and Dissent: The East German Opposition and Its Legacy*

Volume 3 T. M. S. Evens, *Two Kinds of Rationality: Kibbutz Democracy and Generational Conflict*

Volume 2 Micheline R. Ishay, *Internationalism and Its Betrayal*

Volume 1 Johan Heilbron, *The Rise of Social Theory*

The French Melting Pot

Immigration, Citizenship, and National Identity

Gérard Noiriel

Translated by Geoffroy de Laforcade
Foreword by Charles Tilly

Contradictions of Modernity, Volume 5

University of Minnesota Press
Minneapolis
London

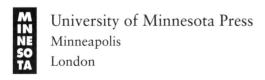

The University of Minnesota Press gratefully acknowledges financial assistance provided for the translation of this book by the French Ministry of Culture.

Copyright 1996 by the Regents of the University of Minnesota

Originally published as *Le creuset français: Historie de l'immigration xixe–xxe siècles.* Copyright Editions du Seuil, Paris, 1988

All rights reserved. No part of this publication may be reproduced, stored in a retrieval system, or transmitted, in any form or by any means, electronic, mechanical, photocopying, recording, or otherwise, without the prior written permission of the publisher.

Published by the University of Minnesota Press
111 Third Avenue South, Suite 290, Minneapolis, MN 55401-2520
Printed in the United States of America on acid-free paper

Library of Congress Cataloging-in-Publication Data

Noiriel, Gérard.
[Creuset français. English]
The French melting pot : immigration, citizenship, and national identity / Gérard Noiriel ; translated by Geoffroy de Laforcade ; foreword by Charles Tilly.
p. cm. — (Contradictions of modernity ; v. 5)
Includes bibliographical references and index.
ISBN 0-8166-2419-4 (hc). — ISBN 0-8166-2420-8 (pb)
1. France—Emigration and immigration—History—19th century.
2. France—Emigration and immigration—History—20th century.
I. Title. II. Series.
JV7924.N6513 1996
325.44'09—dc20 95-52323

The University of Minnesota is an equal-opportunity educator and employer.

Contents

Foreword

Charles Tilly

Any discussion of immigration's history has political overtones. What are they to become, these newcomers: vanishing visitors, victims, villains, or viable citizens? Gérard Noiriel's history of French immigration shows how much the choice among these characterizations depends on the current politics of nationality rather than on the actual social origins or behavior of immigrants. A country whose fertility began to decline very early, France has depended on immigration for the bulk of its population increase since the nineteenth century. It has served as Europe's greatest melting pot, with Poles, Italians, Belgians, Spaniards, and North Africans arriving by the millions. Yet intellectuals and public officials have zigzagged between two contradictory positions on immigration: on the one hand, denying that France had any particular problem with immigrants; on the other, decrying the latest streams of immigrants as threats to the country's unity and viability. Through historical foreshortening, they have constructed a fable of primordial, continuous Frenchness disrupted only occasionally by external invasions.

Noiriel will have none of that. First and foremost, he seeks to put France's public discussion of immigration into historical perspective. In original, reflective, fully documented chapters he analyzes French discussions of immigration history, the legal history of immigration and naturalization, characteristics of French immigrants, their social experience, and the place of immigration in modern French history as a whole. In chapter after chapter we see him patiently disassembling mythologies, carefully reconstructing the story so that, at last, his readers will understand the centrality of immigrants and immigration in French life—public and private—since 1800. In his pages we see a sure-handed, clear-eyed social historian at work. We learn the value of well-executed historical research in understanding not only the past but also the present and the future.

Along the way, Noiriel repeatedly compares French and U.S. immigration and how they have been discussed. Although both the United States and France have fed hungrily on immigration, he points out, the two countries have discussed it in very different terms. While the French have typically either assumed that foreigners would rapidly and unobtrusively join the French nation or objected that the latest arrivals were unassimilable and therefore threatening, Americans have conducted a long, long debate over the relative merits of assimilation and ethnic pluralism. Although the legal systems of both countries have emphasized jus soli—the principle that birthplace and commitment override origins as bases of nationality—Americans have divided more sharply over the extent to which the survival of old-world cultures contributes to effective public life. Preservation of ethnic, racial, and religious diversity has attracted many more advocates in the United States than in France.

As a consequence, the United States has produced a much more ample written history and sociology of immigration than has France.[1] Writing the history of one's own family or group as a way of finding roots and cultivating self-esteem has been a common American practice for a century or so. What is more, discussions of immigration and ethnic–racial divisions figure repeatedly in analyses of American urban, labor, social, and political histories; consider, for example, the many replies to Werner Sombart's misleading but compelling turn-of-the-century question, "Why is there no socialism in America?" (The question is misleading because such nineteenth-century labor movements as the Knights of Labor certainly had a radical, roughly socialist edge. It is compelling because, despite a turbulent history of strikes, rebellions, and labor violence, the United States never produced a mass labor party in the style of Continental Europe or of other English-speaking democracies.) In confronting immigration and its consequences, Americans immediately find themselves asking to what degree "different" also means "separate and unequal." Different versions of the rags-to-riches story inform both critical and self-congratulatory analyses of opportunity in the United States, past and present; to hear strong political overtones, one needs search no farther than the next comparison among blacks, Jews, Hispanics, and recent Asian immigrants.

For a century or so, U.S. historians, sociologists, and social critics have been producing detailed accounts of immigrant experience; Noiriel points out how much more voluminous and varied is that U.S. literature than its French counterpart, and how much more central to public discussion. From Jacob Riis to Daniel Patrick Moynihan, students of immigrant life have used their observations to dramatize arguments about U.S. life as a whole. The greater prominence of immigration in U.S. social criticism probably springs from three roots: (1) the politicization of ethnic, racial, and religious differences in nineteenth-century nativism, urban ward politics, and government actions such as the internment of Japanese-Americans during the Second World War; (2) the salience of racial division during and after the Civil War; (3) the incessant U.S. concern with inequality, its origins, and its consequences.

Noiriel admires and envies the abundance of U.S. writing on immigration, borrowing from U.S. models when he can, but he also performs a service for Americans. In his book, students and critics of U.S. social life will find an exemplary synthesis of historical integrity with political concern. The next time a politician or intellectual complains that recent immigrants pose a threat to the American way of life because they differ so much from the old, Noiriel will be at hand to document the eternal return of that complaint, to expose its usual grounding in political ideology rather than in the cool historical examination of immigration's complexities, and to remind Americans that current discussions of immigration and inequality can benefit enormously from careful examination of the past.

Preface to the English-Language Edition

In a pocket-size reedition of his book on the history of madness, Michel Foucault wrote that a preface was a "declaration of tyranny," "the initial act by which the monarchy of the author settles in" (Foucault 1972, 10). I regard it, instead, as a key element in the necessary explanation by which an author establishes a dialogue with readers.[1] The exercise is even more necessary when a book is published in translation and, therefore, intended for an altogether different readership. Even in cases where the issues they discuss are in some sense universal, most books in the humanities are heavily influenced by the national context in which they were written. This preface reviews the conditions in France, where the book was developed. In addition, on the basis of research I have carried out since, I will discuss the emergence of a new field of historical research, to which this book initially contributed: the "sociohistory of the political."[2] Finally, I end with some suggestions for the development of research comparing France and the United States.

The Immigration Question in France during the 1980s

During the 1980s, the far right—which had virtually disappeared from the French political scene following the Second World War—witnessed a spectacular rise in its electoral following; today, the National Front and its leader, Jean-Marie Le Pen, regularly attract over 10% of the vote. The movement owes its success at least partly to its advocacy of a xenophobic platform that blames immigrants for all of the problems facing French society. More fundamentally, however, as Simone Bonnafous (1991) argued in her dissertation, the National Front owes its success to the fact that many of its spokespersons were able to bring public opinion around to a new way of thinking about immigration. Whereas in the 1970s organizations that defended immigrants' interests developed an aggressive discourse centered on issues of labor, housing, and so forth, in the 1980s they were put on the defensive. Before long, the view that immigrants represented a threat to "national identity," originally launched by the far right, was held by large sectors of the public. While it is true that a vast majority of politicians firmly objected to the xenophobic or racist remarks expressed by the National Front, a kind of consensus eventually settled in, even among such noteworthy historians as Fernand Braudel, that because of their origins (African) and their religion (Muslim), immigrants from North African countries posed specific problems of integration. In this perspective, many commentators began drawing upon historical arguments to prove that the country was confronted with a radically new problem and that French traditions and culture were on the line.

My purpose in writing a book on the history of immigration in France was not to intervene directly in the public controversy but, rather, by setting the historical record straight, to confront these efforts to manipulate the past. I wanted to show that the indifference displayed by French historians on this issue had encouraged nationalist propaganda by fostering a genuine phenomenon of collective amnesia about the extraordinary role played by immigration in the renewal of the French population during the twentieth century. Since the original publication of my book, this point has been widely confirmed by various demographic studies. If not for the influx of immigrants over the past century, the overall population of France would stand at 45 million rather than at 58 million. Approximately 20% of persons born in France have at least one immigrant parent or grandparent. If we add in great-grandparents and the foreign population born outside French territory, we reach a total of nearly one-third of the overall population (see INED 1991), which makes France one of the foremost countries of immigration in the twentieth century. I sought to explain why immigration had taken on such great importance in the recent history of France, analyzed the factors that had contributed to historians' silence on the subject, and examined the republican forms of integration through which these newcomers had become part of the French nation. I did not, however, seek to criticize or rehabilitate multiculturalism or Jacobin centralism; nor did I specifically assess the "success" or "failure" of policies of integration.[3] My reluctance to enter directly into the political debate reflected a desire to preserve the autonomy of what Marc Bloch called the "historians' trade." I, too, believe that while the historian has an obligation to address the political issues of the time, he or she should refrain from developing a "habit of judgment" and keep an analytical distance from the passions provoked by current events (Bloch 1953).[4]

To understand my insistence on this point, one must keep in mind the intellectual climate in France in the mid-1980s. The crisis of the labor movement disenchanted progressive historians. Many became aware that their refusal to distinguish between scholarly reflection and militant statements had sometimes blinded them to the horrors of Stalinism, since they had been unable to take into account those aspects of reality that contradicted the cause they believed they were defending. With this failure in mind, a different relationship between intellectuals and politics was suggested.[5] According to this perspective, the search for truth must be disconnected from political concerns because knowledge of the social world is in itself a potential instrument of political liberation for the oppressed, since the elucidation of the mechanisms through which dominant groups (most notably intellectuals, the principal agents of symbolic domination) assert their power is never in the interest of those groups. Hence my insistence on the stakes involved in the representation of immigration by French historiography for more than a century.

The state of historical research in France in the 1980s is also relevant to understanding the conditions in which this book was written. The issue of immigration, a topic of heated political controversy, was at the time completely marginal in French historical writing. I suggested a number of explanations, especially in chapter 1, for historians' silence on such a key dimension of modern French history. Written in the midst of preparations for the commemoration of the bicentennial of the French Revolution, the book could not fail to mention the role played by historians under the Third Republic in elaborating the collective memory and foundational myths of the period, from which immigrants were by definition excluded.[6] More fundamentally, however, it appeared that these gaps in research were linked to the way in which academic fields were institutionally divided up in the late nineteenth century. A great division formed between the social sciences and juridical–political studies, a process that would in later decades arise in the field of history itself, in the opposition between social and political history. On an epistemological level, this split was a major obstacle to the development of a true history of immigration, given that the immigration issue could only be understood by combining these two areas of study.

Immigration, Citizenship, and National Identity: Problems of Definition

Given the small number of existing historical works on the subject, I chose, rather than to present a necessarily incomplete history of immigration, to delimit the contours of this new area of historical research. Drawing from a vast body of existing literature on migration in general, I set out to define the characteristic elements of what has become known, over the past two centuries, as "immigration."[7] My perspective was thematic rather than chronological, with each of the six chapters devoted to an issue I considered essential. Starting from the widely accepted hypothesis that immigration was closely related to industrialization and the construction of the nation-state, I argued that in the French case, the precociousness and scale of immigration did not simply result from the development of sparsely populated regions (as was the case in such "new" countries as the United States, Canada, and Australia) but was, first and foremost, an outcome of the needs of the labor market. In the middle of the nineteenth century, French large industry could no longer rely on a sufficient flow of labor from the countryside. French peasants, unlike those in other European markets, were able to resist the process of uprooting and proletarianization that accompanied the industrial revolution, for both economic reasons (a majority of French peasants owned their own lands) and political reasons (from 1848 onward, they enjoyed the right to vote and represented the largest electoral constituency in the country). As a result, relying massively on immigration seemed an ideal strategy for supplying the labor market, since it allowed the recruitment of a labor force itself deprived of the economic and political means of escaping proletarianization. In the French case, therefore, immigration developed as a direct consequence of citizenship, as the other side of the republican coin, so to speak.

The importance attributed here to the relationship among immigration, citizenship, and nationality requires that I define what I mean by each of these terms. The majority of social scientists today, following Benedict Anderson's famous book, regard the nation as an "imagined community." Very often, however, this expression is subjected to an idealist interpretation that betrays the author's point. As often happens in the social sciences, most readers seem to have paid greater attention to the book's title than to its content. In the introduction, Anderson wrote that "in fact, all communities larger than primordial villages of face to face contact (and perhaps even these) are imagined." Furthermore, it is the "style in which they are imagined" that makes it possible to distinguish between the national community and other communities (Anderson 1992, 6).

Anderson convincingly argues that national collective representations are special in that they are shared by individuals who, for the most part, do not know one another. He dedicates important passages of his book to the study of instruments of communication (such as printing, publishing, administrative technologies) without which people living far apart would never have come to share those representations. The notion of "imagined communities" makes sense only if it is understood that the collective representations that structure national identity require a preexisting "communicational infrastructure."[8] The key contribution of Benedict Anderson's book is, in this respect, to have shown that national collective representations result from a process of *communication at a distance;* whereas in traditional "imagined communities," collective representations were determined exclusively by face-to-face relations. This does not in itself, however, explain how communication at a distance can generate *specifically national* representations. From the very onset of capitalism, publishing, newspapers, and other means of communication developed on a scale that was not circumscribed by the physical space of emerging "nations." It may even be argued that until the nineteenth century, these instruments of communication at a distance conveyed a system of representations that emanated from another important "imagined community" in European history—one that for a long time challenged national representations: Christianity. National representations eventually prevailed precisely because they were constructed and peddled by the leaders of emerging nation-states.

As Ernest Gellner has argued, these representations are national insofar as their implementation and control are in the hands of the state, which exerts power over a space that coincides with the limits of national territory and therefore affects the population living within those boundaries. (Gellner 1983). While my perspective is in some ways similar to Gellner's, it differs on one crucial point: According to Gellner, the state intervenes in nation formation essentially by destroying traditional oral cultures through industrialization and replacing them with a centralized, written culture spread thoughout the national territory mainly by the school system. This analysis places too much emphasis on cultural factors. Gellner, like Anderson, believes that the bond that unites members of a national community resides in collective representations; the state is seen essentially as the agent that creates and spreads national images and symbols.

The main problem with this approach is that it does not help us truly understand the relationship between citizenship and national identity. Limiting the study of the nation to problems of representation blinds us to the fact that members of a shared national community are united by an objective, material bond. In the modern world, all members of a given nation depend on a single state authority. The legal bond known as *nationality* (in the German sense of *Staatsangehörigkeit,* or the act of belonging to the state) is in fact an extremely restricting institutional relation, codified by law and made concrete in identification documents (the passport). Historically, the application of citizenship principles explains why such a legal bond gradually became so important. Ever since Rousseau's *Social Contract,* citizenship has been defined as the ability of an individual member of a given national community to partake—albeit indirectly—in the elaboration of laws that he or she must then obey. By virtue of this principle, all members of the same national community are bound together, whether they like it or not, since a decision taken by some of them necessarily involves the rest. Whether they realize it or not, they consequently have a great number of interests in common, whether those interests be economic (since their incomes fluctuate according to the exchange rate of their national currency), professional (since in most countries today, only nationals are entitled to work without prior administrative authorization), or related to individual freedom (since only nationals can freely cross the borders of the state to which they belong). As we will see throughout this book, the establishment of this community of interests was crucial to the triumph of collective representations of the French nation, as well as to their extension to all sectors of society.

I should specify, to avoid any misunderstanding, that the term "state" is employed here as the equivalent of the concept "*étatisation*" (becoming *of* the state) proposed by Michel Foucault (Foucault 1982).[9] Indeed, from the perspective of a sociohistory of the political, the state should by no means be confused with the government; it is not a "character" that makes decisions and exerts repression but, rather, a series of social practices that are organized around two processes: the "legalization" and "bureaucratization" of social relations, which are closely intertwined with the establishment of citizenship. On a heuristic level, to analyze the state as a *process* is a means of surpassing the fruitless polemics between those who emphasize structures and those who prefer to see only interactions. The gradual extension of institutionalized social practices—which, I argue, were the essential vehicle for the "coalescing as nations" of European societies from the nineteenth century onward—was the outcome of a multitude of everyday interactions and conflicts among individuals of all social groups. Rather than as an "imagined community," then, it is preferable to define the nation as a *politically sovereign institutionalized community.*[10]

The study of the French Revolution shows that the national bond emerged gradually as a practical solution to the problems of promoting "citizenship." The Constitution adopted in 1791 defined, for the first time, the juridical meaning of the word "citizen" by listing a series of criteria (place of birth, sex, age, level of property) that, within the national territory, identified individuals eligible to call themselves French. It was an abstract definition elaborated by a small group of individuals (the "representatives of the people"), but it affected people throughout the country. For such a definition to become effective sociologically, citizen-individuals had to be identified by name, age, and so on. Since the community formed by these citizens was made up of millions of people spread over a vast territory, the techniques of identification employed by face-to-face communities were inadequate; agents of the state routinely needed to identify individuals whom they did not know directly; hence the need to resort to written documents, the quintessential instrument of communication at a distance. At the time of the 1791 Constitution, however, only the Catholic church held registers through which individuals could be identified. Since priests were mostly interested in identifying members of their own religious community, many of these registers failed to note Jews and Protestants. As a result, putting into practice the notion of citizenship required transferring the control of parochial registers to the state. This is what was at stake when the government established civil status on 20 September 1792 by decree. From that moment on, an individual could only exist as a citizen once his or her identity had been registered by the municipal authorities, according to regulations that were the same throughout the national territory. This is why the government (by a law dated 11 Germinal, Year XI) imposed upon all individuals the obligation to use a single given surname, establishing rules for its use and transmission.[11] Citizenship became possible only through the irruption of the state into individuals' daily lives. It is impossible, as a result, to continue separating the state and civil society, as if they were two distinct entities. On the one hand, given that citizens control the state via their representatives, society is present in the state; on the other hand, the state directly contributes to the making of personal identities by codifying the main elements that define them. The outcome of this dialectical process was that the national bond began to establish itself from the Revolution onward.[12]

The second crucial stage in the emergence of the national bond was the advent of the Third Republic in the late nineteenth century, which saw the quantitative and qualitative improvement of individual rights, not only at a political level but also, and especially, on a social level. Indeed, it is during this period that, under pressure from the labor movement, laws were enacted that transformed the different professional groups into categories of entitled beneficiaries (for example, laws relating to work accidents, weekly holidays, and retirement pensions). This vast juridical–bureaucratic enterprise, which consisted of defining and identifying groups, represented a key moment in the formation of what are usually termed "social classes"[13] and in the institutionalization of migratory phenomena. The social legislation adopted at that time was an essential component of the protectionist policy implemented in response to the economic crisis of the years 1880–1890. For example, foreigners were only authorized to hold a given job if that job could not be performed by a French worker, and so foreigners were no longer, as they had been before, allowed to enter the country freely. Furthermore, most republican social legislation included discriminatory clauses against foreigners. Since women and children, who were not considered citizens, benefited as French nationals from these laws, the new measures led to an increasingly pronounced differentiation between citizenship and nationality, which is one of the main reasons behind the adoption of the 1889 law on French nationality.[14] Given the proliferation of categories created by the new legislation, primitive forms of identification founded on civil status registers were no longer sufficient; hence the importance of the "revolution in identity"[15] that occurred during this period. Thanks to the invention of identification papers that made the juridical bond between citizens and the state concrete, representatives of the administration could rely on instruments that allowed them to act efficiently from a distance. From that time onward, "immigrant" became a specific category within the foreign population, which could, for example, be differentiated from the category "tourist" because the immigrant had obtained a residency permit allowing him or her to practice a trade on French territory. In this way, it became possible for the government to channel migratory flows toward those sectors of industry that suffered from the greatest labor market deficit. Immigration had become both complementary and antithetical to citizenship.

It is from this perspective that I approached the controversial question of the integration and assimilation of immigrants into French society. Sociology teaches us that the integration of an individual into a given group can be measured though the study of his or her participation in the various activities of that group. From this perspective, studying the *integration* of immigrants into the national community presents no particular difficulty. The historian need only evaluate how immigrant populations compare with nationals in terms of income, occupation, and so forth. The question of *assimilation*, however, is much more complex. Fundamentally, the question posed is whether immigrants can succeed in integrating into a national society while at the same time preserving their culture of origin. French republicans have consistently replied that this is impossible, arguing that if immigrants are to achieve equality with nationals on the labor market, they need to master the national culture. Discussing this point requires that we agree beforehand on the meaning of the term "national culture." It is a fact that historical and anthropological studies of "national characteristics" have often contributed to forging the stereotypes from which nationalist propaganda draws its inspiration. In order to avoid these pitfalls without circumventing the problem (as did the Marxists), Norbert Elias suggested that we approach national cultures as historical constructs rather than as heritages: national cultures, he suggests, are the result of dominant groups having used the wheels of the state to extend their own norms to all classes within society (see, in particular, Elias 1991). In this process, France, of course, represents an extreme case. Given the precociousness and the power of the central state, regional languages and cultures lost ground to the cultural norms of the aristocratic and bourgeois elite, norms that had been assembled from the seventeenth century onward within the court society of Versailles. This national culture, consolidated by the Republic, was then transmitted by the school system and major organs of information and, in a more diffuse manner, through norms of conduct (such as figures of speech and table manners), eating habits, and so forth. While this well-known argument seems to me to be generally relevant, its problem is, as Peter Sahlins noted, that it defined national identity as a linear process that begins with the center to reach the base (Sahlins 1989). If we accept that widely dispersed individuals within a national community only communicate among themselves indirectly, this transmission of norms can only result from a series of mediations. In order to be efficient, any form of communication at a distance among those individuals located at the center and those located at the periphery must be made concrete in interactions, that is, in direct, face-to-face relationships.[16] National norms are diffused only when they are appropriated by individuals. In order to achieve this, the resources available to individuals are provided by their local and regional context and related to gender, trade, and so forth. That is why although the French as a group are familiar with the French language, how one speaks that language varies according to whether one is a man or a woman, a worker or a member of the bourgeoisie, a resident of Alsace or of Provence. This is the point I wish to underscore in my approach to the national assimilation of immigrants. Contrary to what is commonly believed, even in France the nation-state did not assimilate individuals of immigrant origin. On the contrary, it is they who assimilated national norms. Social psychology has shown that the personality of an individual is forged in the initial stages of life through the interiorization, most often unconscious, of the norms that prevail in the environment. The children of immigrants are no exception. It may even be that the tendency of the host society to discredit their culture of origin has often accentuated their desire to conform to the national model. Again, in the case of language, the importance of local mediations is clearly apparent in the fact that the children of immigrants speak French in Marseilles with a Provençal accent, and in Strasbourg with an Alsatian accent.

Perspectives for Comparative Research on Immigration History in France and the United States

In my work on French immigration, I often refer to the rich and abundant literature published since the beginning of the century on immigration history in the United States. In doing so, my purpose has not been to undertake a truly comparative historical study of the question[17]—my knowledge of the history of the United States is insufficient—but, rather, to identify certain points of reference. Nonetheless, I would like to speak briefly on the potential value of the perspective outlined here for a comparative approach to the history of immigration.

Many authors, such as William Safran, have contrasted the French model, in which the state is thought to have exerted control over social society, with the U.S. model, in which, in contrast, civil society is perceived as having obstructed the development of the state (Safran 1989). In France, and more generally in Europe, public services undeniably play a more important role in social life than they do in the United States. The problem with this presentation, however, is that it tends to accredit the idea that society and the state are two distinct entities and therefore conceals the process of the *étatisation* of modern society, which was described earlier for France and which also characterizes the United States as a democratic society, even if there are substantial differences between the historical forms taken by *étatisation* in the two countries. This explains why, despite the array of political contrasts that distinguish these two societies, the historical process of the assimilation of immigrants presents many similarities. Let us take, for example, the question of language, a key element in the construction of a collective culture and identity. I have argued elsewhere that, after three generations, the proportion of descendants of immigrants who still speak their language of origin is no greater in the United States than it is in France. In a recent book, Alejandro Portes and Rubén G. Rumbaut underscored that "in the United States, the acquisition of non-accented English and the dropping of foreign languages represent the ultimate test of Americanization," and today still, the children of immigrants prefer to learn English rather than use their language of origin (Portes and Rumbaut 1990, 180f.). The essential difference between France and the United States does not lie in the importance of the phenomenon itself—the proportion of people of recent immigrant origin (over three generations) is roughly comparable—but in how we understand it (on this point see Horowitz 1992). For a long time in France, immigrants were absent from the collective memory, whereas in the United States they were omnipresent (overshadowing African-Americans and Native Americans). In both cases, however, this opposition is related to the way that nation's foundational myths were forged and promoted by the state. In the United States, immigrants were from the outset agents of national construction, whereas in France, they arrived massively after national unity had been achieved. Yet the contrast in collective representations of immigration can also be explained by the different forms taken by the institutionalization of social identities. The example of statistical nomenclatures is a case in point. In France, the republican refusal to consider ethnicity a legitimate component of public life produced a system of classification centered around socioprofessional categories and the juridical criteria for nationality. In the United States, on the other hand, racial, ethnic, and religious criteria played key roles from the beginning in the elaboration of censuses. As I have tried to demonstrate, administrative categories contributed to the forging of individual and collective identities, in other words, to the perception that individuals and groups had of themselves and of others. To classify people, as is done in California, as "non-Hispanic whites," "Hispanics," "blacks," and "Asians" would be considered racist in France, evidence of discrimination among French citizens; to Americans it seems natural.[18] These contrasts in the forms taken by the institutionalization of collective identities created different opportunities for political participation, since immigrants could only mobilize those resources available to them in the context in which they found themselves. This is why, although the stigmatization of immigrant communities is a historical reality in both countries, in France, immigrants responded by mobilizing the resources available to them through their position in the workforce. Their massive involvement in the French labor movement and in the struggle against fascism was an essential factor of their integration into French society. In the United States, in contrast, "the reaffirmation of old distinct cultural identities—whether actual or invented in the United States—has been the rule among foreign groups and has represented the first effective step in their social and political incorporation" (Portes and Rumbaut 1990, 140–41).

Rather than polemicizing to determine whether the American model is more or less democratic than the French one, I think that scholars should regard these models as historical expressions of the institutionalization of social groups that privileged different aspects of collective identity (socioprofessional in one case, ethnic in the other). It is clear that in France, administrative centralization and the extraordinary power of the bureaucracy played a key role in the social and cultural unification of the nation. In the United States, federalism and the preeminence of judges over state functionaries, as well as the late unification of the country and its sheer vastness, worked in favor of diversity. Yet these statements must be qualified for two reasons. First, there are also powerful assimilating mechanisms at work in the United States, albeit in a form different from those in France. The role of the Supreme Court and of major trials, which receive abundant media coverage, is effective in spreading national norms throughout the United States. Conversely, and contrary to what most Americans believe, the French Republic did not seek to eliminate ethnic cultures. The 1901 law on associations provided a legal framework through which communities may celebrate and enrich their culture of origin. What the Republic prohibited was the *politicization* of communities. The defense of cultures of origin could, therefore, not be allowed to constitute a legitimate demand, an object of public controversy. Thus, in France, it was not possible for immigrants to collectively oppose efforts to discredit their culture of origin. But the fact that in the United States over the past century immigrant communities have been constantly obliged to renew their struggle against the stigmatization of being immigrants proves that, despite the politicization of ethnicity, they have not been able to reverse the hierarchy of cultural norms. One of the essential reasons for this failure can be found, I believe, in the process of institutionalization that these communities were not able to avoid. Immigrants began by regrouping locally, forming communities that were bound together by direct links of familiarity but isolated from one another. With the unification of the national territory, the development of the state, and the centralization of political life, in order to obtain recognition of their rights and to defend them, members of these ethnic communities were obliged to expand on a much larger basis. Their members were hence confronted with the problem of communication at a distance that I discussed earlier. They had to designate their representatives and enter into a juridical–bureaucratic process of categorization and identification without which they would not be able to defend their rights. It is in this way, in part, that immigrants came to assimilate the norms prevailing in U.S. society, whether linguistic or any other. Given the rapid decline of the elements that had characterized their culture of origin, the defense of ethnic origins became a largely symbolic means of asserting one's membership in a group capable of defending the interests of its members.

With the very serious crisis affecting the labor movement in France today, the least advantaged groups are left practically without any collective means of defending their interests, and at the same time their situation is constantly deteriorating.[19]

What scholars once referred to as "the social question," that is, inquiry into the sources of social conflict, is rapidly becoming a vast process of administrative management of "social problems" that are recognized as such only if the mass media becomes interested in them.[20] Under these conditions, the resources available in the United States, the community-based forms of mobilization, may represent the last resort for dispossessed people of all sorts throughout the modern world. It should be kept in mind, however, that the politicization of ethnicity, unlike the politicization of socioprofessional groups, is part of a logic that ultimately leads to claims of national independence, for minority norms can only become legitimate and dominant if they are defended or implemented by a state.

Introduction

The writing of history has become a pawn in contemporary French controversies regarding "foreigners." Those who insist that the current situation is "new," "preoccupying," or "distressing" refer to the past to prove their point. While they concede that France has long been a country of immigration, they believe that the integration of foreigners has always been, until now, smooth and painless. Some argue that immigrants in the 1960s were "distributed" throughout the nation, whereas today they are concentrated in "ghettos." Others claim that earlier immigrants came from countries with greater "cultural affinities" to France or that current difficulties are linked to a "crisis of citizenship." Immigrants, once haunted by the desire to become assimilated, now think in terms of cultivating their "difference."

The history of immigration is also used to justify another perspective, which does not necessarily contradict the first: the vision of a country "enriched" by diverse migratory inputs, which President François Mitterrand once evoked before an audience at the Sorbonne[1] and which has become a widespread leitmotiv of "good conscience" on the subject. In this perspective, immigration is seen as "one of the keys of our economic and social history" (Gaspard and Servan-Schreiber 1985, 192), as a "crucial aspect of French industrial and social history" (Le Bras 1986, 192).

In all this tumult, the only voice that remains to be heard is that of historians. Neither from schoolbooks, from standard histories of

France, nor from scholarly works can one draw much relevant material to support an argument on the contribution of immigrants to contemporary French society. Given this context, the researcher seeking to exercise the "historian's trade" (to use Marc Bloch's term) may choose between two options. The first is to ignore these controversies altogether, on the grounds that scholars have no place responding to the pressure of current events. The second is to enter into the debate, in the name of civic responsibility, with the goal of "reestablishing the truth" on gas chambers, the Manouchian affair, racism, and so on.

These are two perfectly legitimate conceptions of the scholar's professional obligation. In this book, I have chosen to explore a third approach: one that does not neglect the burning issues of the present but, rather, claims the right to approach them in a new way; in short, one that defends the autonomy of scholarly analysis. My plea is, therefore, that immigration be regarded once and for all as an issue worthy of historical research, by those who neglect it as well as by those who refer to it lightly. As we will see, over the past century the study of immigration has constantly been subordinated to political concerns and polemics, which have obstructed its emergence as a specific historical object and which have resulted in the marginalization of this area of scholarship. In the shared effort to shake free of these constraints, the retrospective insight of historians can help overcome a narrowly conjunctural perspective; by underscoring the recurrence of phenomena, it reveals laws or patterns that enable us to decipher what is genuinely "new" in the current context. The purpose of this book is not to negate the specificity of a given national or "ethnic"[2] community settled in France, nor is it to underestimate the particularities of each historical conjuncture. My goal is to break with a logic of research that has governed immigration studies until the present and that concentrates on specific cases without analyzing the larger picture. For instance, while the "Jewish problem," the "North African problem," and the "refugee problem" have been isolated, no one has ever sought to understand how each of these examples could help forge a specific object of inquiry called "immigration."

In this endeavor, history can also be used as a tool of criticism. As Lucien Febvre taught us, to study the history of words is to question the most self-evident aspects of everyday life. Perhaps more than any other, the "reality" of immigration is indeed a question of words. An immigrant is above all, to paraphrase Jean-Paul Sartre, someone whom others regard as an immigrant. What this shows is that scientific rigor is neither a gratuitous game nor a form of fetishism. What discourse tends to dissimulate is the very power exerted by the intellectual. As a young North African man once bitterly observed, "to say *immigrant* is to designate someone without honor, who is lost, who has nothing left."[3] The problem is not to state whether we are "for" or "against" foreigners but, rather, to determine why scholars feel authorized to employ terms that cause foreigners to suffer and, hence, contribute to their existence as "immigrants." History, conceived as an effort to "denaturalize" language, analyzes why and how the term emerged in our vocabulary, before its appropriation by the instruments of analysis of contemporary society (above all statistics) and establishment as a "self-evident fact" of everyday controversy. Moreover, what historical inquiry proves is that the issue of vocabulary is even more important for the study of second-generation immigrants. According to a century-old pattern that we will have to explain, we are now experiencing a renewal in the concern for genealogy and for "origins." It is not, as some claim, a question that affects only second-generation North African immigrants (or *Beurs*). History shows that when the criteria defining "immigration" are transferred from the juridical to the cultural or "ethnic" realm, the question of origins becomes a fundamental problem, one that has profoundly affected French political life since the late nineteenth century and that has harmed many people.

I have dwelled on the dilemmas facing research on immigration in order to clarify the intentions of this book. Indeed, an estimated one-third of the population currently living in France is of "foreign" descent.[4] But although I consider this to be empirically important, it is not my intention to rehabilitate a sense of roots, to unveil origins, or to exalt the "plural identity" of France; nor have I attempted to flatter the universalism of the ideology of "human rights." This type of discussion is as superficial as it is recurrent; it is of no interest to me whatsoever. Individuals are free to represent their past in any way they wish, to display or to hide their "ethnic," national, or socioeconomic origins. *Collectively,* however, to take seriously the diversity of the current French population involves *a change in outlook* on the recent past. Immigration can no longer be considered an issue that affects us from without; it must be understood as a problem that is *internal* to the history of contemporary French society. Indeed, to illustrate its problematic, this book could very well have been entitled *Immigrants into Frenchmen.*[5]

Such an approach sheds new light on an array of problems that traditional historiography has neglected. Anthropologists have taught us that in order to give meaning to their lives, all individuals, regardless of the social formation to which they belong, aspire to fit into a coherent narrative of the past, even if it is more or less mythical; they need to belong to a lineage, to be part of a genealogy. In contemporary society, whether we like it or not, historians contribute to the writing of this "novel of origins." As Fernand Braudel wrote in his last book: "To define the French past is to locate the French within their own existence" (Braudel 1988–1990). Beyond simply stating the "truth," to explain contemporary France's indebtedness to immigration is, therefore, to provide millions of inhabitants of this country with the *possibility* of legitimately locating their personal history, or that of their family, within the "master narrative" of French national history. What makes immigration such an important dimension of recent history, however, is that it raises epistemological questions of greater relevance to contemporary France. It is not the immigrants themselves who are particularly interesting but, rather, the *explanatory principles* that must be mobilized if we are to address the unanswered questions of French republican history: what is the relationship of real individuals to institutions (state, party, nation)? What is the role of uprootedness in the formation and the consolidation of a society? How can the issue of "origins" and "feelings of belonging" be incorporated into the so-called history of mentalities? How are criteria of class, nationality, and gender combined in the definition of individuals and of the groups to which they belong?

This book is also intended as a contribution to the current debate on the "crisis" and the "renewal" of history (Roche 1986; Dosse 1987). While such discussions are often quite rich, they nonetheless tend to separate epistemological thought from empirical research, a problem that is not unique to historians. From a heuristic point of view, I find it more useful to articulate theoretical analysis and concrete investigation. Only in this way can it be shown that the "reality" we seek to understand raises fundamental questions for historical scholarship.

In its own way, this study is a tribute to the memory of Fernand Braudel. In his last book, Braudel spoke of the need to "reconcile" history and sociology in a unitary approach to social science. He also insisted again on a point that he had defended all his life: that history should help us understand the present; knowledge of the world of the dead should help the living find their way. The painful thing about this book, however, is that to reach this goal I had to gradually renounce the Braudelian enchantments of my student years and criticize the very foundations of the theoretical edifice he left, because the direction in which it took me was, I realized, misleading.

One

The Denial of Memory

Omission and historical error are central to creating a nation; hence the advancement of historical knowledge is often a threat to nationhood. Ernest Renan, 1882

I hold that we are as much the disciples of those whom we contradict as of those whose words we repeat. Paul Lacombe, 1894

The ability of a field of scholarship to reflect upon itself is an essential factor in its enrichment; why, then, until recently, has historical investigation in France remained blind to immigrant history? By emphasizing, in a rarely cited passage from his famous conference at the Sorbonne, the relationship between memory and history and between history and the nation, Ernest Renan paved the way for an analysis of the mechanisms through which the problematic, concepts, and focus of republican history obstructed the emergence of immigration as an object of scientific inquiry. My goal in this book is not to "unmask the lacuna" or "reveal the shortcomings" of the historiography but, instead, to establish the key epistemological problem facing the social sciences in general. My purpose is to illustrate the pertinence of Michel de Certeau's statement that the scholar's vision always unfolds from a given standpoint, which "by virtue of conjunctures and of shared problematics, makes certain research strategies possible while invalidating others" (de Certeau 1974, 15).

An Illegitimate Object

An index of research in progress, established in 1977, listed 310 projects on the topic of immigration (such as dissertations or Centre National de la Recherche Scientifique [CNRS] or Direction Générale de la Recherche Scientifique et Technique [DGRST] working papers), of which only six were directed by historians or associated with their accredited institutions (departments, laboratories). More recently, a Centre National de Documentation Pédagogique (CNDP) listing of the dissertations on immigration, drawn from the records of the National Library, reflects both the underrepresentation of history and the evolution of fields of interest over a period of twenty years.[1] Whereas a mere fifteen titles addressed the issue between the early 1950s and the mid-1960s, the total grew to eighty during the following decade. The evolution has since then been virtually exponential: Nearly three hundred doctorates have been awarded in ten years.

As we will see, in this, as in many other aspects, the 1950s simply continued an earlier trend that had established the supremacy of legal studies in matters of immigration. We are no longer, to be sure, in the same situation as that of the turn of the century or that of the interwar years, when nearly all doctoral dissertations produced in France were written by jurists; nonetheless, nearly half of the titles indexed between 1951 and 1965 still carried such signatures. The field of sociology made a massive incursion into immigration studies between 1966 and 1974 (accounting for roughly 40% of the output), followed closely, in the recent period, by psychology.[2]

These figures clearly illustrate the modest role played by history in the development of postwar scholarship on the subject. The total number of history dissertations is almost too insignificant for the two first periods under consideration to be counted. Although there was some improvement between 1975 and 1985 (ten out of three hundred titles), the overall output remained marginal at best.

The volume of recent publications on the subject of immigration can be measured by consulting Marianne, the database of contemporary history (whose name itself suggests a nationalist historiographical bias). On the basis of key words covering the main aspects of immigration research for the period between 1979 and 1985, the computer found a total of about fifty references: two books, a few dissertations and mimeographed reports, articles published in one journal of national repute (*Vingtième Siècle*) and one major university journal (*Revue du Nord*); the rest appearing in local journals, foreign publications, or nonhistorical journals. In comparison, an inquiry on ironmasters produced, by itself, a listing of several hundred documents.

It might be argued that immigration appears, here and there, throughout historical writing on other topics. For example, French scholars have often had to consider immigrants when studying workers in dissertations on regional history (Lequin 1977; Noiriel 1982). Others have approached the question from the standpoint of political history, under the influence of Pierre Renouvin or Jean-Baptiste Duroselle (Milza 1981; Schor 1985; Ponty 1985). All of this simply confirms, however, that immigration has yet to be truly apprehended for itself, as a specific object of historical research.

This tendency is even more pronounced in the case of more widely read historical texts. If they do not overlook the subject entirely (Chaunu 1982), the numerous "histories of France" published in recent years dedicate only a few sentences or paragraphs to the issue. These authors hold the demographic question in much higher regard. Invariably, the "explanation" given for immigration is that it helped "solve" the population deficit following the hecatomb of the First World War (Duby 1972).

Immigrants do not fare much better in the sixty-six essays of Pierre Nora's *Les Lieux de mémoire* devoted to the "places of memory" of the Republic and the nation. This is not surprising, given that for the editor, "among the novelties of the country's present-day situation is the presence of a large immigrant population, which does not display the customary traits of 'Frenchness' [*francité*]" (Nora 1984–1986, 3:651).

The absence of immigration is even more remarkable in studies of local or regional history. One comes across written histories of Roubaix in which not the slightest mention is made of the Belgian population, which made up an absolute majority of the population at the onset of the Third Republic (Toulemonde 1966). And in Provence, a mecca of immigration if there ever was one, local historians treat the subject as if it had played a negligible role (Baratier 1969). In the twenty years between 1950 and 1970, the university journal *Provence Historique* produced a grand total of four pages on immigration! My own earlier research on the Lorraine region revealed a similar pattern (Noiriel 1984).

School textbooks display an even greater degree of collective amnesia. Although immigration is entirely absent from some eleventh-grade manuals, most of them summarize it in a few sentences such as this passage from a textbook published by Hachette in 1982: "Demographic stagnation generated an attitude of withdrawal, particularly among foreigners, most of them from Italy, Poland, Belgium, and Spain, who made up 6% [*sic*] of the population. The growing number of political refugees provoked xenophobic reactions. . . . Such attitudes were clearly unjustified, given that from 1935 onward, immigration was the only source of population growth; and that even in areas where unemployment was high, foreigners were called in to perform certain jobs which the French were unwilling to perform." One can hardly accuse the textbooks of contradicting the scholarly literature, which, by and large, discusses the exact same themes. Vulgarization reproduces, in a simplified form, the mainstream historical argument that fails to include immigrants as part of the nation, recognizing only their right to work "in our country" and to perform the unpleasant tasks scorned by nationals.

The contrast between the existing French historiography and that of another great land of modern immigration, the United States, is striking. From the interwar years onward, immigration occupied a crucial position in U.S. scholarship (Brun 1980). In 1959, Oscar Handlin even received the Pulitzer Prize for the sum of his work on the subject (see, in particular, Handlin 1959). Other distinguished historians, such as John Higham, president of the American Historical Association in 1974, owe a good deal of their intellectual reputation to their works on immigration (Higham 1975). The abundance of textbooks on immigration history, and of well-illustrated works such as Handlin's "pictorial history," is an unmistakable sign of a solid research tradition in this domain. Each page of Handlin's work is illustrated by a "place of memory," ranging from the Statue of Liberty to the immigration museum on Ellis Island, and includes portraits of famous Americans with Italian, Polish, Jewish, or other backgrounds (Handlin 1972). Beyond its recognition by U.S. historiography, what stands out for the French reader is the willingness to present the immigration process as a formative aspect of U.S. society and history, as a full-fledged component of the nation; whereas French textbooks argue the opposite: that immigration is an "external" (transitional, new, or marginal) problem, which is unrelated to the historical formation of France and which has nothing to do with the "French" or with their past.

The argument often put forth to explain this contrast—that immigration was, by its sheer volume, a crucial aspect of U.S. history but only a secondary phenomenon in France—does not withstand analysis. In fact, we must be careful not to confuse "ethnicity" with "immigration." While from the perspective of its racial composition, France is indeed different from the United States, the same cannot be said of immigration (understood as a temporary or definitive "displacement" of part of the population from one country to another).

In contrast to the unitary myth of France, U.S. mythology has always tended to inflate the role of immigration in the history of the United States. Even at the height of the flow of immigrants, Jeanine Brun noted that "the population of recent immigrants never exceeded 15% of the total population" (Brun 1980, 19). It should also be kept in mind that in the United States, migratory flows have always been more accurately monitored than in France; in the United States, until the Second World War immigration remained an essentially transoceanic and therefore transient phenomenon, which necessarily came through ports. The permeability of French borders, on the other hand, has always favored a high degree of illegal immigration, which blurred the statistics. The essential point, however, is that immigration to the United States steadily declined in the early 1920s following the promulgation of restrictive laws; whereas in France, the phenomenon became important essentially from that period onward. In 1930, France was the country with the highest rate of foreign population growth in the world (515 per 100,000 inhabitants, compared with 492 in the United States). At the end of the 1960s, France was again among the leading industrialized countries in terms of the size of its immigrant population. Contrary to what is usually believed, over the past half-century the economic, social, and political importance of the immigration issue has been greater in France than in the United States. From a genealogical perspective, the living memory of the "immigrant experience" over a span of three generations (from children to grandparents) is greater today among the French than among Americans. As the *Wall Street Journal* indicated several years ago, the U.S. economy currently suffers from its low immigration rate in comparison with countries like Canada, Australia, or France (7% of the population in the United States is of foreign origin, compared with 20%

in Australia, 16% in Canada, and 11% in France). "The nation," noted the columnist, "could use the rejuvenation which the émigrés, who contribute more to the host nation than they take from it, bring with them."[3] Where the statistics supporting these comparisons were taken is unclear, however, and given that statistical categories differ in the two countries, the argument should be taken with a grain of salt. If the U.S. administrative category "foreign-born" is compared with an equivalent notion in France,[4] one sees that in 1970, less than 5% of the population had recent foreign origins, compared with 12–14% in France according to the 1975 census figures. The discrepancy is particularly illustrative of the far greater role played by first-generation immigrants in France than in the United States. However, other figures indicate that by 1970, the role of the second generation was, proportionally, of equal importance in both countries: 11.8% of Americans born in the United States had one or two parents of foreign origin (U.S. Bureau of the Census 1975). The same year, according to the survey conducted by Alain Girard (1971), nearly 10% of French citizens were in that situation.[5] Therefore, until more specific studies are conducted, we can say that over a span of three generations, the impact of immigration is today at least as important in France as in the United States.

The Nation and the Historian: A Question of Influence

The contrast between French and U.S. historiography is attributable to the history of national formation in the two countries. All Americans, even Native Americans, can consider themselves immigrants. In this new country, still largely unoccupied at the end of the eighteenth century, the nation was conceived from the outset as a process of "merging" different migratory waves into a "melting pot" from which would emerge the U.S. citizen, a synthesis of all the qualities of the world. In France, the same fascination with origins explains the invisibility of immigration in historiography. The "dean of nations" was already largely formed and its foundational myths (above all, the French Revolution) already established when mass immigration began. We will return, in the final chapter, to the role of these initial conditions in defining the conflicting migratory models enshrined by the United States and France. The important thing to underscore here is the discrepancy in the timing of the two models. In the U.S. case, immigration was an early phenomenon and the formation of the nation occurred much later. In the French case, the opposite is true: The "national" phenomenon has a long history, whereas immigration is fairly recent. This chronological contrast has numerous consequences. Some of them stem from the role played by historians (or the role that some would have them play) in those contemporary nations where the commemoration of origins is an essential element of strategies of political consensus. In the United States, the legitimation of Anglo-Saxon domination over other social groups is achieved through the constant reminder of their prolonged presence in the land. Later waves of immigrants position themselves with respect to this "precedence" of "White Anglo-Saxon Protestant" settlement. The social role played by historians in the invention of a mythology of origins is accentuated by the fact that the prestige (and often the interests) of each community depends on its ability to demonstrate the "precedence" of its origins. This may well explain, in part, why historians of Scandinavian origin have been so influential in the historiography of immigration.

In the French case, the consolidation of the foundational myth was structured around the continued resurgence of debates about the French Revolution (Furet 1981). It is clear, from a brief survey of doctoral dissertations awarded in history since the end of the nineteenth century, that this question mobilized a substantial portion of collective research efforts, at the expense of other areas of scholarship. This explains in part why the historiography of immigration has been so poor in France; it is an issue that remains incomprehensible, virtually without raison d'être, from the perspective of the polemic between French scholars on the origins and legitimacy of the Republic. This imbalance is also a reflection of French historians' relationship to politics, a much closer relationship than in other countries. There is a tendency to respond to demands emanating from outside academia and to take for granted that politically important problems are necessarily just as important for scholarship. This is undoubtedly why Renan was not understood when he stated that "to avoid distortion, we would do well to exempt science from giving its opinion regarding questions in which so many interests are at stake.... She has better things to do: Let us ask of her simply the truth" (Renan 1992).

The chronological difference mentioned earlier had many other consequences for the interpretation of society by French historians. The institutions of the French nation (language, administration, and so on) were established long before the Revolution, at a time when

France was more affected by emigration than by immigration. The Revolution and the Empire reinforced the process of centralization and unification, particularly with respect to language. That is why traces of yesterday's France are so widespread in the country we know today. A historical approach focused on the search for traces and material clues, therefore, has much to choose from: monuments, urban architecture, rural archaeology, and toponymy all testify to France's ancient past; and within the "French school" of historical research, such a methodology has always attracted enthusiasts. These very signs of the old, however, tend to conceal the new, as is evidenced by each page of Fernand Braudel's last book (1988–1990). Given the rigidity of preexisting structures, the millions of immigrants who transformed the composition of the French population had considerable difficulty leaving their own visible trace or forging their own "places of memory." Whereas in the United States, Ellis Island—through which millions of European immigrants passed—has become a museum, comparable symbols of immigration in France (such as the selection center in Toul, which recruited the bulk of Central European immigrants between the wars) were razed to the ground, as if a history that fit in so poorly with the mythology of the soil could be magically erased.

Traces of the past are not only to be found in places. Archives, the "memory of the state," and more generally all the tools with which historians construct their research, also carry their indelible marks. Consider, for example, the official statistics produced by the Statistique Générale de France (SGF) and, later, the Institut National de la Statistique et des Etudes Economiques (INSEE). As we will see in this book, they played a considerable role in the development of research on immigration and have had a lasting effect on the way immigrants are perceived, thereby influencing paradigms as well as policies.

When the first attempts to measure the foreign presence in France were made in the mid-nineteenth century, the categories of official taxonomy were already well established. The natural sciences, political economy, and grammar had served as models since the seventeenth century, producing clear and logical definitions, as well as sharp divisions, that laid the groundwork for social classification at the onset.[6] The "French spirit" also influenced legal definitions from the beginning. With the Constituent Assembly, legal thought established a clear distinction between the "national" and the "foreigner," and the Civil Code was a model of legal rationality. The long-standing trend toward centralization effectively undermined "ethnic" communities of origin and facilitated the emergence of a relatively homogeneous "civil status." The revolutionary upheaval discredited not only the old order but everything that harked back to origins, so much so that the first decrees abolishing nobility were also directed against names that evoked people's origins: "An elegant name is still a form of privilege; its credit must be destroyed" (quoted in Sudre 1903, 12). The abolition of corporations was also followed by a series of measures against brands, which under the ancien régime had served as mandatory trademarks. These measures were, of course, soon abandoned, but they nonetheless left their mark on the French legal system (the Civil Code, for example, prohibits the search for paternity).[7]

These are some of the aspects of French history prior to immigration that must be considered to understand the logic of French statistics. Legal definitions were sufficiently interiorized by the middle of the century that the sole criterion invoked to distinguish the French from the foreign was nationality.[8] Just as there is no heading to specifically designate "worker-peasants" in the classification of professions (despite their prominence in the population at the time), the same Cartesian logic excluded mixed categories to designate foreigners (such as "second-generation"). Moreover, language, religion, and "race" were discarded as criteria for classification.

The contrast with U.S. nomenclatures is striking. The continued existence of slavery well into the nineteenth century and the presence of different races on the same soil caused census officials to adopt primarily "ethnic" modes of classification from the eighteenth century onward. Although information regarding faiths later disappeared from general censuses, questions on the language spoken and parents' nationality were maintained. Historians of immigration therefore have access to very detailed statistical data regarding the annual number of immigrants admitted into the United States, by country of origin (U.S. Bureau of the Census 1986). There are also entire volumes of purely historical data, drawn from decennial censuses, which make it possible to count the number of U.S. citizens with one or several foreign parents or grandparents, based on their nationality of origin (U.S. Bureau of the Census 1975). In recent years, as a consequence of the "ethnic renewal," the government has undertaken the classification of individuals according to the nationality of their ancestors (British, French, German, and so on); with, for each group, information regarding such factors as age categories, demographic and professional profiles, and income levels (U.S. Bureau of the Census 1983). In addition, polls have been conducted since 1978 by the National Opinion Research Center in Chicago to determine the memories that Americans have of their ancestral origins, and the results of such surveys have informed the conclusions drawn by history books (Archdeacon 1983). It is clear that through the creation of different statistical frameworks, France and the United States developed entirely different visions of society, of their history and "identity."

Origins and Contract

In comparison to its counterpart in the United States, French historical research on immigration was marred by still another major handicap: the complete lack of interest displayed by social scientists until the 1960s. Sources that might have compensated for the gaps in official records, such as sociological studies, were virtually nonexistent until the Second World War.

To fully understand this point, we must return to the nineteenth century, when a thorough revamp of the university system gave academic disciplines the institutional foundations they had until then lacked. Renan's famous 1882 conference at the Sorbonne, entitled *Qu'est-ce qu'une nation?* (What is a nation?), is a key document for understanding the relationship of French scholars to the national question over the past century. In a hundred pages, Renan summed up the entire range of opinions that could be expressed in 1880 without violating republican legitimacy. Some of Renan's arguments later provided the basis for a genuine national consensus. Against the German position (in the context of the controversy over Alsace-Lorraine), the author argued that to confuse the concepts of race and nation would be deeply mistaken. France being a "Celtic, Iberic, Germanic" country, there could be no pure French race; only a French people (*peuple*), the descendants of a variety of "ethnic" backgrounds that had mixed well before the French Revolution. Discussions of race were necessarily endless, Renan argued, because they brought fundamentally different definitions into play. Whereas a zoologist would define race in terms of "blood," the concept "as we historians understand it, is something which is made and unmade," since human groups are eminently historical subjects. Renan, following in the footsteps of Fustel de Coulanges, preferred the French definition based on "lived" history (shared memories) and mutual consent to the German emphasis on "ethnic" heredity and "dead" history (that is, language). The ambiguities of the French definition, however, explain why it has been the object of so many conflicting interpretations.

Renan distinguished between two contradictory dimensions of the nation. On the one hand, a nation is a "soul," "the outcome, just like an individual, of a protracted history of efforts, sacrifice, and devotion"; "our ancestors," he concluded, "determined who we are." On the other hand, the nation is "a spiritual principle," the "clearly expressed desire to continue living together." And he added: "The existence of a nation (*if you will excuse the metaphor*)[9] is an everyday plebiscite, just as the individual's existence is a perpetual assertion of life"; the nation has no right, then, to assert: "you belong to me, I take you."

These two statements are a good example of how a chain of oppositions can be constructed between past and present, between history and law (or sociology), origin and contract, right and left.

Without going into the political controversies provoked by Renan's argument, it is safe to say that in France, the intellectual debate on the national question (and therefore on immigration) has constantly been caught up in a paradigm structured by the opposition between contract and origin. Having already discussed the direct role played by historians in this debate, I now turn to the analysis of how it affected the social sciences in general.

The Man of the New Social Contract: Emile Durkheim, Founder of the French School of Sociology

Recent studies have underscored the role that Emile Durkheim played in the renewal of republican thought in the late nineteenth century, in particular his contribution to the full expression of the solidarity school and to the legal theories of Léon Duguit (Nicolet 1982). More telling for our purposes, Durkheim endorsed Renan's view that scholars had no place meddling in questions of immediate political relevance. This explains why, at the height of a virulent controversy over "foreigners" in parliament and despite endless debates on the definition of immigration or the impact of the Dreyfus affair, Durkheim and his fellow contributors to *L'Année Sociologique* found it unnecessary to intervene in the name of science. Here again, the contrast with the U.S. situation is striking. The Chicago school, which marked the birth of North American scientific sociology, was preoccupied from the beginning with questions of immigration (including the Jewish question). Until the interwar period, the leading representatives of this school—including Park, Burgess, Wirth—developed research agendas with more or less assimilationist goals, at a time when the daily life of immigrants was made very difficult by a policy of ethnic quotas and by nativist xenophobia. Moreover, Franz Boas, a renowned anthropologist, agreed to participate in a survey on the morphology of foreigners and morphological changes in the second generation, commissioned by an anti-immigrant senatorial committee. The overall findings filled some forty volumes (on criminality, the urban question, and so on) in which the mainstream preconceptions of the time were amply illustrated. The study performed by Boas himself, however, debunked a series of racist arguments, in particular with respect to cranial indicators (on which there were also "experts" in France). He showed, for example, that second-generation anthropometrical measurements of the Jewish population were similar to the Anglo-Saxon "norm," and that the "fusion" was even more pronounced for third-generation immigrants.[10] In a similar vein, an extraordinary five-volume study of "Polish peasants" was published in 1918 by W. I. Thomas and F. Znanieki. The authors, by collecting a wide range of documents (several thousand letters written by immigrants), by putting together very complete "life stories," by drawing from history and from comparisons between the host country and the countries of origin, inaugurated scientific research on the issue of immigration, and most of the studies published in France to this day fall short of its quality (Thomas and Znaniecki 1958).

For historians, these surveys are in and of themselves a valuable source of information; they are still unequaled in France, where the reluctance to intervene in these controversial questions extended beyond the recognition, during the First World War, of the importance of immigration in French society. In this sense, the work of Maurice Halbwachs, who was perhaps the scholar most attentive to the fieldwork of Durkheimian sociologists and who wrote his thesis on the working class, is quite significant. Halbwachs chose to study the "ethnic experience" in Chicago. He produced a detailed analysis based on U.S. statistics, which combined data on the first and second generations with national criteria (for Italians) and religious or "ethnic" criteria (for Jews). It never occurred to him, however, that, as a member of a sociological school that advocated the virtues of comparativism, he might have something to learn from these statistical categories themselves. It is somewhat surprising that Halbwachs attributed the appearance of the Chicago school to the specificity of the immigrant experience in Chicago itself (Halbwachs 1932). At the time, there were as many immigrants in France as there are today, and, while it was perhaps never quite like Chicago, Marseilles, with its Jewish, Italian, Armenian, North African, and Spanish communities (a significant portion of the total population, particularly when origins are taken into account), was also a laboratory of "ethnicity" in the 1930s. What was missing, then, was the sociologist, not the object.

Halbwachs's analyses of the French population, published several years later in a volume of the *Grande Encyclopédie* edited by Lucien Febvre (1935), are of the same stamp. Whereas another chapter entitled "France: A Country of Immigration" described the impact of immigration on French economic life, society, and politics, Halbwachs simply commented on statistics on the evolution of the foreign population and its distribution by nationality, placing the entire question within the context of the demographic consequences of the Great War; yet these figures, however insufficient, could easily have been explored for their relevance to larger issues. While he did call for the improvement of statistical records, it was not to gain a better sense of the foreign population in general but, rather, to apprehend such "collective subjects" as the Flemish and Britons in the name of the survival of the "ethnic personality" of French regions (*pays*), an idea reminiscent of those of Paul Vidal de La Blache and André Siegfried.

The work of Marcel Mauss, Durkheim's nephew and the founder of French scientific anthropology, can be analyzed in a similar light. In a 1927 essay on the new tasks of sociology, Mauss argued that it was appropriate for scholars to intervene in discussions on current events, thereby lending governments a hand by providing them with the insights of science. While he expressed his admiration for the Chicago school and for Edith Abbot's studies on immigration, he nonetheless placed these works within the context of American exceptionalism: "The field of sociology must contribute to the study of the serious and compelling contemporary problems of immigration *in America,* and of emigration *elsewhere*" (Mauss 1969b).

I will not dwell on the reasons that have been invoked to explain the Durkheimian school's reservations about fieldwork; they are related to the "theoretical tradition" of French academia (sociology had to define "noble," "elevated" objects of research in order to be accepted as a legitimate academic field; the task of conducting surveys was left to the staff of the Labor Bureau); to the way that sociological elites were trained (the Ecole Normale Supérieure and the philosophy *agrégation* did not predispose scholars to encounters with immigrants); and to the lack of human and material resources compared with the United States (see, in particular, Karady 1982; Joas 1984).

An additional explanation is required, however, to fully understand the discretion of scientific sociology on these matters. As Vincent Berdoulay (1981) has argued, a majority of the original Durkheimian sociologists were of urban Jewish origin. Despite (and perhaps because of) the fact that it is never directly addressed in Durkheim's work, the question of "origins" probably never ceased to intrigue him, and later Mauss and Halbwachs. Their refusal to take up the issue of immigration in its fullest dimension is perhaps also linked to the revival of the question of "identity" caused by the upsurge of anti-Semitism. If, as Jean-Claude Chamboredon has argued, Durkheim's sociology can also be seen as "a meditation on the correct ways of being an assimilated Jew in contemporary France" (Chamboredon 1984), then his work is not that far from the preoccupations of Jewish intellectuals of German origin, such as Georg Simmel or Louis Wirth, who were more explicit in their approach to the key issues of loyalty to the group of origin, the "marginality" inherent in the status of "foreigner."[11]

To understand the Durkheimian contribution on this subject, it must be analyzed in context. As we will see, the Dreyfus affair was not only a question of anti-Semitism. From the 1880s onward, the legal principles born of the French Revolution were challenged on an extraordinary scale. As a result of the countless bills directed against foreigners that were brought before the parliament, the question of origins became commonplace in French thought. The very year in which Durkheim's *Division of Labor in Society* (1893) was published in France, a law was passed requiring foreigners to prove their identity.

The first Nationality Code, promulgated four years earlier, had introduced partial legal restrictions on naturalized citizens of immigrant origin. Against this backdrop, anti-Semitism, aimed above all against foreign or "foreign-looking" Jews, was on the rise. Alsatian Jews who had fled that region following its annexation by Germany, as well as the massive numbers of Jews who had fled the pogroms in Russia, were ideal victims. As Michel Winock (1982) has shown, Drumont's best-selling book *La France juive,* published in 1886, was grounded in studies by Taine and Renan on the incompatibility of Aryan and Semitic races. Such vulgarizaton reinforced stereotypes on heredity and on the determinism of ethnic origins.

Durkheim's problem (as the son of an Alsatian rabbi) was clearly not to refute Drumont but, rather, to refute the authors who had inspired him. At that time, most of the country's major thinkers, whether on the left or on the right, shared these "ethnic" preoccupations in their French version. This, I would argue, is why *The Division of Labor in Society* should be seen as the most radical critique ever written of the thesis of rootedness in the land (*enracinement*). For Durkheim, the topics most often emphasized by his adversaries—the family, "ethnic group," local environment, worship of ancestors, and heredity—belonged to the past, to the era of "mechanical solidarity," when individuals were subordinated to groups and therefore deprived of true freedom. The modern world, he argued, had witnessed the triumph of organic solidarity. Progress in transportation and greater human mobility had gradually eroded the social function of attachment to the land. Values and knowledge were no longer transmitted directly by the family or through genealogy, from one generation to another, but *indirectly,* the past having become crystallized in the present through the materiality of monuments, of the rules of law, and so on; hence the role of institutions (above all, of schools) in transmitting to "untamed" children (that is, children deprived of heredity) the culture of the society in which they were born. Durkheim also believed that the steady growth of the state bureaucracy accentuated the "uprooting" of individuals from the arenas of mechanical solidarity. Not even the family, as evidenced by the extension of domestic law, was spared by this evolution. Individuals, thoroughly cut off from their origins, increasingly found themselves at the center of a web of threads linking them to the new social structure. They were defined according to their role within a given nation rather than by "blood relations"; hence the need to invent new forms of identification with new intermediary groups, that is, with trade organizations (Durkheim 1933, 1951).

In the final chapter, I will argue that Durkheim's analyses, seemingly hopeless given their isolation in the 1890s, remain quite relevant today as a means of approaching the question of immigration; in contrast, the arguments used against him at the time are no longer credible.

The other major academic field in which the *dominant* tendency is still loyalty to the social contract perspective is law, if only by respect for the fundamental principles of the Constitution inspired by the ideals of 1789.[12] As we will see in chapter 2, however, this has not prevented jurisprudence from becoming increasingly hostile to immigrants.

The "Shameful" Origins of the History of Immigration in France

Until the 1950s, there was little change in the position of the fields of law and sociology with respect to immigration. The tenacious denial by sociologists (we will return to law in chapter 2) can be explained by the ongoing character of the intellectual confrontation that caused it in the first place.[13] Indeed, the position defended by advocates of the social contract is incomprehensible unless it is seen in the context of a permanent confrontation with the "lobby of origins," a group who also claimed to be influenced by Renan and who emphasized notions of race and heredity but in a historical rather than a zoological sense. Maurice Barrès, quoting Jules Soury, gave the best definition of this idea:

> What we represent is nothing more than substantial continuity, the living expression of thought and speech, with its array of gestures, habits, and hereditary reactions through which *the dead uphold the living*; and these specific ethnic and national traits that differentiate the French of France from foreigners, born of age-old variations, are not metaphors at all, but phenomena as real as the matrix of anatomical elements in our nervous system. (Quoted in Sternhell 1985; emphasis added)

This notion of "the past within the present" made a strong impact in France, particularly on historians, whom it tended to flatter and who often invoked it in their writings.[14] It also deeply influenced such diverse intellectual paradigms as those associated with, among others,

René Martial — *immigration*
récent

Siegfried, Vidal de La Blache, Gustave Le Bon, Emile Vacher de Lapouge, and Alphonse Bertillon. As we will see, the Durkheimians
themselves attempted to incorporate it into their sociology.

The Barrésian conception's inability to recognize the role of immigration in the making of French history is obvious. Yet for a long
time—and this is the paradox that would stand in the way of the
scientific construction of the object—advocates of the paradigm emphasizing the primacy of inheritance were the only ones to study immigration as a historical process (usually to underscore its dangers
for "the future of the race"). Three main threads, quite distinct from
one another, can be identified as forming this intellectual nebula.

The most marginal of the three, given that it placed itself outside
the problematic of republicanism, was represented by the advocates
of physical anthropology. Lacking a genuine institutional base, the proponents of this tendency were primarily physicians. Its leading figure
(for our purposes) was René Martial, who repeatedly called for a
genuine immigration policy grounded in a new science—anthropology—defined as a combination of history, biology, and psychology;
a concept that met with some success under the Vichy regime.

Demography was the second area, much more important than
the first, that addressed the question of origins. The founders of this
discipline, Alphonse Bertillon and his brother Jacques, defined the
term "immigration." Having practiced medicine and developed an
interest in physical anthropology, they created a "subdiscipline" that
was primarily concerned with "the future of the race" and the preservation of "French blood." They viewed immigration from the perspective of the "distressing problem of the falling birthrate" in France
and regarded the recruitment of foreigners as a last resort that was
not without its dangers. The legal act of naturalization was perceived
as an act of political arbitrariness, which provided foreigners with a
spurious Frenchness (J. Bertillon 1911).

Another subdiscipline within the field of demography was more
closely associated with statistics. Its representatives had often acquired
mathematical competence at the Ecole Polytechnique, which they then
applied to their studies on immigration. Alfred Sauvy is a case in point;
he published the first population studies of people not necessarily of
French "origin," using elaborate calculations to measure "*francisations*" and naturalizations. Alfred Depoid conducted an in-depth survey on the same topic in 1942, for the SGF, which further broadened

falling birth-
rate caused
immigration
in France

the range of nonlegal definitions of the foreigner (or, so to speak, of the not-quite-French Frenchman) (Sauvy 1927; Depoid 1942). While these studies were not immune from "ethnic" bias (the issue of "undesirables" dominated French thought at the time), they were strictly technical exercises that left to others the task of drawing conclusions.

The third component of the "lobby of origins" was represented by the field of geography. Two men—Emile Levasseur and Vidal de La Blache—played a considerable role from the start by establishing connections with statisticians, demographers, anthropologists, and historians. In his studies of the French population, Levasseur directly addressed the issue of immigration. His commentary of the censuses produced by the SGF, which emphasized the influx of foreigners from the Second Empire onward, was often cited, as were his anxieties about the "problem of nonindigenous cores." Vidal de La Blache, on the other hand, provided a framework and a methodology to compensate for the insufficiencies of sociology. For the contemporary historian, no sources are more valuable for the study of immigration than the geographical journals (in particular the *Annales de Géographie,* founded by Vidal, and the *Revue de Géographie Alpine*) and regional dissertations in human geography that adopted Vidal's methodology. The interest in immigration as a "human phenomenon" and the meticulousness of the field research on which these monographs were based explain why geographers necessarily ran into foreigners. Not surprisingly, this line of inquiry produced the first major nonlegal dissertation explicitly devoted to immigration, a work that remains to this day, for many historians, the most important source on the subject. Written by Georges Mauco in 1932, it made abundant use of the data provided by the SGF from the mid-nineteenth century onward. It also, however, produced a wealth of original surveys conducted by the author himself in numerous French cities and firms; these surveys contained detailed descriptions of the role of foreign workers in the labor market, recruitment policies, everyday community life (for Poles in particular), problems of assimilation and coexistence (for example, in mixed marriages, delinquency, schooling), and so on. Ethnic stereotypes that had developed in the nineteenth century were still very evident in Mauco's work. For example, he spoke of Slavic "atavism" and Italian "impulsiveness" and invoked such phrases as the "danger for the race" (Mauco 1932).

Not unlike the present-day situation, the Great Depression provided the "lobby of origins" with a more favorable conjuncture than it had experienced in the 1920s, when economic expansion had focused attention on issues of recruitment and contracts. The stabilization of immigrants increased their visibility; attention turned to "nonproductive" individuals and to children in particular. Aroused by xenophobic fantasies, the problematic of the family—and therefore of genealogy and "assimilation"—was reinforced. This explains why from the 1930s to the 1950s in politics (see chapter 2) as well as in the social sciences, discussions of immigration were dominated by the issue of "assimilation."

In an international conference sponsored by the League of Nations in 1937, Mauco stated that immigration had been completely neglected in France; he suggested a program of study and indicated possible research directions. Two years later, in collaboration with the renowned French geographer Albert Demangeon (which indicates the degree of legitimacy attained by the subject among professionals), he published a major survey of foreigners in agriculture. This work was important because it applied the Vidalian tradition of fieldwork and collective research to the study of immigration, basing itself on data from volunteer informants, most of whom were schoolteachers. Three thousand copies of a questionnaire were circulated and drew a thousand responses, which were the basis of dozens of monographs. After the Second World War, this method was employed by Alain Girard and Jean Stoetzel in their well-known study of foreigners in France commissioned by the Institut National d'Etudes Démographiques (INED) (Mauco and Demangeon 1939; INED 1954).

In a dramatic illustration of Renan's warnings a half-century earlier, the political stakes involved in the "question of origins" reached their highest point under the Vichy government, amid anti-Semitic policies and the persecution of second-generation immigrants in the administration. Although there is no direct link between the two aspects, it was also the Vichy regime that created the Foundation for the Study of Human Problems (know as the Fondation Alexis-Carrel), with a budget of 40 million francs for the first year and a staff of fifty researchers (Drouard 1983). Between 1941 and 1945, the foundation conducted a series of studies related to population issues; INED (its successor in 1945) later published the results of these studies.[15]

Interestingly enough, the profile of researchers that we identified as forming the "lobby of origins" was still well established at this time. The most important studies were written by a physician-anthropologist (Robert Gessain), a demographer (Alfred Sauvy), and a historian-demographer, whom we will discuss later (Louis Chevalier). The "geographical method" adapted to the study of immigration by Mauco was also well represented. The authors relied on a network of "non-professionals," social workers and leaders of associations. As we will see in coming chapters, these studies are a valuable source for historians, whether it be for the study of Polish refugees in the early nineteenth century or of the everyday lives of Russian and Armenian communities in the suburbs of Paris prior to the Second World War.

These studies were closely linked to political concerns that were regarded as crucial to the country's reconstruction after the war. The articles published at the time by Sauvy expressed a willingness to confront two crucial aspects of the question: insuring a policy of recruiting a foreign labor force and encouraging the assimilation of those foreigners who had long been present in France.[16] This second point was in fact consistent, as we shall see, with the explicitly articulated aspirations of the "second generation" that was coming of age (the children of the great wave of immigrants of the 1920s) and that claimed, in return for its involvement in the Resistance, recognition in the form of a genuine policy of assimilation. A large consensus, however, held that, given the existence of more or less well-defined "ethnic differences," all immigrants were not assimilable. In a letter dated June 1945 to the Ministry of Justice, held in the archives of the Haut Comité Consultatif de la Population, Charles de Gaulle himself—then head of the government—advocated a more discriminatory naturalization policy:

> Ethnically speaking, it is advisable to limit the flow of the Mediter ranean and Oriental peoples who have deeply modified the makeup of the French population over the past half-century. Without having to implement, as in the United States, a rigid system of quotas, we might consider lending priority to the naturalization of Nordic peoples (Belgians, Luxembourgers, Swiss, Dutch, British, Germans, etc.). Reserving a percentage of 50% for such elements is one possibility. (Quoted in Beaud 1987)

To implement this unnamed policy of "ethnic quotas" (which illustrates how the official representatives of a self-defined "nation of human rights" viewed the most recent arrivals of immigrants: Italians, Armenians, Poles), the social sciences were solicited. Indeed, the fields that generally applied legal definitions to designate immigrants were considered incapable of resolving these dilemmas. Gessain, for example, believed that the legal terms "Pole" and "Italian," which defined citizenship of a nation, were inadequate to define "ethnic" realities, particularly in the case, for example, of Armenians, Arabs, and Jews; he considered these names vague at best and in need of serious analysis. Two academic fields were summoned to play a key role in this process: anthropology and, above all, history. The first issues of the INED publications contained an elaborate listing of "research in progress" and announced a "program of research" that has yet to produce any results.

To illustrate that this was indeed a turning point and that the history of immigration might at that time have become an established discipline within the social sciences—with a high priest, a journal, and a colloquium (and the ideal pretext for a trip to the United States)—three fundamental articles published immediately after the war, by scholars who are famous among historians for other aspects of their work, deserve particular attention.

The first was written by Abel Châtelain, the author of an authoritative dissertation on temporary migration in nineteenth-century France. In 1946 and 1948, Châtelain published two articles in the journal of the University of Lyons, *Les Etudes Rhodaniennes*. In the first, he emphasized the "demographic and ethnographic revolution" that France had undergone since the beginning of the twentieth century; particularly in the south, where, he argued, the population structure had been completely transformed (in the city of Marseilles in 1936, for example, he estimated the foreign-born population at one-third of the total). Châtelain added that the legal definition of a "foreigner" was totally inadequate to understand the scope of these changes. As a result, he suggested that "legal foreigners" be distinguished from "ethnic foreigners" (that is, "all individuals of foreign origin"). It is to this group that "geographers must turn their almost exclusive attention, considering that they cannot, unlike demographic economists, be satisfied with legal conventions." Châtelain therefore proposed the creation of a new field—"demo-geography"—the only discipline capable of "approaching the truth, of approaching reality." He conceded that this research strategy was riddled with obstacles, for "to ask people if their parents or grandparents were foreigners comes across as indiscreet and disrespectful of established laws" (Châtelain 1946). Two years later, in two reviews of books on the topic of foreigners, the author clarified his program. Criticizing Mauco for his tendency to rely uncritically on demographic data, he outlined a specific methodology for the field of demo-geography: substitution of geographic units for administrative units (the region rather than the department); aspiration to attain "the most thorough definition of foreigners"; and analysis of the social practices of the first and second generations to identify the evolution of behavior and adaptation. These two last points require a large-scale application of genealogy, anthroponymy, and civil status investigations from as far back as the early nineteenth century (Châtelain 1948). If we add the use of computers, which did not yet exist at the time, what we have is the program of "historical demography," a field that would establish itself a few years later; the essential difference between them is that "immigrants" were replaced by "our ancestors," that is, by the peasants of the ancien régime.

Political science is the second area in which a similar process can be observed. French historians are deeply indebted to André Siegfried, in particular to his analyses of regional political "temperament" and his explanations of the continuity of political behavior. Siegfried also published an article on immigration, which everyone has since forgotten, after the war. He argued, from a comparative perspective, that France and the United States had been confronted with the same problem since the turn of the century. Furthermore, he added, immigration "should not be viewed as simply a circumstantial phenomenon. It rates among the great trends of our time, of worldwide importance and historic implications (Siegfried 1946). For Siegfried, only history could reveal the *laws* determining questions of immigration; history, therefore, had to be summoned to help devise the new immigration policy that everyone was demanding.

To conclude this overview, some credit must be given to the historian who probably contributed the most to the legitimacy of historical research on immigration in France, a professor at the Collège de France who is best known for his studies of the Parisian population: Louis Chevalier. *Documents sur l'immigration,* published by INED following the war, contained several articles in which Louis Chevalier outlined his own platform for historical research. First, he observed that the history of assimilation had never been written in France and that the history of foreign communities amounted to a few dispersed studies, often published by learned societies. He briefly suggested two possible methodologies for a history of immigration: one, reaching as far into the past as the ancien régime, would lead up to the present; another, based on genealogy and in the form of case studies, would draw from the present to understand the past. Chevalier concluded:

> These are just some indications of the studies that need to be carried out and how to approach them. Only through such studies will the causes of immigration and its methods, as well as the different phases of assimilation, be understood. It should be emphasized that the central issue is assimilation; and that if existing studies of foreign populations are relatively uninteresting, it is because, rather than focusing on the transformations of mankind in a given environment, they have failed to distance themselves from purely political and economic concerns. (INED 1947)

The convergence with Siegfried's views is clear.

That such positions were voiced is enough to invalidate the claim that scholars never realized the importance of immigration for historical research. Those who had announced the birth of this new history after the war, however, later abruptly branched out into other directions, without ever explaining the reasons for their attitude. Gessain and Mauco went back to psychoanalysis; Chevalier and Châtelain abandoned immigration for the history of twentieth-century migration, which was more in line with the French academic tradition.[17] Several years later, in his preface to a book by Charlotte Roland (1962), Chevalier provided a bit of explanation: He denounced the "tradition" of French sociology that had always relegated research on immigration "to the lowest echelons of its hierarchy"; he also accused the Chicago school of having left "its loyal imitators in France and elsewhere in a most unfortunate position." Geography was not spared, particularly the Vidalian school, which, according to Chevalier, "abruptly moved from the topicality of facts to the origins, and often the antiquity, of customs, beliefs, and ideas—more readable for certain periods than for others, experimented with in a moment of convulsion, and solidified in some legend or some saying." Finally, the author emphasized the role of circumstances: "There are no ghettos here"; in other words, the French tradition of "assimilation" had made immigration invisible within French society (Chevalier 1962, 7–11). These are all excellent reasons, but they do not explain why the research announced was never carried out. This may be due to the fact that in 1962, it was difficult to defend ideas that a new generation was already in the process of discrediting.

New Immigrations, New Sociologists

From the 1960s onward, economic, intellectual, and political changes made the preceding generation's discourses on "assimilation," "ethnic" incompatibility, and the like incomprehensible, or at the very least unjustifiable. Rather than provoking a genuine scholarly debate on these issues, however, the new situation led to a general neglect of the past. The supporters of the old positions had no choice but discretion; any show of resistance on this point would have forced them to justify a problematic that was born (or, rather, consolidated) under the Vichy government. This explains why, as Drouard (1983) noted, the decades of silence that surrounded the work of the Fondation Alexis-Carrel also obscured questions of assimilation, leading a new generation of sociologists to believe that they were the first to navigate these waters.

The institutional phase inaugurated by the social sciences in the late nineteenth century came to a close in the 1960s. For sociology, this period heralded a practice of scholarship that no longer relied on a handful of individuals but was made up of genuine research bodies, university centers, and scientific institutes with far greater human and material resources than had previously been available. This rejuvenated institutional setting attracted a new generation of sociologists, who had been raised in the atmosphere of social struggle (from the Popular Front to the Resistance and the Cold War) and colonial wars (Algeria in particular). Their intention to view the world differently, exacerbated by the events of May-June 1968, came to the fore. Under the influence of Marxism, many intellectuals now believed that research was meant to serve a cause, neither that of the state nor that of the French nation but, rather, that of the "oppressed," the "wretched of the Earth." In the field of study that concerns us here, a combination of Marxism and anticolonialism paved the way for the creation of a new term, "immigrant worker." With decolonization, two previously unrelated research trends came together: immigration studies per se and studies of the colonial world. The latter had developed autonomously before the Second World War, particularly through the *Revue des Etudes Islamiques* and the Haut Comité sur la Méditerrannée (created in 1937), which published Joanny Ray's work on Moroccans in France. These studies on the colonial world, which were far more "comprehensive" (in their own paternalistic way) than were studies of immigration published during the same period, came under heightened criticism from sociologists from the 1950s onward. Andrée Michel's 1955 work on Algerian workers is a perfect illustration of the changing intellectual mood (denunciation of the capitalist state and of its scholarly supporters, an emphasis on descriptions of the forms of exploitation endured by these immigrants at work and in everyday life, tribute to the unity between French and foreign workers). This particular study represents a moment of transition; its preface, written by Pierre Laroque, still reflected the old way of seeing things. Laroque was the author of a report on the exploitation of colonial workers in France that, under the Popular Front, had been deemed "progressive." But the Conseil d'Etat could not accept the sociologists' criticisms of the role of the state in questions of immigration, particularly with regard to social security. The two points of view grew from distinct epochs, but, as is evidenced by the statistical count of dissertations mentioned earlier, sociology had moved into a position of strength.[18] It should be noted that this new generation of scholars was mainly preoccupied with this equally new generation of immigrants. The survey by Alain Girard and Jean Stoetzel on Italians and Poles, published by the INED in 1953, was one of the last to deal with these nationalities. As for the Armenians and the Central Europeans, who until the aftermath of the war had posed "serious problems of integration" requiring subtle policy making and in-depth understanding, no serious study of them was ever published. Should we conclude that their "problem" had solved itself?

North African workers, and Algerians in particular, became the objects of a growing number of studies, somewhat overdetermined in their focus by the upheavals of the Algerian war and conditioned by an economic context of renewed growth. The characteristics of the first stage of immigration were present *just as they had been in the 1920s* (but to realize this requires some understanding of history): a large majority of single men, considerable turnover, hotels either overbooked or filled by bachelors, and so on. Detailed knowledge of this aspect of immigration had become possible thanks to the range of tools available to sociology, to the growth of fieldwork, and to the abundance of "questionnaires." The result of this approach, totally oriented toward the present, was to further marginalize the advocates of an "assimilationist" problematic. This situation lent itself to the strategy adopted by policy makers with respect to the social sciences, which consisted of contracting for research with a practical and short-term purpose (Amiot 1986). The empiricism of scholarship and its thorough subordination to current events were accentuated. Michel Oriol's survey (1981) of sociological work on immigration following the Second World War revealed the fallout from such an orientation: the compartmentalization of research and the hegemony of economic concerns and of all aspects of the living conditions (evidenced, for example, by studies of housing and of poor adaptation) of these "outcasts," as immigrant workers were fashionably defined.

Yet the classic antagonism between sociology and demography had not completely disappeared. The difference between the approach to immigration adopted by the Center for Sociological Studies, founded by Georges Gurvitch, and that of the Foundation for the Study of Human Problems (later INED) was an affair of nuance. The "populationist" school of thought, in politics as well as in academia, was too old and deeply rooted in French life to disappear altogether. While the interests of INED scholars shifted to the new problematic of the family, at the expense of immigration, discussion of the integration of foreigners remained an important aspect of the research coordinated by Alain Girard. Nonetheless, controversies provoked by such notions as "assimilation" or "maximum tolerance"[19] explain why the young researchers of the INED were more inclined to undertake studies on less sensitive topics. It was the reign of Alfred Sauvy the "economist," of Ecole Polytechnique graduates who were more competent in mathematics than in sociology. The "science" of immigration amounted to a series of clichés and ill-defined models (Courgeau 1970).

Clearly, this new conjuncture was not very favorable to historians. But the fact that research proposals on immigration formulated after the war were so discredited can also be explained by struggles within the "corporation." Indeed, the duel between Braudel and Chevalier at the Collège de France is far from irrelevant to our story. Braudel's review of Louis Chevalier's 1958 *Classes laborieuses, Classes dangeureuses* was a full-scale criticism of the paradigm proposed by the author. In an effort to make the Chicago school's approach acceptable to French intellectual circles, Chevalier applied it to his work on early-nineteenth-century Paris (a period characterized by a strong flow of migrants from the provinces). He therefore advocated a "biological" history (urban pathology), of which Braudel contested the very object; just as he questioned Chevalier's presentation of "immigration" as a key variable "which conditions everything else." Braudel was also doubtful of the book's methodology: Chevalier's reliance on literary texts; his refusal to recognize the all-powerful explanatory value of statistics; his disdain for economic history; and, finally, his sacrilegious preference for "short-term conjunctures," which was totally beyond Braudel's understanding. More than the book itself, however, what most annoyed Braudel was Chevalier's "proud delivery" before the Collège de France and his pretentious vindication of a "manifest," which Braudel regarded as an attack on the field of history (Braudel 1980). In the 1978 pocket-size reedition of his book, Chevalier wrote a preface that implicitly responded to Braudel. According to Chevalier, the dividing line in scholarship of the 1950s had been "between those who had money and those who did not" (implying that "the Americans should have funded my research rather than that of the *Maison des sciences de l'homme*). He then lashed out against demographic history, which he believed was primarily concerned with calculating birth and mortality rates in obscure country villages.

This desertion of the field by historians seemed to justify sociologists' making immigration "external" to past and present-day French society. Foreigners were "at the gates of our cities," to paraphrase one publisher's justification of a new series. The authorities of their countries of origin (who encouraged émigrés to believe that their exile was only temporary) and the French government itself (which encouraged various forms of subterfuge to improve the "flexibility" of the labor market), as well as sociologists from all spectrums, forged a genuine consensus around the image of the immigrant worker as an individual "living between parentheses," as an individual whose presence in France was necessarily temporary.

The first effect of this a priori judgment was to identify immigration with misfortune. Forced by poverty to desert their homes, émigrés could hope for nothing but failure in the host country; hence the recurrence of such themes as uprootedness, solitude, and even madness in, for example, North African literature in France (Bonn 1982). In addition, this led to a genuine cult of difference, particularly widespread from 1968 onward. "Ethnic awakening" was widely advocated along with regionalist and feminist demands. Armenians were now seen as "threatened by assimilation," engaged in a physical and spiritual struggle to "preserve their originality" (Ternon 1983). The leftist interpretation of Foucault perceived the immigrant as a "savage" in the process of "domestication," a victim of the "integrating machine" embodied by the state (Marié et al. 1977). In a curious reversal of the discourse that had once been dominant, sociological publications on this subject often betrayed a tendency to systematically denounce and rehabilitate. According to this logic, the criteria used to define the object had little to do with scholarship; the important thing was to underscore the extreme or "exemplary" character of a given case study. The most unhappy, most exploited, most deserving of sympathy, in short the most *recent* immigrants, received priority. Such criteria for evaluating the importance of an object, upon which the scholar's importance often depended, produced a strange sort of competition: to determine which, for example, among an Algerian, a Jew, and an Indochinese was the least "civilized" of them all. The characteristic substantialist approach of earlier studies on immigration was thereby reinforced, at the expense of a more relational approach; this did not take away from the value of some of these studies.

In the meantime, studies of immigration became trapped in a ghetto. The compartmentalization of the field, the proliferation of "specialized domains" embodied in research centers, shattered research by shattering the object. Scholars who were not "experts" on immigration most often either ignored the question or treated it lightly. By granting "socioprofessional categories" all-powerful explanatory and descriptive value, the statistical apparatus of the INSEE in fact encouraged this trend. A study of social mobility states that "there are undoubtedly few areas where the influence of ascendancy is not visible"; it makes no mention, however, of the role played, in this respect, by immigration (Thelot 1982, 117). One could easily show that most of the articles published in the journal of the INSEE, *Economie et Statistique*, confuse "social origins" and the "professional class of origin."

The sociological perspective, which prefers to view immigration in France through its most recent aspects, continues to reflect a widely held view that present-day intolerance can be explained by the fact that temporary migration has ended and by the realization, by the French as well as by older immigrants, that their settlement in France is permanent. This analysis may apply to a country such as Germany, where immigration is a recent phenomenon, but it fails to grasp the uniqueness of the French situation. The "older" immigrants in question are in fact only a small minority of those aged sixty-five or older. At the beginning of the economic crisis in 1975, only 37,000 of the 300,000-plus foreigners in this age group were of African, American, Asian, or Oceanian origin, whereas 265,000 were European. There were one-tenth as many "older" Algerians as there were "older" Italians, and one-sixth as many as of "older" Poles. In 1982, the proportion remained one Algerian for every five Italians in the age group of sixty-five and older. European nationalities, on the other hand, represented the older migratory waves, and most had settled permanently in France. It is difficult to conflate them with the Gastarbeiter of former West Germany.[20]

Attention shifted back to questions of assimilation (although the term remained taboo) with the economic crisis and the interruption of immigration and its corollaries (such as permanent settlement and increased visibility of the family). Given what we have seen, the disarray among sociologists is quite understandable; their main arguments ("difference," the radical "foreignness" of the other, the evils of the "integrating machine," and so on) were now manipulated by the advocates of a return to jus sanguinis who shouted "*La France aux Français!*" The issue of bilingualism in schools (which Sauvy had already raised in the 1950s), problems of integration faced by the second generation, and questions regarding the future of the French population reappeared. Furthermore, a remodeling of statistics was once again suggested in order to create tools of information that were less subordinate to a juridical logic. In the constant back-and-forth movement that characterizes discourse on immigration, the present-day balance is once again tilted on the side of origins, "ethnicity," and history. The scientific (but also the political) challenge is to manage to finally overcome these age-old vascillations.

Questions for Fernand Braudel

The fact that immigration has never until now been a recognized object of historical research is also linked to epistemological considerations. I will end this chapter by examining such factors, through the work of the historian who left the greatest mark on contemporary research: Fernand Braudel.

The most interesting aspect of Braudel's final work, *L'Identité de la France,* is that it can be read as a genuine palimpsest in which the major forms of historical writing, from the work of Jules Michelet to those of the Annales school, are intertwined. The first theme that is of interest to us here is, of course, the point of view adopted on immigration. Unlike many books of the same sort, Braudel's work does not evade the question. Yet everything seems to indicate that immigrants did not belong to the history of France for him either. The chapter on immigration is entirely built around the opposition between "us" and "them." Older waves of foreign migration are of course discussed, but they reinforce the commonly held belief that "the assimilation of these foreigners, who were our close neighbors, was relatively rapid" (Braudel 1988–1990). Braudel apparently considered this such a self-evident fact that it was useless to spend time on it: "The list of 'foreigners' having... become members of our community would be too long." In fact (and this is another example of the danger I mentioned in the Introduction), the sole aim of this historical reminder is to underscore the "problems" of present-day immigration: "I believe it is the first time that immigration presents the country, on a national scale, with a kind of 'colonial' problem." This does raise the notion that history should serve to understand the present, but it raises it in such an impoverished form that the historian to whom we owe so much is virtually unrecognizable. Braudel, who had insisted more than any other historian on the fact that "the entire past lies in the present,"[21] felt authorized to encapsulate in a single sentence an explanation of how our present is affected by the history of immigration: "by 'absorbing' foreigners," France "became materially and culturally richer." The reader who wonders how one becomes richer by absorbing, in other words how one goes from "them and us" to "them *in* us," will find no response in the three volumes of *L'Identité de la France.*

Braudel's followers might argue that these gaps would have been filled had the author not passed away, that forthcoming volumes would have discussed the issue in more detail, and that the weaknesses of the work are due to Braudel's old age. I believe, on the contrary, that the very conception of history that Braudel defended is what prevented him from answering these questions. It is clear, first of all, that the thirty-five pages on immigration, out of nearly a thousand, were tacked on to the substance of the work. The essence of the argument lies in anecdotes, which are, of course, well-meaning but unrelated to the structure of the book. This can only be understood in light of the conception of historical time (the famous "*longue durée*") that Braudel relentlessly defended all his life. This is the first thread I would like to draw from the hank of *L'Identité de la France*.

What the countless reviewers of this book did not emphasize enough was the fact that it contained traces of a polemic, now almost a century old, between sociologists and historians over the very definition of the object called "history." In his introduction, Braudel criticized narrative history in the name of a scientific practice of the discipline. He justified his interest in space and time by invoking the need for "indispensable comparisons, forms of experimentation; I mean, experiments conducted according to a preconceived plan, which I may resume at will regardless of the elements studied" (Braudel 1988–1990). The learned reader in sociology will easily recognize the influence of Durkheim in this epistemology, which extols the virtues of comparativism. Durkheim is, in fact, cited by Braudel, who identifies with his view that history and sociology differ only slightly. One man who played a fundamental role in the conflictual dialogue between history and sociology, however, is not even mentioned: François Simiand. The point of departure was the famous controversy that, at the turn of the century, opposed Simiand and Charles Seignobos, leader of the "historicizing historians" (to paraphrase French philosopher Henri Berr). This controversy eventually grew into the foundational myth, so to speak, of the Annales school—and of Braudel in particular.

Although to dwell at length on these issues would distract us from the gist of our study (cf. Noiriel 1995), a word on the object of the quarrel is necessary. Simiand's goal was to wage a battle against the "idols"—political, individual, and chronological—of the "historians' tribe," particularly those historians (Lavisse, Seignobos, Langlois) who, at the time, dominated both the field and the university. More important, Simiand challenged the historians' idea that social realities are purely subjective and individual, requiring the researcher to reconstruct the motives of individual actions and hence preventing history from attaining the level of objectivity of the physical or biological sciences (Seignobos 1901). For Simiand, in contrast, there were no fundamental differences between scientific fields of inquiry, and what the historians' argument really betrayed was their congenital empiricism and their inability to distinguish, as philosphers had done since Kant, between reality and the object of knowledge. In physics, as in history, he continued, reality can only be attained through the mediation of human subjectivity; but the process of abstraction, far from destroying or being "disloyal" to reality, is in fact what makes it a scientific object. For science, the object is constructed rather than given, and it is through the process of objectivation that laws are derived. But if the object is constructed, then all the elements that define it must be articulated and structured accordingly. History's claim to dominate the social sciences in general, on the grounds that it is the only field capable of establishing the link (*Zusammenhang*) between different aspects of reality, is therefore unfounded. For Simiand, this so-called link is a simple artifact of presentation, the expression of a textbook logic (agriculture first, industry second, and so on). If the object is constructed, then of necessity relations must exist among the different elements. Experimentation consists of comparing, of making elements vary in order to correctly evaluate these degrees of necessity. While the search for causality (which Simiand discussed in detail in another conference) and experimentation each have their specificities, they are not in principle different in biology and in history. Historians must strive to develop "laboratory conditions" of their own. Another logical conclusion, given the conception of the object, is that "no science, not even the most advanced, selects an object or tackles a question randomly among the facts which come under it" (Simiand 1903; see also 1906). This last point had already been raised ten years earlier by a historian whom Braudel regarded as one of the greatest ever: Paul Lacombe. Alarmed by the spectacular upsurge in historical research, an accumulation, in his words, of "appalling magnitude" (the "dispersal of history" decried by many today is clearly nothing new), Lacombe believed that only by viewing things relationally could the importance of different phenomena be determined. But this theoretical operation could not, he argued, be performed by just anyone. He distinguished between two equally legitimate but quite different genres within what we call "history": "history as art," "accessible to the mass of humankind" and reserved for enlightened amateurs; and "history as science," the "task of our time," whose goal is to understand the world in which we live (Lacombe 1894).

In the context of contemporary debates on the "crisis of history" and the field's relation to science, even a schematic reminder of the arguments held by proponents of "history as science" is enlightening precisely because they were caricatured by the Annales school in its foundational years. Contrary to what some authors have claimed (Dosse 1987; Pomian 1986), the "founders" of the Annales school did not put into practice Simiand's program. In the inaugural lecture he delivered at the Collège de France, Braudel offered a critique of "history as science," arguing that it had "failed" because it claimed to "predict the future," because it viewed itself as "prophetic" (*sic*) (Braudel 1980). In fact, a curious misunderstanding, which originated in Lucien Febvre's time, provided the Annales school with a "scientific" justification (via the prestige of sociology) for its rivalry with the historians at the Sorbonne; in the process, the ideas defended by Simiand were introduced in such a way as to make them acceptable to scholars in the field.

There is ample evidence for this. Despite Febvre's proclamations on "the historian inventing his object" by resorting to "very complicated techniques" (Febvre 1953), his *practice* of history is by and large characterized by empiricism. What distinguished the writings of the Annales school from so-called factual history, or *histoire événementielle,* was that they framed their topics differently (economic history, history of "mentalities"); but the *objects* were still drawn from the "prenotions" of common sense. That François Simiand and Maurice Halbwachs upheld their critique of historians in general, without making an exception for the Annales school, attests to this point (Simiand 1932; Craig 1979).

It has become fashionable to reduce scholarly polemics to their strategic aspect, attributing them to "corporatist interests" or to "the imperialism of disciplines." But this continued quarrel between Durkheimians and historians is also grounded in real issues. Simiand, like Lacombe before him, maintained that it was impossible to "practice history" (in the scientific sense) by simply describing everyday phenomena. On the other hand, the "theoretical" renewal proposed by Lucien Febvre was in fact a pretext to broaden the field of historical investigation. "We have no history of Love; let's think about it. We have no history of Death" (Febvre 1953). In statements such as these, Febvre defined the premises of a history of "mentalities" and of what became known as "*la nouvelle histoire.*" The point here is not to approve or disapprove of the field's evolution but to show that from the point of view of Durkheimian sociology, *constructing* an object of scientific inquiry requires more than including miasmas, daffodils, tears, or even the Mediterranean within the purview of the word "history." Would we really serve the cause of science, Norbert Elias wondered maliciously, by "extending historical research to the 'life story' of a dog, a flower bed, or a randomly picked person" (Elias 1983)? In the end, the main criticism directed by sociologists at historians is that they tend to confuse the *construction* of a scientific object with the *historicization* of notions drawn from "common sense." Indeed, Braudel's unwillingness to challenge the apparent obviousness of current events is the most glaring problem with his approach to immigration.

Another very common approach in Braudel's work can be traced back to the work of Simiand at the beginning of the century. Simiand believed that to identify "scientific laws" would require proving that the phenomena observed occurred repeatedly and regularly and that the "conditions of laboratory observation" remained identical in each case; hence his critique of *histoire événementielle* and his assertion that only "serial" or "quantitative" history is scientific. Throughout his life, Simiand sought to prove the validity of the positions he had held in his youth; he became a reknowned specialist of the statistical method and a spokesman for the "economic historians" at the Ecole Pratique des Hautes Etudes. But whereas Simiand as an epistemologist never quite convinced the tribe of historians, his research in the field of economics gave birth to a genuine school of thought, with Braudel and Ernest Labrousse as its leading figures. In the end, Simiand gave the dissenters among historians what they were looking for: a specific field of inquiry called "economic and social history." This expression met with such success in the 1930s that it became a catchphrase of language and thought. The expression seemed so natural to historians that, after Lucien Febvre, no one thought of analyzing it critically. There were centers of economic and social history, journals entitled *Annales d'Histoire Economique et Sociale* and *Revue d'Histoire Economique et Sociale,* as well as a vast anthology to which a large number of historians contributed and which was directed by Labrousse and Braudel: *L'Histoire économique et sociale de la France* (The economic and social history of France). The expression was constantly used in books, articles, and colloquia. What it designated, however, was simply an economic history, a fact that Febvre revealed. The term "social" was added to the title of the Annales because it was vague enough to "cast the net as wide as possible."[22] The paradox is that the creation of a social history *in its own right* was forsaken as a result of criticisms from . . . a sociologist! Experts in economic history readily admit that their field is indebted to concepts forged by economists; similarly, demographic history would not have been born without the help of the demographer-mathematician Louis Henry; and political history owes a lot to André Siegfried. But historians have never regarded sociological concepts (with the exception of a few Marxist expressions) as essential to a genuine social history.[23] This resulted from the presupposition that "economic structures" by themselves could provide insights into the foundations of society. The economy was seen as the "backdrop of the social scene"; as Jean Bouvier told the audience at a famous colloquium on "social history" chaired by Labrousse (Labrousse 1967), "without prior economic analysis, all that is left is description, and explanation recedes." Yet sociology was never invoked to justify these assertions, and for a good reason. Simply adding "mentalities" to "the economic and the social" restored the very logic of "tally history" for which Simiand had criticized Seignobos: the all-purpose table of contents found in so many textbook histories of France.

By disassociating (against Simiand) the structure of the object from a quantitative approach, "economic and social history," aided by prestige and with the help of computers, came to regard science as a matter of numbers. Louis Chevalier was correct in stating that much of demographic history's scientific legitimacy stems from this presupposition. It therefore became possible to introduce a third "level," in a sense the top floor of the edifice: *l'histoire des mentalités*. "The serial approach," wrote Pierre Chaunu, "provides a superior tool for the analysis of quality, . . . an outline of the history of civilization" (Chaunu 1974, 67). But because Simiand's objectivism was incapable of defining a rigorous approach anywhere except in the economic realm, the quantitative method was ultimately swept away by the "history of mentalities." This was a full-scale return to the kinds of things against which Simiand had constructed his entire paradigm: "haphazard exemplification," the historicization of a priori commonsense notions framed as "new objects," and so on. To use Paul Lacombe's terms, we might say that "history as art" replaced "history as science." It is true that Braudel expressed reservations about the "history of mentalities" (his knowledge of Simiand's thinking was sufficient to avoid the confusion between aligning series of figures and constructing a scientific object). Nonetheless, the construction of Braudel's *L'Identité de la France* is characteristic of "economic and social" approaches in general: volume 1, "space" (we will return to this point); volume 2, "men and things," that is, demography and the economy (the volume dealing with the "social" aspect was scheduled to come later). This articulation of the object is no different from that of the "table of contents" approach of, for example, Henry Hauser (agriculture/industry/commerce), which is still the rule in textbooks today.

It is Braudel's conception of time that determined the essence of the epistemological debate over history in later years, at the expense of the discussion of the historian's trade developed by Marc Bloch.[24] We might argue that this conception is nothing more than a variation on the image of superposed shelves. In his early work, Braudel likened "*longue durée*" to "immobile time" in the physical realm, "*moyenne durée*" to "economic and social conditions," and "*temps court*" to the epiphenomena of the "*événementiel,*" of the "mental"; he stood by this model for the rest of his life. Ernest Labrousse, whose work displayed the same three-way structure and the same arrangement in tiers (Labrousse 1967), exerted a much greater influence on modern history than did Fernand Braudel, but both authors assumed that the mental lagged behind the social, which itself lagged behind the economic. It comes as no surprise that immigration, primarily conceived as a "political" problem, received only superficial attention in *L'Identité de la France*; anything else would have been surprising.

It is important to emphasize, once again, that the very richness of this paradigm explains the "oversights" of an entire epoch of historical research. Because the social always dragged behind the economic, the political, or the demographic, key questions of sociological thought were barely touched upon by historians. Witness, for example, the periodic resurgence of debates on the relationship between the "individual" and the "collective." More than any other discipline, history was marked by the holistic a priori of French thinking, in which the two notions are systematically confused. It would be interesting to look at all the *Histories of France* published from Michelet's times to the present and to make an inventory of all the metaphors that describe France as a person. We find them in the writings of the "historicizing historians" of the Sorbonne as well as those of the Annales school. In his dithyrambic celebration of Braudel's thesis, Lucien Febvre himself wrote: "For the first time a sea, or rather a web of seas, is promoted to the dignity of a historical actor" (Febvre 1962, 169). For the director of the journal *Annales,* each of the parts in the study represented an aspect of the "person" (that is, the Mediterranean): for example, the analysis of the "environment" was a "physical portrait." Similar metaphors have appeared in recent publications. For Pierre Chaunu, "France is a person, and the mystery of a collective personality is no more dense than that of the persons we ourselves are, by virtue of our biological being" (Chaunu 1982, 10). In his introduction to the first volume of *Les Lieux de mémoire,* Pierre Nora explicitly likened the individual to the collective. Later in the book, the nation is defined as an "*être là*" ("being there"), as "becoming conscious of itself," as "retrieving itself as a past," as "discovering itself," or as "experiencing itself in its geographic being" (Nora 1984–1986, 1:vii, 3:648). These formulations illustrate the extent to which French historians have interiorized the categories of the positivist tradition in French legal studies, which goes back to Jean-Jacques Rousseau's Social Contract and culminates in the theory of the "nation as a person," of which Adhemar Esmein (1896) was the foremost defender. Moreover, this theory was disparaged by the legal establishment itself, in particular by Léon Duguit (1907), early in this century.

Fernand Braudel explicitly states, in his last book, that France is not a person, but his entire paradigm remains bound by a holistic conception, as his references to psychoanalysis and the very title of the book attest. The criteria chosen to define the object are what make it possible to distinguish social history from political history. According to the aforementioned principles of "history as science," "France" cannot be a point of departure if the object is genuinely constructed, nor can "the nation" be considered a given, as something that is "always already there." Social history starts out with real-life characters, real individuals, or, as Max Weber calls them, "elementary atoms"; it then conceptualizes, or constructs, them in such a way that the initial "prenotion" "the nation" might disappear altogether or be redefined on the basis of articulations grounded in reason.

To understand the stakes involved in this question, we must return to the polemic between Simiand and Seignobos. Febvre, and, especially, Braudel so accustomed us to view Seignobos as a toiler in the archives, bogged down in his *histoire événementielle* and his cult of "great men," that we often feel exempt from reading his thoughts on methodology. These writings not only contain an approach to historical time that is much closer to Braudel's than might be expected (see Mairet 1974), but his objections to Simiand are precisely a criticism of Durkheimian holism and the risks it involves for research: "In the field of history, it is quite perilous to allow oneself to write the biographies of imaginary beings such as the church, royalty, the stock exchange or speculation." Later on, Seignobos added: "The phenomenon is expressed by an abstract noun—for example the market, the textile industry mechanization—and this abstract term is used as if it designated a real being" (Seignobos 1901, 150, 224). By dismissing these objections outright and calling them "nominalist jokes," Simiand in fact reinforced a very French tradition, inherited from Auguste Comte, that consisted of thinking exclusively in terms of collective entities. As Simiand was quick to point out, Charles Langlois and Charles Seignobos were even less able to pursue the debate, for their historical works betrayed the same presuppositions (Langlois and Seignobos 1898).

This is undoubtedly because Seignobos was not the sole inventor of his arguments. He borrowed from the analyses produced during a debate similar to the one that was going on at the same time in Germany (in fact, the authors often explicitly refer to the work of Georg Simmel). Throughout the twentieth century, however, the "French school" of historical thought ignored a line of thought that amounted to the most vigorous critique of objectivism in the social sciences, with the exception, perhaps, of Charles Morazé, whose 1942 refutation of Simiand's theoretical analyses was in part inspired by Max Weber's sociology. Indeed, in his epistemological works, Weber was firmly opposed to the "naturalist monism" of those who regarded biology as the absolute model of science. For him, on the contrary, there was a radical difference between the physical sciences, which sought to determine general laws, and the humanities, in which general laws were the least valid because they were the most lacking in content. The greater the extension of a concept, the more it is abstract and draws us away from reality. That is why Weber defined the concept as an attempt "to put some order in the chaos of facts." The "comprehensive sociology" that he advocated sees the individual as the basic unit of research, the only one capable of deconstructing the "personified concepts" of the state, the party, the church. Norbert Elias also dwelled frequently on these issues, underscoring the scientific obstacles linked to the researcher's use of everyday language and criticizing "the reified use of the concept of 'institution' [that] hides the individuals behind them." He also denounced the attitude that consists of "taking Nations rather than individuals as units" (Elias 1978). If this were simply a quarrel between experts, there would be no point in outlining the different points of view. But the methodological choices that it implies are of key importance. As this book will abundantly illustrate, the historical study of immigration—it is easy to understand why—requires the deconstruction of the nation as a collective entity and the adoption of an approach that begins at the level of individuals.

Braudel's holism is also deeply rooted in another line of thought, an additional clue to which we now turn. I am referring to the geographical thought of Vidal de La Blache. As Vincent Berdoulay noted in his analysis of the relationship between historians and the Vidalian school, "the holistic approach, the search for collective entities and other related notions, were fundamental aspects of Vidalian thought" (Berdoulay 1981, 185). This approach is illustrated by a crucial metaphor used by the geographer and his followers: "regional temperament" (character, disposition), a notion that Siegfried (who had been a student of Vidal) introduced to political science and political history. As we know, Vidal's influence was fundamental to the historians of the Annales school, in particular Lucien Febvre and Fernand Braudel. The latter inherited a theme, is particularly visible in *L'Identité de France,* that was developed by Vidal in his famous *Tableau géographique de la France* and that is derived from the dogma of "the people's rootedness" in French soil. Vidal shared the distress of an entire generation confronted with the disintegration of ancestral lands (*pays*) in the face of industrial change; hence his belief in the importance of "roots." In his conclusion to the *Tableau géographique de la France,* the geographer expressed confidence in the abilities of the "national temperament" to *resist* the upheavals of modernity. He also assigned geographers a quasi-militant mission to reassure the country by placing the accent on its "continuities" over time: "More than ever, the careful study of what is fixed and permanent in the geographic reality of France must guide our work" (Vidal de La Blache, quoted in Guiomar 1984, 591).

L'Identité de la France is profoundly marked by this philosophy of rootedness. But Vidal also provided the core of the book's architecture: "extended time" (*temps long*), that is, the physical environment as it has been organized by humanity from the most ancient times. Like Vidal, whose propensity to leap abruptly from the most ancient history to the most recent period was criticized early on by Louis Chevalier, Braudel argued in *L'Identité de la France* that French history had ended at the moment when industrialization began. A simple breakdown of the number of pages devoted to each issue reveals his extremely limited interest in contemporary and industrial history, not to mention legal, administrative, and political history. Perhaps we should interpret this as a reflection of Braudel's limited knowledge of subfields other than modern history. Fundamentally, however, what we find is an approach similar to Lucien Febvre's, whose main concern was to understand how the French nation was *formed,* how the "fusion" of ancient "races" led to unity and to the apotheosis of the Revolution. The "frames" were in place, the rest could only be a matter of "surface," of epiphenomena. That is why Fernand Braudel grants so much importance to a Vidalian methodology of traces in physical space: toponymy, the form of villages, weather vanes on the roofs; the full register of rural history and anthropology is mobilized.

If Braudel placed so much emphasis in his last book on an approach to geography that was at least fifty years old and that remained oblivious to subsequent advances in the field (Péguy 1986), it is because this approach provides the only possible solution to the central problem of his book. The entire project of *L'Identité de la France* is to prove that people believe themselves to be free when in fact they are completely determined by history. The book is replete with expressions that betray the author's obsession with this issue. It is both the vindication of an entire life's work (the central thesis of Braudel's writings is that the *longue durée* conditions the present) and the expression of another approach to history, that of Renan, Lavisse, and, especially, Barrès, an approach that sees the French today as simply the continuation of their ancestors. Given that for Braudel history stops around the end of the eighteenth century, the rest is nothing but a steady dotted line leading up to the present. In this perspective, whenever the landscape fails to reveal "traces," it is replaced by a geographical map; hence the author's uncharacteristically uncautious enthusiasm for the book by Hervé Le Bras and Emmanuel Todd, *L'Invention de la France* (1981), which postulates the continuity of the "French anthropological system" on the basis of a series of maps drawn by a computer.[25] Braudel and Chaunu thought highly of this controversial and questionable book because it identifies the missing link between the most distant past and the present day. This link is the family, therefore the lineage and genealogical continuity. "Everything starts with the family, almost everything can be explained through it," Braudel argued (Braudel 1988–1990); and Pierre Chaunu added: "There exists at least one common cement that binds the different parts of France: the duration and continuity of a population that goes far back in time"; hence the postulated filiation with "those who preceded us, and whose genetic trace we carry within us" (Chaunu 1982).[26] This deep-rootedness of the French population, the cornerstone of the theoretical edifice, is asserted rather than demonstrated. The statistical data from which were drawn the maps presented as "visible evidence" by Le Bras and Todd have only one flaw, and that is that they are limited to migration *within* France. It has been many years since André Beltramone (1966) demonstrated, with supporting statistics, that immigration, or the uprootedness of some, explains the roots of the others. The two phenomena must, therefore, be studied *together.* If we take seriously the statistic that establishes that one-third of the inhabitants of France today have foreign roots, the all-encompassing role of the family as an explanation of continuities and traditions falls apart.

One would also have to reexamine the studies of nineteenth-century historical demography from the perspective of mass immigration. For example, Jean Dupâquier's study (in Dupâquier and Dupâquier 1985) of the 8,000 couples married during the First Empire and their descendants is somewhat distorted by the a priori notion that the French population is deeply rooted in the past. As one collaborator in the study observed, the choice of patronymics beginning with "Tra" as a basis for selecting individuals, while it worked for the native French, was quite ill adapted to foreigners (the Vietnamese, for example, were overrepresented). Furthermore, the methodology adopted by the authors of the study, which banks on the *longue durée* and the continuity of lineages from the early nineteenth century onward, does not allow an adequate estimation of the extraordinary renewal of the population as a result of immigration. The complementary study of naturalized citizens deals with only a tiny portion of those individuals of foreign origin that this research excludes.[27]

The current fascination with genealogy reinforces the notion of an ancestral continuity in French lineages. One finds ample evidence of this by simply browsing through the pages of the luxurious *Gé-Magazine,* which includes several historians and anthropologists among its contributors. This publication is a constant hymn to "our ancestors": "When our ancestors paid the commoners' tax"; "when our ancestors were young"; "when our ancestors voted"; "our ancestors' toys." Almost every issue of this monthly magazine contains articles that take for granted that our predecessors were rooted in the soil of France, with patronymics smacking of "our" countryside.

Yet a return to Durkheimian sociology provides other tools for apprehending the question of the "past within the present," in terms better adjusted to contemporary society.

Maurice Halbwachs went the furthest in the exploration of the theoretical track, particularly in his work *On Collective Memory,* in which he attempts to articulate the "past within the present" with the thought of the other master of his youth, Henri Bergson. His research reflects the idea that individuals and the social groups to which they belong leave a profound mark on the space within which they live. But, unlike Fernand Braudel, he believed that the closer the past, the more visible is its trace. Furthermore, Halbwachs did not limit the definition of traces to their effects on the landscape. On the contrary, he argued that in modern societies, people have a tendency to isolate themselves from the physical environment that surrounds them. The imprint of the past is therefore particularly visible on established forms of collective life (state organizations, parties, trade unions) and on the constructed forms in which they reside (ministries, town halls). The past is also condensed within all the written and diagrammatic documents that a society preserves; it leaves its mark in the very flesh of individuals, "in the expression of figures, in the aspect of places (where they live), and even in the ways of thinking and feeling which are subconsciously preserved and reproduced" (Halbwachs 1992). His most important theoretical innovation is his effort to explain how the passage from individual recollections to collective memory actually occurs. Using very simple sentences, Halbwachs introduced the phenomenological thought that was developed in Germany by Edmund Husserl and Max Weber into a problematic that had until then had remained very "French." He exposed, for example, the fundamental role of the "lived" and "subjective" experience of individuals in the analysis of symbolic processes. This is a good point of departure for understanding why flags, monuments, and commemorations can arouse the enthusiasm of certain individuals and groups while leaving others indifferent; how powerful mobilizations are built and maintained, but also end up getting away from those who have an interest in manipulating them. Research in these directions will enable the history of both national and "nonnational" phenomena to move beyond the usual "pedagogical" a priori and the history of mentalities, and renew itself altogether.

Because he refers to Emile Durkheim, we might have expected Braudel to use these analyses to enrich his approach to "the identity of France." There are two major reasons, I believe, why he did not do so. The first is that the Durkheimian conceptual framework cannot be reconciled with the problematic of deep-rootedness in the land; as we saw earlier, it was in fact constructed *against* this problematic (which is at the center of Braudelian explanation, at least in his last book). The second reason is that the work of the founder of scientific sociology contained the seeds of these, in many respects contradictory, developments. One furrow, tilled by François Simiand, facilitated the growth of economic history, of the "*longue durée,*" and of objectivism. Another furrow, plowed by Halbwachs, encouraged the development of a more individualist and subjective sociology. Perhaps it was impossible to conciliate the two. Drawing on Simiand made it impossible for Braudel to understand the value of Halbwachs's work. But his blindness was reinforced by the competitive games between academic fields. The Annales school, constructed in reaction to the "psychologicalizing" history of Lavisse and Seignobos (which remained dominant at least until the 1950s), was not prepared to accept an approach that reevaluated the role of individuals and of their subjectivity. Furthermore, "Annalists" were compelled to distance themselves from a sociology that had made no secret, before 1914, of its expansionist designs. Whereas the thought of Simiand could be annexed (at the cost of the deformations described earlier) by privileging the eminently historic concept of *longue durée,* Halbwachs's problematic was far too sociological to be admitted. Even prior to the publication of *La Méditerranée,* Halbwachs had developed a decisive critique of *longue durée.* Criticizing historians for restricting all phenomena in a single time frame, he argued that each social group, each "object" constructs its own duration; that there consequently exists no unit of measurement "in itself" (Halbwachs 1992). Braudel could not accept such a conception, for it ruined a theory—conceived to ensure the hegemony of his discipline over the social sciences in general—that claimed that the time of history (and therefore of the historian) was the yardstick for all other durations.[28] Braudel, therefore, showed a lack of interest in the work of Halbwachs, whom he dismissed and catalogued as "dogmatic" in one half-sentence of his *Ecrits sur l'histoire* (Braudel 1980).

These are some of the objective reasons, reasons beyond human weaknesses, that explain the great paradox of the Annales adventure to this day. Conceived from the start as a historical endeavor designed to help understand the present, the Annales school was incapable of building the necessary tools for this ambition. Braudel lacked, wrote Jacques Le Goff, "a serious methodological basis" with which to undertake a social history of the contemporary period worthy of that name. And he added that for ten years, the journal of the Annales school had vainly attempted to put together an issue on the subject (Le Goff 1986).

Before we can begin to forge these tools that the Annales school failed to provide us, before we can lay the groundwork for a history of immigration, we must borrow freely from the whole array of social sciences.

Two

The Card and the Code

By the way, what was his nationality? He looked at his passport. Ah yes, Greek citizen. Amusing. Albert Cohen, 1930

Because they are rooted in the self-evident workings of the economic and technological division of labor, most people generally understand such categories as "working class" or "manager." Conversely, because they are completely inscribed in the legal opposition between French citizen and foreigner, the terms "immigration" and "immigrant" convey a range of considerably less well-understood meanings. To write social history in these terms therefore requires that we ask ourselves how such an artificial vocabulary (which, I argue, was virtually unknown only a century ago) became so familiar to those who use it and to those it designates. It is often overlooked that legal registration, identification documents, and laws are what, in the final analysis, determine the "identity" of immigrants; this identity is therefore enshrined, we might say, in "the card and the code."

Immigration: A Republican Invention

The Era of "Foreigners" (1789–1889)

Claude Lévi-Strauss (1952) observed that all societies have terms to distinguish between "good" and "bad" individuals (that is, between members and nonmembers of the group). Under the ancien régime, foreigners were considered legally inferior. They were deprived, for example, of civil rights (mainly of the right of succession), although by the eighteenth century these practices had fallen into disuse (Mathorez 1919–1921). Given the nature of feudal law, however, "foreigner" was a very different concept than it is today. In reality, "foreigners," as we now understand the concept, have only existed since the French Revolution. Two major actions of the Constituent Assembly thoroughly transformed its definition: On 4 August, by eliminating privileges, the assembly also founded a national community with a specific Constitution and legal system. Nationality came to represent, in the words of Jean Portemer, "the criteria used to set a foreigner apart." In the same period, the principle of equality among all individuals was solemnly proclaimed by the Declaration of the Rights of Man and the Citizen. "Foreigners would thereafter enjoy rights as individuals and be placed in a position of equality within the national community" (Portemer 1959, 535). Early on in the Revolution, two fundamental legal principles were introduced that, for the next two centuries, in an infinite variety of ways, determined the rights of foreigners. This is not the place to review in detail the history of this legal framework, which has been extensively studied elsewhere. We should simply note that despite the Declaration of the Rights of Man, discriminations against foreigners reappeared during the period of intermediary law and were consolidated in the Napoleonic Code. Foreigners were already deprived of civil rights; those who had not obtained (by decree) "admission to domicile" or who did not belong to a nation having signed a treaty of reciprocity with France also found themselves excluded from a number of civil rights (such as rights of succession or adoption). By virtue of article 272 of the Penal Code, a foreigner arrested for vagrancy could be led, voluntarily or by force, to the border. The principle of expulsion was introduced into French law on 28 Vendémiaire Year VI. It was confirmed, and its organization written into law, on 3 December 1849, and it remained in force for nearly a century. Regarding naturalization policy, the jus soli of the ancien régime and early phase of the Revolution was replaced by jus sanguinis.

A social history of law must go beyond the analysis of legal texts; it must seek to understand the extent to which legal norms affected the daily lives of the people at whom they were aimed and to determine the resources, in persons and equipment, required by their application. One piece of evidence is the interest that this aspect of law generated within the legal corporation. Until the beginning of the Third Republic, it is clear that very few brilliant minds showed an interest in the question of foreigners. At a time when the "civilists" of the School of Exegesis still monopolized education and practice (Arnauld 1975), commentary on the Civil Code was a favorite exercise among jurists; yet such discussion was virtually silent on foreigners. At the beginning of the Second Republic, the question was again downplayed by members of the bar, and an examination of jurisprudence betrayed the "uncertainties of legal experts" (Gand 1853). N.-J. Legat wrote in his *Code des étrangers* (Code of foreigners; 1832) that it was "virtually impossible to provide a fully accurate legal definition" of a foreigner. "Only the circumstances indicated by the law can determine whether or not an individual should be regarded as a foreigner." The author indicated the glaring contradictions, with regard to matters of naturalization, that were contained in the law itself and shared by such renowned ancien régime jurists as Jean Domat.[1] The concept "foreigner," which from a jurist's point of view remained rather vague, certainly did not connote the hardships of working-class life that it does today. In 1861, L. Lehmann listed a variety of reasons why foreigners would want to come to France: for its pleasant climate, to finish their education, for curiosity or because they love to travel, or perhaps to engage in commerce; not a single mention was made, however, of work in factories or in the fields.

Leaving aside the issue of law, the same can be said of the "social" literature published at the time, when the "labor question" was an issue but the "problem of foreigners" was not. When Audiganne traveled through France during a period of massive foreign immigration, he saw neither Belgians (Flemings) in the north nor Italians (Piedmontese) in Marseilles (Audiganne 1860). Studies by Louis Reybaud and monographs published by followers of Frédéric Le Play did mention these foreign populations, but they did not make a special case of them. Immigrants were perceived as being a part of society, just as were the *compagnon du Tour de France,* the native of Auvergne, or the highlander down from the Alps. The representations of "laboring classes" and "dangerous classes" described by Louis Chevalier, which were predominant until the beginning of the Third Republic, originated under the July Monarchy and were based on the concept of "class" (Le Play 1856, 1859; Reybaud 1863), as was the notion of "the people" (*le peuple*) that emerged with Victor Hugo and Emile

Zola and that preceded the "new perspective" of the turn of the century (see, for example, Le Play 1856, 1859; Reybaud 1863). The scholarly literature also reflected a vision of an overpopulated country, and the high birthrate was often identified as one of the causes of working-class misery (Giresse 1867). As Moheau argued in the late eighteenth century, France's misfortune resided in its status as a country of *emigration;* foreigners present on French soil should therefore not be mistreated, lest such behavior provoke retaliatory measures against the many French citizens around the world.[2]

Clearly, the concepts "immigration" and "foreigner" as they are applied today were totally absent from scholarly literature in the nineteenth century. Over the course of the century, the lack of interest displayed by jurists in this question seems to have been accentuated by the progressive relaxation of constraints on foreigners. That the evolution of customs, the triumph of liberal ideas, and, especially, progress in transportation would lead to a suppression of police controls was almost a leitmotiv of the juridical literature published during the Second Republic. Some authors noted that the 1851 ruling by the prefect of the Seine, which required foreigners to make themselves known within eight days of their arrival to obtain a residency permit, had fallen into disuse. Others regarded as null and void the old revolutionary law penalizing landlords who housed foreigners without declaring them to the authorities, since this offense was not even mentioned in the Penal Code (Portet 1882). With the establishment of free trade and the international conventions of 1860 and 1861, the principle of freedom of circulation for merchandise was extended to people; restrictions in this area were regarded as a thing of the past (Danguillecourt 1875; Hepp 1862).

The liberal Empire is also famous for having loosened the rules on naturalization. An 1867 law decreased the length of the "trial period" required before a foreigner could apply for citizenship and eliminated virtually all the temporary restrictions imposed by the state on newly naturalized citizens. The acquisition of French nationality automatically conferred full citizenship rights on the individual (Folleville 1880).

A "blurred" vision of the foreigner was also common throughout the lower echelons of the administrative and judiciary systems. The National Archives abound with examples of efforts by the Interior and Justice Ministries to clarify the meaning of the naturalization law in order to ensure its correct application. In 1810, the prefect of one department granted citizenship to an individual after one year of residency in the country instead of ten (NA F2 I 441). In 1831, the interior minister had to remind the prefectorial corps of the rules that applied to naturalization, in order to prevent the "frequent errors" he had observed from happening again (NA F7 12238). In 1856, the same government official scolded the prefect of Meurthe-et-Moselle for failing to correctly spell the surnames and birthplaces of naturalized individuals (DA MM 6 M 296).

The resources made available for the application of the law were often scarce. Canadian historian M. R. Marrus wrote that prior to 1870, refugees enjoyed a certain margin of freedom given that a "strict control" of their movements

> would create enormous difficulties for small Western bureaucracies. . . . Even if the authorities wished to expell foreigners, they would have little chance of succeeding. In the absence of fingerprints, identity photographs, efficient files or a modern police network, refugees could easily cross borders and live in relative peace in the country of their choice. (Marrus 1985)

The argument was true for all categories of foreigners. The registers of hotels and inns were more poorly kept than ever. In Nancy, as early as 1826, they were replete with insulting or ridiculous markings, which the police chief strove to eliminate (DA MM 4 M 136). Although civil status had existed for a long time and was carefully regulated in the Civil Code, it often remained difficult to prove one's identity.[3] Until 1880, "professional criminals constantly swapped names among themselves," wrote Pierre Durand. "The police were forced to rely solely on the memory of its agents" (Durand 1910, 53). For foreigners, the problem was made worse by the fact that they often came from countries where civil status was practically nonexistent. Even naturalized citizens often found it difficult to prove their new status, either because their declarations had been recorded by mayoralties on loose sheets of paper that had been lost or because the official statement was not properly conveyed to the *Bulletin des lois*.[4]

Additional evidence that "foreigner" had not yet emerged as a specific category can be found in the statistical registers, which list the individuals arrested over the course of each month. Even in a department such as the Bouches du Rhône, under the heading "foreigners" were listed both individuals born abroad and those who came from another department and carried a mandatory "internal passport." Brawls in the "heated" neighborhoods of Marseilles between "Italians" and French citizens were mentioned in the reports, but without the slightest sign of xenophobia. For example, in 1857, although the fights had resulted in several deaths, the municipal police official wrote: "The various assassinations committed during the month of December did not disturb the public peace. The assassins were all arrested and put at the disposal of the law" (NA F7 3942). Under the heading "the state of foreigners," the archival files for the period preceding the fall of the July Monarchy contain, aside from statistical data, nothing more than ritual phrases attesting to the foreigners' "good conduct" and to the fact that "no complaint has been filed against them." The French police made a point of honor of concluding its reports with an assessment of "public peace."[5]

It should also be noted that at the time, "being French" did not entail substantial privileges. Unlike adult French citizens since 1848, foreigners were, of course, deprived of the right to vote and excluded from public service jobs; a law passed in 1850 prohibited foreigners from opening schools, and a decree in 1852 denied them the right to become newspaper editors. But these restrictions did not add up to much in most people's daily preoccupations. On the other hand, the gradual liberalization of access to "civil rights" played a key role in making conditions equal for all; for example, the law on mutual aid societies dated 15 July 1850 said nothing of excluding individuals who were not French. Furthermore, despite their diversity, the municipal regulations on charity bureaus in major French cities tended to emphasize the length of an individual's stay in the community rather than his or her nationality of origin. The explanation for this is that "social rights" were still, at the time, the material and ideological province of "Christian charity," and the "poor" had no fatherland (Houzé de L'Aulnoit 1885). Although in periods of crisis foreigners were sometimes the first to bear the brunt of selective assistance, in the north during the 1840s, for example, this was by no means the general trend (Lentacker 1973).

In the workplace, before the law of 1898, "our nationals received no favors from the law; there was complete assimilation, in terms of work accident compensation, between a foreign and a French worker" (Martin 1908, 10). Despite repeated controversies over the question of individuals who had been admitted to residency on the grounds of reforestation, article 105 of the Forestry Code did not exclude foreigners, and consequently the judicial system systematically confirmed their rights (Médecin 1909).

As we will see, not to be French was in some ways an advantage; noncitizens were, for example, exempt from military service, an obligation that the populace particularly resented.

The combination of the principle of admission to domicile and jus sanguinis permanently established the existence of intermediate categories of individuals who could not be definitely classified as "French" or "foreign." This situation had already been a cause for concern in the Ministry of Justice under the July Monarchy. The procedure of admission to domicile, defined as a kind of "quasi-naturalization," was considered a "dangerous semblance of naturalization that places the individual in a situation where he is torn by two countries" (NA BB 11405, quoted in Echinard 1973, 271). As reliable a jurist as Daniel de Folleville wrote that

> many individuals, established in France from father to son from time immemorial, have not been naturalized per se, but nonetheless enjoy the status of Frenchmen.... Some may occupy public jobs, even participate in parliamentary assemblies or municipal councils by virtue of an error on the part of the voters who believed them to be French." (Folleville 1880, 190)

How remote this picture seems to a twentieth-century observer.

Immigration: The Word and the Idea

Simply thumbing through old dictionaries reveals that the terms "immigration" and "immigrants" were practically absent from the legal as well as the sociological literature prior to the 1870s. Jean Dubois (1963) made no mention of these terms in his work on the French political and social vocabulary used in the first years of the Third Republic. They were also absent from the *Littré* dictionary, although they did appear in its 1876 supplement. Pierre Larousse's *Grand Dictionnaire universel du XIXe siècle,* published in 1865 and 1876, ignored the immigration issue altogether. The word, as well as the notion, were absent even from the dictionary's first supplement, published in 1878 to "repair the omissions" caused by the appearance of new terms during the twelve years it took to prepare the first edition. Only ten years later, with the publication of the second supplement, did immigration finally make its appearance in the "*Grand Larousse.*" In an article entitled "Migrations," written in 1878 for the *Dictionnaire des sciences médicales,* Alphonse Bertillon noted that the term "immigration" had "only recently" been introduced.

Unlike the term "foreigner," the word "immigration" was part of a lexicon that emerged at about the time of the Third Republic. Moreover, its two French derivatives, *immigré* and *immigrant*—two terms that are often nowadays used interchangeably—did not originate in the same intellectual circles. Whereas, as we have seen, the word "foreigner" belonged to the legal vocabulary, the term "immigrant" entered through fields of scholarship that were profoundly transformed during the 1880s as a result of their gradual institutionalization. The term first arose among statistician-demographers, under the leadership of the Bertillon family. In the definition provided by the aforementioned *Dictionnaire des sciences médicales* (1878, article entitled "Migrations"), Alphonse Bertillon defined "immigration" as a process illustrating the arrival of an immigrant "in the new country of adoption," and he then stated that of all countries, "it is in France that the least is known about migratory flows." To this assertion directly aimed at geographers and demographers, Bertillon added another intended for statisticians, statesmen, and entrepreneurs: "From the perspective of social accounting, a Nation is similar to a factory. Whether it is people or things that are produced, the keeping of books is subject to the same rules and obligations: One must record exactly what *enters,* what *exits,* establish the *balance* of this two-way movement and *verify,* according to the *state* of the register and the products in the store (inventory or counting), the accuracy of the account of *movements* (what comes in and what goes out)" (emphasis in the original). This method informs "the foremost authority (factory boss or head of State)" of the company's performance.

The definition put forth by the *Grand Larousse* was based on the demonstration by the SGF that the number of foreigners residing in France had tripled in the span of three decades. This was interpreted as compensating for French unwillingness to have many children, but it was not seen as a political risk, since France's "capacity for assimilation" was "large enough" to absorb these foreigners.

This analysis of the lexicon of immigration puts before us a familiar set of problems that were characteristic of industrial society as France encountered it in the late nineteenth century.

Statistician-demographers found themselves at the crossroads between several disciplines that gained extraordinary power and influence during this period. The French statistical apparatus developed substantial material, human, and conceptual resources during this period (INSEE 1977). Since 1851 (with a hiatus in 1856), quinquennial censuses had counted the foreign population according to sex and nationality, and the range of available statistics became increasingly diversified. The *Bulletin hebdomadaire de Paris,* the Criminal Justice administration, and the Court of Seine all provided statistical data about foreigners. The period also witnessed the proliferation of international statistical congresses oraganized for the purpose of harmonizing definitions, procedures, and censuses.[6]

In a matter of years, progress in the demographic sciences (Dupâquier and Dupâquier 1985) combined with advances in statistics produced a radical transformation of analyses regarding the makeup of the French population. In their works on the subject, such noteworthy scholars as Emile Levasseur, a statistician-demographer, focused on the issue of the "declining French birthrate," a problem that was considered "worrisome" and for which a series of publications sought a remedy; immigration was seen, in this perspective, as a makeshift solution (Levasseur 1889).

At the same time, the field of political economy also underwent decisive changes. Past theories, which were defended by the *Journal des Economistes* or *La Réforme Sociale,* were challenged in the pages of Anatole Leroy-Beaulieu's journal *L'Economiste français.* In his own work, Leroy-Beaulieu lashed out against the indifference of traditional political economy toward problems of immigration and colonization. The polemic with protectionists that was spearheaded by this firm advocate of liberalism helped to establish immigration as a serious issue (consider, for example, the famous debate on the protection of the labor market). As one author observed in 1898, "in these past years, with the rise of the labor question in particular, the presence of foreigners in France has been examined from an economic standpoint that no one had thought of before" (Barrier 1898). This sudden interest in immigration was not unrelated to the growing autonomy of economics within the curricula of law schools. A considerable growth in the number of dissertations in economics occurred in the final years of the century. That the immigration question had gained a measure of legitimacy is attested by the political economy essay question formulated in 1901 by the *agrégation* exam[7] in law: "Must the national labor market be protected against foreign immigration?" (Bigallet 1901). The field of legal studies was also affected by these changes. In the 1880s, during which the monopoly of "civilists" was challenged by the rise of new branches within the legal sciences (such as social, commercial, and administrative law), the reign of "distinguished experts" declined in the study of law. On a doctrinal level, the offensive launched by the so-called "publicists" led to the first major change since the Civil Code. The importance of "the immigration problem" was one argument, among others, put forth by scholars in search of recognition within the new branches of legal studies. In his treatise on naturalization published in 1880, Daniel de Folleville vigorously advocated the development of private international law. He deplored the fact that, in French universities, there were no courses on "peoples' rights," and he proposed an urgent, large-scale reshaping of courses on administrative law and on political science (Folleville 1880).

In certain fields of inquiry that had not yet been clearly defined, such as "criminal science" (on the margins of law, philosophy, and morals), immigration statistics were widely used as evidence of the "scientific" quality of the discipline (particularly in the works of Gabriel Tarde, Durkheim's main opponent). Explanations based on "ethnicity," chiefly defended by Lombroso in Italy, were very influential in France as a result of recent discoveries—in physical anthropology, psychology, and biology—that emphasized issues of heredity and race. Transposed into the political realm, these themes provided arguments for new definitions of "nationality" (Barrès 1893).

The law of 1889, widely regarded as the first expression of a Nationality Code (Le Sueur and Dreyfus 1890), illustrates the breadth of the change that occurred in the 1880s. In 1882, Senator Batbie proposed a law that, without reforming the existing legal framework for naturalization, regrouped the different texts on the subject that were dispersed throughout the legal literature. In 1884, in the midst of this "revisionist campaign," which by and large reiterated past positions, a congressman from the north, Maxime Lecomte, advocated amending military law to declare that the children born in France of French-born foreigners would automatically be French when they reached adulthood. The proposal went to the Senate, where a new naturalization law was being examined. The Batbie bill was modified to take this new element into account, but the senators rapidly realized that the bill was contradictory from a legal point of view. The issue was then entrusted to the Council of State. Given that this institution was dominated by "civilists," the bill was stripped of all of its clauses that were deemed contrary to jus sanguinis. The members of the council argued that recent anthropological studies had underscored the role of race in the formation of the national character (Agel 1889). The bill returned to the Senate in 1886 completely rephrased, and public opinion reacted with an uproar to its announcement. The flights of fancy expressed by the Council of State met with widespread opposition because they failed to take into account the real problems of French society. By this time, the debate had already become focused on second-generation immigrants' access to French nationality. The main issue at stake, military service, generated two debates of fundamental importance. Nationalist and anti-German elements argued that because of France's demographic decline, alternative sources for military recruitment had to be found. The argument used to justify the urgent need for a reform of nationality law was that Germany boasted seven times as many naturalized citizens as did France in a foreign population one-seventh as large (Cordier 1887). A similar argument held that to accept the maintenance, from one generation to the next, of a foreign population settled in France would create a "*Fremdenfrage*" comparable to that of Russia or the Austro-Hungarian empires. The law therefore had to be reformed to end the emergence of "nonindigenous cores" (*noyaux allogènes*), that is, ghettos, in French society.

The second major argument expressed through the controversy over military service was linked to the economic crisis. Since employers often hired workers whom they were certain would not leave, foreigners, who were exempt from serving several years in the army, enjoyed a competitive advantage over French citizens in the labor market. The requirement for mandatory military service for all French citizens, passed in the early 1880s and implemented in 1889, made this problem even more acute. This explains the logic behind a bill to reform nationality law; the bill's author, Maxime Lecomte,[8] justified his project before the Chamber of Deputies in these terms: "The fact that for eighty years, generations of foreigners have resided on our territory while conserving their autonomy, and without sharing the same national defense interests as French citizens, is dangerous and must be reversed."[9]

The Senate went on to examine a new bill that incorporated two major innovations: Children born in France of foreigners themselves born abroad would become French citizens upon reaching adulthood. Children born in France of non-French parents who had also been born in France (a situation later referred to as "double jus soli") would be automatically considered French, without the possibility of declining.

Adopted by the Senate, the new bill was passed by the Chamber of Deputies with slight modifications that further reinforced the principle of *jus soli.* Eight years of discussion had culminated in "new legislation" adapted, as one senator put it, to "a new social situation."[10]

This law, which some considered "liberal," also made concessions to the advocates of "race" and "heredity." In a departure from the mainstream principles upheld under the Second Empire, naturalization no longer entailed immediate access to the totality of rights enjoyed by citizens. For a period of ten years, a recently naturalized Frenchman could not aspire to run for parliamentary office. The "internal borderline" between the "national" and the "foreign" was clearly delineated by the Nationality Code, in which jus soli was confirmed and admission to domicile was marginalized.[11] This was in fact a rationalization of the law, in that it abolished the intermediate legal category that had designated people who had acquired, generation after generation, the ambiguous status of being semi-French and semi-foreign.

To be properly understood, the 1889 naturalization law must be viewed in relation to another controversial issue of the 1880s: the question of "identification documents," which was directly addressed, for the first time, in a decree dated 2 October 1888. This problem brings us to the world of police procedures, which was more familiar with memoranda than with laws, and where many disputes were resolved informally. To clearly understand this world, therefore, requires a careful study of the archives. In such a context, as we will see, a given "conjuncture" (with its fortuitous circumstances and the array of "fundamental" problems it conceals, such as economic crisis and the rise of nationalism), can crystallize into material measures and lasting institutional forms that make any return to the past impossible. From 1884 onward, parallel to the debate on the nationality question, another parliamentary controversy broke out over the "taxation of foreigners." In less than thirty years, a total of about forty bills related to this issue came up before the chamber. The main argument put forward by its advocates was that French workers had to be protected from the competition of foreign workers and that the latter (or their employers) should therefore be required to pay a special tax, also presented as "compensation" for the exemption of foreign workers from military service. The government of the Third Republic repeatedly rejected these claims, which so contradicted the republican values of the French Revolution that they were equally decried by such diverse individuals as Martin Nadaud and Maurice Rouvier. But the fundamental explanation for the failure of these projects is that they contradicted the freedom of movement clauses written into treaties signed between France and dozens of other nations. To adopt such measures would have led to France's exclusion from the international "community of Nations" (Bernard de Jardin 1899). On numerous occasions, the veto emanated directly from the Ministry of Foreign Affairs.

The labor shortage generated further conflicts of interest, which intensified toward the end of the century. The spokesmen for large industry and agriculture frowned upon any measure that might cause the departure of a badly needed contingent of foreign laborers.

An eleven-member parliamentary commission was finally named in October 1886.[12] To solve the international problem, the commission suggested that all foreigners be required to declare their residence in France at the town hall nearest their home, which would record the information in a special register. The municipal authorities would, in turn, deliver an official document attesting to the proper registration of each individual.

The willingness to protect the labor market was therefore wrapped in an apparent effort to facilitate identification control procedures. This scheme was not simply aimed at circumventing the obstacle of international treaties; it also represented, at that particular moment, a collective realization that the millions of foreigners residing in France were not, in practice, subject to the slightest census count. This is eloquently expressed in an important and oft-cited report to the chamber written by a deputy named Pradon. Describing the situation of foreigners in France, Pradon wrote:

> There is not the slightest hint of a past record; even that social label and basic indicator of one's identity, the name, is uncertain. It varies according to need. How can the person's claims be verified? What if that person carries no identification, or if the documents he displays are false? There is nothing we can do. This is why so many investigations targeting foreigners are abandoned.[13]

Other similarly inclined authors viewed taxation as a means of identifying and counting foreigners present in France:

> The residence tax will scare no one away, but for its application to be effective, the past record, address, profession and morality of each foreigner must be investigated; which implies close surveillance, and would grant the police prerogatives to expell individuals considered unworthy of residing in France. (Bérard 1886, 38)

The controversy continued for several years in the press and in parliamentary debates without producing concrete measures. The accession of General Georges Boulanger as the head of the War Ministry, however, provoked a sudden acceleration of events. In the context of the Schnoebelé affair, the administration, shaken by the rivalry between the ministers of war and the interior, became caught up in a veritable war scare (see NA F7 12581, 12582). From 1886 onward, the Interior Ministry was the object of harassment by the military, which sought to increase coordination between the two services for the control of foreigners. Faced with the inertia of the police, the War Ministry mobilized the gendarmerie. Between March and May 1887, foreigners suspected of espionage were listed separately: of the others, those available for military service received a special mention. Prefectures around the country protested the attempt to use the police services to organize a "territorial secret service." The prefect of the Alpes-Maritimes, for example, in a letter of 18 February 1887, denounced the "confusion of powers" implicit in this initiative and warned that "the generals" might rapidly become "the true authorities in command of civil servants."

The Interior Ministry had to move quickly in order to avoid being stripped of its prerogatives. On 9 February 1887, a confidential memorandum requested that prefects in strategic locations keep an eye on newly arrived foreigners, "for the time being." The order suggested that hotel keepers be reminded of the July 1791 law concerning the inscription of foreigners in the appropriate registers.[14] Finally, after several months of hesitation, the decree, which closely resembled the bill brought before the parliamentary commission, was published on 2 October 1888. Within six months of each other, the two measures that to this day remain the cornerstone of the identity of foreigners came into legal and administrative existence.

On Different Manners of Playing with the Border

Given the written and oral satisfaction expressed by political leaders following the adoption, in 1888 and 1889, of measures intended to solve the immigration problem, one might suspect that the polemics that had raged during these years would fade away themselves and seek other causes. On the contrary: The solution created the problem. The issue of the "identity of foreigners" was only beginning.

The unrelenting dynamic that (along with the legislation passed by the Vichy government) set the stage for more contemporary controversies has three causes whose long-term effects can be examined. The first is the intensification of international relations. Technical progress (in transportation and in armament) and the exacerbation of nationalisms reinforced what Norbert Elias has called the "chain of interdependence" (the threat of war or terrorism) and legitimated any policy of identifying foreigners.

Furthermore, given that foreigners were by definition excluded from all forms of political participation directly concerning them (except through their country of origin), they had only one way of protesting policies of which they disapproved: flight. The creation of a legality creates the possibility of illegality, that is, of "illegal" immigration. Immigrants were confirmed in their social role, which consisted of eternally pursuing someone else's identity.

Finally, in times of crisis, measures taken to close off the labor market not only affected working-class immigrants on a large scale but were also felt by the middle classes and among the liberal professions. The "social demand" for strict identity controls of foreigners was accentuated. The substantial electoral payoffs of such a policy did not go unnoticed in political circles (with, as we will see, variations according to parties and epochs).

By the 1890s, these three causes had already played a key role in extending the discussion of the possibility of taxing foreigners. Immediately following its announcement, the October 1888 decree was decried as insufficient. In Paris, many foreign workers avoided making the required declaration; the hotel register police, busy with other tasks, lacked the resources to ensure the enforcement of the law (Bernard de Jardin 1899). Above all, the decree's opponents underscored the fact that it failed to solve the problem of competition in the labor market. These three factors explain the promulgation of the law dated 8 August 1893, whose stated goal was both to "ascribe a civil status to foreigners" and to efficiently protect French workers from foreign competition. The law repeated the terms of the October 1888 decree, but it was aimed above all at foreigners with a professional activity in France. In order to obtain a license, a foreigner arriving in a community to take on a job would henceforth be required to register at the town hall or police station. Non–wage earners, idlers, and tourists remained subject to the 1888 decree. To be able to register, each immigrant had to present proof of his identity in the form of a birth certificate. If the person was born in a country in which formal civil status was not established, he faced the obligation of having an identity document validated by a consulate. This formality had to be renewed at each change of residence. A certificate of registration was delivered to the beneficiary at the cost of a fiscal stamp, and failure to present it to the police in the event of an identity check led to expulsion. Diplomats were exempted, border dwellers needed to go through the formality only once, but seasonal workers were required to renew the certificate of registration each year.

In five years, a new era had been ushered in. For the first time, as Janine Ponty has noted, a distinction was made between laboring and nonlaboring immigrants; it was, in short, a first step toward the modern-day "immigrant worker" (Ponty 1985).

Despite the opposition of the large industrialists and farmers and the official protests of neighboring countries, the parliamentary fervor continued. No sooner had the law been approved than a deputy from the north announced a new bill that would oblige border dwellers to make a weekly declaration (NA C 7323). The ease with which foreigners managed to sidestep the law at this stage provided opposition members of all persuasions with an ideal argument to denounce the carelessness of the government. At this stage, "nomads" became a primary target of the authorities.

At the end of the century, wanderers were submitted to a very rigorous census. In April 1908, Georges Clemenceau demanded strong measures to force wanderers to adopt a fixed identity. Their future for the next half-century was finally determined by a 1912 law. Travelers, who until then had fallen under legislation concerning vagrancy, were now required to carry an "anthropometric identity booklet," which, along with entries showing their civil status, included the following entries: "the height of the waist and chest, the size, length, and width of the head, the bizogomatic diameter, the length of the right ear and of the left middle and little fingers, and the color of the eyes. Spaces will be reserved for fingerprints and for the two photographs (face and profile) of the booklet holder."[15] "For the first time ever in our modern legal system, a text is introduced that gives the administration the possibility of denying individuals not only the right to reside but also the right of entry, on the grounds that their presence is deemed dangerous" (Dallier 1914, 58). The important thing to notice here is that the law specifies "nomads" but is in fact aimed at foreigners. Generally overlooked by studies on the history of wandering populations, Dallier strongly emphasized this point in his work. Although international agreements signed by France prevented the authorities from overtly recognizing it, "the promoters of the 1912 law were in fact aiming at foreigners" (Dallier 1914, 56). At first applied to individuals who combined the unworthiness of both the "nomad" and the "foreigner," the "card" (in its modern version) would soon be required of immigrants in general.

The First World War, which radicalized distrust of all non-French individuals, was the golden opportunity. A bill presented in 1915 criticized the insufficiencies of the law of 1893 and demanded that at the end of the war, an identification card be required for all foreigners residing in France. "This card will mention, very obviously, the nationality of its holder, his civil status, his photographic description, his profession and it will carry his signature." The document was soon also required to carry the person's address and a visa renewable each year (NA C 7725). This proposal became official policy through two decrees announced in April 1917. The identification card became mandatory for all foreigners above the age of fifteen residing in France. A card with a special color was created for wage earners in agriculture and industry.

From 1918 onward, a series of memoranda and decrees added the final touches to the identification policy applied to foreigners, proceeding by "trial and error" on the basis of the various interests involved.[16] The scale of these transformations is apparent in the law dated 11 August 1926, which abrogated that of October 1893 and formally incorporated earlier changes. The certificate of registration became a full-fledged identity document, in the form of a card complete with the "bare-headed portrait" of its bearer. Data indicating an individual's profession was added to information about civil status. It became necessary to have a work contract in order to qualify for a job, and a person's occupation (agricultural or industrial) was specified. Renewable every two or three years, the card was to be stamped within forty-eight hours of a person's arrival in a community and of any subsequent change of address. The card was valid anywhere in the nation, but the slightest change in one's sector of job activity required a completely new document. The reimposition of a fee (which, according to the authorities, was not a tax but "payment for a police service") ultimately reinforced the distinction among three categories of foreigners: Some (domestic employees, chauffeurs, artisans, tradespeople, and the like) were not considered "workers" and hence paid the full fee for their card. Workers, on the other hand, were entitled to a discount, provided they had entered the country legally; those whose status had been regularized after their entrance paid the full fee. Last, there were those for whom the fee was waved, particularly in cases when a certificate of indigence had been obtained. Tourists received special treatment, and in 1928, a card was established for people living in frontier zones. Since the distinction between French and foreigner had become increasingly clear, numerous subcategories were reestablished as concessions to those with a vested interest in the matter.

Again in the 1930s, it was through the card that the authorities satisfied the claims of social groups who held foreigners responsible for their misfortunes. In 1934, entrance into the country was further restricted by the refusal to issue cards for a period exceeding eleven months, and the automatic extension of permits beyond an initial five-year period was called into question. In August 1935, artisans were required to carry a special identification card that mentioned their trade and was valid strictly for the exercise of that profession within a given department. The Popular Front made matters worse by ratifying the "artisans' card." These restrictive measures were periodically reinforced throughout 1938; and on 12 November, foreign shopkeepers were required to carry a document indicating their profession on the front page. In addition, a "health passbook" for foreigners was established in June 1938.[17]

What this proves is that conditions were quite propitious for the xenophobic and anti-Semitic legislation drafted by the Vichy government. Indeed, an identification card was instituted for Jews as a prelude to the police raids (Marrus and Paxton 1981).

The return to democratic government in 1945 did not, however, lead to a revision of the prewar legal framework. Despite the distinction introduced between residence permits and work permits, the breakdown by categories (temporary, ordinary, privileged) remained unchanged. Furthermore, the 1938 requirement for foreign shopkeepers' I.D. remained in effect, and most liberal or administrative professions were still inaccessible to foreigners. If, as a deputy told the National Assembly in the mid-1980s, the system of residency permits has remained largely unchanged since the war,[18] it is because its stability and efficiency are guaranteed by fifty years of experience. Recent debates have proven that the issue of immigration is inseparable from the question of "residence permits."

The history of the Nationality Code is closely related to that of the I.D. card. As will soon become apparent, to this day legislation on nationality has generally been conceived within the framework of national boundaries as they stood in the late nineteenth century. The political game consists of controlling this space to its fullest extent and rephrasing increasingly subtle definitions that are ambiguous enough to allow government high-handedness. Here again, 1893 was a watershed year (which proves that any reform of the card had an impact on the code). The adoption of the "double jus soli" principle was immediately followed by a government-sponsored bill in which two restrictive measures were introduced. A child born in France of a French-born foreign mother could decline the new nationality when he or she reached adulthood and was therefore no longer automatically considered French (this law changed in 1973). This clause was in part a concession to countries of emigration, which feared the "annexation" of their citizens by France, but above all, it was a reflection of the xenophobic climate that overtook the country in the 1890s. This is evidenced by the second reform of the Nationality Law in 1889. In some cases (which cannot be reviewed in detail here) the authorities could henceforth deny French nationality to a person considered "unworthy" or undesirable. This new state prerogative caused an uproar in both the National Assembly and the Senate. Antonin Dubost (who sponsored the 1889 law) predicted that this breach would be exploited by the government to further increase its involvement in nationality-related issues. On the right, Thellier de Poncheville noted that the one thing the bill neglected to do was clarify what the government meant by "unworthy," which paved the way for its arbitrary implementation.[19] Opponents of the bill were not entirely mistaken in fearing that state intervention would constantly grow in its aftermath. The 1945 code, by adding "failure to assimilate" and "serious physical incapacities" to the list of justifications for denying French nationality, further legitimized the practice. With the exception of the clause on physical incapacities, all of these measures were ratified by a law passed in 1973, and few contemporary politicians seem to find anything wrong with them.

The economic expansion of the 1920s and the ensuing shortage of labor brought liberal trends back to the fore. A 1927 law distinguished between "naturalizations" as such (which inspired a decree aimed essentially at first-generation immigrants) and "acquisitions" (a term tailored for the second generation). Most of the new measures dealt with naturalization per se: the legal age of eligibility was reduced from twenty-one to eighteen years, "admission to domicile" was abolished, and the length of the waiting period shortened to three years. To satisfy the "populationists," the law stipulated that a French woman who married a foreigner would retain her nationality, meaning that her children would be born French (and, it was hoped, proud of it).

The arguments brought out in the ensuing parliamentary discussion were basically the same as those expressed in 1889. For Charles Lambert, one of the main authors of the bill, the goal was to provide France with 100,000 additional soldiers and avoid the emergence of nonindigenous cores. For advocates of jus sanguinis, the project was too liberal, for it amounted to the indiscriminate granting of French nationality. As the rapporteur observed, the new code would have been defeated had the state not assumed new prerogatives to limit naturalizations. While the new bill was not a simple repetition of the 1895 Michelin law (which proposed to ban the descendants of foreigners from public office for four generations!), it nonetheless reinforced restrictions on naturalized citizens. Their ineligibility for office was extended to all elected offices. Furthermore, the law ratified the possibility of being stripped of one's French nationality, which dated back to the First World War (Salmon-Ricci 1929).

Legislative measures throughout the 1930s were replete with cheap concessions to the prevailing xenophobia. The law of 19 July 1934 broadened the scale of restrictions by excluding foreigners from all government-paid jobs. Once again, what was said was said, for although the Popular Front eliminated retroactivity, it reinforced the measures taken in 1934. This restrictive policy was aggravated by a series of decrees enacted in November 1938: A naturalized citizen had to wait five years before obtaining the right to vote, and a mandatory French-language exam was added to the requirements for naturalization. Edouard Daladier justified these measures by stating that it was necessary to overcome naturalization's "excessively 'automatic' character. . . . We must distinguish between good foreigners and undesirables" (AEF B39915; Bonnet 1974). By simplifying the procedure for government appropriation and establishing detention camps for the expelled, the government inaugurated a policy that the Vichy government would simply take a step further. A law dated 22 July 1940 initiated reconsideration of naturalizations decreed since 1927, a measure that affected 15,000 people (Marrus and Paxton 1981). Jews and native-born French with one foreign-born parent were banned from employment in the administration. Here again, post-Vichy legislation did not imply a significant policy change. Regarding the Nationality Code, Justice Minister René Pleven believed that by simply introducing a more logical classification, he had "consecrated earlier legislation."[20] Minor amendments notwithstanding, the principles of 1889 and 1927 were indeed ratified. Exclusionary employment policies remained in effect, as did temporary bans on the right to vote (for five years) and eligibility (ten years). During the Cold War years, governments made frequent use of a legal framework that enabled them to deprive second-generation immigrant activists, who were massively enrolled in movements led by the Communist Party, of French citizenship.[21] Only in 1973 did real change begin to occur, reflecting larger transformations in French society. Yet the amendments proposed by the special commission created at that time continued to meet with strong government resistance. René Pleven, concerned that access to French nationality might turn into a "free-for-all," vetoed the reduction to five years of the waiting period for naturalization. The justice minister stood firmly by restrictions imposed on naturalized citizens, which Jean Foyer referred to as a "wart" in the legislation, "the maintenance of which would hark back to the law of 1934."[22] The new law abolished voting restrictions, but the period of ineligibility was only shortened; a majority of deputies were convinced by the argument that "political representation based on a person's former national origin" should not be encouraged. Only in 1978 were all professional restrictions abolished, and restrictions on naturalized citizens' eligibility were lifted in 1983.

When Words Mean Deeds

The preceding pages have shown that the existence of "cheaters," "illegal" or "undocumented" individuals, was one of the arguments most frequently invoked to justify the reinforcement of strict regulations on identification. This leads us to a crucial aspect of the history of "the Card and the Code": the means employed to ensure the application of legal and political decisions. From the perspective of social history, this is a good opportunity to discuss how the performative efficiency of discourses analyzed by linguists is achieved. From the perspective of history, immigration is a good illustration of Pierre Bourdieu's point that a whole set of sociological conditions must be met in order for "words to become deeds" (Bourdieu 1982).

Evidence from police archives points to the numerous obstacles encountered by officials in their efforts to implement new identity control procedures. In February 1888, a confidential memorandum requesting that prefects require hotel keepers to register foreign guests met with widespread resistance, particularly from the hotel keepers themselves. The special commissioner for the south wrote in May 1888: "Nowhere did I find a single register consonant with the newly prescribed model. All are ancient and poorly kept." Two years later, he reiterated his observation: "In many localities, travelers are not summoned to reveal their identity" (NA F7 12581; see also Néré 1959). From 1889 to 1893, no fewer than nine memoranda addressing this problem were sent to the prefectures by the Interior Ministry. Mayors also balked at obeying instructions that increased their workload. Judging from prefects' response to a memorandum inquiring about reactions to the law of October 1893, opposition in many departments emanated from elected municipal authorities (NA F7 12584). In Doubs, for example, the law was "hampered not by ill faith but, rather, by the inertia and negligence displayed by mayors, many of whom were slow to grasp the complicated play of recent measures regarding foreigners." A similar explanation was given in the case of

Gard: "In many areas, the declaration registers for 1888 are poorly kept, and sometimes they have outright disappeared or been lost in the archives of the town hall." The reports also underscored the incompetence of mayors. In Aisne, "municipalities have not always correctly interpreted the terms of the 2 October 1888 decree"; some thought that young people employed as domestic servants were not affected by the law, others failed to take minors into consideration, and so on.

Another common observation among prefects was that the adaptation of the immigrants themselves to such noncustomary practices was slow. Widespread violations of the law were reported in the first few years following its promulgation. Even in Cantal, by the end of a year one-half of the foreign-born population (80 out of a total of 162) had failed to comply. In the ward of Briey (Meurthe-et-Moselle), 280 such cases were reported on 31 May 1889. The list of individuals whom the police referred to as "unsubdued" included cartwrights, day laborers, farmers, and miners. The nature of the "offenses" registered by the subprefect are eloquent: "believed she was French"; "does not speak or understand French"; "was unaware of the decree"; "did not think of doing it" (DA MM 6M 296). Same thing in Aisne: "Many who had lived in the community ever since they were born thought they were exempt from the prescribed formalities. People who had resided in France for a long period of time were also convinced that the law did not apply to them" (NA F7 12588). Or in Gard: "In a way, foreigners who had resided for several years in major centers had acquired acceptance; and having mixed with the bulk of our fellow citizens whose language and customs they adopted, they were unwilling to abide by the law" (NA F7 12584).

These immigrants had settled permanently in France much earlier, and they represented a majority of the foreign population. "Birds of passage," on the other hand, were constantly moving and changing residences; neither they nor people with legal problems or simply without "papers" responded to identity controls. Efficient means of applying the law had to be found for these unstable individuals, whom public opinion indiscriminately regarded as "nomads."

This question took on particular importance in the late nineteenth century, when the identity paradigm was undergoing fundamental changes. As Carlo Ginzburg (1989) has noted, from Giovanni Morelli's method of distinguishing between authentic and falsified paintings to Conan Doyle's *Sherlock Holmes* and Freud's explanation of neuroses, a new epistemological paradigm was emerging that was based on the interpretation of signs. Although Ginzburg failed to mention this, what must be emphasized in the case of France is that this reordering of thought and practice was centered around the issue of foreigners. Although he is not a well-known figure, one of the men to whom the twentieth century owes the most is Alphonse Bertillon, the inventor of "*bertillonage*" and of the "spoken portrait"; the creator, in other words, of modern techniques for identifying individuals that have become basic to the policeman's trade.

The Bertillon method is based on files of individuals' photographs and on a series of measurements of the human body (in particular, the nose, mouth, eyes, and ears, but also the skeleton), systematically indexed and classified so as to construct typologies. Similarly, *bertillonage* attaches great importance to the physical stigmata that help identify an individual: mutilations, handicaps, skin marks, deformations linked to certain professional activities, "racial" or "ethnic" characteristics (Bertillon 1896; see also Niceforo 1907, chapter 8, "Le Signalement scientifique"). The essential hypothesis is that every human being has an individuality that can be identified by physical characteristics. (In 1888, the Englishman Galton introduced fingerprinting techniques, which by their simplicity eventually supplanted earlier methods.) The new approach also benefited from scientific advances in photography, from progress in forensic medicine, and from the triumph of statistics and of physical anthropology.[23] These scientific trends did not occur in a vacuum; they were accompanied by an equally profound evolution of ideas.

The problem of recidivist criminals rendered elusive by their changing identities triggered the development of this new identification system. It was mainly to end this situation that the prefecture of police in Paris adopted the Bertillon method in 1882, establishing a Judicial Identity Service and then extending the procedure to the rest of the country. This decision marked the end of a prolonged controversy, which had originated under the Second Empire, over the use of photography as a means of identifying individuals. In 1871, the minister of marine and colonial possessions wrote his colleague of the Interior Ministry, to request the implementation of his recent decision to systematically photograph recidivists whose sentence exceeded six months. In his response, the minister of the interior explained that the penitentiary administration had begun considering the use of photography in 1893 but that it had decided against it at the advice of the prison inspection administration. The latter took the position that the measure was appropriate only in "very exceptional cases" and that vigilance was necessary to avoid abuses. To apply this measure to all prisoners "would unlawfully worsen their sentence and add one more obstacle to their rehabilitation." Furthermore, because physical change occurs at all ages, photography was considered an unreliable means of identification (NA F7 12078). (Bertillon would later prove that, in fact, the human skeleton is fully developed by age twenty.) When the efficiency of the system had done away with police skepticism, it was the magistrates' turn to express reservations.[24] It is undeniable that the virulent campaign waged in the press and in parliament against police "incapacity" to keep track of foreigners played an important role in the adoption of new methods. Is it a coincidence that the first systematic application of *bertillonage,* the "anthropological identity booklet," was aimed at nomadic populations? Early on, countless photographs of banned individuals filled the albums kept by the judicial identity service. Anthroponymic files identifying "foreign anarchists" had been established at the turn of the century.[25] The system was soon extended, however, to "ordinary" immigrants. The archives contain numerous files with titles such as "description of suspects," "individual notes on suspects with regard to nationality" (inscribed in logbook B by Boulanger), which included questions pertaining to the civil and physical identity of persons, complete with photograph and fingerprints (see, for example, NA F7 12591ff.). In many cases, a simple breach of the law of 1893 or of the 1888 decree was enough to cause a person to be included in these lists. In one extreme case, a sixty-five-year-old Italian man inexplicably found himself on the list of suspects; he had lived thirty-five years in a community in Alpes-Maritimes, had lost a son to a war on the side of France, and had daughters married to French customs officials (NA F7 12587). The important point here is that *bertillonage* was not simply a technique; it was a new state of mind, a perception of the world and of others. The comparison between police reports at the beginning and at the end of the nineteenth century is eloquent; the assumption of "tranquility" was replaced by the a priori designation of "suspect" or "symptom." The rationalization of police work created an entirely new technology based on the interpretation of signs. This administrative normalization of *description,* a product of Johann Lavater's physiognomy, which was derived from commonsense "typification," undoubtedly contributed to modifying the perception of the "Other." A person's "lightness of complexion" or "foreign accent," for example, became objective, "scientific" indicators of his or her "foreignness."[26] Handwriting was not spared by this hermeneutic. During the Dreyfus affair, Alphonse Bertillon brandished the results of a graphological exam as "proof" that the Jewish officer was indeed guilty. The bureau of criminal investigation obtained the centralization of census returns concerning foreigners, on the grounds that "the handwriting on the returns, which is often that of the individual questioned, is in many cases likely to facilitate identity searches."[27]

This "paradigm of the trace" implied that an ever increasing number of facts had to be recorded regarding each individual. Numerous parliamentary debates on foreigners underscored the paucity of available surveys. In 1882, Talandier argued that a bill to reform the law of December 1849 could not be discussed due to the lack of reliable statistics on expulsions (NA C 7323). Later, a parliamentary commission created to discuss the competition of foreign workers in industry requested that the Labor Office gather facts on this issue.[28] It is therefore no coincidence that in order to facilitate serious statistical studies, a centralization of data accompanied legal efforts to keep track of foreigners. From 1891 onward, the data collected by the police were compared with those of the SGF. For the first time, a statistical study focused specifically on foreigners and was published separately. The collection of statistical data increased steadily thereafter, particularly under the Vichy regime.

In order to measure the impact of the changes brought about by the system of I.D. cards, it is worth mentioning that the description contained in the document was not the only element of identification. The material structure of the card itself was also a sign. Its color, for example, played an important role from the card's inception in 1917 onward. Green indicated an immigrant industrial worker, chamois an agricultural worker. As social categories were diversified, so was the palette: yellow for agricultural workers, grayish-blue for industrial workers, green for nonworkers, blue with red ink for artisans, orange for shopkeepers. After the war, red became the color of temporary residence permits, green the color of ordinary identification cards, and blue the color of "privileged" foreign residents. The fact, that over a period of a half-century, numerous debates and meetings were devoted to this issue proves that it was not a question of detail or poetic fantasy. In 1933, the ministers of the interior and of labor argued over the color of I.D. cards. The latter, upset with not having been consulted, criticized the choices of his colleague, preferring a green card for agriculture and the color manila for industry; both colors were already used for social security cards and were familiar to employers. New colors, he argued, might create confusion and encourage fraud. Under the Popular Front, the controversy focused on the color of the ink used to inscribe the word "artisan," which was considered illegible. The card, it was argued, had to be easily identifiable in order to facilitate controls. The text also had to be as legible as possible, and the individual's profession was to appear in big letters on the cover page. In 1933, the Interministerial Commission on Immigration met to criticize the project adopted by the Interior Ministry: The terms "agriculture" and "industry" were not sufficiently visible on the document. The commission demanded "straight letters, in a straight line, so as to form, in a sense, the title of the document." In November 1936, the minister of the interior suggested that "the term *artisan* be printed in very large typographical characters, so as to catch the eye immediately." Under Vichy, the term "Jew" was written in large letters.

Just as it was vital that no individual be allowed to pose as another, the substitution of I.D. cards had to be prevented. The inventors of the card had naively used "ordinary paper, (and) forms composed with graphic symbols that are readily available to the public" for "less than three thousand francs"; hence the recurrence of fraud. During the 1930s, almost every major city apparently had its underground printing office (EFA B 39914-39916). In 1933, an industrialist from Rives was therefore selected to produce a special type of paper, "the pulp of which is tinted so as to produce a chemical reaction." The year 1937 saw the appearance of watermarked paper, and today, the card has become "unfalsifiable."

The use of the so-called wet stamp, which testified that an immigrant had paid his tax, also required close vigilance. Originally borrowed from a "unique series" and therefore available on the market, the stamp was repeatedly stolen or diverted and had to be modified. In 1935, a special tax label was adopted, but it was unsatisfactory because prefecture employees spent too much time applying it.

Ultimately, the entire layout of signs on the blank page of the I.D. card was debated. In June 1937, for example, the issue was where to move the word "prefect," the rectangle containing the grantee's signature, and the dotted circle to be stamped by the prefecture. The unending process of adjusting the foreigners' I.D. card was accompanied by a steady increase in administrative knowledge. In such an eminently empirical enterprise, progress can only be attained by trial and error. In 1924, the government instructed: "Practice has shown that it was preferable to replace not only the photograph as prescribed by the decree dated 2 April 1917 but also the card itself, rendered useless by wear and tear." Officials later observed that issuing a folded card rather than a single-page one would help reduce fraud and that in order to avoid blurring identification data, glue was preferable to staples as a means of applying the photograph. This process of trial and error eventually culminated in the present-day I.D. card, the product of years of accumulated administrative experience.

What I have described here is an aspect of the process that resulted in the adoption by the police of "scientific identification" techniques: the rationalization of administrative surveillance. Many other cases might be mentioned to illustrate this process, whose history remains to be written. Consider, for example, the problem of foreigners' movements. Upon their arrival, immigrants obtained an identification card at the border recruitment office. It soon became apparent, however, that they did not always continue on to the place of employment indicated in the work contract. The authorities therefore decided to issue a simple pass at the border, which the local mayor or police commissioner was to transform into an I.D. card upon the worker's arrival.

The expulsion of foreigners was also rationalized. Prior to the train and the airplane, the conventional mode of transportation was the paddy wagon. In Savoy as late as the 1880s, however, the road stopped in Briançon, fourteen kilometers from the border; the constabulary and the expelled foreigner had to walk the rest of the way. Elsewhere, in Marseilles for example, the paddy wagon escort took several days, and often weeks, to pass, leaving ample time either for escape or for a diplomatic reversal of the expulsion order (NA F7 12076). Taxation in kind also played an important role in the new logic of identification. Used as a political device to ensure the protection of the labor market, it soon became a key aspect of the system of identification, allowing it to "function by itself." In 1891, the criminal investigation department explained that its project to extend the Service de Contrôle des Etrangers, submitted for approval to the Interior Ministry, would not cost the state a penny. The total sum of fines collected by the Treasury for violations of the 1888 decree amounted to 38,000 francs; "far from weighing on the budget," the system actually provided "a source of revenue" (NA F7 12585). This was supplemented by the income derived from the tax stamp itself, which in 1893 had reached 200,000 francs per year (Médecin 1909). Since this argument was often used to persuade municipal authorities (who cashed in on some of the returns) to apply the law, "finance laws" would periodically attempt to raise the tax, provoking such waves of international protest that the government was often forced to back down.

The key factor, however, was the reorganization of police services that accompanied the steady increase in personnel. In a manuscript note dated 1891, the criminal investigation department stated that the Service de Contrôle des Etrangers had taken on great importance and that this "development had not been foreseen in August 1889, when three employees were assigned to staff the service"; hence the proposal for a new organization chart and a staff capable of handling the extra workload, which "the new legislation examined by the parliament" might increase even further. According to the director, to ensure an efficient system, a chief editor was needed at the head of the service; five employees were needed to verify figures and to record transfers (that is, for example, deaths and departures), admissions, reintegrations into French nationality, and naturalizations. Five assistants would have to be hired to classify forms (five hundred per day and per employee), to note police or court convictions, and to maintain files on "suspects from the perspective of nationality" (2,800 such individuals had already been recorded) (NA F7 12585). A thorough history of the service would reveal the pursuit of this expansion during the ensuing decades. Following the creation of the Office of Judicial Identity, a Central Bureau of Identification Cards for Foreigners, a Refugee Service, and an Expulsion Service, among others, were created. This evolution had an impact at the level of each prefecture and was accompanied by a proportional extension of police personnel.

Centralization and specialization were other aspects of this process of bureaucratic rationalization. The new Nationality Code, issued in 1889, introduced a new procedure. Since mayors were considered unqualified, declarations would henceforth be made to justices of the peace, who would then transmit them to the chancellery. In 1933, when the paper used for identification cards was changed, their manufacture was entrusted to experts of the General Board of Stamps (the Direction Générale du Timbre).

The centralization and expansion of such services explains the growing number of ministerial memoranda regulating procedures down to the tiniest detail (including the proper way to erase the fiscal stamp!). Red tape, which invaded the ministries and archives, became essential to these new modes of administering the verification of identity. For each category of suspects, there was a file and a statistic; each official act produced a copy for the archives, for the "memory" of the state in the event of dispute, loss, or theft. Written production, therefore, also had to be rationalized. In the late nineteenth century, a new era began in the formal history of police archives, with the proliferation of standardized forms (such as acknowledgments of receipt and standardized naturalization or expulsion files). Extensive use began to be made of printed forms. Manuscript texts were increasingly replaced by anonymous typewritten reports.

The authors of the 1888 decree defended it by invoking the need to grant immigrants the same type of civil status as French nationals had. The French administration therefore intensified its efforts to give a new "Christian name" to workers from other lands. It was, in the logic of republican law, a way of pursuing the struggle to eliminate all traces of origins.[29]

Virtually all of the naturalization laws were accompanied by polemics between the advocates and the opponents of the *francisation* of names. In the interwar period, an intense struggle opposed those who, along with the newspaper *Le Figaro,* believed this process to be dangerous on the grounds that "an infinite number of wogs ("*métèques*") hide themselves behind French names" (24 June 1927), and those who held, on the contrary, that a foreign-sounding surname of a naturalized citizen "was prejudicial to our prestige abroad."[30]

Similar concerns were voiced during the 1945 vote on the Nationality Code. One writer expressed concern in the journal *Population* that "except in the countryside, the form of people's names was relatively variegated." In his list of the names of the soccer players on the French team, he found only five true Frenchmen. In a demonstration grounded in historical phonetics, the author defined a "French type of surname," easily recognizable by the absence of "an accumulation of consonants." He therefore advanced several proposals for *francisation*: the *i* in Italian names would be changed to a *y*, the *o* to *eau* (to make them sound more Vendean, or even Chouan?). This raised, the article continued, a serious problem: What was to be done with the Poles? To replace the *i* in Polish names by a *y* would do nothing to improve their situation. No matter, "perhaps Wanilewski could be approximatively replaced by Basile" (Juret 1947).

Following the Second World War, several laws were drafted to further regulate the question. *Francisation* was defined more specifically. For surnames, the measures proposed a "necessary modification to make them lose their foreign character," and for given names, the objective was to replace foreign names with French ones.[31] It was in everyday administrative practice, however, that foreign surnames most often fell victim to the "*machine à franciser.*" Janine Ponty noted, with respect to Polish miners, that difficulties in communication between civil service agents and workers often led to errors, such as confusing an individual's given name and surname or simply misreading the surname. A host of whimsical transcriptions were recorded: "The group of letters *szcz* became *srez, sc* or *er*" (Ponty 1981). In the case of Armenians, *francisation* occurred in civil service registers through the suppression of terminations, or through the transformation of the *i* of terminations into a *j* or an *e; Boyadjian,* for example, became *Boyajean* (Keuroghlian 1977). The same observations are true for Italians in the communal registers of Var: "Giraudo became Giraud, Vimeï became Vimey or Vimet, Viale became Vial" (Mauco and Demangeon 1939, 385). The consequences of these mutilations for the "identity" of immigrants will be discussed in the next chapter.

To Each His Immigrant

Just as it has been said that for each Bambara there was an ethnologist and vice versa (J. Bazin, quoted in Amselle 1985), so it may be shown that as ever growing sectors of French society became interested in the "existence" of foreigners, the "reality" of immigration became self-evident to most. Behind the material forms, behind the "papers" and the institutions, there were always people. We have seen, for instance, that the "card," an idea that did not exist in 1880, ended up mobilizing considerable interests. One after another, the Interior, War, Justice, Foreign Affairs, and Finance Ministries got into the act, as did consuls, mayors, deputies, and a vast array of public officials. Arguments arose between services and between the different echelons of the state apparatus.[32] In short, a multitude of individuals were now directly affected by the Card and the Code through which the identity of foreigners was materialized. The stakes were perhaps greatest at the level of petty civil servants. For the elite, the question of foreigners was one issue among others; for the base, in contrast, what was at stake was the very existence and definition of each appointment. Charles Cornette, civil registrar, and André Andréani, division chief in the prefecture of Alpes-Maritimes, were cases in point; it is thanks to the "problem of foreigners" that they were admitted into the exclusive club of book authors. There was a need for simple texts that would explain the complexity of the legislation to the other second-rank civil servants and avert errors in its application. "During the verification of civil status registers, carried out under the direction of distinguished magistrates, I observed that the records concerning foreigners were not updated as regularly as would be desired," explained Charles Cornette in the preface of his book (Cornette 1889, preface). These words summarized the full meaning of a life and professional consciousness, which, as we will see in the next chapter, did not always work in the interest of the immigrant.

Immigrant: By Virtue of What?

We have traveled only part of the distance on the long road leading to the current legal definition of immigration. An examination of the texts that govern the question today reveals the extraordinary level of complexity it has reached since the Second World War.[33] The law of 17 July 1984, which "simplified" earlier dispositions by creating two types of cards (the one-year temporary certificate of registration and the residence permit, valid ten years and theoretically renewable), in fact illustrates the complications caused by an increase in the number of administrative branches involved after the Second World War. Without entering into the details, which have been concisely examined by the jurist C. Nguyen Van Yen (1987), we should note that the law established temporary "student" cards, others specifying the profession practiced in France, and still others defining the individual as a "member of a family." Likewise, according to article 15 of the 1945 ruling, residence cards are allotted to persons who are able to justify a sufficiently long presence in France, who have family ties in the country, or who are defined as "refugees." In contrast to the status of "temporary resident," the status of "permanent resident" allows the practice of any profession without administrative authorization and protects its holder from procedures of expulsion or escort to the border, except in cases of "absolute urgency."

It should be specified, however, that a series of special cases exist for both types of permits. The employment situation is not an obstacle for "highly qualified" foreigners (such as university professors or senior executives) seeking a wage earner's temporary certificate of registration (*carte de séjour temporaire*); nor can a request for such a certificate be denied if the individual comes from another European country and has lived for some time in France or is considered (regardless of the definition provided by international law) a "quasi-refugee" of Vietnamese, Khmer, Laotian, Lebanese, or Portuguese nationality. The same privilege is granted to members of immigrant families who reside legally in France. A series of special cases also exist for the issuing of residence cards. These are "rightfully" granted to members of the aforementioned groups, to foreigners who have served in the French army, to "political refugees," to individuals who having lived in France since childhood (that is, who arrived prior to the age of ten).

At the risk of boring the reader, we must add individuals with a special status to this list. Members of the European Economic Community (EEC), for example, need only a declaration (rather than an authorization) to carry on a professional activity in France. They possess a specific residency permit: the community residence card (valid five years), which also provides them with added protection from measures of public order. They have access to the procedure known as "family regrouping" without administrative control, whereas other foreigners need to declare the length of their stay and justify adequate housing conditions and resources.

The Algerians form a category in their own right. Following the Evian accords, the situation of Algerians who arrived in 1968 had to be clarified. Their permit consisted of a "certificate of residence" that was valid for five years and that carried the annotation "wage earner." For "historical reasons," their case was handled by the Interior Ministry rather than by the administrative services in charge of immigration. Family regrouping was conditional upon showing a document certifying one's address (delivered by the municipal authority) and a medical certificate.[34] With the decolonization of black Africa and with Gaullist hopes for the creation of a vast economic and cultural space under France's hegemony, other specific sets of rules were defined. A 1960 agreement, for example, offered citizens of the former French colonies of Africa total freedom of movement (upon simple presentation of an identification card from the country in question) and complete assimilation with the French (including into the labor market). Despite repeated efforts to place immigrants from Gabon, Central Africa, and Togo on the same legal ground as other immigrants from "nonprivileged" countries, they maintained, theoretically at least, their original advantages. Similar particularisms resulting from decolonization are apparent in legislation on the Nationality Code.[35]

To explain how we arrived at this legal and administrative imbroglio, two decisive factors in the definition of immigration must be invoked: the development of the welfare state and the intensification of international relations.

As we have seen, the blurred line of demarcation between French and foreign was illustrated in the nineteenth century by the absence of discrimination directly linked to material advantages. Writing on the eve of the First World War, one author noted that politicians of the early nineteenth century were so willing to grant equal legal rights to foreigners that "being French" did not yet offer any particular advantages. Not surprisingly, the advent of universal suffrage modified this situation. The distinction between "rightful claimants" to political expression by the ballot, on the one hand, and everyone else, on the other, was no longer defined according to economic criteria as it had been under the monarchy; it was based on a status defined by national belonging. For people who were not part of circles accustomed to employing such concepts as "the nation," "sovereignty," and so on, the right to vote was the first tangible form of "citizenship" (outside of the military question, which was perceived differently by different sectors of the population). This right could not be perceived as merely theoretical, for it implied a vast process of material organization and the creation of "electoral lists," as well as village- or neighborhood-level mobilization. The dividing line between members of the club and outsiders became quite tangible. The rapporteur of the December 1849 law on the nationality and residence of foreigners justified new legal restrictions in these terms: "Circumstances seem all the more to warrant caution that... the advent of universal suffrage enhanced the importance of the status of French citizenship."[36] Because of the restrictions placed by Napoleon III on true political democracy, the full consequences of new forms of political life did not become apparent until the Third Republic.

There were no discriminatory clauses in the first "social laws" (the limitation of child labor in 1841, the drafting of a system of labor legislation in September 1848). "These prescriptions were aimed at workers in general, without excluding foreigners, for it was not yet understood that there might be dangers involved in allowing foreign workers to benefit from positive legislation; they might then arrive in flocks and compete with nationals on the labor market" (Didion 1911, 60).

Although the laws on hygiene (1893), on the length of the workday for women and children (1892 and 1900), and on a weekly break from work (1906) did not establish a difference between French and foreign, most of the major social laws passed in the late nineteenth century did. The elasticity of the notion "national sovereignty" served as a justification for excluding immigrants from all forms of collective expression. An 1884 law prevented them from playing leadership roles in trade unions. Furthermore, the 1890 law on security and the 1894 law on relief and retirement funds deprived them of the right to vote and of eligibility in the mines. The laws of 1892 (on conciliation and mediation) and 1907 (on the conciliation board) discriminated against them in similar terms, as did the laws of assistance (which replaced "charity"). The 1893 law on free medical care was, unlike previous legislation, reserved for French nationals; and jurisprudence, as Council of State records for February 25 1897 show, accentuated such measures (as was often the case in this period) by prohibiting access to hospitals for foreigners. The law of 1905 on the elderly and crippled was no exception. Interior Ministry memoranda addressed to the prefects left no doubt as to how the authorities interpreted the law. One of them specified that in cases in which "an old man or a cripple who is not in possession of French nationality has been admitted into a commune," the prefect must "intervene to put an end to this formal violation of the law (quoted in Didion 1911, 110). Similarly, most of the forty-two bills on elderly retirement brought before the parliament contain dispositions against foreigners. Finally, the 1910 law on retirement pensions for workers and peasants automatically insured foreigners, whereas French nationals were given a choice.[37]

The most significant example is the law of 1898 on work accidents. The real responsibility for the gradual discrimination established by jurisprudential interpretations lies in the law's own lack of precision (Martin 1908). In cases of work accidents, the family of a foreign worker could not claim compensation benefits unless the family members lived in France (a rare situation for temporary migrants, who were numerous during this period), and if a disabled worker wished to return to his country of origin, he would lose his pension and receive a sum amounting to three times a single pension payment. That same year, Great Britain passed a law on work accidents that showed virtually no discrimination between foreigners and nationals. What happened to the "country of human rights"?

The 1898 law on work accidents caused an uproar in countries of emigration. In the Belgian parliament, representatives denounced its "nationalist and chauvinistic" tendencies. For the press, "the French Republic has reestablished the law of fortune.... [Foreign workers] are declared unfit to take advantage of the right of conventions that Pothier, 120 years ago, regarded as natural law." For this writer, the measures were "monstrous" and invited retaliation, "if the madness and obstinacy of France made such a campaign necessary."[38] The French government offered two main justifications for these measures. First, it was argued that France was a country of high immigration and was more advanced in terms of labor law than were most other nations. Legislation more favorable to immigrants would provoke a wave of new arrivals at a time when there was a shortage of jobs. This problem, which illustrates both the interdependence among nations and the "law of unequal development," remains to this day an obstacle to political liberalism in the formulation of immigration policy.[39] The second reason brings us back to the central theme of this chapter: the construction of an immigrant identity. The government's refusal to pay pensions outside French territory was due to a concern for public finance rather than a lack of generosity. How were the authorities to determine whether the disabled foreigner was married, if he had children, or if those who came forth as "rightful claimants" were truly related to the victim? And if the worker returned to his country, how could the administration keep track of him? How could his death, or possible emigration to France, the United States, or elsewhere, be verified?

Some of these forms of discrimination still persist today.[40] Over the years, however, they were attenuated as problems of record keeping, definitions, and evidence were progressively resolved. Two major series of determining forces may be discerned in this process: international relations, increasingly relevant to questions of immigration, and the interests of the various groups that make up French society. In the constant interplay between labor supply and demand that characterizes modern immigration, countries of emigration have one powerful weapon at their disposal: They may threaten to prohibit their citizens from emigrating to France, a threat that, on various occasions, has been brandished by such countries as Italy, Poland, and even Algeria. The most powerful countries could also resort to various other types of pressure (economic or diplomatic, for example) in order to obtain more favorable treatment for their emigrant workers. The definition of immigration and of immigrants was constantly extended by international law through bilateral treaties and international conventions.

Prior to 1914, France had already signed several accords with large countries of emigration (with Italy in 1904 and 1906 and with Belgium in 1906). This trend was accelerated following the First World War (1919, treaty with Italy and Poland; 1920, treaty with Czechoslovakia) and the Second World War (between 1963 and 1965, treaties with Tunisia, Morocco, Portugal, Turkey, and Yugoslavia). These treaties sanctioned the principle of equality of working conditions, wages, and so on between foreigners and nationals and established the reciprocity rule with respect to rights. In the name of reciprocity, immigrant workers gradually came to benefit from the legislation of the welfare state.

The Franco-Italian treaties reveal how international accords also contributed to the definition of immigrants. In 1919, the French government regarded the reciprocity rule with respect to assistance as too favorable to Italy, given that few French citizens resided in Italy. The treaty therefore introduced several distinct cases. If an Italian worker had resided in France for a total of more than forty-five days or for a period of at least five consecutive months, the cost of assistance was to be covered by the host country. To receive sickness relief, a worker had to account for at least five consecutive years of residence. In the case of assistance to the elderly, disabled, and incurably ill, the length of the required uninterrupted presence in the host country was set at fifteen years (Baille 1927).

It is clear that international discussions established the *length* and *regularity* of residency as the criteria determining who was a rightful claimant and who was not. This is, undoubtedly, of central importance to understanding the strategies deployed by the individuals involved, who found themselves forced to determine their position in relation to these norms in their plans for the future (to leave without anything or to settle in a foreign land). Furthermore, given that they failed to foresee many of the concrete situations that arose, such general accords were sure to provoke disputes. The 1919 treaty, for example, did not specify the *starting point* from which to measure the amount of time spent in France (or in Italy, in the case of French émigrés). Consequently, a new agreement in 1924 defined as evidence of residence in France, in article 6, the identification card for foreigners, the card attesting to one's trade, and inscription in an enrollment register. In the absence of these documents, an administrative inquiry was required. The need to record or register one's identity in order to become a "rightful claimant," written into the 1924 diplomatic agreement, was reinforced by the conditions imposed by charity offices for the acceptance of an applicant. To benefit from assistance to the elderly in Provence, one had to produce no less than fourteen official documents (including a birth certificate, a medical certificate, a health certificate, certificates of nationality and of residence, a report of police inquiry, a mayoral certificate attesting to one's income level). We can see how the issue of "papers" took on increasing importance in immigrants' lives.

The numerous disputes that accompanied these international negotiations and the growing number of foreigners unable to claim even their government's intercession in their favor (refugees and stateless individuals, as well as all those whose government had not signed such a treaty with France) explain the growing number of international accords on the subject of immigration. In 1892 the first sanitary convention was signed in Venice to protect recruiting countries from epidemics of cholera. In 1900, another congress laid the groundwork for an international association for the protection of workers; the congress of The Hague in 1905 was concerned more specifically with free legal assistance; that of Copenhagen in 1910 with issues of relief aid.

The 1924 International Convention of Rome produced the first precise definitions of the terms "emigrant" and "immigrant."[41] This trend was intensified by negotiations on the situation of refugees (such as arrangements of 1926 and 1928, conventions of 1933 and 1938) leading up to the international recognition of "Nansen passports," which made concrete the refugee's legal separation from his former country and defined his obligations with respect to the laws of the host country. The 1951 Geneva Convention sharpenend the definition of a refugee in international law;[42] the 1954 convention in New York defined "stateless" individuals. In general, the movement in favor of an international legal framework for immigration grew considerably following the Second World War, particularly with respect to "human rights." The Council of Europe played a leading role in this process. International conventions on immigration issues are regularly called by European ministers; the European parliament issues "recommendations" to EEC countries, encouraging a "social policy" toward foreigners. Each country now finds itself caught up in a multitude of bilateral accords or international conventions (France and Spain have signed the greatest number). This recent emergence of a broadly respected framework within international law places increasing limits on the role played by national states in the implementation of immigration policies.

These negotiations, which have taken place over an extended period of time, explain one of the most unique features of immigration law—a genuine mosaic of "specific cases," "exceptions to the rule," and "special regimes." This process also illustrates that, in order to defend their interests as immigrants, individuals have no other choice but to address the representatives of their country of origin (when they have one). This is one of the reasons why immigrants, in France even less than elsewhere, have never formed an actual "social group"; unlike those social groups that emerged from the technical division of labor and that gradually managed to obtain representatives and to forge means of struggle and symbols of their identity, thereby forcing the state to take their specific interests into consideration.

The Impossible Immigration Policy

Still, however, domestic political and social struggles have contributed—despite the exclusion of immigrants from them—to the historical construction of a definition of immigration in France. Following the passing of the 1898 law on work accidents, the attenuation of discrimination toward foreigners was not due only to international protests.

Opposition soon appeared in France itself. "On 7 May 1899 in Bayonne, workers from the different building corporations protested against the law, which they believed favored the employment of foreign workers" (Martin 1908, 64). The incipient Ligue des Droits de l'Homme et du Citoyen added its voice to that of the trade unions; in parliament, the parties of the left denounced the effects of the law on "national work." Politicians realized that "raising a hue and cry against the donkey" was not enough to make a policy; the already complex interdependence imposed limits on xenophobia, even from a French point of view. For the labor movement, a sustained demand for equality in wages and working conditions between immigrants and French nationals was a means of conciliating both internationalist claims and the defense of French workers.[43]

That police or taxation measures, in a society that had turned its back on the ancien régime, did not constitute a policy was diffusely expressed prior to 1914; it was forcefully proclaimed on the eve of the First World War by Adolphe Landry, in a bill, submitted to the Parliament in December 1915, that was a full-fledged program for the postwar period. Landry began by criticizing the numerous taxation projects, which he believed aggravated the labor shortage in agriculture and industry. Even before the war devastated the labor market (one-and-a-half million workers disappeared), the author of the project had announced that the labor shortage problem would reemerge after the war, that massive immigration would be necessary, and therefore that the country would need a true immigration policy. Landry put forth a number of broad proposals for such a policy. Before 1914, private recruitment agencies had shown their weaknesses; Landry therefore saw liberalism as an inappropriate solution. It was, he argued, the state's responsibility to orient incoming flows of immigrants to areas where labor was needed. Furthermore, political leaders would have to devise a strategy of assimilation for the new arrivals, in order to avoid the formation of nonindigenous cores that might "alter our race." The measures Landry proposed in essence amounted to examining, from a physical and moral point of view, applications to emigrate to France (NA C 7725).

Given Landry's personality (he was a reputed demographer and future minister), large segments of the French ruling class in all likelihood shared his stance on these questions. Indeed, Landry's program became policy before the end of the war, when the government took charge of recruiting operations, of the selection and housing of colonial workers, and of immigrants recruited for the purposes of war industry (Mauco 1932).

At the parliamentary level, the question of immigration was problematized only after the war. Each major party—according to its electoral constituency—developed its own point of view, and the resulting positions have remained virtually unchanged to this day.

The breadth of needs, the problems faced by French society as a result of the sudden inflow of two million foreigners (particularly, as we will see, with respect to welfare) explain the vigor of the interwar French political controversy. Countless books were published on the issue, a chosen theme of various polytechnical engineers (Pairault 1926). Upper-level civil servants and high-profile politicians, such as Albert Thomas, Edouard Herriot, and Jean Tardieu, wrote prefaces that underscored the importance of the stakes involved (Paon 1926; G. Lefebvre 1929). As a study published in this period noted, whereas the term "immigration" had been rarely employed prior to 1914, after the war it became part of everyday language.

In the brief periods during which the left—which mainly represented the interests of the wage-earning classes—was in power, it established mechanisms that were aimed at controlling private enterprise's recruitment of immigrants. In the early 1920s, the Confédération générale du travail (General Confederation of Labor; CGT), through joint bodies in which it participated (such as placement bureaus) obtained a right of inspection in order to prevent foreign competition from entering the labor market. In 1926, the Left Coalition created a High Commission for Immigration, which Raymond Poincaré dissolved only months later. The Popular Front established the first, short-lived State Secretariat for Immigration, with Philippe Serre at its head.

Right-wing organizations, which represented the interests of owners (especially in agriculture) and industrialists who had a vested interest in foreign labor, played a much more central role in immigration policy prior to the Popular Front, when they exerted almost unshared power. Overall, they took a stance in favor of private enterprise. This was not an expression of American-style "liberalism," however, for they were the first to demand state intervention in the form of police and administrative control. Their primary objective was to closely adapt the inflow of foreign labor to the needs of the French economy. This explains why from the early 1920s onward, the exercise of state tutelage over the recruitment process was seriously disparaged. The Société Générale de l'Immigration, run by large industrialists, controlled most foreign recruitment during the interwar period, earning comfortable profits in the process (the society's capital rose from 2 to 20 million francs between 1924 and 1930).

The role of the state therefore seems to have been much more limited than Landry's program had stipulated. The Foreign Affairs and Interior Ministries respectively took control of diplomacy and public order, which was not fundamentally new. The Labor Ministry, in contrast, extended its influence through the newly created Service de Main-d'oeuvre Etrangère (which in the 1920s employed some 120 people). We have already discussed its role in the establishment of foreigners' identification cards for agricultural and industrial workers to avoid competition in the labor market. The same concern for regulation of the labor force explains the tutelage exercised by the Labor Ministry over the departmental placement bureaus. Furthermore, it retained part of the recruitment tasks, in particular at points of entry (Toul, Modane, Marseilles, Perpignan, Hendaye, Le Havre) where identity, health, and work contract controls took place.

At the time, social policy was a marginal and archaic aspect of administrative activity. In the Loire during the 1920s, a mere five employees handled social cases for the entire department. Not until 1930 was a "foreigners'" service created in the prefecture's office of social affairs. In the 1920's, Marseilles provided welfare for 13,000 elderly, 3,000 of whom were Italian. Of the 6,000 families who benefited from large family allowances, more than half were Italian, as were 20% of the patients hospitalized with free medical assistance. In 1926, of a total budget for relief aid of 17.7 million francs in the Bouches-du-Rhone, some 4.6 million francs were spent on the Italian population alone (for the Loire, see Bonnet 1974; for Marseilles, see Baille 1927). The situation was the same in the iron and steel basins of Lorraine. It was the crisis of the 1930s and the cost of unemployment that precipitated the bankruptcy of an age-old system of managing "poverty" (Noiriel 1984).

With the state unable to meet the need, most social welfare emanated from private sources. The Service Social d'Aide aux Emigrants, created after the war as the French branch of the International Relief Organization, organized several dozens of medical social workers and visiting nurses active in the main regions of immigration. These women, who possessed a very Christian sense of self-sacrifice, were often the wives or daughters of wealthy bourgeois men or aristocrats, and their social role consisted of "doing well," "relieving misery," while their husbands devoted themselves to the exhausting task of managing the affairs of the world. In 1927, most of the relief associations were regrouped within the National Commission of Assistance to Migrants led by the untiring Madame Chevalley (Bonnet 1974). The new role of the church with respect to immigration was more directly illustrated by the work of Cardinal Chaptal, the "foreigners' archbishop," who was director of the newspaper *L'Etranger catholique en France* and waged an energetic struggle against expulsions during the 1930s. In 1939, a Protestant association, the CIMADE, was created with similar welfare objectives.

Following the Second World War, a scenario emerged that was identical to that of the interwar period. In 1945, the state firmly reestablished its control over immigration. The newly created National Immigration Office (ONI) was the instrument of public oversight of all recruitment and placement questions concerning the foreign labor force. Furthermore, these questions were regarded as only one aspect of a global immigration policy, which also included a plan for integrating the foreign population into French society. This program of "assimilation" was in fact an extension of the one that had been partially applied in the late 1930s.[44] The key institution associated with this policy of "assimilation" was the Haut Comité de la Population (High Committee on Population), and the main person was Georges Mauco, who was in charge of immigration issues in the Haut Comité, general secretary from 1937 to 1953 of the Union Scientifique Internationale sur les Questions de Population, and a cabinet member of the Immigration Secretariat within the French government. In a colloquium organized by the International Labor Organization (ILO) in 1937, he outlined a program for the assimilation of foreigners that was implemented following the war (Mauco 1937).

It comes as no surprise that the question of immigration was narrowly linked to the evolution of policies concerning the family, which underwent an extensive process of institutionalization from the 1950s onward. This is evidenced by the creation of a Ministry of Population in 1945. Foreigners were placed under the authority of the Direction de la Population, which itself was made up of five subservices: on the family, mutual aid, settlement, and naturalizations (which, significantly, no longer depended on the Ministry of Justice). The very names given to these services illustrate the process of extension of the state's activities beyond the traditional spheres of police and labor and a political willingness to integrate immigrants. This was clear evidence of the overriding influence exercised at the time by the "populationist" tendency (led by Alfred Sauvy and Michel Debré) in political discussions on the reconstruction of France. It was the experience of the problems faced by the country following the First World War that oriented the thinking of policy makers, many of whom had held positions of power long before the Second World War. Having kept in mind the difficulties that large industry had encountered in the 1920s in labor recruitment, they were convinced of the need to stabilize the foreign-born labor force in the large industrial basins, a process that could only be accomplished by a policy of integration through the family.

But this assimilationist policy also reflected the concessions made to the second generation produced by the migratory flows of the 1920s. The role played by foreigners in the Resistance, the appearance of organizations in which immigrants played an important role, such as the Comité d'Aide et de Défense des Immigrés (CADI), forced the authorities to take their primary demand—integration—into account. Several bills suggesting the creation of a status for foreigners were debated following the war. In 1945, for example, a group of deputies led by Vincent Auriol and Gaston Deferre revealed the motives of their initiative in favor of immigrants: "To obtain the settlement of this labor force is not only just, it is also in the utmost national interest. Settlement should take on the form of assimilation, with a vast majority of immigrants being absorbed by society."[45] The vicissitudes of the Cold War prevented the project from being carried through. Nonetheless, the history of this period left traces in the legislation. The Nationality Code approved in 1945 reflected this assimilationist spirit. The new residency permit also established a preferential treatment for those foreigners who had resided in France for the longest period, by creating a category of "privileged residents."

From the 1960s onward—the Armand-Rueff report of 1959–1960 is often considered a turning point—the liberal and technocratic tendency imposed its views in government, to the detriment of the "populationists." The new economic conjuncture, marked by unprecedented expansion, once again focused attention on issues of supplying the labor force with deskilled and, above all, "flexible" workers. The authorities more or less explicitly encouraged the industrialists' strategies of by-passing ONI oversight. With the new status defined for Algeria after the war, the owners became interested in a "native" workforce that had not until then been considered profitable, but whose recruitment now had the advantage of not being subject to state control. The key weapon, however, was the encouragement of illegal immigration, which the procedure of a posteriori regularization encouraged. Thanks to this procedure, a large part of the immigrant labor force recruited after the Second World War avoided control by the ONI (see in particular INED 1975; Granotier 1979). The initial phase of institutionalizing "social" policies with respect to the foreign population was hindered during the ensuing decades for these very reasons. The authorities, without fundamentally revising the measures taken in the late 1930s and immediately following the war, renewed their traditional reliance on the private sector for social policy toward immigrants (even if it meant financing all or part of the organizations established to this end). This is what occurred in the case of the Fonds d'Action Sociale (FAS), created in 1958; the SONACOTRA, created in 1956; and the ADRI (which produced the television program "Mosaïque"), created in 1975. This attitude explains why the vast "social" domain that lay fallow was gradually taken over, especially after 1968, by far-left activists, who replaced Madame Chevalley and her "visiting nurses" but on an entirely different scale. A multitude of associations in support of foreign workers appeared in such areas as reception, housing, literacy, and legal assistance. While investing considerable energy in a policy of aiding the newly uprooted populations, which must not be underestimated, these activists also struggled to obtain institutional recognition (Marié 1977). Gradually, these volunteers became civil servants who contributed to redefining the "social" and broadening the sphere of state intervention (consider, for example, the "shantytown" scandal that led to the 1970 law on unsanitary dwellings, a law that produced the transit projects and the zones of priority urbanization as we know them today).

Although further research is required on these questions, it is understandable that the number of social groups with a vested interest in immigration grew during the interwar period. This might be viewed as one of the primary reasons for the present-day visibility of second-generation immigrants. Periods of crisis generate a necessary transfer: Society and government direct their interests away from the sphere of production and focus on "reproduction" (in Marxist terms); in other words, the shift is from the foreign-born worker to his family and children. Those who previously participated in the process of institutionalizing "aid to migrants" are encouraged to "reorient" their concerns toward the new generation. Viewed from this perspective, the growth of the administrative division of labor is what makes inventing a new definition of immigration so crucial.

By outlining the "genealogy" of the Card and the Code—which are at the heart of the definition of contemporary immigrant identity—this chapter has sought to *apply* a sociological principle that tends to remain theoretical and that defines the present as a "materialized" or "incorporated" past; for, as Norbert Elias wrote, "sociological theories which are not verified by the work of empirical sociology are good for nothing" (Elias 1983).

I have thus come back, by a different path, to the basic argument of Fernand Braudel's last book: We cannot understand or act upon the present if we know nothing of the past that overdetermines it. This is a lesson that all those—politicians and others—who are today concerned with "problems of immigration" would do well to ponder; failure to do so will surely expose them to new rebuffs.

Three

Uprooted

If you go straight, you will fail the screening,
If you go left, you won't cross the ocean,
If you go right, you will remain DP[1] *all your life,*
If you go backward, your head will be cut off.
Ukrainian poem, 1948

Who will knock at the door of my house?
An open door, come in
A closed door, a den
The world knocks on the other side of my door.
Pierre Albert-Birot, 1983

This book takes issue with Jules Michelet, Paul Vidal de La Blache, Fernand Braudel, Pierre Chaunu, and the countless historians who, in the past, excelled at celebrating the virtues of deep-rootedness in the land. The ancestors invoked in this book are the uprooted of France's history; they are remembered dearly by many in France, but they are absent from its history textbooks and are seldom included in the celebration of our national commemorations.

Because "from the new group's point of view, he is a man without a history" (Schütz 1964), the foreigner is someone who, by definition, has no roots. My purpose here is not, however, to narrate the history of "people without history" but, rather, to shed light on a *process* that, by its very recurrence, can only be said to have a history in the sense described by Shakespeare: one replete with noise and fury but void of meaning, and hence full of consequences for History.

Fragments of Memory

> At the sound of the gramophone, we ate the *pastourma* and the *soudjouk,* we drank the *raki* and the *sarop* while singing the *amané* of separation. Then, with Milonas leading the way, the small group took the road of the Gold Horn through the narrow streets of Yedik Pacha, perched on top of a hill that glowed in the light. To abandon Istambul on this day of spring, one had to possess the experienced soul of an exile. (Lépidis 1973, 15)

> African tourists arrived by plane or by boat, Turks or North Africans crossing the border on foot, Asian "families" arrived by train with false I.D.'s, illiterate Moroccans as seasonal agricultural laborers, Yugoslav tailors sitting at their sewing machine in the workshops of the Sentier, unemployed workers real or disguised, waves of students . . . "illegal" immigrants vary greatly in origin, itinerary, situation, and trade. (*Le Monde,* 6 August 1987)

> Improvised stokers, volunteer shepherds or horse drivers, all illegal and huddled between piles of sacks and cases of coal, fishermen's helpers on sailing ships strangely lured toward the Balearic Islands by a current leading to the coasts of Languedoc, to *La Nouvelle,* for example; often exhausted, the *Chleuh* and his comrades disembarked one fine night, when the signal was given, on the coveted soil. (Ray 1937, 138)

> *Union populaire de Tir,* Le Creusot, 18 March 1935. I request, honorable Mr. Consul, that you send me as soon as possible the passports of citizen K., for he needs them, unconditionally and without delay, in order to change his identity card. (Letter from a Polish worker, in Miroz 1979, 63)

> When they return on their vacation, it is summer, streets are crowded, there are festivities, joy is everywhere. Before I learned, I thought it was always like this in France, that they had brought all the joy with them. (An Algerian immigrant, quoted in Sayad 1975)

> The orphanage, not knowing my surname, gave me the first and last names of my grandfather; he was called MARGOSS, so I therefore became MARGOSS-IAN. (Margossian 1975, 23)

> A
>
> Ablamowicz, Dominique, *Lithuania,* Paris
> Abramowicz, Jérôme, *Volhinia,* 1st reg. of Crac., France
> Adamkiewicz, Thadée, soldier, 4 of line, London
> Adamkowicz, Mathieu, sec. lieut., 19 of line, Brives (Corrèze)

Adamowicz, Joseph, b. in Horowicze (Grodno), sec. lieut., 13th reg., Bourges (Cher)

Adamowski, Joseph, b. in Cracow, sub. lieut., 2 of line, Brives (Corrèze). (Krosnowski 1837–1838)

People know each other, call each other by their first names or nicknames; customs officials, bus drivers, café owners and ice cream or French fries vendors: The border resembles a village fair, and one wonders what it means anyway. (Lentacker 1973)

The undersigned Portuguese émigré respectfully requests that you have subsidies distributed to him in Dunkerque, where he currently is. (Letter by a Portuguese refugee, 1833; NA F7 12112)

Do you see that little timorous man over there with the black lorgnette? He used to be a reputed gynecologist in Berlin. Now he wanders the streets of Paris with his bag and sells artificial flowers. (Hans Sahl, quoted in Schramm and Vormeier 1979, 152)

BARUCH. Major Jewish drama in six parts. This exciting drama can be viewed by all audiences. It offends no religious or political susceptibility. (Movie advertisement in the rue Saint-Sabin, Paris, quoted in Valdour 1929, 135)

I remember the terrible sight of a large group of wounded who were about to be expelled. The Senegalese infantrymen, blackjacks in hand, pushed them back. A screaming and imploring human mass swept back to avoid the bodies. (Testimony of F. Montserry, minister of the Spanish republican government; in Grando et al. 1981, 57).

1. The race and natural nationality of peoples are not taken into consideration, only the nationality of the state.

2. From an international perspective, there does exist an Austro-Hungarian nationality, but not, as indicated on the forms in question, a purely "Austrian" or purely "Hungarian" nationality. The Czechs living in France cannot accept the summary and imaginary title of "Austrians." (Letter from a group of Czech citizens to a French census official in 1896; NA F2 I 1694)

We are here, impatient
Close to the border awaiting the hour of our return
Watching for the slightest change
From the other side of the border, feverishly
Questioning each newcomer
Forgetting nothing, surrendering nothing, forgiving
Nothing of what happened. (Brecht 1966, 102)

Arafane, you are leaving for Taracounda. Here: Say hello to everyone, tell them that we are in good health. When we become rich we will let them know. It is for them that we are here. (Malian poem, quoted in Jacque 1985, 107).

In the end he wondered where the real Poles were. As for he and Paulette, they felt French. But in a family where German was more spoken than Polish, and Polish more than French . . . It's hard to make sense of it all. (Drelon 1982, 49)

1897–1899: tunnel in Switzerland
1899: Joeuf, Homécourt, Auboué mines (Lorraine)
1900: Fontoy, Hayange, Rohrbach mines (annexed Lorrraine)
1901: Algrange, Roechling, Rohrbach mines (Germany)
1902: Audun-le-Tich, Villerupt, Hussigny, Knutange mines (Lorraine and Germany)
1903: Auboué, Joeuf mines (Lorraine), return to Italy
1904: Moutiers, Auboué, Esch, Micheville mines (Lorraine and Luxembourg)
1905: Micheville (Lorraine), return to Italy
1905–1908: Landres mines (Lorraine)
1909–1910: Piennes mines (Lorraine)
1910–1911: Paris subway
1911: return to Piennes. (Extract from a worker's passbook, cited in Noiriel 1982, li)

If I am called Chinese, I don't mind, I'm not Chinese. I'll only hit someone if he calls me a halfbreed. (Indochinese from a camp in Noyant, quoted in Simon 1981, 484)

It was a strange document in the form of an accordion, covered with stamps and multiple figures, which read like a horizontal papyrus. The place of birth was deformed: SAVAS instead of SIVAS, as was the name: TOKALARIAN instead of TOKATLERIAN. Yet the last time we asked him to write it, he took care to spell in capital letters. Did the staff member make a mistake when he copied it down? (Lépidis 1973, 27)

Each year during the ceremony of Recollection, these flags bestow a fraternal salute upon the monument that lists the names of those who disappeared, without having witnessed the realization of the independence they dreamed for their homeland. (Defer 1932)

The majority of prisoners from this nation, who come through the department by groups of two, three, five, and even six hundred, without shoes nor clothing, covered only by a few rags or shreds of covers and of tapestry, are almost unable to walk, particularly since the season made the paths difficult. (Description by the gendarmeric of Seine et Marne of a convoy of Spanish prisoners crossing France in 1812; quoted in Aymes 1983, 183)

I stayed two years at the Chevilly-Larue shelter. I was housed in building 3 (there were six buildings) and there were eight of us per apartment, four per room. Our beds were bunked two by two; the dining room, kitchen, and bathrooms were shared. No shower, gas, or hot water. (Boumedine Zaïd, quoted in *Les Temps Modern,* 1984, 1692)

How a German social democrat became a Senegalese infantryman and a French resistant. (Günther Markseheffell, quoted in Badia 1982, 66)

In Gennevilliers, for example, in certain shacks of what is called the Arab village of Grésillon, a small battered bed in a dormitory costs thirty francs per month. Elsewhere, the right for four people to sleep in a basement costs forty-eight francs per person and per month. (*Le Temps,* 8 December 1926)

And so it is that France penetrates all of us to the bones. (Algerian émigré quoted in Sayad 1975, 55)

The Chinese and the Scandinavians, the Spanish and the Greeks, the Brazilians and the Canadians, each felt at home on the banks of the Seine. No obligations, one could speak and think freely, laugh, scold, each person lived as he pleased, sociable or solitary, lavish or thrifty, in the clouds or unconventionally. (Zweig 1943, 157)

They come regularly in gangs, each led by a foreman. They carry long lanceolate cisterns, as well as a cooking pot for the group's polenta. They spend up to six months in Corsica to perform heavy rural labor and earn 1.75, 1.90 and sometimes 4 francs. Almost all of their wage is taken back to Italy. (Le Conte 1908, 172)

My parents put together what they had, which was not very much, and on the morning of 23 June 1911 my parents, my young brother and I, were on the road for Valence, where we took the steamer, a mixed cargo that carried oranges to Cette. (Spanish immigrant in Hérault, quoted in Azas 1981, 90)

In the interstice of this grey sliding, I catch a glimpse of the war of attrition of death against life and of life against death. Death: the gears of the assembly line, the imperturbable sliding of cars, the repetition of identical gestures, the task never completed. (Linhart 1981, 12)

Poincaré, Poincaré, when will I be among your inhabitants? (Vidal Nahoum, recalled by his son, sociologist Edgard Morin, in the 1986 colloquium *Le Migrant*)

In those days, they left the various villages by gangs of twelve or fifteen, on foot, singing along the roads to the sound of an accordion. We called them the *Fransmannen* and the children announced their arrival from afar, as they approached: "*Les Franchimans! Les Franchimans!*" (Flemish agricultural worker recalling his father, cited in Anglade 1976, 65–66)

Their dilapidated houses, worn out by prolonged exposure to the great storm, are covered with what was once tar-lined paper, by old waxed canvas and used doormats; they are all patched up and caulked with pieces of tires, tin cans, scraps of iron, bits of zinc. (Armenian housing at the Oddo encampment in Marseilles; Naudeau 1932, 149)

REPUBLIQUE FRANCAISE. CITY OF SAINT-OUEN. RECOGIDA DE LAS BASURAS.—L'ALCALDE. (Municipal announcement regarding garbage collection in Saint-Ouen, quoted in Mauco 1932, 345)

The ship was brought to a halt. The arrival of the pilot vessel was greeted with cheers. To everyone, the French flag that flew on the mast represented the ultimate goal. They cried: "*Vive la France!*" (Medzadourian 1975, 24)

French, in this neighborhood of Cette, is nothing but a foreign language. (Bertillon 1911, 48)

There were twenty-five of us, from various villages, including my brother who is now in Lyon. It is not difficult to cross the border in Portugal. All it takes is a walk from eight in the evening to eight in the morning. (Portuguese immigrant quoted in Petonnet 1985, 34)

He is capable of remaining still for several hours, without seeming the slightest bit bored; immobile for hours, crouched oriental-style or with his knees against his chin, his head leaning forward, resting in the palm of his hand, his eyes closed, his back against the wall of his house in the lonely alley or on the sidewalk of his street in the summer, in his room in the winter. (Description of a Moroccan immigrant's "free time"; Ray 1937, 184)

The idea that I was leaving my youngest brothers and sisters, my dearest loved ones, my fiancée, brought tears to my eyes. (A Polish émigré woman working in France as an agricultural laborer, quoted in Ponty 1985, 283)

When, at a bend in a path, the "heroes of Poland" were spotted approaching a town, cheers broke out and spontaneous demonstrations occurred. An air still warm from revolutionary transformations welcomed the arrivals; and looking toward this distant and beloved France, they said: "Governments change, dynasties pass, but nations remain." (Sokolniecki 1910, 74)

We had to constantly besiege the staff of the police prefecture in order, to obtain that our residency permits be extended for fifteen days or a month, and sought to bribe those intermediaries who spoke slightly better French in order to approach the wickets. (Doctor Olievenstein, quoted in Schramm and Vormeier 1979, 214)

Friends, we have paid a greater price than can be be imagined. (Statement of boat people attacked by pirates, quoted in Jacque 1985, 71)

He held the face upward and observed the lining of the eyelids. He looked sulky. He whispered into my ear, no need to insist. Granular conjunctivitis. The twentieth case since this morning. Next please, Kotia? Kotia is already there, and after her there is another one. The same decisive auscultation. The eyelids. The muscles of the neck. Kotia has a swollen throat; a predisposition to the goiter. The doctor tears up the report. A voice is heard in the next room. Pregnant women shouldn't bother to present themselves before Myslowice. They will be denied a counter-visit and their transportation costs will not be reimbursed. (The recruitment of Polish workers by French companies in the interwar period, according to Le Febvre; quoted in Noiriel 1984, 166–67)

And pairs of brown eyes, some gloomy and others joyful, watch as the blue-tinged mountains, often crowned by white, beyond Cape Matifou—the Djurdjura, the Kabylia—gradually disappear. (Muracciole 1950, 9)

Perhaps I would understand what was going on if there were a rule to the game, if communication were established between the administration and the administered, but that is probably asking the impossible. (Nakamoura, a Japanese translator living in Paris, on the problems encountered in the renewal of a French residency permit; *Le Monde* 5 February 1987)

Suddenly the man who accompanied us said: "*Estamos en Francia.*" It was still night; I felt that non-existent line, the border, behind us. I felt it almost physically. (Paco Ibanès, quoted in Grando et al. 1980, 249)

My work is filthy, a *poison* that enters my stomach. (Algerian immigrant quoted in Sayad 1975, 65)

Before boarding the boats, those who were leaving said, for the last time, good-bye to the parents and friends who had come to see them off. They shed tears, exchanged best wishes, and promised, without really believing it, that they would some day be reunited; they kissed, hugged for the last time; families that had until then been united, were thus forever separated. (Medzadourian 1975, 13)

One day, who knows why or how, the *Wandertrieb* fell upon souls in the remotest parts of the Balkans, Germany, and Sicily: they had to come to Paris, they had to have seen this marvelous city where such fine wages could be earned, where they could have so much fun, where work would be abundant. It was a haunting thought, a mirage, and they departed alone or in groups, directly or in stages, married or single, young or old. (Schirmacher 1908, 34)

> My father had obtained tickets for the last departing boat, an old Russian steamship called *Aphon.* Unfortunately, the port of Novorossisk was caught in the ice, the northwesterly wind was blowing fiercely. No ship could get underway. And the Bolsheviks were approaching the city. Were we going to let ourselves be overtaken this time? (Troyat 1987, 27)

> A. V. Vedenski, went abroad in November of last year, departed from Sotchi; seeks her sister I. V. Guefding. Please send news to Mrs. Munck Strand, Boulevard 66, Copenhagen, Denmark. (*Les Derniers Nouvelles,* of 1920, quoted in Gousseff and Saadier 1983, 337)

> Was their family ever lapidated? Were they ever chased away from their home? Have they experienced the suffering of forced exile? That obligation to break one's life like a branch of dead wood? (Lépidis 1973, 55)

Writing

To speak of the "immigrant experience," we must write history in a manner entirely different from the bland, soothing, and even reassuring narratives of consensus that are so typical of the peasant *longue durée* and to which we have been accustomed by the leading experts of French rural history. As an entry to this chapter, I chose to reproduce certain "excerpts from memory," bluntly, as I found them; their contradictions and their diversity themselves attest to the richness of that "other France." For the scholar who belongs to the national group and uses the dominant language, to speak of "foreigners" inevitably poses a serious problem. To write about the Other is to practice a form of annexation, by confining him to the prison of a syntax and a lexicon that are not his own and that have, quite often, caused him to suffer. This, for the historian, is the crux of the theoretical problem raised by Marc Bloch, when he noted that history's reputation as an enjoyable pastime put the field at a scholarly disadvantage (Bloch 1953). The popularity of "life histories" is related to the fact that biography, reconstructed and reinvented by and for writing, lends itself particularly well to reader identification, to populism, and to nostalgia. But at times, in the eagerness to write the history of people without history, the historian all too often overlooks his or her own "otherness," or forgets that, to paraphrase the poet Arthur Rimbaud, "I is another" ("*Je est un autre*") (Lejeune 1980). When an immigrant's life history is told, the problem is redoubled by the rift between the scholar and the biographer's "subject," a rift that is widened not only by the difference in their social status but also by national belonging.

How are we to overcome this "logic of representation"? A key step is to realize that the problem exists. The self-satisfying consensus of rehabilitation, to be sure, must be disrupted. But we may go further still. Historians are not exempt from the task of inventing new forms in order to adapt them to the nature of their object. One source of inspiration might be found in the formal imagination of great writers; the French *nouveau roman,* for example, invented an array of techniques for breaking with traditional narrative. And if immigration is viewed, like colonization, as a "war of inscription," then we might find inspiration in Claude Ollier's writings on Morocco, his original calligraphy, new arrangements, and diverse narrative forms (see Khatibi 1987; Ollier 1981).

It is true that in the social sciences, the constraints on writing are somewhat greater. But here again, the historian may draw from the frequent innovations of sociology. An exemplary case of this is Abdelmayek Sayad's alternative approach to the "foreigner":

> The purpose of sociological discourse is not to attenuate the *opacity* of authentic discourse, by resorting to linguistic and ethnographic notes or by providing the reassurance of comment. Authentic culture fully mobilizes the resources of a culture, as well as an original language, to express the experiences which that culture or language ignores or denies.

Sayad therefore prefers to juxtapose two discourses, that of an Algerian immigrant narrating his experience and that of a sociologist whose role is to produce scientific knowledge (Sayad 1975).

An essay such as this one cannot provide a detailed description of sustained primary research. The reader will find traces of these concerns, however, in the deliberate exclusion of illustrative quotes throughout this chapter and in the rejection of an excessively "integrated plan" divided into overly "articulated" parts, complete with "clever" transitions; all of which would, in the end, conceal the gaps, ruptures, and dismemberments of the process described.

Gastarbeiter

In industrialized societies, work is what "gives birth" to the immigrant, and it is through work that he exists. When work disappears, the result is the immigrant's "death," his negation or "nonexistence"

(Sayad 1979). Figure 3.1, which depicts the changes in the size of the foreign population in France since the mid-nineteenth century, corroborates this definition. In periods of economic expansion, Simiand's A phases, the number of immigrants rose significantly (under the Second Empire, in the 1920s, and again in the 1960s). In phases of stagnation (B), the foreign population either remained stable or regressed (in the late nineteenth century, the 1930s, and the late 1970s). The recurrent nature of the "immigration problem" can be explained by the fact that foreigners are always subjected to the host country's cycles of economic activity.

Examination of the available statistics clearly indicates that the demand is for "producers," rather than simply for immigrants. Without analyzing census figures in detail, we will compare the three moments in which the foreign presence in France appears to have been highest: 1891–1901 (when professional statistics on immigration first appeared), 1931, and 1975.[3]

A preliminary remark is that the foreign-born population in France has always been overwhelmingly male. As early as 1866, for every 100 women there were 136 men, although in 1891 the number had fallen to 113. The situation is the reverse for the French population in general, in which women always slightly outnumber men. By the end of the 1920s, the difference was even more pronounced, with 156 male for every 100 female immigrants (among native French citizens there were 90 men for every 100 women). A half-century later, for every 100 foreign-born women, there were nearly 150 foreign-born men; in comparison, for every 100 French-born women there were only 93.5 French-born men.

The examination of age pyramids reveals similar tendencies. The most overrepresented age brackets were always the most productive. In 1891, male children aged less than ten years comprised 18.2% of the male French-born population, compared with 11.4% of the foreign-born population. Young men between the ages of twenty and twenty-nine, on the other hand, made up 16% of the French-born population and 22% of all immigrants. The data for 1931 and 1975 confirm these tendencies. The foreign-born population always included fewer young men and fewer elderly, whereas adults in their prime were more numerous. This trend is also perfectly evident in the rate of activity by national group, which was six to eight points higher among foreigners during the peak periods under consideration.

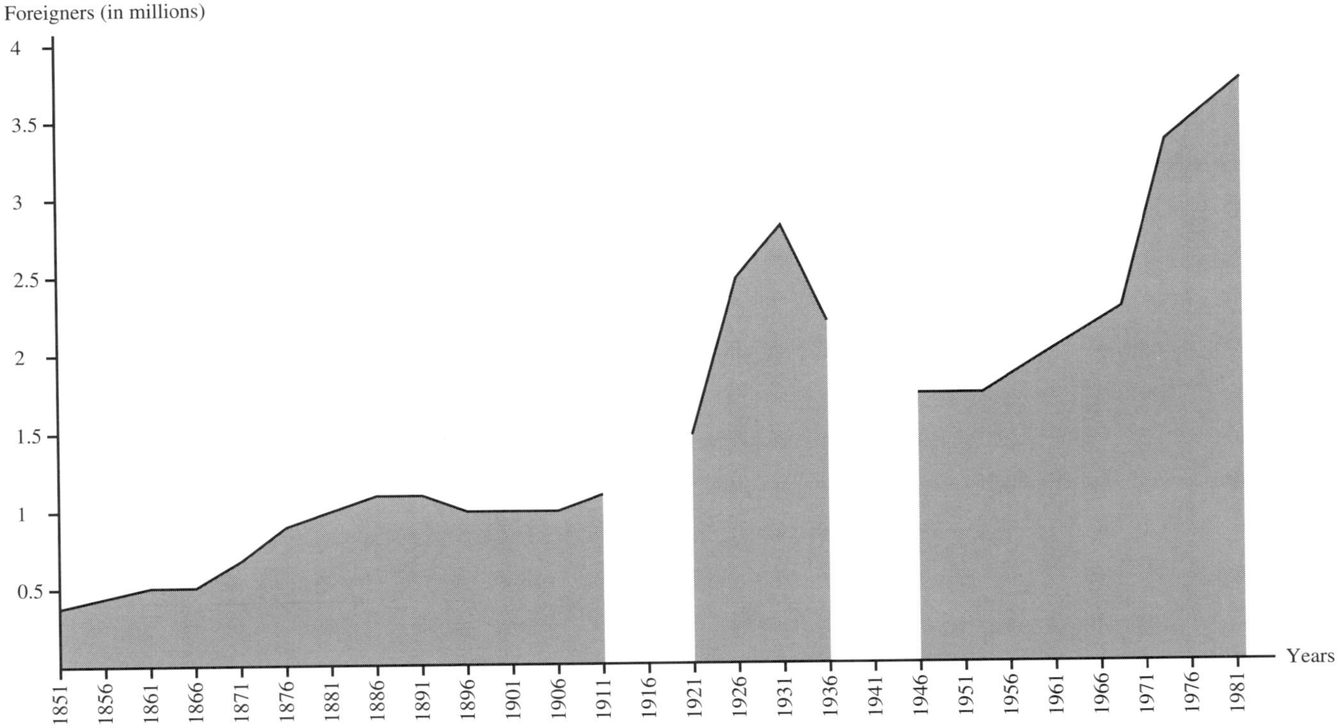

Figure 3.1. Evolution of the foreign population in France according to census figures, 1851–1982. (Data are unavailable for 1856, 1916, and 1941.)

These census figures reveal another general tendency of the French Gastarbeiter: immigrants were convened, recruited, and retained to work jobs that were characteristically turned down by nationals. Native Frenchmen scorned three basic categories of work.

1. The first encompasses tasks that rely on the physical strength of unskilled workers. Such jobs were widespread in agriculture and were generally performed by seasonal laborers whom the census figures fail to mention; yet more than 100,000 of them entered the country between the late nineteenth century and the 1960s. For a long time, the rural areas from the north and to Ile-de-France were cultivated by Flemish seasonal laborers, known as *franchimans*. They appeared in May for the splitting and hoeing of beets and harvested in July and August. They ended their season by lifting potatoes and beets and sometimes participating in the production of sugar. In the south, the grape harvest was unthinkable without the help of tens of thousands of Spanish seasonal laborers. In the fields of Provence, the picking of flowers, lavender, and olives became the specialty of Piedmontese immigrants during the *belle epoque*.[4]

The destabilization of the economy in the first half of the nineteenth century, which we will discuss in chapter 6 explains the extreme shortage of agricultural workers that plagued rural areas throughout the country from the 1890s onward. Agricultural firms were, as a result, the first to collectively recruit immigrant workers. In the years preceding the First World War, incoming Poles gradually displaced the Belgians. The testimonies of agricultural emigrants collected in Warsaw do not quite live up to the myth of "traditional French hospitality": workdays from sunrise to sunset; exhausting tasks, particularly because of antiquated tools; housing and hygiene conditions far below those enjoyed by certain Polish agricultural workers in Germany and often more miserable than in Poland itself (see Ponty 1985)

Physical force was also highly sought for factories. More than pure muscular strength, however, what was especially required was a capacity to endure the trials of exposure to drastic conditions. As a result, foreign workers were always more numerous in insalubrious activities. In 1901, they comprised 12% of the labor force in the chemical industry, often up to 20% in galvanoplasty, and 23% in the making of vegetable oils. The massive arrivals of the 1920s were oriented mostly toward these sectors. In the mines, the proportion of immigrants went from 6.4% in 1901 to 42% in 1931. That year, they made up 20% of the labor force in the chemical industry and 30% of the embankment workers. During the 1960s, immigrants were always given the most trying jobs, which remained numerous despite technological transformations: the food industry, foundries, and especially construction, in which one out of every four immigrants was employed in 1975.[5]

The third sector of hard work was comprised of jobs in the "secondary labor market" (see Piore 1979, 106). At the periphery of large industry, these activities tended to survive precariously and with little capital. They were the mecca of illegal immigration, places where owners took advantage of the workers' illegal position to impose workdays that often exceeded twelve hours. The garment and clothing industries were the centers of this form of exploitation, which in late-nineteenth-century Paris could be seen in the Marais among Jewish hatmakers. Prior to the 1960s, Belleville was the other Jewish neighborhood that owed its livelihood to these marginal activities. The same was true for the Armenians in the suburbs of Paris (such as Issy-les-Moulineaux) and for the Yugoslavians and Turks who worked for the firms based in the neighborhood of Sentier (see Green 1985; Roland 1962; INED 1947b; Moulier Boutang et al. 1986).

2. The second pole of attraction for immigrant labor was at the cutting edge of technological progress, in areas where the machine had made a mere appendix of man, at the mercy of its rhythms and whims. In the Roubaix textile industry under the Second Empire, for example, the Belgian labor force was concentrated in areas where work was mechanized, such as the cotton mills (Reardon 1977). Similarly, in the shipyards of La Seyne-sur-Mer, the flow of Italian workers (who were as numerous as the French by 1888) occurred after the reorganization of the work process and its adjustment to the requirements of large industry (Martinencq 1982).

In the interwar period, the mechanization of the large foundries of Lorraine transformed the moulder's job into that of a semi-skilled worker, which explains the massive presence of Italian and Polish immigrants (Noiriel 1984). A half-century later, the automobile industry had become another case in point. Standardized mass production, by creating numerous semi-skilled jobs, drew largely from the immigrant labor force. In 1973, one-third of the workers in this branch were foreigners.

3. Domestic work was the third area reserved primarily for foreigners. This is often overlooked when we discuss "immigrant work-

ers," perhaps because the domestic labor force is essentially made up of women. Yet the study of this sector reveals a trend that has lasted throughout the century: regardless of the period under scrutiny, workers employed in "domestic service" represent roughly 5% of the overall French-born working population. In the case of foreigners, the proportion exceeded 10% in 1901, and oscillated between 6 and 8% from then on. The specificity of foreigners is even more visible when the data on women's work is compared. In 1901, nearly one-third of the foreign-born female workforce was employed in domestic service; in 1931 the ratio was roughly the same (28%, the same as the current level) whereas in that same year, only 11% of employed French-born women worked as servants.

The least-valued trades are found in the most depreciated sectors. Not only are foreigners employed in industry, but they most often occupy blue-collar jobs. In this respect, the accentuation of this working-class status is the only discernable evolution in the entire century. Slightly more than half of the immigrants belonged to the working class in 1901, more than two-thirds in 1931, and three-fourths in 1975. Not only was the proportion substantially lower among native-born French, but the percentage of blue-collar workers in the overall working population was low: 34% in 1901, 40% in 1931, 36% in 1975. Conversely, foreigners were not common in the more highly valued positions, such as white-collar jobs and liberal professions, which employed a small fraction of the immigrant population. Here, too, the more refined the analysis, the more detail appears in this logic of domination. The generic term "peasant," for example, conceals vast inequalities of status. In 1891, nearly one of every five foreign workers was employed in agriculture (47% in the case of French-born workers); but among foreign agriculturalists, only 18% owned their land, compared with 50% for the French. The ratio was similar in 1931 (29% of foreign agriculturalists and 61% of French-born agriculturalists owned their land).

In industry as well, although statistics are lacking to distinguish between different strata within the working class prior to the Second World War, all our sources (contemporary surveys and historical monographs) prove that the foreign labor force monopolized the inferior jobs that were classified prior to 1945 as "semi-skilled." According to this logic, when French-born workers are found in depreciated sectors of production, they are in positions of authority or management (for example, as engineers or foremen), or at the very least are highly skilled (for example, maintenance workers). By isolating the professional category of *ouvrier spécialisé* (semi-skilled worker), INSEE statistics made it possible to distinguish between different levels of hierarchy within the working class, which broadly coincided with the reality of segmentation on a national scale. In 1975, for example, 55% of foreign-born wage earners were in the semi-skilled category, compared with 20% of French-born workers.

The profile of the foreigner in contemporary France can now be drawn with some precision: brought in to perform a job, he is a rather young man, almost always a blue-collar worker engaged in the most physically and nervously exhausting forms of work, either in industry or in agriculture. Foreign-born women are fewer in number and less often employed as wage earners; when they are, it is usually as servants to the French, from the Flemish or Piedmontese maids of the late nineteenth century to the Polish maids of the interwar period and the Portuguese maids of today.

The Space of Nationalities

The statistics presented in the preceding pages describe the "average" foreigner; in other words, one who in reality does not exist. When this abstract entity is deconstructed, however, the diversity of situations is extraordinary: There are multiple "ethnic" and national groups, colonial workers, refugees, stateless people, border dwellers, seasonal laborers, and on and on. Because it is difficult to construct a classification without excluding any group, many studies isolate a single nationality that is more or less explicitly presented as "representative" of the whole. Such an approach is only justified if it begins by locating the group under study within the "social space" formed by the totality of nationalities present in France at a given time. To do this we can now rely on computer technology and, in particular, factorial analyses of correspondence. In a study underway at the laboratory of social sciences of the Ecole Normale Supérieure, Yves Chauviré and I have reviewed, in this perspective, the essential statistical data provided by the censuses for the three years during which the immigrant population was most numerous (1901, 1931, and 1975). Although they represent only the first stages of this research, the simplified diagrams published here (Figure 3.2) nonetheless illustrate the "framework of nationalities" that characterizes each of these

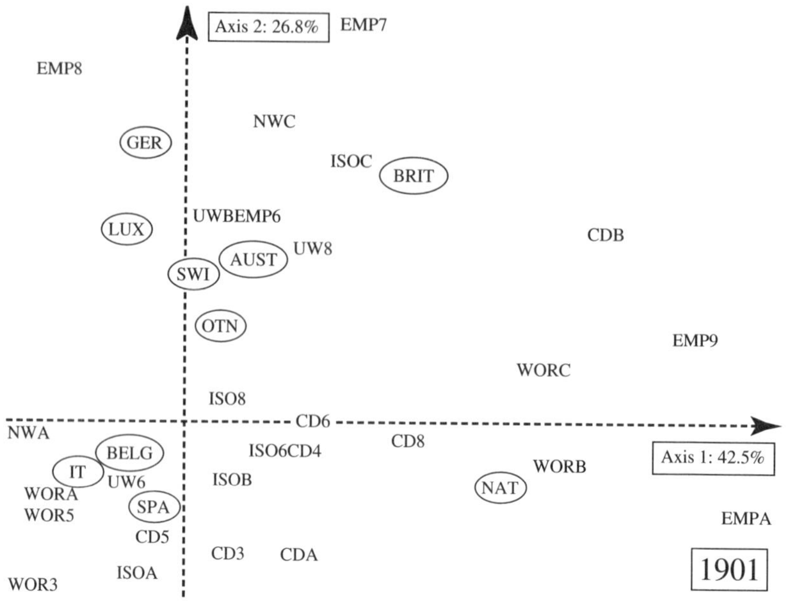
Axis 2: 26.8%
EMP7
EMP8
NWC
GER
ISOC
BRIT
UWBEMP6
LUX
CDB
AUST
UW8
SWI
OTN
EMP9
WORC
ISO8
NWA
CD6
CD8
BELG
ISO6CD4
Axis 1: 42.5%
IT
WORB
UW6
ISOB
NAT
WORA
SPA
WOR5
EMPA
CD5
CD3
CDA
1901
ISOA
WOR3

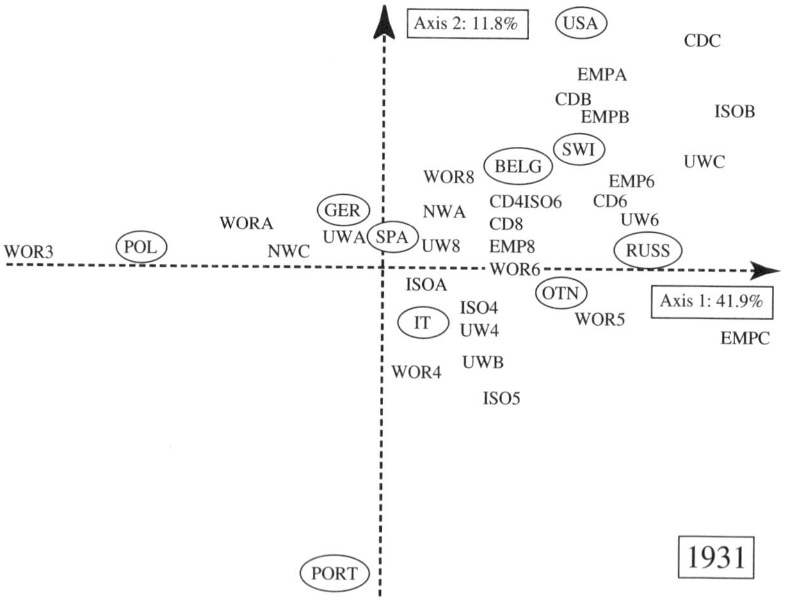
Axis 2: 11.8%
USA
CDC
EMPA
CDB
ISOB
EMPB
SWI
BELG
UWC
WOR8
EMP6
GER
CD4ISO6
CD6
WORA
NWA
UW6
CD8
WOR3
POL
UWA
SPA
NWC
UW8
EMP8
RUSS
WOR6
ISOA
OTN
Axis 1: 41.9%
ISO4
IT
WOR5
UW4
EMPC
UWB
WOR4
ISO5
1931
PORT

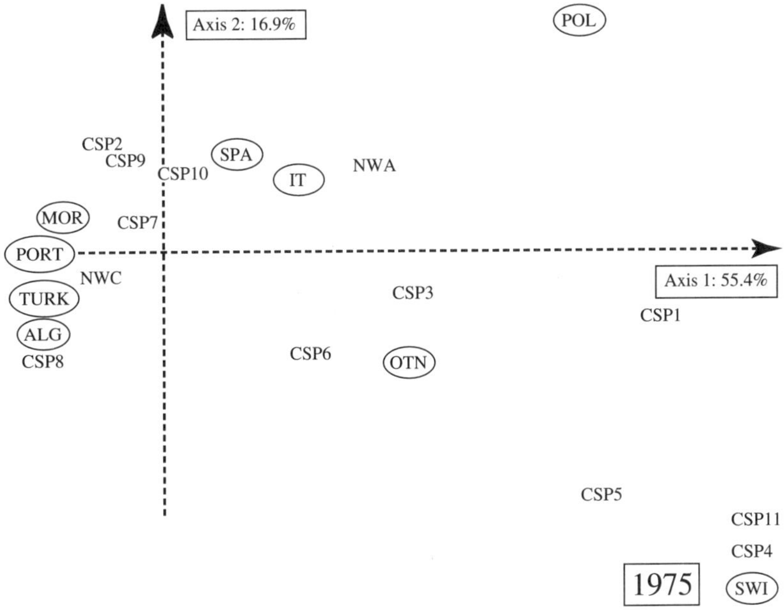

Figure 3.2 Factorial analyses

Abbreviations for nationalities and variables

IT: Italians; GER: Germans; LUX: Luxemburgers; SWI: Swiss; AUST: Austrians; BRIT: British; NAT: Naturalized citizens; OTN: Other nationalities; BELG: Belgians; SPA: Spaniards; POL: Poles; USA: Americans; PORT: Portuguese; RUSS: Russians; MOR: Moroccans; TURK: Turks; ALG: Algerians

Variables employed for 1901, 1931, and 1975. NWC: Nonworking children; NWA: Nonworking adults

Variables employed for 1901 and 1931. CD: Company directors; EMP: Employees; WOR: Workers; ISO: Isolated workers; UW: Unemployed workers; 1: Fishing; 2: Forestry-agriculture; 3: Mines and quarries; 4: Manufacturing and production industries; 5: Cargo handling–transportation; 6: Commerce, banking, entertainment; 7: Liberal professions; 8: Domestic health care; 9: Public services

Variables employed solely for 1901. CDA: Company directors 1 + 2; CDB: Company directors 7 + 9; EMPA: Employees 1 + 2 + 3 + 4 + 5; WORA: Workers 1 + 2; WORB: Workers 6 + 8; WORC: Workers 7 + 9; ISOA: Isolated workers 1 + 2; ISOB: Isolated workers 3 + 4 + 5; ISOC: Isolated workers 7 + 9; UWA: Unemployed workers 1 + 2 + 3 + 4 + 5; UWB: Unemployed workers 7 + 9

Variables employed solely for 1931. CDA: Company directors 1 + 2; CDB: Company directors 3 + 5; CDC: Company directors 7 + 8 + 9; EMPA: Employees 1 + 2; EMPB: Employees 3 + 4 + 5; EMPC: Employees 7 + 9; WORA: Workers 1 + 2; WORB: Workers 7 + 9; IOSA: Isolated workers 1 + 2 + 3 + 8; ISOB: Isolated workers 7 + 9; UWA: Unemployed workers 1 + 2; UWB: Unemployed workers 3 + 5; UWC: Unemployed workers 7 + 9

Variables employed solely for 1975. CSP1: Agriculturalists; CSP2: Agricultural workers; CSP3: Executives in commerce and industry; CSP4: Liberal professions and high-level management; CSP5: Middle-level management; CSP6: Employees; CSP7: Foremen, skilled workers, apprentices; CSP8: Specialized and unskilled workers; CSP9: Minters, seamen, fishermen; CSP10: Service employees; CSP11: Artists, clergy, army, and police. [Translator's note: "CSP" means "catégorie socio-professionnelle," or simply, in English, "profession."]

three moments.[6] The relation between the position of a given nationality within its framework and the length of its presence in France is clear. In 1901, the oldest foreign groups were the English, the Germans, and the Austrians, representative of the "artisanal" wave of the first half of the century. The Belgians represent the first major wave associated with the industrial revolution. In 1886, they represented 40% of the total of the immigrant population, but they were gradually surpassed by the Italians as the century came to a close. In 1901, Italians were the most represented but also the most recent group. That is why we find them at a pole of the first factorial axis of inertia opposite the pole of "naturalized" citizens, which we have introduced as the symbol of integration into French society (see chapter 4). The Italians are influential in determining the second axis, opposite the English and the Germans. In short, two clusters can be distinguished in the diagram: One is comprised of recent immigrants, Italians, Belgians, and Spaniards, who belong to the working class (both agricultural and industrial); the other, in the upper and right-hand regions of the diagram, is represented by national groups linked to the tertiary sector ("service employees"), whose settlement in France dates back the furthest and which contains a substantial portion of inactive adults.[7]

The migratory flow in the 1920s and its consequences for the restructuring of the framework of nationalities in France are reflected in the diagram for 1931. Here again, notwithstanding the sustained recruitment of Italians, it is the most recently arrived nationalities that play a key role in the orientation of the axes of inertia. The first axis opposes the "other nationalities"—a category comprised of foreigners with little numerical representation and whose professional composition is therefore influenced by the administrative sector (consulates, various services)—to the Poles, who are very strongly identified with the working-class mining trade. The vertical axis (third axis of inertia) is particularly influenced by the presence of the Portuguese, who are linked to the blue-collar trades in manufacturing and production industries and who may be opposed to the Americans, who are characterized by a high number of inactive adults, independent service workers, and employees of private industry. Yet, as the example of the Russians illustrates, other factors than the length of presence in the country may intervene to determine the position of a nationality within the whole. What we have here is an illustration of the impact of "political," and no longer simply economic, immigrants—that is, refugees. Although their massive arrival is as recent as that of the Poles, the higher social backgrounds of the Russians moves them away from the center of the diagram, nearer to the categories of "employees" and (usually independent) "shop managers."

The diagram for 1975 shows a repetition of the tendencies described for the two earlier periods. The first axis of factorial analysis is heavily marked by the arrival of massive waves of immigrants from the 1960s onward (Portuguese and Algerians; Turks and Moroccans to a lesser degree), immigrants who are very clearly included among "semi-skilled workers" and who also find themselves opposite the category of "other nationalities" dominated by employees and employers. The groups that had predominated in earlier waves had either disappeared due to their small number (Belgians, Russians) or now occupied a very different position than they had in the 1930s. This is the case for the Poles, whose singularity resides in the importance of the inactive adult population.

These three diagrams illustrate a global trend in long-term immigration. Each new migratory wave was characterized by individuals from a few numerically dominant nationalities who occupied, for a time, the most marginal positions in society but who took advantage of new flows to "conquer" less off-centered positions. It must be noted, however, that the limits imposed by the legal definition of the "foreigner" allow us to evaluate only the social mobility of the first generation, which preserved its nationality of origin. As we will see in the next chapter, the phenomenon is even more visible if we view it from the perspective of the second or the third generations, whose members are for the most part legally French.

Ebbs and Flows

The problem with representations like those in Figure 3.1 is that they are linear reflections of homogeneous flows. They do not take into account the variety of individual movements, the constant come-and-go that characterizes immigration and of which the "fragments of memory" cited at the beginning of this chapter give some idea.

It is important to emphasize that the foreign or foreign-born population settled in France today represents only a tiny portion of the millions of immigrants who, at one time or another, tread French soil. No statistic is capable of measuring the scale of the phenomenon of persons who return to their country of origin. In the United States, despite the considerable obstacle represented by the ocean, an estimated one-third of all immigrants returned to their homelands between 1908 and 1957. In France, until more detailed research is carried out, we have only clues, but they tend to prove that returns were even more significant. According to Georges Mauco, between 1920 and 1935, of two million immigrants who legally entered the country, one million eventually returned (Mauco 1937). The results of a survey conducted in the employment registers of the iron mines of a community in the Meuse indicate that between 1906 and 1945, 28,000 different names were recorded for a workforce that never surpassed a total of 1,800 miners! (Harbulot 1977).

As we have seen, it is the cycles of economic activity of the recruiting country that give the general tempo of the ebbs and flows. But what makes the adjustment of the labor force to the changing needs of the national economy so difficult is that other logics, other strategies disturb the ideal tempo for capitalist rhythms. To understand these logics and these strategies, we must turn now to those countries that supplied the labor force.

Sayad, in describing the "three ages of Algerian emigration" to France, indicated the basic trends of the process of rural emigration toward industrial centers. In the "first age," the community to which the migrant belongs is sufficiently structured to escape the destructive effects of emigration. Algerian peasants use the stay in France as a means of overcoming the crisis of rural society (for which, in this case, colonialism is largely responsible). The emigrant is chosen by the community, who delegates him for a limited time and entrusts him with a "temporary mission" on the other side of the Mediterranean, in order to provide the peasant group with the resources it needs (particularly in currency). In this "first moment" of immigration, the rhythm of departures is determined by the requirements of agricultural activity. The émigré generally departs after the ploughing period in late autumn and returns for the summer harvest. Hence a migratory tradition gradually settles in. The émigrés regularly take turns so as not to end up "contaminated" by industrial society. The creation of migratory channels and of a network allow the migrant to find a host environment in France. The presence of this community, the brevity of stays, and the weight of norms acquired in the society of origin all combine to protect the émigré against the aggressions (and temptations) of the host society.

But, as the French saying goes, "the worm is in the fruit." Indeed, while emigration is a temporary solution that relieves rural misery, it also contributes to the dissolution of collective values and to the destructuring of the group. The migratory process favors the development among Algerian peasants of a spirit of calculation and the use of currency. It brings about a modification of lifestyles by reinforcing individualism, which makes the constraints of collective life increasingly unbearable. The process of "deruralization," which everything helps accentuate, is brutally accelerated.

The "second age" of Algerian emigration is characterized by the group's disarticulation. The emigrant is no longer delegated to insure the survival of the community. He leaves to attempt to improve his own personal lot, to escape from the pressure of others in the community, compelled by a desire for "social revenge" on his compatriots who humiliated him or to whom he is inferior. This emigrant tends to be younger than earlier emigrants; he remains in France for a longer time; the crisis that provoked his departure makes him much more vulnerable in the face of the new world.

The "third age" is often that of definitive emigration. The émigré is in the process of becoming an immigrant, who shares a number of needs and certain values of the host society but remains quite marked by the world from which he came. This creates a tendency to regroup, to promote community-based organization, to live in isolation; a trend that is favored by the increasing presence of women and the appearance of specifically Algerian shops and artisanal trades (Sayad 1977).

As numerous sources and studies testify, this is not a purely Algerian phenomenon. Everything seems to indicate that the logic of the "three ages" is in fact ageless, a reflection of one of the terms of the unequal relationship between an industrial and a rural society. As even a cursory reading of the biography of Maurice Nadaud illustrates, the situations of the mid-twentieth-century Algerian émigré and that of the bricklayer in the Creuse a century earlier have much in common: the same control by the village community at the onset, the same temporary delegation of a member of the group to the region of Paris in order to solve the problems internal to rural society (purchase of lands, dowry, indemnification of the young). The adaptation of rhythms of migration to the necessities of rural society, the establishment of recruitment channels, the presence of "colonies" from Auvergne in certain neighborhoods of Paris, everything is similar, even the xenophobia and scorn of Parisians. Moreover, from the Second Empire onward, immigrants showed a tendency to extend the duration of their stay (second age), and the great depression of the 1880s ultimately provoked the permanent settlement in the capital of the majority of migrants from Creuse and the extinction of the process (Italians replaced migrants from Auvergne) (Nadaud 1976).

The logic of complementarity between rural and industrial labor, characteristic of what historians call "proto-industrialization," was particularly widespread and tenacious in Italy. According to Emile Témime (1990–1991), the Piedmontese and Tuscan communities, no longer able to subsist on their internal resources alone, were forced in the late nineteenth century to send emigrants to the south of France; hence the establishment of lasting networks and of "migratory traditions" that often resulted in the emergence of typical crafts, many of them still alive today (Catani 1987a). With respect to immigration from Bergamo, a little-known article published in the 1930s described with great precision the diversity of interests at stake and of the types of migration that can coexist within a single region. Massive emigration appeared in the 1860s. Italian unification ruined local craft industries as a result of Lombard competition. But the new migratory flows were rooted in a much older tradition that was reactivated and enriched. The communities located in the mountains were occupied by lumberjacks who left for the "season," going to Switzerland and France (Côte d'Or, Franche-Comté, and the western Pyrenees in particular). In the late nineteenth century miners working in the United States and increasingly in France (in the Briey basin) converged on the valleys. Laborers recruited by large public works industries, to dig the tunnel of Saint-Gothard (1882) and to build hydroelectric dams in the French Alps, were recruited from the same localities. In the hill areas, temporary migrants tended to be employed in the building trades. Many of them participated in the reconstruction of the north and of the Paris region (particularly in Aubervilliers). The plain of Bergame provided seasonal agricultural workers and settlers (some of whom settled in the southwest in the early 1920s). Textile workers also came out of Bergame. It was they who formed the small Italian colonies of the interwar period in the Eure, particularly the Meyre project in Vernon (Bertoquy 1934).

This example illustrates the diversity of the forms of Italian emigration, the attraction exerted by France, and the tendency of these temporary migratory waves to turn into permanent settlements, particularly with the aggravation of the agricultural crisis in Italy.

The Italian case is a perfect illustration of the "three ages" process, but the process can also be found in other rural regions. In Belgium and Spain, temporary seasonal migration also tended to transform itself into permanent immigration. The Turkish example shows that the logic of the "three ages" still exists in the most remote regions of Anatoli. The demographic explosion and the parcelling out of land provoked the departure for Europe of migrants delegated by the village community. But there again, the process ultimately undermined the group by stirring rivalries between the wealthiest and most influential families who remained and the "lords of Germany," semi-skilled workers at Volkswagen whose savings positioned them as nouveaux riches in the village.[8]

It is true that, depending on the period, the country of origin, and the host country, we find cases that correspond more or less to the "ideal type" according to the theory of the "three ages." An infinite number of different combinations are possible, determining countless different portraits of immigrants, from the seasonal laborer who leaves his village for a few weeks at a time to the miner who abandons his home forever to settle in a northern mining village or a housing project in Lorraine. I might add that not all immigrants were affected by this process, which implied a more or less drawn-out transition in the transformation of the peasant into an immigrant worker. In France today, many foreign workers were transplanted much more brutally from one universe to the other. In Poland in the 1920s, for example, the major economic and political crisis and the collective recruitment carried out directly by French companies on the spot left people with very little opportunity to even partially control the migratory process. In other cases, the passage from rural to urban society was already largely underway, or even completely accomplished, prior to immigration. The decline of traditional societies provoked a rural exodus toward the major cities of the country (in Algeria, this phenomenon coincided with the "second age" of immigration). Difficulty in finding work or low wages determined a second upheaval, this time in the host country itself. Immigration sometimes affected a group that was already largely engaged in working-class life. The massive arrival of Flemish immigrants in northern France in the mid-nineteenth century resulted from a very deep crisis in the textile industry in Flanders; in the following decades, it was the crisis in the coal industry that provoked the exodus of the miners of Borinage toward France.

In certain cases, reasons other than economic forced workers to leave their country. The thousands of Jewish workers from Central Europe who arrived in France in the late nineteenth century were mostly skilled workers in the small clothing industry who in France resumed their original activity.

The latter point brings us to another key factor in explaining the ebbs and flows that characterized the foreign population: the role of refugees.

From the affluence of Polish, Spanish, Portuguese, and Italian exiles under the July Monarchy to the arrival of large numbers of Southeast Asians in the present day, each failed (or successful) revolution, each dictatorship, each genocide forced millions of people to seek asylum in France. At least five waves of Spanish refugees, often of conflicting opinions, have entered France over the past century and a half, including Carlists, republicans, and Basque activists. The high point was reached in 1939 when 300,000 people fleeing Franco sought to survive by crossing the border into France (Stein 1979). The same process was repeated in the twentieth century for Russian refugees. Revolutionaries fled the Czar at the beginning of the century and were followed by White Russians fleeing the October Revolution; another wave of refugees persecuted by Stalin followed the Second World War. As we will see later on, the forced "cohabitation" of political activists of the same nationality but of opposite opinions was not unrelated to the difficulties that they had in preserving an "identity" loyal to their country of origin beyond the first generation. For the moment, the important point is that for refugees or political immigrants, the desire to return is even more pronounced than for other foreigners; hence the frequent come-and-go of Armenians, for example: They arrived in massive numbers in France in the 1920s; some of them went home following the Second World War (to Soviet Armenia), only to return (or attempt to return) several years later.

The rhythms of economic activity, the logic of rural groups, and the international political conjuncture are the key factors explaining the instability that characterized the world of immigration. To these must be added one final factor: the hazards of the stay in France. Numerous testimonies describe the disappointment of exiles and of refugees who discovered that the "fatherland of human rights" did not exactly resemble the image that the history texbooks of their country had given them. Furthermore, those who expected to get rich fast were rapidly disappointed by the reality of industrial work in France. Most often, however, they refused to admit it when they returned home, hence reinforcing the collective "blindness" that the migratory process kept alive (Sayad 1975).

All of this explains the extraordinary turnover of immigrant communities in times of economic expansion, although it is difficult to determine how much of the turnover is due to internal movements from one firm or one region to another, departures for other countries of immigration, and "definitive" returns, which often preceded new departures.

To the turnover of disenchanted immigrants we must add the instability of "professional" travelers, the champions of *Wandertrieb*, constantly in search of new skills, a more gratifying job, or new adventures. Most commonly found in the nineteenth century, these nomads did not disappear in the twentieth. Accustomed to clandestinity, they could often be found in activist political circles; they tended to be bachelors and chose this way of life, a stage that since the Middle Ages has been called "youth," or the period preceding settlement into a trade, a place, and a family life.

These combined elements defined the famous law formulated by Ravenstein in 1885 before the Royal Statistics Society of London (a law that, in the case of France, would nonetheless deserve to be seriously modified, as we shall see): The migrant most often traveled short distances but preferred major urban, industrial, and commercial centers. This explains why the number of immigrants in a given city was proportional to the available opportunities, and hence to the size of the city itself (see Duchac 1974). This preference for large cities explains why Paris and Marseilles, to name the most noteworthy, have hosted so many migrants over the past century. Moreover, foreigners had an interest in cities located on or near a border. In Lorraine, for example, Italians preferred to live in the communities closest to Luxemburg or Germany, which allowed them to escape more easily from the police or to dodge the fluctuations of the exchange rate and unemployment by passing in a flash from one country to another (Walter 1935).

Ruptures, Camps, and Encampments

The immigration experience always begins with a voyage that is both the symbol and the actuality of the transition from "before" to "after." Crossing the border is a crucial moment in this adventure. Oral surveys and written testimonies illustrate the extraordinary precision with which immigrants remember the vicissitudes of their trip: the date, place, and time of departure and each movement and gesture of everyone involved are core elements of many life histories told by Italian immigrants, as well as by Central European Jews, in Lorraine.[9] The story (oral or written) almost always contains an epic dimension, which underscores the numerous obstacles the immigrant encountered and overcame: a ship caught in the ice or in the storm, a mountain infested by wild animals and riddled with armed customs officials.[10] There is an eminently mythical dimension to this; it is a "novel of the origins" designed to inscribe the new genealogy in the host country (see chapter 4). Yet these testimonies also reflect a very real dimension of the immigrant experience. In this sense, a broad geo-history of borders remains to be written. It would show that the main places of crossing between the "inside" and the "outside," the French "interior" and "exterior," were the stage for often dramatic struggles between those who guarded the gates and those who wished to enter: Spanish refugees turned back by Senegalese infantrymen in the Pyrenean mountains; Italian illegal aliens crossing the glacier Théodule on foot near the Cervin, swimming from Vintimille to Menton, rowing from Sardinia to Corsica; not to mention the Algerians embarked in the baggage compartments of the rafts headed for Marseilles, or the boat people hunted down by pirates in the southern seas (Grando et al. 1981; Mauco 1932; Jacque 1985).

The voyage, an inaugural act, is only the first step in the obstacle course of immigration. The arrival is a second crucial moment. It, too, has its own specific space: temporary camps.

The term "camp" today automatically evokes the image of Dachau or Buchenwald, in other words, of Germany; it is assumed that this has nothing to do with France's "collective memory." However, although they never reached the same degree of atrocity as those established under Nazi rule, French camps have a long history, a history that mainly involves foreigners. Jean-René Aymes (1983) described the deportation under the First Empire, from various regions of France, of 50,000 Spanish prisoners and 2,500 hostages, many of whom perished in the dungeon of Vincennes or in the forts of Bayeux, Brest, or Briançon.

In France, the First World War inaugurated modern forms of confinement of foreigners from enemy powers. It was then that the first detention camps appeared in various parts of the country.

From 1938 onward, Spanish refugees were parked in the camps of the southwestern region. "Sand lined by the sea and by barbed wire," wrote Charles Tillon of the camp in Gurs, where the housing was made of wooden shacks and which contained two washrooms for 1,400 people. Under Vichy, the charm of French hospitality in Gurs and Argelès was brutally revealed to anti-Nazis from throughout Europe and to Jews in particular. Thousands of people—"the scum of the earth" described by Arthur Koestler—died there (Schramm and Vormeier 1979; Koestler 1941).

These were, some will say, extreme cases in extreme periods. This is true, provided we understand them as caricatures of a much larger, albeit less dramatic, process. The history of immigration is also the history of people being forcefully set apart: isolation in a given area while awaiting an entrance exam. The establishment of an organized immigration policy inaugurated the mechanism of "decompression sieves," a kind of purgatory between hell and paradise where John Dory recruiters separated the good from the bad, those "in order" from those "without papers," the "healthy" from the "ill." Only illegals (and many became illegals to avoid this cruel ritual) managed to avoid the probationary exam, although they would have to confront it if they wished to regularize their situation.

In 1930, Georges Mauco estimated that 70% of the immigrants who entered France were controlled by the police and sanitary officials. One-fourth underwent a double selection process, first by the administration and then by the employers. A good example is Meurthe-et-

Moselle, which held hundreds of thousands of immigrants from Central Europe, most of them Polish.

Located in the annex of a barracks, three kilometers from the station (a distance that the immigrants often had to walk after a voyage of several thousand kilometers), the camp's facilities were totally insufficient: not enough medical supplies, showers that did not work, lack of personnel. The sanitary conditions during the trip and the stay (which could last up to a week) were so poor that during the medical verification exams (following a first exam at the time of departure) immigrants had to be thoroughly deloused. The promiscuity was such that women gave birth "in public" in the dormitories; there was insufficient space and money to build an isolated block. The repeated protests of the Polish government forced the French authorities to make several improvements. The center, a blot on the conscience of the "land of hospitality," was closed in the 1930s and was later destroyed (like many other camps, of which only cemeteries remain) (Noiriel 1984). But the process of selecting the foreign labor force was pursued following the Second World War, using improved techniques (psychological and technical exams, instruments for measuring physical strength).

All of these tests preceded the immigrants' arrival in the "encampment": the embodiment of precariousness, of the temporary situation that it was hoped that the act of migrating would be. Most immigrants lived in these areas at some point (and some of them remained all their lives) in order to survive. A quick analysis of the types of housing available to single men leads us from the ageless furnished rooms in Paris under the July Monarchy and in the major industrial cities of the post–Second World War period, to the shelters for bachelors made famous by the firm Sonacotra and encampments for seasonal agricultural laborers: shanties and wooden shacks. Descriptions of the rooms, hotels, sheds, and boarding houses for "bachelors" kept by a "mother" (the *bacana* of Italian miners in Lorraine prior to 1914) tell of overcrowding, of beds occupied in turns day and night, of the absence of comfort and even of basic hygiene (Köll 1981; Lentacker 1973; Michel 1955; Carreno et al. 1972).

The situation was no better for foreigners who came as families. Indeed, immigration is characterized by the sudden arrival of large populations in a specific area (a sector or a region of economic expansion) at a given time (the "boom" creates an immediate demand for workers); hence the permanent mismatch between the demand when all these people arrive and the housing situation. The recurrent trend in the literature on the subject, amplified by a certain complacency (particularly among hygienists) is the description of "slums," which presented several different facets.

First, there were the slums for refugees. They consisted of makeshift encampments, most often located at the edge of major cities. Marseilles, during the interwar period, had several of these centers. The Russians had a neighborhood of wooden sheds behind the Saint-Charles train station, and the Armenians fleeing the Turkish armies were assembled in the Oddo camp, which delighted journalists (though not historians) in search of the picturesque. Such "refugee shelters" can still be found today. As always, they are filled with the latest waves of immigrants, who are today the products of decolonization; for example, the Harki camps in southern France and the camps for the repatriated settlers of Indochina, such as Noyant-sur-Allier, which had 2,000 inhabitants. More recently, a ritualized "refugee obstacle course" has been developed for the surviving boat people: following initial formalities in "zones of transit," they are taken to "temporary shelters" that are spread throughout France (Naudeau 1931; Simon 1981; Hassoun and Tan 1986).

For the millions of ordinary immigrants who do not have refugee status, the terms used to refer to this precarious space are "insalubrious neighborhoods," "ghettos," "shantytowns," and "transit housing projects." Again, a study of the forms of collective housing available to immigrant communities would demonstrate that the same basic mechanisms were reproduced in each period of massive influx. The Flemish neighborhoods of Roubaix in the 1860s, the Italian miners' housing projects in Aboué around 1910, the Jewish neighborhoods of Belleville or the Marais during the belle epoque and the années folles, and the buildings and shantytowns of Algerian and Portuguese immigrants in the 1970s all have in common overpopulation due to the scarcity of housing and decrepitude due to low wages that force the immigrant to be satisfied with the most ancient and poorly kept (or unkept) buildings. Hence, on whatever piece of devalued land was available (waste grounds in particular), the immigrants built their own towns of scrap and fragile materials (such as wood or corrugated iron): precarious, uncomfortable shelters that would ultimately leave as few traces as did the camps, swept away by the powerful impact of new urban policies. Indeed, nothing is left of the belt of shantytowns that surrounded Paris in 1930, of the Armenian shacks in Issy-les-Moulineaux, or of the "Spanish quarter" in the city of Marseilles.

The primitivism of the housing goes hand in hand with the poverty of the infrastructure: muddy pathways instead of real streets, little or no electricity, no sewage nor any system to provide drinkable water; hence the syndrome of urban pathology under the July Monarchy, which Louis Chevalier described at length: hypermortality because of epidemics and characterized by extreme infant mortality rates (twice as high as the national average for immigrant families living in industrial zones between the two wars and in the 1960s) (see Reardon 1977; Köll 1981; Zehraoui 1971; Green 1985; Michel 1955; Granotier 1979; Ducellier 1981, 1982; Chevalier 1978).

Uprootedness

Uprootedness is one of the causes and one of the main forms of the urban pathology analyzed by the sociologists of the Chicago school. In their monumental study of the Polish peasantry, Thomas and Znaniecki—after having studied future immigrants in the primary groups that structured their community of origin—underscored the disorganizing effects of migration. The extensive monograph that makes up the third volume of their work emphasizes the destructive effects on the individual of an overly abrupt passage from one type of society to another completely different one, where the norms of individualism prevail (Thomas and Znaniecki 1958). There is no equivalent study for the French version of this process. However, what we do know proves that uprootedness was not a phenomenon confined to the immense cities of North America.

In general, uprootedness can be characterized as the individual's loss of the essential references and support base with which integration into a "community" would have provided him. Maurice Halbwachs, André Leroi-Gourhan, and Bruno Bettelheim have shown, in their respective domains, the importance of spatiotemporal frames for the psychological and social equilibrium of the individual. Any transplant (whether due to geographic or psychological change) leads to a more or less pronounced feeling of uprootedness. But in contemporary societies, in which the nation represents the essential group to which people belong, the sense of uprootedness produced by immigration (in the sense we have defined in this book) is particularly strong. For collectively recruited immigrants, the initial trauma of separation is followed by the destructive effects of selection procedures in specialized centers. The newcomer's life history is recorded (on a police questionnaire); he is photographed, weighed, and fingerprinted and then given an identification number. All of these operations—to which we might add body searches, auscultations, delousing, and so on—characterize, according to Erving Goffman (1961) the institutional rituals whose goal is to sever an individual's ties to his or her past. For immigrants, these procedures make it even more difficult to bear other characteristic signs of being in an unfamiliar world (*dépaysement*), not the least of which is solitude.

On the average, the Algerians studied by Ashène Zehraoui (1971) were separated from their wives for eight years. A majority of the Spanish immigrants who arrived in the Paris region during the same period to work as servants came in couples, but at the cost of splitting up the family. Of three hundred individuals surveyed, only ninety-two were not separated from their children (Inspection Générale des Etudes de la Seine 1967).

In the interwar period, Georges Mauco (1937) drew attention to the psychological evils of isolation for Polish agricultural workers, holding it responsible for acts of insanity that the tabloid press had widely reported in 1928. A recent study carried out in a village of Seine-et-Marne confirms these remarks. The instability of Polish agricultural workers contrasted with the rootedness of French peasants and explains the absence of an established pattern of sociability; whereas in the mining towns of the north, the collective life of Polish communities flourished (Gossiaux 1984).

Archival sources and autobiographical testimony illustrate the drama of the solitude experienced by that other category of immigrants, refugees. From the early nineteenth century onward, they tended to come together to pursue their political struggle in exile. For example, in the case of Italians under the July Monarchy, there were four types of refugees corresponding to the different waves of emigration that had occurred in the preceding half-century: The *contumaci* (who had been sentenced to death or to prison and had managed to escape), the *outlaws* (who had been sentenced to banishment, such as the Romagnan revolutionaries of 1831), the *fuorisciti* (who had emigrated to avoid arrest), and the *voluntary émigrés,* who had obtained permission to leave. Most lived in the poor neighborhoods of the capital, in particular the fourth arrondissement. Despite the subsidy paid by the French government (1 to 1.5 francs per day and per person for over 1,500 Italian exiles in 1831) and the aid of philanthropic institutions run by wealthy émigrés (such as the *Comité de Secours pour les Réfugiés Italiens Indigents*), they generally lived in poverty, organizing "collective canteens" or leaving the city to reduce their food expenses. A majority of these refugees suffered from the "moral atmosphere of bourgeois France. . . . Flipping through the letters of most of these émigrés, they are so quick to compare the life of vanity enjoyed by the French with the pure passion and simple *alla mano* ways of the Italians, that one would think they had all read Stendhal" (Crémieux 1936). Yet those who managed to remain together in Paris had the least to worry about. Indeed, at the time the French government forcefully dispersed most exiles throughout small provincial towns. The National Archives hold numerous files containing letters from Portuguese, Spanish, Polish, and other refugees begging the administration to bring them closer to their compatriots or to their families (see, for example, NA F7 12112, 12078). In the twentieth century, the situation of refugees was even more difficult, and their isolation was undoubtedly greater. The suffering that accompanied the loss of their homelands was well interpreted by the film industry. Andrei Tarkovski's *Nostalgie* or Hugo Santiago's *Les Trottoires de Saturne,* for example, described the role that music played for the exile in search of his roots. It is also understandable that among Argentinians, the tango was much more than simply a popular dance. Indeed, more than any other form of expression, the tango "extolled the initial wound of exile, buried illusions, the inability to defy the present" (Jorge Lavelli, *Le Monde,* 13–14 November 1983).

The available sources also illustrate the difficulties of learning a new language for an adult population that was usually confined to the ghettos of work, with little time for evening classes. Regardless of the period, the French spoken by first-generation immigrants was, after a few years, characterized by a mixture of two languages that could not be disentangled, which proves that immigrants were torn between two worlds without really belonging to either (Sayad 1975). Even Italians, whose "linguistic proximity" to French is too often assumed, experienced persistent difficulties in pronouncing such vowels as *oe* or *y* (Vegliante 1987). In my own oral research in Lorraine, I encountered numerous elderly people living in retirement, some of whom had lived in France for up to a half-century and who still mixed Italian words (in fact borrowed from regional dialects) with French words (Noiriel 1984). The studies published by INED in 1947 and 1953 recorded the same phenomenon, for both Russians and Poles. (Girard and Stoetzel estimated that among the latter, only two out of ten spoke French correctly at that time, twenty years after they had emigrated.) The process evoked by novelist Azouz Begag (1986), whose immigrant heroes use terms such as "*taumobile*" and "*boulicia*" (police), was, therefore, quite widespread.

This illustrates the position of inferiority in which immigrants found themselves; for life, their very language betrayed their foreign origin. This problem was most acute in the initial phase; the immigrant's poor grasp of the language was aggravated by other areas of ignorance about the host society, making him or her a perfect victim. This is a phenomenon that has often been described with respect to the "jungle" of major U.S. cities, but countless examples can be found in France as well. In Marseilles in the 1920s, Armenian refugees were enlisted upon their arrival by "supervisors" who, with the complicity of certain employees in the port, taxed these poor souls from five to thirty francs simply to obtain access to dockwork. As a receipt, each refugee received a tramway ticket! (Turabian 1928).

This brings us to another characteristic aspect of the uprootedness of immigrants. In addition to the shock that followed the transfer from one society to another, the discovery of the fast world of assembly lines and the complicated topography of subway lines (Boudjedra 1969), they often had great difficulty understanding the new dominant norms.

In the Name of the Father

In oral surveys, it has been found that the immigrant's memory of the first hours or of the first days spent in the country is quite vivid despite the corrosion of time; this is because the adventures of the initial encounter left as strong an impression on immigrants as did the trip itself or the examination in the recruitment center. It is in those early hours or days that a newcomer discovered the fundamental importance of identification papers, which would profoundly affect his or her entire life as a foreigner. This point is so omnipresent in oral surveys and in written testimony, regardless of the individual's social origin, that it would in itself merit an entire chapter. The impact of "I.D. papers" is significant because legal identity is based on a symbolic system that is often unknown in the country of origin. As we saw in chapter 2, "the Card and the Code" reflect the specific needs of highly differentiated societies in which the "chain of interdependence" extends far beyond national boundaries. The I.D. card is, in a sense, the material proof that one is set apart from other individuals. Indeed, given the anonymity and individualism characteristic of modern Western societies, the an individual's identity is not defined within a framework of his or her familiarity or relationships. An Algerian in his village—and this is true for all immigrants who come from rural societies—was someone familiar, someone who was called by his name. An integral part of his group of origin, his identity was known to all; there was no need for papers when a man's word engaged the honor of his name. By abruptly imposing the norms of juridical identity specific to Western societies, the immigrant was required to instantaneously accomplish an act that it took the French centuries to internalize, in a drawn-out process that culminated in the triumph of civil status. For the immigrant, his or her very surname is often at stake. In traditional Cambodian society, for example, there is no given name–surname distinction. The *Jhmoh,* the single term that designates an individual, is not based on the relationship with a parent but invokes, instead, the circumstances of one's birth. Similar problems were encountered with foreigners from countries considered culturally closer to France. In Portugal, for example, the transmittable surname is that of the mother followed by that of the father; often, however, in an effort to simplify the procedure, the administration records only the first of the two surnames, thereby dropping the true patronymic, the father's name. This is one of the effects of an increasingly complex bureaucratic machine that needed to rationalize, that is to simplify, the written identity of individuals (the ideal code being one number attributed to each person). Immigrants whose native language was not based on the Greco-Latin alphabet fell victim to a "translation" of their surname to adapt it to the orthographical norms of "*francité.*" We have seen that the interaction between a foreigner and a representative of the administration frequently led to the amputation of the immigrant's name; to this we should add the effects of the drama that led to exile in the first place. For the orphans of the Armenian genocide, as was the case for refugees who had had to falsify their identity in order to flee, arrival in France meant that they would have to adopt a new name and a new identity. These fundamental changes were all the more important for the immigrant because he or she was constantly required, by law, to display "papers" each time the police checked for identification. In times of crisis, the renewal of the I.D. card was called into question. All of the sources I have consulted illustrate the deeply felt anguish caused by the arbitrary practices of officials, a fear of first being suddenly relegated to the world of illegals and of then being expelled. Even without crises, the issue of papers has always been present in the lives of immigrants and has become ever more significant as the bureaucracy has become more rigid and demanding. The institutions with which a person interacts all require evidence of that person's identity. Suddenly awakened to the world of red tape, immigrants are subjected to much more of this routine harassment than are French citizens; they are required to present more documents in everything they undertake. Since they tend to belong to the most economically disadvantaged groups, they are confronted more often than are others to the services of social security, hospitals, family allowances, and public assistance. The frequent administrative errors in the spelling of their names or in noting their civil status further increase the time spent clarifying and waiting in line.

It is therefore not surprising that many oral or written testimonies are obsessed with this question. As Erving Goffman noted, an individual's legally guaranteed, established identity and his or her psychological identity are closely related; it is therefore not suprising that persecution can lead to madness, as in cases encountered by psychoanalysts in which the "illness" is nothing but a quest for recognition, expressed by the presentation of a multitude of "papers."

Stigmas

It is also at the moment of their arrival that immigrants discovered what it really meant to be "foreigners," subjected to the judgment of those whose norms they were supposed to adopt. In Monceau-les-Mines, one of the favorite popular pastimes was to watch the Polish convoys arrive. The newcomers were looked over mockingly, with their semi-military costumes, their large baggy trousers, their greenish tunics from another age, their boots, and their leather caps with the peak folded over their foreheads. Comments abounded on the women in camisoles covered with multicolored shawls, with colorful checkered hankerchiefs over their heads. In the housing projects of the north, women exchanged their impressions on furniture and on the costumes worn by the newcomers. Men openly sized up their hips and chests. But the height of this little-known form of "working-class sociability" was reached when the Poles went down into the mines dressed in white. There was nothing "Slavic" about this practice; it was simply that these immigrants, who had been uprooted at least twice already, had learned in Westphalia that discipline and impeccable cleanliness went together (Miroz 1979; Drelon 1982).

When they went to church, Polish immigrants again found themselves in an uncertain situation with respect to local customs. In their country, one stood through church ceremonies; the benches were reserved for the elderly and the crippled. Confused by the comforts of French Catholicism, they were afraid to sit down lest they occupy an undue seat, and they stood in a group in the entrance in front of the door, blocking access to the church. This attitude, as well as their costume and their habit of kneeling right in the middle of the nave, transformed the holy place into a sideshow and provoked laughter among the parishioners (Poszwa 1930). The situation was not very different in the synagogues. Jean Tchernoff, in his description of the Jewish communities of Paris prior to the First World War, distinguished between assimilated Jews, with their dignity, top hats, and calm gestures, and new immigrants, devoured by mysticism, "persecuted Jews" who "gesticulated furiously, swaying their bodies" (Tchernoff 1938, 3:14).

The literature on immigration is full of these sorts of descriptions, which prove that while the stigmatization of foreigners took on various forms, it was by no means specific to one or another ethnic group or nationality; it was not a "Jewish problem," or an "Arab problem," nor was it related to "religious," "cultural," or "physical" particularities. These examples underscore the importance of that which cannot be learned, of "manners," of body language and gestures that automatically distinguish a Frenchman from a "foreigner." In short, what is truly incorporated and exhibited to signify the boundary between "them" and "us" is the entire historical past of the nation.

Several types of individual reactions can be observed in response to the discrediting of oneself that the judgment of the Other provokes. Revolt is one of them. It is one of the factors in foreign criminality, which is already favored by uprootedness. More often, however, the foreigner seeks to conform to the new norms. Here again, the literature abounds in concise examples. In Belleville in the 1930s, for love of a pretty French woman, a young Armenian immigrant tries to transform himself into a genuine "cheeky Parisian urchin"; he convinces himself that he has always loved the "Six Days" and the accordion waltz (Lépidis 1973). Intellectuals adopt various other strategies. To understand puns, for example, and the subtleties of "French humor"—thereby winning over those who laugh—they might assiduously read *Le Canard enchaîné* for years as part of an effort to become integrated (Valensi and Wachtel 1991).

But most of these efforts end in failure. Alfred Schütz (1964) described the social mechanism of the irremediable distance separating the foreigner from the national. Foreigners can only "translate" their new environment in terms that are familiar to them, and the model is provided by their group of origin. This translation is, however, usually inadequate, and the efforts exerted to become a full-fledged member of the new "club" tend to be futile or to appear suspicious.

For immigrants of middle- or upper-class backgrounds, who are often refugees, uprootedness is frequently aggravated by a downgraded professional status. For example, according to some sources, one-third of Russian immigrants had received a university education, and three-fourths a high school education in Russia (Repiton 1986). A large number—although fewer than legend claims—were members of the aristocracy who had fled the October Revolution. Many novels written by Russian émigrés recount the difficulties they encountered in their attempt to remain on a level with the French elite. Henry Troyat's father, a wealthy merchant from Caucasia, was unable to fully establish himself in the world of French commerce, partly because he was not trusted. The capital his name had accumulated thanks to the social efforts of several generations was suddenly devalued. A poor understanding of the commercial laws of the new country and of its language were additional obstacles that explained the family's repeated failures (and the desire for social revenge expressed by the son, as we will see).

Anonymity represented a loss of symbolic capital for those who had experienced fame in their own countries, and even more dramatically so among exiled writers, which proves that names, like currency, are part of a whole that is structured along national lines. Writers and musicians who were well known in Russia found no public in France and lived in misery. This was the case, among others, of Bunin, even though he had won the Nobel Prize for literature in 1933. The trauma of downgraded professional status, in addition to uprootedness, most often provoked an attitude of withdrawal, and only the chimerical hope of a return home gave many the strength to go on living. Some of these refugees, officers and intellectuals, swelled the ranks of the working class. In Creusot, they were hired as unskilled workers in the Schneider factories, where management complained of their propensity for "neurasthenia"! Others were sent to Tarn-et-Garonne to cultivate the land, but they were described as "living in expectation" and accused of abandoning their crops (Troyat 1987; Banine 1968; INED 1947a; Mauco 1932; Mauco and Demangeon 1939). This attitude of renunciation so often observed among first-generation immigrants, this tendency to abandon certain practices, is also a strategy to avoid stigma. In the example cited earlier, Louis Poszwa argued that jeering in churches led to the rapid "dechristianization" of part of the Polish population in France, a decline of religious practice that can also be observed in other communities (Poszwa 1930; Cholvy 1982). Similarly, by their attitudes foreigners sought to avoid potentially embarrassing situations. Today, many Southeast Asian refugees dread being confronted with places that are "loaded with history" and are therefore weary of old buildings with customs and modes of occupation that have been codified for a long time. The rules are unfamiliar to them; prefering "modernity" (which is not a specific characteristic of Asian culture), they tend to withdraw into the immense anonymous skyscrapers of the thirteenth arrondissement of Paris: a new area, which therefore has no history; a place where, consequently, it will be easier to start their own history over again (Hassoun and Tan 1986).

Another series of attitudes characteristic of stigmatized foreigners consists of playing with appearances, with an outward display of identity. Once one suddenly realizes that one's mere physical appearance, in other words, the simple act of being oneself, generates fear, laughter, or aggression, and that one cannot avoid confronting those with whom one interacts daily, one may seek to defuse the potential for conflict by "rites of interaction." An Armenian from Valence recalled that when he entered a café and was stared at like a wild animal, he ostentatiously crossed himself, which meant: "Don't be afraid of me, I am of the same religion as you, I am your brother" (Keuroghlian 1977).

Beyond pacifying gestures, another possibility is to play on looks by modifying one's physical appearance. Here again, the literature abounds with examples. Eve Dessare (1976), for example, wrote that her mother, a German Jew who had fled the Nazis, was constantly a butt for French administrative harassment. In order to wheedle an extension of her residency permit from the ill-tempered clerks of the prefecture of Paris, she had no other choice but to powder her face so as to "look more French."

To seem more like local people, a name change was another possibility. This was a frequent occurrence in the nineteenth century, when the administration had fewer means of control than it does today, and especially in times of xenophobia. In Lyons in 1894, for example, following the assassination of President Sadi Carnot by an Italian anarchist, many Italian immigrants had the *i* or the *o* removed from the end of their names (Dupin 1900).

Under the Vichy government, the Jews attempted to escape persecution by trading German-sounding surnames for elegant, better-sounding French ones. Lotte Eisner explained, for example, that she had borrowed her new identity, *Escoffier,* from Prosper Mérimée's *Carmen.* The name sounded very French, but the term "*escoffier*" means "to kill." This is a good example of the ultimate resistance put up by individuals who were obliged, in order to survive, to renounce entire aspects of their identity (Palmier, in Badia 1982).

Among Themselves

Individuals of the same national or "ethnic" origin commonly came together in an effort to escape the confrontations of everyday life; security and relative tranquility were found in the intimacy of sameness. Statistics available from the nineteenth century onward do not support the idea that immigrant "ghettos" emerged only after the Second World War. As early as the Second Empire, foreigners were concentrated in the most dynamic large industrial areas, such as Roubaix, the popular suburbs of Lille (Wazemmes, Saint-Sauveur) or Marseilles. Later on, each new wave of immigration was reflected by the appearance of new ghettos: in the mining areas of the north and of Lorraine, in the Paris region, in the Alpine and Pyrenean valleys. The figures reflect this concentration of foreign-born labor: 85% of the immigrants in the department of Loire lived in the arrondissement of Saint-Etienne in 1930; three-fourths of those surveyed in Meurthe-et-Moselle worked in the arrondissement of Briey; two-thirds of the immigrants of Moselle lived in three arrondissements of Thionville and Metz; 90% of the Armenians of Drôme lived in Valence; and so on. At the national level, in the 1930s, 1,700 communities had a foreign population that approached or exceeded their total French population (Mauco 1937).

It must be emphasized that those who recruited the foreign labor force were responsible for the formation of these ghettos. The organized importation of workers has always been intended to satisfy the needs of large companies. From the late nineteenth century to the 1970s, heavy industry was the prototype of this logic. The type of working-class space that was formed on the model of the factory town provoked a large-scale process of segregation among zones of work and of immigration, agricultural zones, and the commercial and intellectual metropolises. Meurthe-et-Moselle is a particularly striking example of this, but there are many others.

The same process of segregation occurred on industrial sites, for various reasons. The massive arrival of immigrants tended to provoke an exodus among the current inhabitants. This was the case for the peasant population of the villages of the northern and eastern regions that were transformed into mining zones, but it was also true of such areas as the Old Port of Marseilles, where the inflow of Neapolitan fishermen from the nineteenth century onward caused the locals to move out to other neighborhoods. In regions where the established populace managed to preserve control over their homes, those coming from without were kept at a distance. In the mining towns of Meuse, as in Noyelles-sous-Lens, worker-peasants and notables remained rooted in the old village, and immigrants occupied the newer housing projects (Sportiello 1981; Harbulot 1977; Dubar et al. 1982). In some cases, grouping individuals in specific neighborhoods or zones according to "ethnic" criteria was a strategy explicitly defined by employers anxious to reinforce the homogeneity and stability of the labor force. The nature of recruitment (whether family-based or individual) played an indirect role in this process, for the type of housing (projects, shelters) prevented virtually all contact with the existing population. In the iron and steel industry of Lorraine, the job segmentation and the corresponding arrangement of built-up zones (the greater one's skill, the higher one's chance of living on the hilltops) accentuated the grouping of foreigners, since they were also, for the most part, unskilled (Noiriel 1982). The conjunction of economic and "ethnic" criteria in the formation of ghettos was a widespread phenomenon. In Bordeaux, typical of large cities, the prefect noted in 1930 that three-fourths of the immigrants were concentrated in two neighborhoods, not by deliberate choice but because housing was less expensive and better situated with respect to the trades practiced by the city's foreign workers (NA F7 13518). In Decazeville as well, proximity to the workplace was a key factor explaining the massive presence of immigrants in the eastern and southern parts of the city (near the mining shafts), whereas the western districts were residential, commercial, and French (Tomasi 1975).

As we can see, although the assimilating discourse of public officials has constantly stressed the dangers of nonindigenous cores and repeatedly suggested ways to disperse newcomers throughout the country, the higher economic interests of the nation led to the exact opposite result.

This propensity to cluster was also consistent with the aspirations of most immigrants. This is particularly clear in cities, where individuals enjoy much more freedom of movement than they do in more paternalistic regions. Once an initial core of individuals had settled after years of seasonal migrations, informal channels of self-recruitment were formed on a family or village basis. Over several years, a genuine community could form in this manner, sometimes continuing for decades to grow from the same sources. In the Longwy basin, the mining commune of Hussigny lived for three-fourths of a century in symbiosis with small villages located near the border between Marches and Romagna, such as Santa Agiti or Pennabili. The iron and steel mining town of Villerupt drew most of its present-day population from the communities of Ombria such as Gubbio. The same process has been described with respect to the Italian community of Nogent-sur-Marne. Similarly, in Vénissieux, Italians originated from Latium (a community of Frosinone), Spaniards from the localities of the Murcia-Cartagena region, and Kabyles from Dra-el-Mizan. Also in the interwar period, the Italian community of Grenoble included some 3,000 natives of the community of Corata in the Pouilles. The same process occurred following the Second World War: Moroccans recruited in the Paris region during the 1950s came from the

Agadir area; in the 1960s, countless migratory networks linked the small villages of northern Portugal to the industrial communities of the Parisian suburbs (S. Bonnet 1972; Videlier and Bouet 1983; INED 1940; Hily and Poinard in Abou-Saada and Milet 1986).

The process of self-recruitment was therefore a key factor in the establishment of colonies of foreigners. For those immigrants who could not reach France through community channels (collective recruitment, refugees), any flukes in their initial settlement were subsequently corrected by later movements, adding to the important degree of instability described earlier. Information circulated by word of mouth and written correspondence, often leading to enclaves based on regional or "ethnic," if not always village-based, identity. The efforts of Southeast Asian refugees to remain among themselves is a good illustration of the persistance of this process. At first dispersed throughout the country by the authorities, over a period of years they had for the most part returned to Paris (Hassoun and Tan 1986).

It is possible to briefly sketch a typology of the various immigrant "communities" (in the broadest sense) established in France over the past century. Where foreign settlement is very recent, artificially imposed from the outside (by employers or by public officials), and heterogeneous, collective organization is weak or nonexistent. This is often the case in the first phase of industrialization; for example, in the iron industry in Lorraine prior to 1914 or the "pioneer" zones of the Alps during the construction of hydroelectric dams. Transit centers and repatriation centers are examples of artificial concentrations of individuals with nothing in common except their misery. Given the longer duration of their presence and greater homogeneity, so-called foreign colonies dominated by one "ethnic" or national group tend to present a greater degree of cohesion. Several types of urban foreign colonies can be distinguished. Colonies located in the center of town were frequent until the 1930s. The flow of immigrants often caused an ecological reorganization of the whole; old decrepit neighborhoods were abandoned by their former inhabitants, who settled in more recent, less congested zones of urbanization. In Roubaix, four streets housed at least 75% of the city's Belgians in the 1880s, and the rue de Longue-Haie was a genuine foreign enclave. In Halluin, Flemish immigration was so dense that it provoked a veritable displacement of the linguistic border in a previously Francophone zone (dominated by dialects). Ghetto neighborhoods, which Flemish workers virtually never left, were thus delimited by language (Reardon 1977; Hastings 1986). In Marseilles during the second half of the nineteenth century, the flow of Neapolitan fishermen, who literally took over the Old Port, led to the exodus of locals and the gradual establishment of an intensive community life, each Italian village from which the fisherman had emigrated being reproduced by street or by neighborhood (Sportiello 1981).

The groups assembled on the basis of tertiary sector trades (craftsmen, shopkeepers) formed another type of immigrant community in the downtown districts. The Marais and Belleville—neighborhoods through which most new Jewish immigrants from Central Europe passed from the turn of the century until the 1960s—are the best examples of this type of community life in Paris. Similarly, in Valence during the 1930s, 90% of the Armenian population lived in the old craft and commercial center (Green 1985; Roland 1962; Garagnon 1955).[11]

With the urban renovation of the 1960s, these downtown communities either disintegrated or were driven out to the periphery. The prevailing type of foreign communities became the suburb. Nonetheless, it must be noted that suburbs were already very common by the interwar period. Again, professional activity determined the profile of the urban environment. This was essentially a population employed by large industry, gathered around the large factories. With his characteristic racial prejudice, Jacques Valdour described the diversity of workers who flocked to the gates of the Renault plants in the interwar period. Georges Mauco, in a somewhat trembling tone, described the colony of 3,000 Spanish workers settled in the *plaine* Saint-Denis; the Moroccan community of Aubervilliers, the Arab village of Grésillons in Gennevilliers; a world that had never, until recently, attracted the attention of historians. Vénissieux is another particularly interesting example because it perfectly illustrates the evolution of these urban groups. With the integration of former waves of immigrants, what used to be "peripheral" became increasingly central. The extension of suburban communities absorbed and modernized the "slums" of the interwar years; but encampments appeared on the new periphery in the 1960s, such as zones of priority urbanization (ZUP), immigrant housing projects such as the Minguettes, where the 9,000 apartments hastily constructed in tall buildings have become a focal point of social unrest (Valdour 1929; Mauco 1932; Videlier and Bouet 1983).

Urban communities were not the only expression of foreigners' tendency to seek a familiar haven in which to withdraw. One of the most unique features of the French situation is the importance of that degraded form of city planning, the working-class housing project in heavy industry, which until recently attracted major concentrations of immigrants, one wave after another; from Polish mining towns in the northern regions to Italian districts in the east to the "phalenstery" of Ugine in the Alps, and the Péchiney projects in Gardanne, Provence (Ponty 1985; Noiriel 1984; Faidutti-Rudolph 1964; Sabran 1973).

Colonies of agricultural workers are yet another example, of which we have very few recent studies. While agricultural workers rarely managed to form well-structured groups, this was not the case for sharecroppers and farmers, who were for the most part recruited in the regions of the southwest to farm the lands that had been abandoned by French peasants. In the villages of Gers or Lot-et-Garonne, one often finds settlers from Switzerland, often quite well-off, living among themselves, sending their wives home to give birth, refusing assimilation, and working hard to earn enough money to return home. Italian communities are more common, as a result of the systematic recruitment policy carried out by the French authorities in the 1920s. They sometimes display original forms of group life, such as the Bergamitan colony of Blanquefort, a kind of extended community comprised of fourteen families (more than 160 people) in a village that when they arrived had totaled only thirty inhabitants (NA F7 13518; Marcel-Rémond 1928).

Finally, a different type of foreign colony was made up of groups of aristocrats or intellectuals settled in France. Countless novels have described the cosmopolitan Paris of writers and artists in the 1920s, Americans being generally the most visible (Hemingway 1964; Fitzgerald 1973). Sea bathing, which was fashionable in the early nineteenth century, inaugurated a form of idleness that attracted many wealthy foreigners to the coasts of France. In Normandy, Brittany, and Bordeaux, the British dominated the worldly scene, introducing tennis, golf, and bridge as snobbish entertainment. A similar lifestyle was found on the Côte d'Azur, although there was a greater diversity of origins (Corbes 1962; Dupeux 1974; Le Roy 1955).

Foreigners always felt, regardless of the period and regardless of the form, the need to group together as a way of escaping from the daily aggressions of an unfamiliar world. Louis Wirth argued that the role of the ghetto was to ensure the transition between two worlds, that of the country of origin and that of the host country, by attenuating the shock of transplantation (Wirth 1928). The isolated life most typical of the third age of emigration is illustrated by the appearance in the community of activities that are intended to ensure the survival of the group: shops and crafts, but also an array of more or less legal activities ranging from the illegal labor recruitment agency, with its network of smugglers and country correspondants, to "protective" or "mutual aid" organizations such as the Mafia in the United States. The monographs we have show that in a given community, the earliest arrivals often take advantage of their experience to take charge of these intermediary activities. First among them are the cafés, privileged places of sociability among foreigners, in particular for single men, where labor market information is exchanged, where news from back home circulates both ways, and where meetings are organized. A shopkeeper could also draw advantages from his situation by always being available (for example, by giving credit or by being open on Sundays and late at night) and by stocking up on products "from back home." Tailoring, hairdressing, and shoemaking were also trades that were rapidly invested by foreigners whenever there was a sufficiently large community.[12]

In addition to its economic function, "ethnic" business played a substantial role in reinforcing community life by creating ties among members of the group. This is a collective form of "self-presentation," embodied in the very arrangement of the spaces where the activities took place: a shop window or a back room. An entire *histoire des mentalités* could be based on the study of signs, of facades, of the interior arrangement of establishments such as cafés and shops. It would reveal the strategies of assimilation and their evolution over time: Take, for example, the cafés owned by Italians or Algerians called "*Chez Roger*" or "*Au petit Paris,*" whose entire symbolic arrangement (the exterior facade, the disposition of the tables and counter) is in accordance with French norms. Conversely, others present themselves as places of refuge for the "among ourselves," to attract customers who are in search of an atmosphere from back home (Italian restaurants, Arab cafés). However, the proliferation of outward signs of exotocism is more often a concession to the judgment of the Other than a proof of loyalty to one's origins.[13]

The links maintained with those who remained back home help keep alive the hope of returning. Such ties took on various forms according to the period and the circumstances of immigration. Progress in transportation and the appearance of paid vacations multiplied opportunities to return home, individually or in groups; consider, for example, those "Italian" villages of Gers where, during the 1950s, families traveled each week to Venice (INED 1954). Two other ways of maintaining a relationship with one's place of origin—which were also ways of telling oneself and others that immigration was only temporary, time in parentheses—consisted of transferring savings and exchanging letters.

The transfer of a portion of one's wage to the family back home is a constant of the history of immigration. Even when the sums saved were infinitesimal, the money order was mailed as a symbolic gesture (Sömme, in Gani 1972; INED 1981). Thomas and Znaniecki were justified in paying close attention to the study of the correspondence of Polish immigrants in Chicago. On the basis of thousands of documents, they were able to establish a typology of letters, based on the conjuncture, the social background of the immigrant, and how long he or she had been in the host country. The exchange of correspondence was one of the forms of social obligation with which immigrants had to comply. Its expressed, borders notwithstanding, the persistent solidarity among members of the family and strengthened the group's existence within the exile community itself; hence the ritual character that the writing in these letters often took on and the specific form established by tradition (Thomas and Znaniecki 1958).

To my knowledge, there are no studies of this sort for France. Jean-René Aymes's work on Spanish deportees under Napoleon I studies the correspondence sent to the families who remained in Spain. It is clear, in this case, that the levels of resistance to assimilation through writing vary according to the social origins of prisoners. Commanding officers write in a firm, traditional language, anchored in its archaisms, that resists contamination by French. Words that have no equivalent in French are underlined as a means of stressing the impossibility of assimilating them; it is also a way of covertly expressing the complicity between educated people and of stating one's patriotism by refusing to alter the mother tongue. Among simple soldiers, however, the more the Spanish employed is poor and hesitant, the more the invasion of French is manifest (Aymes 1983).

This is not the place to enumerate all the cultural forms that reflect efforts within immigrant communities to keep their values of origin alive. For reasons discussed earlier, this phenomenon is especially the case in the private sphere and is therefore not apparent to people outside the group.

It is known that eating habits are the elements of the culture of origin that maintain themselves for the longest time. Interior decoration is also a reminder of the traditions of origin: large devotional images in the homes of Italians in the south during the 1950s; brightly colored engravings and strips of embroidered fabric on the walls of Polish homes; not to mention the furniture, which, for those who managed to bring it with them, evokes memories of the house where they were born or raised (S. Bonnet 1965; Mauco 1932). The conditions of these foreign communities, the lack of infrastructure, of decent housing, and so forth, sometimes had the positive effect of providing the immigrants with a significant latitude for maneuvering in their efforts to re-create their country abroad. It might be supposed that these self-construction practices played a fundamental role in community stabilization in all epochs. Jacques Barou (1987) recently showed that, in the sixteenth arrondissement of Marseilles, homes were built for Algerian immigrants in the 1950s according to the traditional practice of villages in the mountans of Kabylia. It was a collective activity that required the cooperation of the extended family, according to the model of the *touiza,* a contract of reciprocal assistance that the inhabitants of a village owe each other.

The logic of the "gift" and the "counter-gift," of the favor that puts an obligation on its beneficiary and therefore binds the group together, is very common in immigrant communities, even though it took on various forms according to the possibilities of the place and time. It is in this perspective that we must understand the widespread practice by Southeast Asian refugees today of the *tontine,* a form of group loan to an individual on the condition that he return the favor.

Community life also had its constraints, illustrated by the control that the community feels entitled to exert over members of the group to avoid its dissolution. The best example of this is undoubtedly the issue of mixed marriages. In the early 1970s, over 70% of the Algerian women who married in France did so with members of their own community. Among Armenians in the 1930s, the same desire to control women's marriages could be observed. The choice of a spouse was "arranged" by parents or friends and required the approval of the elder, in endless late evening meetings (Sayad 1975; Keuroghlian 1977). At the national level, in 1930, mixed marriages (French/foreign) made up barely one-half of the total of foreigners' marriages celebrated in France (Depoid 1942).

These informal community practices generally resulted in a very diversified associative activity. In the absence of a global study (see, nonetheless, the research directed by Catani 1987b), it is very difficult to go beyond the description provided by the sources examined here (public archives and testimonies of the time). First of all, it is important to distinguish, as it is generally done for the French movement of voluntary association, between nineteenth-century organizations and more recent ones. Indeed, prior to the legislation of the welfare state, the main function of voluntary associations was to tend to the needs of their members in case of sickness or accident. As we saw in the preceding chapter, segregation between Frenchmen and foreigners was not very pronounced in these organizations. That is why many mutual aid societies that were organized along trade lines included members from a variety of different countries. Most such societies, however, were locally based and recalled the village from which the immigrants had come. This is what Philippe Videlier in 1985 called "intermediary communities of origin" ("*Unions amicales*"), which brought together individuals of shared origin and were led by craftsmen (in Vénissieux, for example, there were mutual aid societies of tinsmiths). In the late nineteenth century, in La Seyne-sur-Mer, Italian shipyard riveters also had their own mutual aid societies (Martinencq 1982); the same was true in Paris in traditional trades (see *l'Unione Italiana, la Giovale,* and so on, mentioned by Schirmacher 1908).

From the First World War onward, the immigrant voluntary association movement took on the form in which we know it today. Small autonomous societies were increasingly integrated within larger national movements; the issue frequently became a political issue of major importance between the country of origin, which used associations, or contributed to their creation, in order to channel the patriotic feelings of its citizens, and the host country, which increasingly kept an eye on these organizations.

At that time, all voluntary associations had similar characteristics, regardless of the nationality they represented: They were either sporting, cultural, professional, or mutual aid associations. Through these structures, the group could publicly manifest its existence through celebrations and competitions and by circulating newspapers and magazines in the mother tongue.[14] The voluntary association movement was organized in a relatively hierarchical manner. Most often, the local structures were dependent on a national leadership that provided substantial financial support. The Poles during the interwar period displayed the most complete associative structuration of all immigrants in France. Numerous local associations (forty-two in Bruay-en-Artois alone, each with its own banner) were gathered into a local committee for each locality, and all local committees were represented in a central committee; in 1930, this central body had a total of 100,000 members and represented five hundred different voluntary associations (Mauco 1932; Ponty 1985). In the recent period, the closest to the Polish example is the Portuguese voluntary association movement, with a hundred organizations in 1975 (Hily and Poinard, in Abou-Saada and Milet 1986).

The key question is, of course, why, in each period, certain nationalities developed many voluntary associations whereas others remained disorganized (the Italians compared with the Poles in the interwar years; the Algerians compared with the Portuguese today). One explanation is to be found in the degree and the nature of assistance provided by the authorities of the country of origin. Today, the vitality of the Portuguese voluntary association movement is linked to institutional support from the government of Portugual. The emigrant who sends his earnings home and who votes in elections is so lauded that a holiday is dedicated to him; official "Lusitanian identity" (*lusitanité*) is cultivated for outside use. In the interwar period, the Portuguese enjoyed an exceptional situation, when the French government departed from its republican traditions and accepted the presence of Portuguese schoolteachers and priests, who were often, in collaboration with the consulate, the genuine representatives of the community. In the Italian case, on the other hand, the support of the authorities in Italy simply fanned political struggles, which had been, for many immigrants, the cause of their departure. That is why, despite the intense consular activity—in support of sporting *Dopoloavora* societies, cultural *Dante Alighieri* societies, branches of Italian veterans' organizations—the Italian authorities did not succeed in promoting as widespread an interest in voluntary associations as did the Portuguese. Individuals who did not have access to sufficient logistical support from their country of origin (either because they were too numerous in France or because they did not have, or no longer had, a state) were therefore at a disadvantage in the construction of voluntary associations. Nonetheless, the existence of a well-established migratory tradition toward France could compensate for this, as in the case of Jews. The generations of Jewish immigrants who had become integrated into French society in the early nineteenth century (particularly the Rothschild family) lent their support, willingly or reluctantly, to immigrants from Central and Southern Europe in ensuing decades, thus relieving their misery in times of crisis (Hyman 1979). The Poles were, to a lesser extent, the beneficiaries of a similar phenomenon. The refugees of 1830 who became established in France (such as Prince Czartorsky, whose grandson was married to a French woman) encouraged the introduction and settlement of the earliest contingents of Polish immigrants prior to the First World War (Ponty 1985).

The nature of immigration was a factor that either stimulated or curbed the development of a voluntary association movement. When those recruited were mostly bachelors (which was often the case for the least-represented nationalities, such as Chinese, Turks, and Pakistanese), their characteristic instability prevented the establishment of a durable movement. Conversely, the massive recruitment of workers with their families (the case of the Poles in the 1920s) was a factor favorable to voluntary associations. Another element had to do with the associative experience of the immigrant prior to his or her arrival in France. One of the rare studies we have of Ukrainians (in English) shows that many rural dwellers, prior to having emigrated, were deeply involved in community movements, in particular, peer group and agricultural cooperatives (of which there were 6,500 in Ukraine in 1914). The group could, as a result, more easily adapt to the new conditions of emigration. Within a few years of their arrival, there were four nationwide Ukrainian associations in France, the largest one representing thirty-two localities and claiming 2,000 members in the 1950s (Anderson and Anderson 1962a).

Similarly, the vigor of the Portuguese associative movement is often explained by the intensity of community practices in the villages of origin, bound by a common history, patron saint, and festivities. That is where the organizational talent so usefully reconverted with immigration is born. The social origins of immigrants must also be taken into consideration. In a matter of years, the Russians succeeded in establishing a very diversified voluntary association movement: professional associations based on the trade practiced prior to exile (made up particularly of intellectuals and liberal professionals) or after exile (the general union of taxi drivers, with 900 members in 1930); military associations, which were very numerous and were grouped for the most part in a general union that claimed 10,000 members in 1934; scouting groups; a popular university; and numerous charitable goups or organizations for aid to refugees. It is obvious that one of the key factors of this intense activity was the privileged social background of many elites and the presence of a wealthy aristocrat who provided funding for these movements (consider, for example, the retirement home founded in Sainte-Geneviève-des-Bois by the Princess Mestchersky) (Repiton 1986).

Another element that is relevant to the variations of associative mobilization is the intensity of what people had in common to commemorate. The force of religious conviction and of nationalism for those who knew what it was like to no longer have a state (the Poles) or for those who were victims of a genocide (the Armenians) are powerful factors of associative fervor. On the other hand, as a result of late unification, for Italian immigrants prior to the Second World War the feeling of belonging was more regional. The experience of political turmoil at home did not facilitate consensus but, rather, tended to divide the members of a given immigrant community (for example, fascists versus antifascists).

This last point brings us to a very important aspect of immigrant associative movements in France. Contrary to what might be expected, community organization did not always reinforce group life. Even when the basis for consensus was very broad, as in the case of the Armenians, there were serious internal dissensions within the voluntary associations themselves. Almost always, Armenian, Russian, or Italian associations were split according to their political leanings. While this phenomenon, still visible in the Algerian case in the 1950s, has since been attenuated, its importance should not be underestimated. It proves that "communities" unified under a national lable often exist only on paper. Paradoxically, it is also the sign of a high degree of loyalty to the mother country, given that despite the misfortunes of exile, priority is given to reproducing the polemics of earlier times. The cleavages at the associative level are often a reflection of deeper underlying animosities among people who, seen from outside, appear to be similar. In Valence, Armenians from Constantinople have nothing but contempt for the peasants of Anatolia. In the Polish working-class communities of the northern regions, relations are often strained between "Westphalian" Poles (from Styria or Carinthia) and "Russian" Poles. Similar rivalries oppose northern and southern Italians in Lorraine (for example, see NA F7 13436; Keuroghlian 1977; Drelon 1982; Noiriel 1984). Social origins in some cases explain the internal cleavages in immigrant communities. In Paris under the July Monarchy, German political refugees who were close to Karl Marx did not always get along with the thousands of craftspeople who had come from the same regions. A half-century later, revolutionaries who were hostile to the czar (for example, Lenin) had virtually no ties with the Russian proletariat in Paris (Grandjonc 1974; Green 1985).

The forms of consolidation of feelings of "sameness" described here produced commemorative practices that represent the apotheosis of group life; they have left more traces in all the regions of France than is usually recognized: from letters, books, and photographs held in public archives or by families, to plaques, stelae, and commemorative monuments, not to mention cemeteries, museums, places of worship, and even the graffiti still visible in what is left of the French equivalents to Ellis Island."[15] To index, catalogue, and save from oblivion these "places of memory" is, to be sure, one of the urgent tasks of immigration history; particularly now that the last survivors of the post–First World War waves of immigration are slowly passing away.

In conclusion, I will simply say that the commemorative practices of immigrant communities illustrate the peculiar situation of foreigners who found themselves torn between two worlds. Unlike the collective memory of those who are "at home" in France, celebrations are not, for the immigrant, a manner of cultivating rootedness in a place where the group is assumed to have always lived. They are above all a means of sustaining the collective hope of a return to "somewhere else" or to "the old days"; hence the somewhat artificial character of celebrations in exile, which is accentuated by the fact that they take place in an environment that, despite sustained efforts to re-create a home, is not really theirs.

Inevitably, then, the feeling of being in transition affects even the most intimate aspects of everyday life. A collective research program currently underway in Lorraine of the different ways of being French illustrates the forced degradation of ritual practices. Among the Kabyles of Morocco, one week before a major celebration, the women whitewash the walls of their homes and wash, clean, and embroider clothing. They go to the baths on the final day and spend the night applying henna to the hands of the young girls and to the feet and hands of the women. When the moment comes, they dress in brand new clothes and attend to the entire family. In Lorraine, the celebration is still practiced, but "it is always sad because we think of the family that stayed back home." Moreover, whereas in Morocco everyone partakes in the preparation of traditional pastries, the individualization of schedules characteristic of industrial society tends to disturb this ritual practice. Mothers are left alone to make the pastries.[16] Similarly, when immigrants seek to re-create the environment in which they were born, they run up against insurmountable obstacles. The Kabyle homes of Marseilles are not really Kabyle homes. It is true that their overall disposition, and particularly the interior courtyard that is the private space of women, is reproduced. But the combination of disorientation and economic necessity due to poverty resulted in the haphazard choice of construction materials. Despite all his or her efforts, the immigrant cannot reproduce the architectural opposition between a main column and a central beam that symbolizes, in Kabyle culture, the complementary opposition between the feminine and the masculine (Barou 1987; Bourdieu 1990). The reconstituted home is a home without a soul.

Four

Battered Roots

Let us pledge, she said
And they had pledged.
They would be amnesiac parents
anyway before their children.
Simone Signoret, 1985

Dear comrades of when I was eight years old, what has become of you in our stout years? Do you remember that soccer game, that name that made you laugh, that child weighed down by an awkwardness you so stubbornly attributed to his foreign origins, your geographic innocence in locating his birthplace in Ali Baba's cave? Henri Verneuil, 1985

The integration or assimilation of foreigners is the other major problem that a scholarly approach to immigration must seek to comprehend. As we saw earlier, research on this theme was discredited quite early on in France. As things stand, we are therefore particularly ill equipped to take it up here. In this chapter, I argue that this question should be viewed as an extended process rather than simply as a conjunctural phenomenon and that any study of French identity must take it into consideration. The title of this chapter in the original French edition ("En toi France, *mes racines meurtries*") was borrowed from an eminent second-generation Polish immigrant named Janus Holdert (1977); it is an eloquent illustration of the gap separating immigrants from their children. While the former are deeply affected by the trauma of exile, the second generation (all second generations) must confront the difficult task of reestablishing roots in a society where they were born and raised.[1]

Processes of Stabilization

The End of the "Noria"

Figure 3.1 shows that the three great periods of massive immigration coincided with moments of settling in, of stabilization, which for millions of immigrants meant the end of the "noria," that is, of any illusion of returning home. At each economic crisis, these people discovered that they could no longer hope to live permanently in their country of origin, which was equally affected by the adverse economic situation. To survive, immigrant workers had to struggle to keep the very job that they had always dreamed of leaving. In addition to crises, which we will examine in more detail in the next chapter, fortuitous circumstances also explain settling in. After having been tossed around for years by the absurd jolts of world history, foreigners often aspired to more stable waters. Even in cases in which a migrant's travels had been motivated by an irrepressible desire to "see the world," there came a time when the migrant, getting older, began to desire a change of life. It often took only a stroke of luck, an unexpected encounter or an opportunity after so much misfortune, for "our ancestor" to finally settle on the land.

Take, for example, Spanish prisoners under the First Empire, simple soldiers, who were generally unemployed in their own country and who had found a trade in France. "They do not hide," one prefect wrote, "that they are happier in France than in Spain; and if peace were to be made with that nation, those who have found a profession or learned a trade would presumably become naturalized" (quoted in Aymes 1983, 316). The same process occurred among seasonal migrants of Hérault a century later; after a few years, many of them "bought a piece of land, which they relentlessly cultivated. Through hard work and savings, they expanded their property and settled down definitively" (Azas 1981, 403). Stabilization was often the result of the wife's arrival or of a marriage in the host locality. Many of the Italian workers I interviewed, who had arrived in the 1920s, admitted that they were fed up with the solitary "canteen" lifestyle and that they had asked their wives to join them in France, thereby breaking with the original strategy, which had been to remain "single" for a short period and save as much money as possible. A half-century later, Ashène Zehraoui noted similar attitudes among Algerian immigrants in his study of the Paris region (Noirel 1984; Zehraoui 1971).

A recurring theme in the writings of theoreticians of "paternalism" such as Frédéric Le Play, and a theme that was constantly reiterated by large industrialists prior to the 1930s, was that women were the main "agents of stabilization" of nomadic workers. Indeed, whatever the historical period, it is clear that immigrant workers who married, and therefore planned to have children, changed their habits. They spent less time in cafés because they were no longer single and could scarcely afford it. Tired of canteens, they sought to establish their own homes. The "greatest of solitudes" was attenuated; their daily routine (for example, their meals and laundry) improved. A new logic took form. As Pinçon has noted, with the stabilization of the population, housing became more decent, whether it be in working-class districts or in low-cost public housing where the process of community grouping often culminated.

Whereas foreigners characteristically envisioned their exiled lives as a transitional period, settlement, even when it was forced upon them, often led to a change of values. Paradoxically, the more a person *was* an immigrant, the less he or she, in fact, acted like one. Indeed, day after day newcomers were overcome by "whiffs of Frenchness." This conversion (which for the first generation was never complete) took the form of integration into the working class. The testimony provided by Joseph Bonato, an iron miner in Lorraine, is a good example of how one's daily work could become encrusted as deeply as if it were part of one's skin: "My hands had become all hard, to the point where I no longer dared to wash my face for fear of hurting myself. Whenever I shook a hand, the person would stare bewilderedly at mine after shaking it. . . . My fingers slowly lost their agility at playing the clarinet" (Bonato 1960, 57).

In refugee intellectual circles, a similar evolution is often described in novels: for example, the protagonist would catch himself one day smoking Gauloises cigarettes; he would begin to dream in French and to say "*chez nous*" whenever speaking of France (see, for example, Troyat 1958).

A good measure of the first generation's gradual distancing from the country of origin is provided by the sums of money sent back home to the family. In the 1930s, as today, the crisis led to a clear decline in the sums transferred. Another unmistakable sign was their newfound interest in the quality of the environment in which they lived. In the working-class projects near Mantes, there was a trend toward the "replacement of the small inside courtyard, which made these homes similar to those back in Morocco, by an additional room.... Small gardens were kept, as well as hen houses and a few sheep or goats. A genuine village life developed, just like the one back home" (Bekouchi 1984, 95). This is a good illustration of the process described earlier, in which one's loyalty to one's origins shifted according to the needs and projects accompanying permanent settlement in the host country. Houses seem to have played a key role in the long run. For example, despite its decrepitude, despite the lack of a paved roadway and of public lighting, Moroccan workers refused to leave the Gerville housing project, which they had arranged to their liking. Not one of its inhabitants chose to build in the nearby development, as had a considerable number of residents of the neighboring ZUP of Val-Fourré. The same had been true a half-century earlier in Valence: "Small houses (with gardens) sprang up year after year along the streets adjacent to the rue Arago (rue Wilson and others) built by Armenian workers who, precisely, did not have access to the working-class projects of the Société Lyonnaise des Soieries Artificielles" (Bastien, quoted in Keuroghlian 1977, 51). The same process occurred in the Paris region: In Issy-les-Moulineaux, half of the Armenians owned their homes in 1950; in Nogent-sur-Marne, the old center of the city, which was falling into ruin, was completely renovated by Italians (INED 1947; Couder 1987).

The role of housing in the permanent settlement of immigrants was also very apparent in heavy industry from the beginning of the century through the 1950s. Industrialists managed to stabilize the labor force that they needed by financing most of the working-class housing projects in the northern and eastern parts of France. The owner, or "tenant-for-life" (in exchange for "submission" to the law of the company), could plan for the future, set concrete goals for improving or enlarging his home, and so on. Furthermore, even if the new house did not resemble the one in which the immigrant had been born, it represented a kind of transition between two ways of life; from this point of view, the garden played a key role (in Lorraine, the Italians grew basil).

The sale of garden produce and the rental of one's home was also, for people who lived in a constant state of need, an important source of income. The house was, in this sense, an element in the strategy of "social promotion" that the first generation followed and to which those who lived in large residential blocks could not aspire.

When first-generation immigrants settled permanently in the host country, it often led—particularly when the immigrant was still young—to a changeover in of his or her centers of interest and to a greater investment in what had until then been regarded as a temporary work situation. As Charles Sabel (1982) argued for the United States, a frequent strategy consisted of seeking a more stable position, with the hope of gaining "skilled" worker status. It is difficult to tell, from census figures, how widespread this phenomenon was, for the classifications used are too broad to apprehend a universe in which everything occurred on the scale of the "infinitely small." An agricultural worker might aspire to the status of sharecropper or farmer; sometimes, a worker's meager savings even allowed him to purchase a small plot of land, which was at first insufficient for subsistance but which could then be enlarged. This pattern of social mobility was even more frequent in artisanal trades (such as dressmaking or metalworking), for which the ultimate goal of becoming independent justified the greatest of sacrifices. Mobility from one generation to the next is more difficult to estimate in the area of large industry. For example, in the iron and steel industry of Lorraine, beneath the generic term "unskilled worker" lay a wide range of differences in status. Italian or Polish workers struggled for years to escape from unskilled work in the mines, by seeking jobs in factories that were also unskilled work but that were less dangerous and less physically exhausting (Noiriel 1984). This type of "horizontal mobility," which was usually over short geographic distances and within the same area of employment and which was often accompanied by efforts to obtain decent housing, to tend a garden, or to receive a retirement pension, was often enough to occupy a lifetime's energy; it left people with little time to reflect philosphically on their "roots" and their "identity"!

Despite its flaws,[2] the survey conducted by Alain Girard and Jean Stoetzel (INED 1953) is one of the rare sources available for the concrete evaluation, over a longer period of time than the interval between two censuses, of professional mobility among first-generation immigrants in France. Moreover, it presents the additional advantage of indicating variations in these patterns according to the host environment. The authors selected four geographic zones, which, I think, reflect labor market segmentation as it applied to the foreign labor force in the 1950s (see chapter 6): two for Italians (construction workers in the Paris region and settlers in southwestern agriculture) and two for Poles (northern miners and agricultural workers in Aisne). Although the population sample is relatively small (about a hundred people interviewed according to trade), the questionnaire provides information on the key importance of the host environment in the immigrant's stabilization process. This cannot be stressed enough, given the distortions introduced in this area of study by a "culturalist" approach that defines "identity" independently of the everyday necessities faced by foreign workers. We will return later to the information contained in this survey regarding the relationship to the country of origin. As far as professional aspects are concerned, it is clear that immigrants encountered a more favorable situation in large cities. The Italians of the Paris region, who at the time of the study averaged more than twenty years' residency in France, quite often had managed to improve their status, in comparison not only with their status in their country of origin (where a majority had been landless peasants) but even with the status of the job originally obtained in France. A majority of workers who arrived prior to the Second World War managed to progress within the building trades themselves; as for the artisans and shopkeepers surveyed, most had begun their professional lives as workers. In the case of the latter trades, however, it is clear that (statistically), they had to meet certain conditions in order to improve their chances of becoming independent: Compared with workers in the building trades, a greater proportion came from families already established as artisans and shopkeepers. The length of their stay tended to be greater than among workers, their average age was higher, and their life history was characterized by a high degree of prior geographic and professional instability. While these are undeniably signs of the effort expended, they also reflect the realistic objectives available to hard-working immigrants in their new environment. The Italians of Lot-et-Garonne were confronted with an entirely different set of obstacles. Most of them arrived at an older age than did their counterparts in the Paris region; they had been lured by a recruitment campaign organized by the French government to counteract the "desertification" of the southwest, and they characteristically lived in isolation.

While all had gone through a period of instability and experienced some degree of upward social mobility (access to property or to the status of farmer), they remained confined to a rural environment. As early as the first generation, the generic term "Italian" referred to a number of very different lifestyles. In Seine, the family budget was managed by women for 76% of workers in the building trades, compared with 23% for the settlers of Lot-et-Garonne. Fertility rates varied considerably: 1.8% for Italian workers in the building trades in Paris, and 4% for those of Lot-et-Garonne. Polish immigrants, most of whom arrived during the same period, confronted the environment in very different, and often less grateful, ways. Whether in the mines or among agricultural laborers, upward social mobility remained very limited for the first generation. With respect to miners, although the professional classifications chosen for the survey are not specific enough to evaluate the forms of horizontal mobility described earlier for workers in the iron industry of Lorraine, they nonetheless indicate that a majority of Polish workers remained confined to the same professional universe: underground miners. At the time, they very rarely gained access to positions as supervisors or foremen. Agricultural workers in Aisne displayed the same professional stagnation; more than twenty years after having emigrated, 125 of 129 people surveyed still earned their wages in agriculture.

As was the case for Italians, however, there were important contrasts between these two Polish groups. Among agricultural laborers, fertility was higher (3.4 surviving children per family, compared with 3.2 among miners in the north), the role of women was less confined to housework (78% of those surveyed declared that wives managed the budget, compared with 91% among miners), and there was a greater degree of residential instability (22% had never moved from one commune to another, compared with 50% among miners). These differences were accentuated for children and in cultural practices, underscoring the key importance of the social environment in which immigrants took root.

Mixed Marriages and Naturalizations

Mixed marriages and naturalizations are undeniable signs of the desire to establish oneself in the host country. Figure 4.1 shows the constant rise, from the early nineteenth century onward, of marriages involving foreigners: from a few thousand such weddings annually

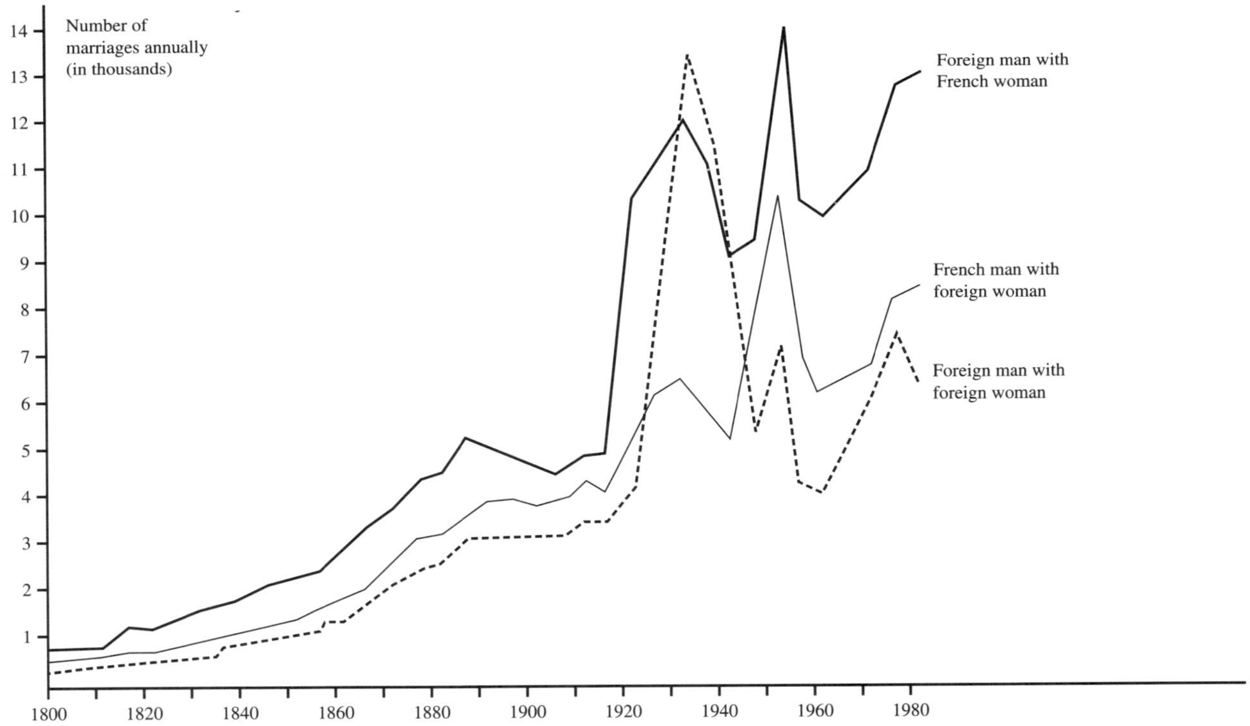

Figure 4.1 Marriages of foreigners celebrated in France, 1800–1980. (Data from Depoid 1942; Muñoz-Perez and Tribalat 1984.)

under the First Empire, the total rose to over 25,000 per year (out of 315,000 marriages) in 1981. These curves reflect a number of recurring trends. Marriages between French women and foreign-born men were always more numerous than those between foreign-born women and French men. This is not surprising, given the high proportion of men in the foreign population. The sudden rise of the curves following the First World War reflects the practice of "compensation," which was typical of the generation of women, born between 1890 and 1910, who were deprived of French spouses because of the war. Another observation is that whereas throughout the nineteenth century, there were always slightly fewer marriages between foreigners than between a French man and a foreign-born woman, this tendency was reversed following the First World War; each massive arrival of immigrants provoked an increase in the number of marriages between foreigners in France. This essay is not the place for a detailed study of the phenomenon; such a study remains to be written.[3] Statistical data show that beyond the close correlation between the rhythm of mixed marriages and migratory impulses, rates vary from one nationality to another. The influence of historic flows of immigration is apparent here; indeed, the highest rates of mixed marriages are always found among those national groups with the longest history of settlement in France. In 1920, 37% of immigrants married to French women were Belgian; in 1930, Italians took the lead and (given the extended duration of Italian immigration) kept it until 1981; in that year, they were surpassed by the Portuguese (Italian men made up 13.8% of the total compared with Portuguese men's 14.1%) and equaled by the Algerians (13%). Individuals who upon their arrival married almost exclusively within their national community, such as the Poles in the 1920s, continue to do so today only in one of every three cases. If for 1975 we examine the percentage of foreigner men married in France to French wives, the figures almost exactly parallel the chronology of migration, increasing as length of stay in France increases: 80% of marriages of Italian men are mixed, 66% in the case of the Spaniards, 27–28% in the case of the Portuguese and Algerians, and 14% in the case of Moroccans. Given the extent of the sociological data that marriage brings into play, these figures are tantamount to a quasi-physical "law" that xenophobic fantasies will never succeed in changing and that reflects nothing more than the work of time.

There is another factor, besides the length of settlement, that plays an important role: socioprofessional status. To illustrate this point, I have prepared two diagrams (Figure 4.2) comparing the rate of mixed marriages for each nationality in 1931 and 1975, and the rate of white-collar workers in the economically active population.[4] In the diagram representing the figures for 1931, a diagonal line links two opposite points represented by Polish (few "white-collar workers" and few mixed marriages) and Swiss immigrants (more than 80% of mixed marriages and 18% of white-collar workers). The other nationalities are lined up along this axis according to the length of their presence in France, with the exception of the Russians, who would have been close to the Poles had the date of arrival in France been the only factor chosen for comparison; in fact, they display an average rate of mixed marriages (approximately 40%) and a high proportion of white-collar workers (more than 12%). It is clear, then, that the social origin of immigrants is a key factor in the choice of a spouse.

The diagram representing the figures for 1975 shows the same diagonal line. The Swiss, however, are no longer represented (nor are the Belgians) because the waves of immigration to which they belonged have died down, and as a result, they were partners in an insignificant number of mixed marriages. As for the Poles, they are among the leaders, slightly behind the Italians, for mixed marriages and slightly ahead of the Italians for the number of management positions. New immigrant groups, however, are found at the bottom left corner of the diagram, with Portuguese and Algerians following each other closely. The lowest point in the diagonal line is represented by the latest arrivals, the Moroccans (only 14% of mixed marriages).

The influence of trade and the region of settlement on each nationality's propensity to marry inside or outside the community of origin is clearly visible in the aforementioned study by Alain Girard and Jean Stoetzel. Agricultural workers, whether Polish or Italian, tend to marry among themselves (93%); the rates are slightly lower for workers: 91% for Polish miners in the north and 73% for Italian construction workers in the Paris region. Once again, one finds a clear contrast within the working class itself between settlement in a large city and settlement in mono-industrial regions. Yet the prize for the most mixed marriages goes to the Italian shopkeepers of Seine, one-fourth of whom are married to French women.

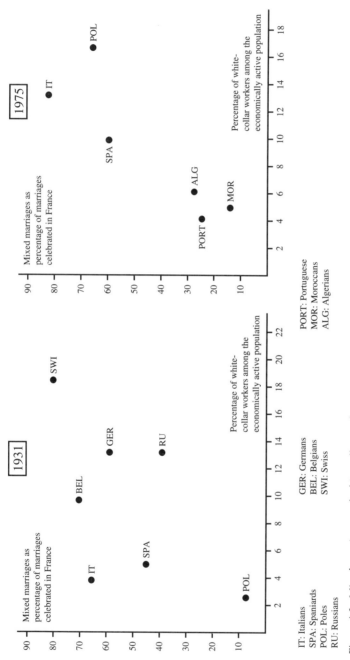

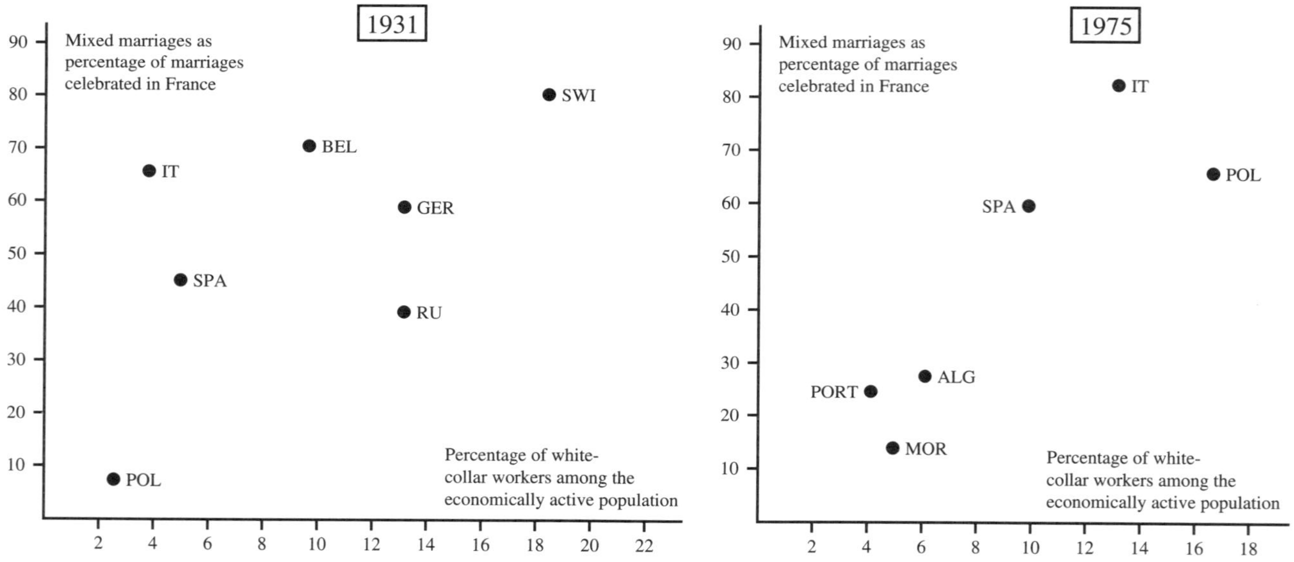

IT: Italians
SPA: Spaniards
POL: Poles
RU: Russians

GER: Germans
BEL: Belgians
SWI: Swiss

PORT: Portuguese
MOR: Moroccans
ALG: Algerians

Figure 4.2. Mixed marriages and white-collar workers

This survey reveals a striking fact with respect to the general figures for mixed marriages examined earlier: the average rates by nationality are substantially lower. Whereas according to the general statistics, in the late 1920s nearly two-thirds of Italian immigrants married women of another nationality (usually French), no other group included in the study, which was conducted twenty years later, came close to that figure, not even the shopkeepers of the Paris region. This phenomenon may be due to the immigrants' location: in the border zones of southeastern France, for example, where a majority of Italians have lived, often for several generations, the rate of mixed marriages is greater because the community is much larger. The same is true of Spaniards in the southwestern provinces.

There is, however, another reason for this. The legal notion of "foreigner" does not distinguish between "generations" as defined by sociologists. Hence marriages between two people of the same origin, one naturalized (and therefore French) and the other legally foreign, may be classified as "mixed marriages." In the iron and steel basin of Lorraine, my research in the civil status archives reveals that many so-called mixed marriages in fact involved two members of the same community, the surnames being an unmistakable sign of a person's origins (Noiriel 1982). Most of the studies on the subject, which rely not only on administrative statistics but also on fieldwork, observe similar patterns. As Pierre-Jean Simon has noted, a close analysis of marriages between "Frenchmen" and "Asians" in the Noyant-sur-Allier repatriation camp shows that they are often between individuals who are of the same ethnic group but with different legal statuses. A monograph on marriages in the mining region of Freyming-Merlebach (Moselle), which compared marriages according to the participants' surname and birthplace, showed that between 1954 and 1964, 10.6% of marriages involved a foreign-born man and a French woman, but nearly one-third of the marriages between foreign-born men and French women were in fact marriages between foreign-born men and French women of foreign origin (see Nicolay 1987).

According to the available case studies, then, the rate of mixed marriages does not necessarily reflect the rapid assimilation by French society of long-standing waves of immigrants.

The analysis of naturalizations and other forms of *francisations* produces similar conclusions. There are, not surprisingly, practically no serious historical studies on the subject. The essential work is still the demographic study by Pierre Depoid (1942), commissioned by the SGF. But it adopts an exclusively statistical perspective and is obsessed with counting the foreign-born in France; an ambiguous agenda, as is evidenced by the way it was used by the Vichy government!

If we examine each procedure of acquisition of French nationality (by decree and by declaration) since the 1889 code, we observe a very large increase in the number of both from the late nineteenth century to the present, with two high points immediately before and after the Second World War (the numbers of acquisitions per quinquennial period went from roughly 60,000 in the late nineteenth century to 220,000 in the early 1970s and to nearly 400,000 in the late 1930s). Figure 4.3 distinguishes between acquisition by decree (naturalizations and reintegrations, that is, resumption of French citizenship) and declarations (which involve, in particular, miners born in France). There were always more acquisitions of French nationality by decree than by declaration (except under Vichy), and the two curves basically trace a similar pattern. At first glance, then, the diagram illustrates the structural effects mentioned earlier, which I have explained by the successive cycles of inflow and stabilization of major waves of immigration. Whether in the 1890s, in the period extending from the late 1930s to the early 1950s (not including the exceptional circumstances of German occupation) or in the current period (which according to the diagram begins in the late 1970s), the curves display the same "peaks," illustrating the decisive role played by the stabilization phase of recent migratory waves.

These statistics must, however, be interpreted with care. Indeed, in the years following each modification of the legislation on nationality, the number of decrees and declarations rose substantially. This illustrates an essential point: These two curves reflect not only the desire to become French but also the evolution of the broader legal and political approach to immigration. A detailed analysis would demonstrate that since the nationality question is above all a question of consent, even secondary or indirect changes in the legislation directly affected the statistical count of acquisitions. For example, the promulgation of the first Nationality Code in 1889, which provoked a radical change in the legislative approach to nationality, was not without statistical consequences. Until the end of the Second Empire, there were never more than a hundred "letters of naturalization" per year; by the late nineteenth century, the number of citizens naturalized by

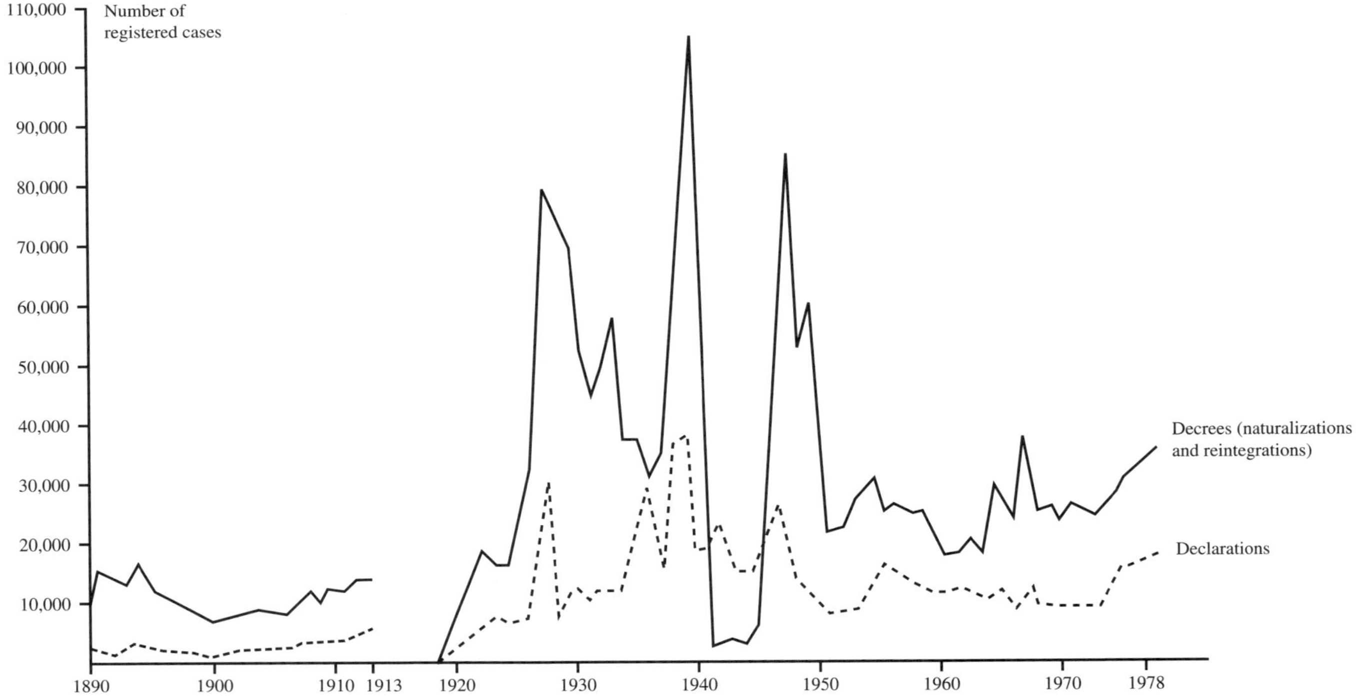

Figure 4.3. Acquisition of French nationality, 1890–1978. (Data from Depoid 1942; Marangé and Lebon 1980.)

decree (not counting children) oscillated between 2,000 and 6,000 per year, and between 15,000 and 30,000 in the interwar period. In other words, the 1889 code represented a shift from a problem concerning only a few members of the elite to a "mass" problem. Another illustration of the statistical effects of legislation is the evolution of the relation between naturalizations and reintegrations in the total number of acquisitions by decree. Prior to the law of 1927, reintegrations represented up to 20% of the total. In most cases, these were French women who had lost their nationality of origin by marrying a foreigner and sought to get it back. The 1977 code allowed women involved in mixed marriages to maintain their French citizenship, which caused a rapid decline of the number of reintegrations.

The history of naturalizations from the perspective of each nationality of immigrants demonstrates that the length of settlement is a key factor in the rate of naturalization within each community. An analysis of the percentage of naturalized citizens within groups of the same origin (which I calculated schematically by adding the number of naturalized citizens to that of foreigners), reveals that those nationalities that settled in France the earliest (Swiss, Belgians, Austrians, Germans) are also those that display the highest rate of naturalization.[5] Italians and Spaniards are at the opposite end of the spectrum. In 1931, the same pattern favored the Belgians and the Germans. The Russians, despite their relatively recent arrival, again stand out as having undergone a high rate of naturalization (more than 13% of the total community of origin). The Poles, on the other hand, seldom acquired French nationality (2.6%). Things had changed by 1975. The "Polish community" in France totaled slightly less than 200,000 people (a figure that includes only Polish nationals and naturalized Polish-born immigrants), but 60% of these people were of French nationality. Conversely, at the same time, a mere 1% of the Algerian community had been naturalized. The main conclusion to be drawn from the 1982 census, with respect to that of 1975, is that the number of naturalizations declined for older immigrant groups (Italians, Poles) and rose substantially for Algerians and Portuguese. Clearly, new migratory waves were beginning the same historical process as that experienced by those before them. All those who speak of the "crisis of citizenship" and the refusal of the newly arrived to integrate would do well to meditate on these figures.

The analysis of professional sectors and jobs in which naturalized citizens were a majority provides a key to understanding this phenomenon. Regardless of the historical moment (turn of the century, interwar years, or contemporary period), to be naturalized meant to improve one's statistical chances of gaining access to living conditions better than those endured by immigrants. The 1901 census indicates that the proportion of naturalized workers in the overall labor force was greatest in metallurgy and mining, as well as in banks and insurance companies. In 1906, a foreigner had slightly more than a 50% chance of being a worker, and a naturalized citizen slightly less. Conversely, 19.5% of naturalized citizens were company executives and 10.8% were white-collar workers, compared with 11.7% and 7.7%, respectively, for foreigners. This same reality is reflected in the 1931 census and confirmed by that of 1975. Whatever the sector in which they worked and whatever their professional category, naturalized citizens found themselves in an intermediary position between foreigners and native French citizens. This does not mean, of course, that the concrete reality experienced by individuals is always reflected in the statistics. Yet a safe hypothesis, in the light of evidence from many studies, is that the choice or refusal of naturalization is related to the types of advantages with which such a decision is associated.

Despite all that has been said and written on the steadfastness of Polish "nationalism," there is no community position common to all Poles on the issue of naturalization. Only 5% of the agricultural workers in Aisne are naturalized, compared with 23% of northern miners. Among Italians, the percentage ranges from 13% (construction workers of the Paris region) to 41% (artisans and independent shopkeepers of Seine). This is another illustration of the primacy of interest over philosophical or "ethnic" considerations. The reaction of Italian shopkeepers was, in fact, identical to that of middle classes everywhere: They fought hard to obtain the small piece of property that was their livelihood. Just as a French shopkeeper placed an armored door on his store to avoid theft, a foreign shopkeeper sought naturalization to protect himself from being expelled from France and having to start all over. The wage-earning Italian bricklayer, on the other hand, had little to lose, given that no one was out to steal his job. Along the same lines, it is easy to understand why people who aspired to jobs "protected" by legislation would want to become French. In Marseilles, the law stipulated that two-thirds of seafaring positions had to be held by Frenchmen; hence the high rate of naturalization among fishermen (Sportiello 1981). Many Italian-born employees of the commune or local county had also been naturalized in order to obtain their jobs. Another factor encouraging this process was the desire to conserve or acquire an advantage reserved for nationals. For example, among those Polish miners who acquired French nationality in the interwar period, some had done so to take advantage of the Loucheur law, which facilitated access to property (Holdert 1977). Other factors—one needs a good knowledge of working-class culture to fully appreciate these—are linked to forms of sociability. Among the Belgians of the north, there was a high rate of naturalization among Belgian "*coulonneux*"[6] in the north because the law required the owners of carrier pigeons to be French (Lentacker 1973). In the Lyons region, it was the 1901 law on associations that forced many Italian workers who managed their mutual aid societies to become French (Bonnet, in Duroselle and Serra 1978). Present-day observers often distinguish between immigrants of the past, who looked forward to acquiring French citizenship, and present-day immigrants, who, it is argued, epitomize the so-called crisis of citizenship. To quote from a novel by Simone Signoret, however, is not enough to prove a point.[7] Although it is true that young immigrants nowadays are not very enthusiastic about fulfilling their military obligation, in reality this is a very old situation among immigrants worldwide. As we saw in chapter 2, this issue was constantly raised, particularly in the border regions, and the resulting legislative changes culminated in the first nationality code in 1889 (Depoid 1942). For later periods as well, despite the new constraints provided by the law, the archives are full of official complaints regarding this matter. It is undeniable that the high proportion of naturalizations among Polish miners in the north is related to the events of the Resistance; the same is true for Italians in Lorraine. Naturalization does not always, however, provide evidence of integration.

As Faidutti-Rudolph has noted, "naturalization is often desired by nonassimilated, recent immigrants who want to be left alone to freely choose their profession and their place of work; it is neglected by older immigrants who are completely assimilated and have forgotten that they are not French" (1964, 371). These remarks are not meant as a substitute for in-depth empirical analysis; their purpose is simply to underscore the complexity of the situation and to warn against drawing conclusions without serious prior study. This is not to say that the issue of naturalization poses itself in the same terms today as it did years ago. It is presumably less urgent, for someone who aspires to a given status or simply wishes to be left alone, to become a French citizen than it was in such a period of disheveled nationalism as the interwar years. Nor does this mean that all nationalities throughout history have approached the question in the same fashion. Indeed, that the new waves of immigration that began after the Second World War came from French colonial possessions created an entirely new situation. For the first time, individuals (Algerians, in particular) whose family lives had been shaken by wars waged by the French were faced with the question of naturalization; as the interview published by Abdelmayek Sayad illustrates, this raised problems of consciousness that were particularly acute.[8]

The Second Generation: In Search of a Definition

Defining the second generation poses a difficult problem for scholars. First of all, it is impossible to rely solely on official nomenclatures. In France, censuses do not establish the same distinction as U.S. censuses do between "native" Americans and Americans with one parent born abroad; this distinction has very often been applied to sociological studies and has created those "mixed" categories for which there is no equivalent in France: "Italian-Americans," "Hispanic-Americans," and so on. In France, the expression "second generation" has only been widely used for the past ten years; it is applied essentially to the children of North African immigrants popularly referred to as "Beurs" (a derivative of "Arab" in back slang), who now have the honor of being listed in the dictionary. In fact, the expression "second generation" came from outside the realm of scholarship and has yet to receive a specific definition, which for some is reason enough to disqualify the concept. I believe, however, that it is very important to propose an objective definition of the second generation, not only to designate individuals but also to illustrate a historical and sociological process that cannot be apprehended by existing analytical frameworks. My goal here is to separate the concept from the context of public controversy and to develop a more reliable definition, one that addresses the problem in all of its aspects. Once again, a historical perspective is required, for which plenty of sources are available. Indeed, it is incorrect to say, as we hear so often, that interest in the second generation began with the emergence of *Beurs.* The term "second generation" appeared in nineteenth-century legal writings on nationality law, for example, with reference to the problem of abandoned children, during the polemic surrounding the drafting of a new Civil Code. In all periods characterized by the stabilization of migratory waves, an intellectual current that I call "the lobby of origins" has consistently raised the issue. More important, however, French cultural heritage is replete with literary works that, in one form or another, discuss the issue of the "identity of youths of foreign origin" that is so hackneyed today. It is paradoxical, to say the least, that so many sociologists are bent on questioning youths (who couldn't care less) about their "identity" while ignoring the extraordinarily sensitive accounts of the immigrant experience that are available in French literature.

The "First Phase of Socialization": A Decisive Experience

On a more general level, the term "second generation" designates individuals who have been exposed to a sociological process, to contradictory forms of socialization, at the crucial stage of fundamental acquisitions: childhood. Of course, it is an issue that does not apply strictly to immigration. Because our societies are constructed on a national basis, however, immigration lends itself more specifically to the problem. On the one hand, a child is initially socialized within the culture of origin, by the family and often by the group; in other words, by first-generation immigrants who still live in the relative isolation of the "community." On the other hand, the same child is exposed to the dominant norms of the host country by other children of the same age (the age of cruelty in which nothing is hidden) and by representatives of various institutions—schools in particular, but also welfare bureaus, pediatric services, and so on. Their main difference from the first generation is therefore that the confrontation between the society of origin and the host society occurs at a key moment of decisive apprenticeships. The legal definition that distinguishes between French and foreign is therefore inadequate. Among these youths, many are French (or will be when they reach adulthood) because they were born in France; others are foreign because they arrived in the country when they were very young, but they have nevertheless received French primary schooling. The fundamental problem here is to understand how children interiorize the attitudes of adults and assimilate their norms (see, in particular, Cicourel 1974), and how this initial mismatch affects their personality later on. It is difficult to find "evidence" of this (in the sense that positivist historians give to the term) because the question is virtually incomprehensible from the point of view of the host society and can only be expressed from within the immigrant group. This is one of the main explanations for the discrepancy, until the 1960s, between the well-meaning literature (administrative reports and surveys) in which the "assimilation" of children was always presented as successful and unproblematic—a mythology that is still sometimes peddled by historians today—and the oral and written testimony of those who experienced the painful process of "assimilation" first-hand.

Based on these sources, we may identify several major themes that broadly exemplify the second-generation experience. It is primarily through his or her group of origin that an immigrant child becomes familiar with the outside world. First, there is the mother tongue and all the experiences associated with its acquisition—the language learned on Grandma's knees, as Lucien Febvre put it; then there is the universe of odors and tastes, transmitted in particular through cooking. Given that the father was often away at work, the role of women here is key. Mohamed Bekouchi noted that at home, "the mother was the keeper of tradition. It was she who transmitted to others, within her social space, customs and ways of life" (Bekouchi 1984, 127).[9] The interior decoration of homes harked back to the mother country: "a sitting-room and small round tables to eat all together from the same dish, with neither fork nor knife but only bread." Table manners, norms related to the occupation of space, to hygiene, and to body techniques, which are powerful sources of identification and mimicry, were transmitted subconsciously. Fathers also had ways of transmitting a part of themselves to their offspring. The construction or arrangement of the home reflected settings and modes of organizing space that were carried over from the mother country. For the children of immigrants, this transposed "home" became the house of their birth, with all its symbolic consequences. Gaston Bachelard wrote: "Beyond memories, however, the house where we were born is physically inscribed in each of us. It is a group of organic customs. Twenty years later, despite all the anonymous staircases, we would renew the reflexes learned with the first staircase; we would avoid stumbling on that slightly awkward step" (Bachelard 1964). In addition to this space that each second-generation immigrant carries with him or her for life, there is the cult of the country of origin, which the father might purposely keep alive. The voluntary activities of immigrants are very often directed at children. In Lorraine during the 1950s, Ukrainian schools were explicitly presented as ways of making sure that young people did not forget their roots. Italian fascist associations in the interwar period sent their children to Italy to attend summer camps. The Poles made their children participate in folkloric celebrations; former officers or soldiers of the Czarist army dragged their offspring to commemorative meetings (Noiriel 1984; Ponty 1985; Troyat 1958). Withdrawal into the family, widespread among settled immigrants, accentuated this phenomenon. Parents repeated the "novel of their origins"—life before leaving, the experience of departure and voyage—to their children, over and over again.

Yet, in a way that was inextricably intertwined with this process, the second generation was simultaneously subjected to the norms of the host country. Parents themselves contributed to this. In these times of fashionable nostalgia, it is often forgotten that many immigrants wished to break completely with their past. Even today, expressing their profound rejection of a country in which they experienced only misery, many Italians in Lorraine will say: "I wouldn't trade Italy for a glass of water." Those who were confronted by the trauma of war or persecution often seek only one thing: to *forget*. There were families in which parents never mentioned their previous lives in front of their children, which exacerbated the latter's desire to know more about their past. In any case, a person's "novel of origins" is always full of contradictions. Its function is both to magnify what one was before and to legitimate an act of emigration that one is no longer perfectly certain was well-founded. The immigrants' desire to establish roots in the host country, which leads them to take on new professional challenges, explains their widespread tendency to present their migratory narrative in heroic terms. Inventing a "novel of origins" is an essential precondition for starting over, and it legitimizes the foundation of a new lineage.

It is also a way for immigrants to rehabilitate themselves in the eyes of their children, who perceive that the norms of the host society constantly disparage their family.

The ambiguity of the transmission of parental norms is evident when parents repeatedly insist that their children do well in school;

when they repeat over and over again that they have made sacrifices to enable their children to succeed; when they speak French at home (albeit poorly); or when they "preach" that their son or daughter must submit to the host country because "this isn't our country."[10] This attitude of self-denigration is perceived, more or less confusedly, by the first generation as the only way to guarantee the integration of their children into the new society; it is further accentuated by the role of "representative" that the child takes on in the family's dealings with official institutions (for administrative letters, social security, and so on), on the grounds that he or she speaks better French or is more "presentable." But it is in school that immigrant children truly discover the inferiority of their situation. Often, what they perceive as discrimination because of their origins is in fact due to their economic situation. Most of the available testimonies reflect a feeling of inferiority that combines elements of exclusion from the "national group," and of exclusion because of social status (that is, poverty).

What is at work here is a kind of symbolic "expropriation" of the feeling of "home." Given that most people identify the country in which they live as their "home," hence relating the abstract concept of "nation" to their familiar environment, the xenophobia picked up by children from parental conversations ("you are eating our bread"; "go back to where you came from") takes on dramatic proportions. Whereas first-generation immigrants could always look forward to a possible return "home," for the second generation there is a contradiction in terms: "home" is France. Furthermore, economic stigmatization does not only affect low-income immigrants. What characterizes immigrants of all social classes is that they often find themselves in a position of inferiority with respect to others who supposedly enjoy the same social status. Children of working-class immigrants, the wretched among the poor, feel bad about walking barefoot or wearing patched clothing; whereas the "poor" in higher-income brackets resent not being able to display signs of their social success. In his autobiography, Henry Troyat spoke of the humiliation he felt at the Lycée Pasteur in Neuilly-sur-Seine; he was ashamed of his shoes, which were "colorwashed with Indian ink," but also of differences in customs and of the widespread, automatic acceptance of the superiority of French norms. Invited to lunch by a classmate, he observed: "The first surprise was the cantaloupe as the first course. At home, the cantaloupe was considered a fruit and served as dessert. On the other hand, the cheese that we were accustomed to serving as an hors-d'oeuvre seemed destined for the end of the meal." To this culinary disorientation, Troyat adds the recollection of the disconcerted look on his hostess's face when he kissed her hand; such scenes give some idea of the problems that for years haunted the consciousness of middle-class, second-generation immigrants (Troyat 1987).

Yet the main difficulties were encountered in the schools themselves. Children often discovered the inferiority associated with their origin when they entered the school system. In one of his novels, Benigno Cacérès tells the story of a Spanish child in the region of Toulouse prior to 1939, whom his friends called a foreigner and who personally requested a birth certificate from the authorities to prove he was French: "How, then, could he be a foreigner? Emmanuel looked at himself in the mirror in search of traits that might make him different from us. He found nothing. When he went to bed at night, he carefully observed the color of his skin. There was nothing peculiar about it." The child finally looked to the schoolteacher for an answer: "Why am I a foreigner?" (Cacérès 1970, 74). A half-century later, Azouz Begag, who was raised in a shantytown near Lyons, tells a similar story: "It was in primary school that I learned the rules of the game. I played on both counts. During classes I could wear the blouse of a French kid, then I became a *gône*[11] again like everyone else" (Begag 1986). The role of the school appears at two different levels. On the one hand, it is a place of conflict among immigrant children and their French counterparts, who play an important role regardless of their number. In her memoirs, actress Madeleine Robinson recalled that her schoolmates mocked her patched clothes and her original name, Svoboda, which betrayed her Czech lineage (Robinson 1978). In an altogether different context, Inès Cagnati, a local novelist, told the newspaper *Sud-Ouest* the story of the suffering endured by an Italian immigrant girl in a closed French rural environment: "Their universe was hostile, aggressive; they didn't want us there. I understood neither its language nor its rules; nor did I know what I had to do, not even to earn their tolerance, but at least to deserve their forgiveness for being myself, for being different."[12]

Outside the walls of the school, the hostility of French children sometimes met collective resistance by children of an "ethnic" or national group. Novelist and critic Cavanna, for example, tells of the "*ritals*" (Italians) forbidding their brethren to socialize with French kids, and more recently, Azouz Begag was considered a "traitor to the Arabs" because of his successful performance in school.

Things worked differently within the sacred confines of the school, given the symbolic power of the institution and of its representatives. There are a wide variety of examples, which differ according to the period, the nature of immigration, and the local context. For example, women of foreign origin who went through school in the interwar period often use extremely violent terms to describe their experience. In a previous book, drawing from the study of a corpus of letters, I gave several examples of this attitude for Italian women in Lorraine.[13] It is also visible in the articles published by the newspaper *Sud-Ouest* in which, forty years later, Inès Cagnati still proclaimed her hostility toward a teacher whose hatred, she wrote, "rained on Italians with the tenaciousness, the violence, and the certainty of pesticides." Film director Henri Verneuil's 1985 autobiography also contradicts the myth of the "smooth" assimilation of prewar immigrants: He described the cruelty of French schoolchildren, who always kept him at a distance, denying him integration by constantly drawing atttention to his "difference."

It is clear that during the 1930s the rampant xenophobia studied earlier and the proximity of the Second World War (Italians were the enemy) led to a degree of government inflexibility that is no longer found today. Yet other factors came into play, which illustrate the subjective character of memory (despite the genuine feelings described). We may hypothesize that in immigrant groups living in isolation, children were relatively protected by the community in the first years of their life; hence the violence of the shock when it came time to go to school, which was not felt quite as strongly, for example, by Italian children whose fathers worked in the building trades of the Paris region. Moreover, women are by far the most outspoken about the experience in their accounts, perhaps because, living at the center of domestic reproduction, they lived in even greater isolation from French society than did men (especially before 1939, when there were still few wage-earning women). Another important point is that teachers did not mean to cause feelings of exclusion among their pupils. In primary school, for instance, it was normal practice to take attendance each morning, to name those who were present and identify those who were not. Yet for immigrant children this ritual could be a source of anxiety, for if the teacher failed to pronounce their names correctly, their classmates would burst into laughter. In this type of situation, as Erving Goffman argued in his sociological analysis of the stigma, anything the teacher might do to "defend" such pupils would only aggravate their exclusion from the group. Georges Medzadourian, who came from a middle-class Armenian family and is now a doctor, never forgot his Parisian school experience between the wars: "Made fun of and misunderstood by their comrades, with names that were difficult to pronounce and unable to express themselves, they (young Armenians) often came home in tears and refused to go to school the next day." Whenever immigrant children found themselves in overwhelmingly French classes, on the day of the history or geography lesson on their country, their classmates would ignore the teacher's efforts and turn to face them, making them the "representatives" or "defenders" of a country that they knew only through the parents' descriptions (see, for example, Troyat 1958).

In primary school, at least until the 1960s, teachers frequently played a "moral" and "hygienist" role; those who have not experienced it find the symbolic damage of this role difficult to fully comprehend. Rules of hygiene (for fingernails, ears, hair, stained clothing, and so on) and "French-style" norms of politeness expose the full range of an immigrant child's acquired identity, which is heavily influenced by parents (and the mother in particular), to the destructive irony of the French children and teacher.

The end result is the self-hatred so often described in the testimonies and novels produced by immigrants, both in France and the United States. This desperate willingness to adapt to the dominant norms of the host country could be expressed in various ways. A group of young Portuguese immigrants admitted in an interview that they were ashamed to reveal their nationality to their teachers; North African youths expressed a desire to become French to escape this stigmatization.[14]

Numerous examples can also be drawn from the realm of literature. Humiliated by her comrades, Eve Dessarre admitted: "I would have given anything to not be distinguished from these French girls my age" (Dessarre 1976, 156). In his novel *Les Eaux mêlées,* Roger Ikor wrote of his character Simon, a Russian Jew who emigrated prior to the First World War: "He ranked even Yiddish, which was as much his native tongue as was French, among the most shameful dialects" (Ikor 1963, 478). Elsa Triolet, in a novel that (not coincidentally) was published around the same time, evoked a similar situation with her character Sacha, the son of a Russian émigré who ends up hating his father because of his accent and his rolling pronunciation of the letter *r* (Triolet 1955, 64). This example describes another expression of self-hatred, also mentioned in a novel by Simone Signoret: "There was no one left around who could recall the sickly ugliness of her poor Polish mother, an illiterate and fearful woman whom, as a child, she dreaded meeting at the door of the primary school located on Saint-Ferdinand street" (Signoret 1985, 83).

Those who would not or could not accept this law of the jungle often adopted a provocative attitude, overtly expressing what they were criticized for. This explains many of the cases of "poor discipline in school." They might be likened to Madeleine Robinson's attitude as a young schoolgirl, when she took pride in hearing her teacher mispronounce her original name, Svoboda (meaning "liberty") (Robinson 1978).

These examples clearly demonstrate the importance of the problem in the formation of the child's personality. Both the stigma and the defense mechanism against it are fixed in the person's identity and continue to influence his or her everyday interactions with other people. In the French and U.S. literature that deals with this issue, the second-generation immigrant is often described as being always alert, quick to avoid or to ward off situations that are reminiscent of initial aggressions. Childhood is, indeed, a crucial time in the acquisition of techniques for avoiding and retaliating against whatever might cause an already threatened identity to be questioned. Another example of this is the testimony provided by Henri Verneuil on the split personality common among children without a country, and on strategies of symbolic flight from the hostility of the world, such as causing "one's solid state to melt down . . . so as to recompose it later on" (Verneuil 1985, 137).

Questions of "Authenticity"

Not only testimonies, which are often biased, but also a number of academic studies indicate that the question of "origins" continues to be a problem when an individual belonging to a stigmatized second generation reaches adulthood. The most common attitude is denial. Albert Demangeon and Georges Mauco concluded that in the 1930s, most foreign children living in the rural world wanted their origins forgotten. Similarly, Ludovic Naudeau wrote of those whom he referred to as the "Italo-Français" of Var that they hid their previous nationality (Mauco and Demangeon 1939; Naudeau 1931). Given the long-standing tradition of immigration in southern France, such an attitude was widespread well before the outbreak of the First World War. G.-B. Arnaudo noted that in Marseilles, the first victims of xenophobia during the events of 1881 were the Italian workers who had their names changed to make them sound more French: "Cervino" and "Bottaglia" became "Cervin" and "Bouteille." He noted, furthermore, that French citizens of Italian origin were the most virulent advocates of witchhunts aimed at "macaronis" (Arnaudo 1881). This supports Faidutti-Rudolph's statement that "sometimes all that is left in the second generation are the complexes that make these newly enfranchised Frenchmen virulent nationalists, precisely because they are conscious of having chosen their fatherland; they may even turn Italo-phobic" (1964, 372). Serge Bonnet (1972) also observed this type of behavior among former Italians who had been assimilated with respect to their compatriots in the Mezzorgiorno. As Colette Petonnet noted in an entirely different context: "Any question regarding the foreign sound of a patronymic is avoided . . . : 'We don't know, it goes back a long way' " (Petonnet 1985, 27).

In *Anti-Semite and Jew,* Jean-Paul Sartre (1948) illustrated the process of stigmatization by describing the two main forms of defense against anti-Semitism available to Jews. The first is to take the part of an "authentic" Jew, that is, one who is loyal to the Jewish tradition; the second, which according to Sartre is much more widespread in France, is to be the "inauthentic" Jew, who betrays (abjures) his people in order to become better integrated into the dominant society. By broadening these analyses to all forms of stigmatization, Erving Goffman (1961) showed that the process is characteristic of society in general, that it spares no one and is inherent in every individual's relation to legitimate norms. Applying Goffman's distinction between "discredited" individuals (those unable to hide their handicap) and "discreditable" individuals (in whom the stigma is not readily visible), we might say that members of the second generation belong to the latter category, for in general they have the possibility of not claiming, or even of hiding, their heritage; whereas first-generation immigrants never manage to erase all signs of their initial experience.

A good way to measure this is by looking at the language spoken. A bit like those illiterate people described by Goffman who wear big glasses to look more knowledgeable, the children of immigrants are often eager to speak a flawless French (or one they consider flawless). William Labov (1972), who studied the linguistic behavior of second-generation Italians in New York, emphasized the hypercorrectness that their use of the language betrayed. I observed (without fully analyzing them) similar linguistic features in Lorraine, where a second-generation Italian could often be identified simply by his or her very pronounced local accent.[15] Because of this denial of origins, the adult second-generation immigrant often wants to leave the childhood ghetto. In a famous book, Louis Wirth (1928) described this process in Chicago. Most often it is the children who discover that their parents live in a ghetto, because they more frequently come into contact with the outside world. Their parents' world suddenly seems cramped, dated; hence their realization that their condition is "distinct" from that of their original social environment, and this collectively translates into a change in where they live.

It is in some ways difficult to compare this to the situation in France, if only because of the different size of cities. Nevertheless, the process of "leaving the ghetto" is quite real. Specific studies are lacking, but an in-depth ecological analysis would show that while new migrants tend to live in the same area upon their arrival, the second generation undergoes a process of both socioprofessional and spatial mobility. In Marseilles, the first generation often lived in the neighborhood of the Porte d'Aix, but the Italian example illustrates a process of dispersal throughout the city from the second generation onward. In Paris as well, Central European Jewish immigrants most often arrived in Belleville, but their children migrated toward the suburban areas or neighborhoods of the capital. In the rural world, Bernard Kayser observed that the children of the Italian agricultural workers massively employed in the countryside of Provence tended to move to the Riviera and to change their occupation (Carreno et al. 1972; Roland 1962; Kayser 1960).

This physical upheaval generally brought about a radical change in lifestyles. In Mantes, white-collar workers of North African origin, who tend to marry French women, have become completely adapted to the French way of life and live a considerable distance away from concentrations of working-class North African immigrants (Bekouchi 1984). In a different context, Yannick Stopyra, who, like his father, is an international soccer player and whose grandfather was a Polish immigrant, explained that his father, who belonged to the second generation, was unwilling to transmit the slightest bit of Polish culture to his own son (the Breton name is revealing). According to him, too many Poles who lived in ghettos of the northern mining towns had subsequently shown difficulties in adapting.[16]

But there were many other ways of escaping the ghetto: for example, naturalization, intermarriage, and changing one's surname. According to Erving Goffman (1961), any change of name, whatever its motive, introduces a breach between individuals and their former world. Indeed, the written testimonies we possess often suggest a dilemma in this respect. The authors make it a point to emphasize that the procedure was forced upon them. For example, the famed novelist Henry Troyat, whose father had already been forced to change his name in order to flee Russia, followed the advice of his publisher; the latter thought it necessary to avoid having "the novel . . . published under a foreign-sounding name." The choice is not an easy one, and it unavoidably becomes a matter of conscience. "I felt that if I published my novel under another name, I would be renouncing authorship. The book would separate itself from me and become the work of a total stranger." In the end, however, the author took his new identity (which was also that of a new life) upon himself and had the change of surname legally confirmed (Troyat 1987, 168). In Madeleine Robinson's case, it was the producer of her first role who asked her to give up her name. She did—was it possible to miss the chance of a lifetime?—but not without regret, for that name "belonged to my father, my Slavic Don Quixote whom I loved dearly" (Robinson 1978, 63). To change one's name is also to symbolically renounce recognition as part of the group. Indeed, the patronymic is the elementary sign of identity that those who are subjected to xenophobia instinctively recognize as a sign of unity. As Henri Verneuil (Achod Malakian) said of an Armenian classmate: "The last syllable I was so familiar with clearly indicated that he wore the marks of my tribe: we were of the same origin" (Verneuil 1985, 239). While this is an issue paticularly for artists, other groups are also confronted with it. Today, for example, in respectable hair salons, owners often require their employees of North African origin to change their names so as not to offend customers.

Other, equally pressing, reasons sometimes lead individuals to make this choice. Among the most conclusive reasons is undoubtedly the attitude of many German Jews following the Second World War. For example, a law school graduate naturalized after the war, who was haunted by this issue of the patronymic for most of his life, said: "One of the most obvious ways to make oneself noticed is by the name, and I didn't want my children to have the same problems as me. I requested and obtained my name change in 1949." But, several years later, new regulations on identification cards forced him to carry the given name that appeared on his birth certificate, Rudolph. He therefore had to undergo new administrative procedures to change his given name as well (quoted in Badia 1982, 131). This testimony recalls a vast debate that affected émigré communities following the war over whether antifascists who had taken on war names, which were usually quite French, should preserve them or not. A majority argued at the time that it was best for them not to make themselves noticed; "why should the victim be made more vulnerable?" (that is to anti-Semitism). According to Father Glasberg, "a young boy, German or Polish refugee, who wandered around France under the name of Bousquet or Duplesis not only sought to appear French, but felt French for having so long equated his personal cause with that of his country" (Glasberg 1946, 239).

While the dilemma typical of the second generation was exemplified by a conflictual relationship to one's parents, which explains the frequency of "teenage crises" in immigrant communities, it often takes on a more collective turn. To remain in the field of literature that we have abundantly solicited here, we might mention the case of Emile Zola. The son of an Italian émigré, he "rediscovered" his family when his fame was already established, as a result of a letter sent by a cousin after she had read *L'Assomoir.* In the letter, she reminded him of his origins and asked him to renew relations with his family, but Zola did not reply. In his correspondence, he spoke of "distant" Italian relatives. His family, who had remained in Italy, was deeply shocked by this indifference. In the context of the Dreyfus affair, the French writer's Italian origins were questioned both by Drumont and by Barrès. The smear campaign that soiled the memory of his father forced him to carry out research to reestablish the truth and led him to travel to Italy. Welcomed as a symbol of Franco-Italian friendship by his Italian acquaintances, he received many letters of encouragement from Italy during his imprisonment. Following his death, an Italian writer even attempted to attribute his "literary genius" to his "Italian roots." In the preface of the book in which all of this Italian correspondence is published, the author reflected on the reasons for Zola's reservations about his family and about a country that had shown him so much sympathy (Ternois 1967). According to the logic discussed earlier, it might be said that his "Italian friends" put Zola in an embarrassing position by lending credence to the arguments of those who questioned his Frenchness in order to discredit him. It was therefore difficult for him to publicly claim his Italian origins (particularly in a literary world where the issue of "heredity" was so fundamental). Roger Ikor, in the novel quoted earlier, showed that the son who had "denied" his language and was ashamed of his Jewish family was nonetheless often confronted with the problem of loyalty to his origins. "Once in a while, a dart stung him in the skin": It was verbal anti-Semitism, in its most benign form, that reminded him so often of his origins and that prevented him from being "just like everyone else"; hence his carefully calculated replies, which allowed him to assume the distance from his parents without seeming like a coward when faced with insults, even though, as Henri Verneuil admitted, this often implied some degree of "treason" (Verneuil 1985, 102).

The specific problems of socialization encountered by the children of immigrants are evoked to explain two opposite forms of social trajectories: delinquency and spectacular social promotion. In both cases, proof is rather difficult to establish. In France, statistics of criminality have never distinguished between first- and second-generation immigrants as defined earlier. While recent data seem to indicate that there are many youths of foreign origin among delinquents, socioprofessional background is still a key categorization (Chamboredon 1971). Further research is necessary to determine the extent to which the Chicago school's approach to this question is pertinent for present-day France. René Gallissot (1985) has argued that in the interwar period, community control was efficient enough to prevent young immigrants from going astray. As Henri Verneuil noted with respect to Armenians (but this goes for other nationalities as well): "They reserved their faults, their weaknesses, their divisions, their unruliness for internal use.... For more than a half-century, no examining magistrate subjected any of them to the Penal Code" (Verneuil 1985, 102). (This, according to records deposited in the National Archives, is only partially true.)

French scholars were even less prepared for the study of social mobility among the children of immigrants. INSEE statistics being what they are, no overall survey of this issue is available for any period. Psychologists tell us that being "divided" between two worlds is a factor that enriches the personality, which might explain the frequent success of second-generation immigrants in artistic circles (but this might also be a result of their "thirst for social revenge"). The fact that there are actors, singers, or writers of foreign origin who are well-known celebrities, however, does not make a statistic. In other professional circles, nothing can be concluded on the basis of a few examples. Stephen Steinberg (1981) has argued that in the United States, "explanations" of the social rise of second- or third-generation Jews in terms of "ethnic or cultural specificities" were more based on mythology than on scientific criteria. The few available studies on the topic (Roland 1962; Bensimon and Della Pergola 1984) suggest that the same may be true for France. Once again, however, given the gaps in the research, we have only scattered bits of information drawn from monographs. The second generation, whether it be of Italians in Strasbourg, Armenians in Valence, Central European Jews in Belleville, or Poles in the coal mining regions of Moselle, seems to be well-rooted in the working-class (see Ricklin 1965; Roland 1962; Garagnon 1955; Nicolay 1967).

The survey carried out by Alain Girard and Jean Stoetzel provides us with additional pieces of information. We have seen that from the first generation onward, stabilization occurs in a specific environment that molds individuals, to the point where the criterion of nationality loses its pertinence with time. This phenomenon is simply accelerated for the second generation. The advantages offered by the big city for upward social mobility are accentuated for the children of immigrants; while 35% of the sons of construction workers of Italian origin are themselves workers, 23% are employees and 15% are pursuing an education. The future of Italian shopkeepers' children is even brighter (16% become workers and 14% become employees, but 31% become independent artisans or shopkeepers and 14% pursue an education). The contrast with Italians from Lot-et-Garonne is striking: 75% of their children grow up to be agricultural workers like their parents, and none become employees! Among the children of Poles, there are substantial differences that correlate with the environment of settlement: Among the sons of miners, 25% go on to become miners as well, 21% are workers, and 4% are employees. In contrast, the children of agricultural workers in Aisne mostly become either agricultural workers themselves (40%) or workers (24%); only 2% become employees (INED 1953). What these figures indicate is not professional immobility, as it might seem at first glance, but, rather, the changes occurring within the working class itself.

A statistical study based on civil status records and censuses, combined with numerous oral surveys, shows that in the iron and steel–producing area of Lorraine, whereas first-generation immigrants remained overwhelmingly confined to unskilled jobs, very often second-generation immigrants became skilled workers, either by learning on the job (for workers such as blast-furnace operators or smelters) or by acquiring a Certificat d'Aptitude Professionnelle at the apprenticeship center and obtaining maintenance positions (as, for example, mechanics or adjustors). The numerous surveys conducted by Faidutti-Rudolph in her dissertation reveal that a similar process was at work among the Italians of southeastern France. In Chedde (Val d'Arve), for example, 42% of first-generation immigrants worked in the chemical industry, 26% in the building trades, and 6.5% in the mechanical and metal-working industries. For Italians born in France (who were therefore members of the second generation), only 25% worked in the chemical industry, 22% in the building trades, and 20% in the more prestigious metallurgical and mechanical industries. In Savoy, in the community of Villard-Bonnot, the chemical industry employed 20% of those born in Italy but not naturalized French, 16% of those who were naturalized French, and only 3.5% of Italians born in France. Conversely, among employees, only 4.5% were non-naturalized Italian-born, 3.5% were naturalized, and 14% were Italians born in France; hence the obvious conclusion: "The length of settlement in France affects professional classifications more than does the geographic origin" (Faidutt-Rudolph 1964, 241; Noiriel 1982).

Clearly, the concept "second generation" has a double significance: it refers not only to national origins but also to the profession. This is not a characteristic unique to French society; Herbert Gans (1982) described the same process among Italian workers of Boston's

West End.[17] If we compare the second generation that became active in the 1930s or immediately following the war with the second generation that is currently searching for a place in the labor market, it appears that it is the means of professional integration and the forms of social mobility that should be closely examined; what is at issue is not just jobs but integration into the overall scheme of working-class values and ways of life.

We are beginning to gain a better understanding of the role played by second-generation immigrants, for reasons linked both to their class position and to their national origin, in working-class political mobilization. In most cases—and this is understandable in light of what we said earlier about the way that the children of immigrants were socialized—the second generation tended to support what appeared to be the quest for "radical" political organization, often advocating violence. In the north, it is clear now what the election of Jules Guesde and the advances made by the Parti Ouvrier Français (POF) owed to the Belgian second generation; the socialist leader's detractors even sought to discredit him by calling him the "deputy of the Belgians" (Reardon 1977; Lentacker 1973). In the 1920s, the great collective mobilizations that shook such textile centers as "Halluin-la-Rouge" proved that the French Communist Party had filled in for the POF. Its social base and mobilizing power owe as much to the working-class condition as to the Flemish origins of the workers (Hastings 1986). Serge Bonnet has shown the close correlation in Lorraine between the increase in the Communist vote in the mining and steel-producing communities and the growing number of voters with Italian surnames (S. Bonnet et al. 1962). An in-depth study that would do more than simply juxtapose individual cases is necessary here as well. Yet everything seems to indicate that even a historical phenomenon as important as the Resistance needs to be reread in light of immigration history. In Lorraine, "shedding one's blood for France" was the best symbolic means of erasing the stigma of origins and of publicly asserting the collective integration of the group into the contested French community.

"To Recover One's Roots?"

These data, however fragmentary, show that integration into French society occurs through establishment in specific geographic and professional environments, most often within the working class, to the point where the legitimacy of the definition of "second generation" seems to lie in the dual significance of the phrase: second generation by national origin and second generation of workers. The question that immediately comes to mind is, of course, to what extent these children of immigrants were "assimilated" by French society. After having provoked much discussion, any question of this sort has become taboo among French scholars, while at the same time nourishing political polemics.

To approach it calmly, we must move beyond the false paradigm within which the entire discussion is framed ("to live with our differences" versus reinforcing the Jacobin mold). Once again, we must be careful to regard it not as a "North African youth problem" but, rather, as one that has confronted French society in general for the past century. That is why I have chosen to focus on the study of foreigners who arrived in the 1920s and their descendants, for whom a study of the processs over three generations is feasible; it is too soon to subject the lives of those who arrived in the 1960s to full-fledged empirical analysis, which is perhaps why so many fantasies still project themselves onto their future.

The first question that needs an answer is whether expressions of the culture of origin survive the experience of settlement in a new country. A statistical analysis that Laurence Bertoïa and I conducted, based on 1,000 naturalization files in Meurthe-et-Moselle (from 1889 to 1939), distinguished between first- and second-generation immigrants according to their age upon arriving in France (those who arrived prior to adulthood were regarded as belonging to the second generation). We observed that 40% of the applications for naturalization were submitted by individuals who had arrived in France before the age of twenty-one (not counting those who were naturalized at the same time as their parents). This is one illustration of the stronger desire to assimilate found among second-generation immigrants. We saw earlier that a number of mixed marriages occurred as early as the first generation, and available statistical studies show a steady increase with the following generations. To take the example of communities traditionally viewed as deeply committed to their native traditions, such as the Armenians (whose "assimilation" many in the 1930s believed would take decades), Geneviève Bardakjian has shown that between 1925 and 1929 Décines (an important center of Armenian immigration in the southeast of France) had a 1.4% rate of mixed marriages;

between 1930 and 1939, it rose to 6.4%; from 1960 to 1969 it reached 51.9%; and in 1970–71, 73.2% (Bardakjian 1973). The rapid evolution is striking. A survey conducted by Doris Bensimon among the Jewish population of the Paris region confirmed this trend: One of eight marriages was mixed in 1935; this had increased to one of three in the late 1950s and to every other marriage in the early 1980s. Had the study established a clear distinction between generations in the sense we understand it here, the rate of mixed marriages would undoubtedly have been even higher (Bensimon and Della Pergola 1984). A personal study carried out by Jan Gruszynski (1977) estimated that among Polish immigrants, one-third of the members of the second generation married within the same "ethnic" group. Raymond Boudon (1963) and his team came up with the same percentage (32%) in their study of mixed marriages in Ostricourt. Girard and Stoetzel, in their survey of Italians and Poles (1953), emphasized the differences according to regions of settlement. For agricultural workers in Aisne (where there is no genuine "Polish community"), the rate of mixed marriages among the second generation reached 55%, whereas it was only 24% for the miners of the north. The same differences were observed with respect to Italian second-generation immigrants: 56% of marriages were mixed among workers of the Parisian building trades, 84% among shopkeepers and artisans of Paris, and 51% among agricultural workers of Lot-et-Garonne. Social status and the size of the group formed by members of each nationality heavily influenced mixed marriage statistics. But the tendency elsewhere was to establish closer relations with local French communities, even if mixing was not as thorough as is sometimes claimed. Other indicators, which require systematic verification, suggest a gradual renunciation of native cultural practices among immigrants settled in France. In the community of Ostricourt, the number of French names given by Polish parents to their children burgeoned from 44% in 1935 to 73% in 1945, 82% in 1955, and 98% in 1960. These figures speak for themselves. Religious practice tended to decline as well. The study by Girard and Stoetzel shows that twenty years of presence in France led to an erosion of fervor in communities that had been very religious when they arrived. It also emphasizes the corrosive role of cities and the influence of dechristianized French working-class norms. In the Paris region, 34% of Italian workers declared themselves to be practicing Catholics in 1953, compared with 61% of the agricultural workers of Lot-et-Garonne. Among the Poles, religious practice seems to have been better preserved (66% among agricultural workers of Aisne and 63% among miners of the north). But from the second generation onward, it declined (for all professions) to 30%. The same trend affected Armenians and the Jewish population of Paris. Charlotte Roland, in her study of Belleville, strongly emphasized this point: "Most people in the second generation are completely detached from the religious traditions that were so important to their parents' native society, and with which the latter are still very familiar despite the loosening of their own practice" (Roland 1962, 265). She estimated that one of ten second-generation Jews (whose parents had immigrated during the interwar period) still practiced their religion; most of them were owners or executives. Her explanation for this "obstinate refusal" is that religious practices remind these people of their origins and establish differences between them and their fellow Frenchmen. According to Roland, this attitude results from the stigma inflicted upon them by the dominant society, which is interpreted "as rejection from the adopted community" and experienced as self-demeaning.

We might conclude from all this that one of the main criteria defining the second immigrant generation is its desire to become integrated within a society that it defines as its own; and the obstacles encountered provoke a more or less pronounced rejection of anything that recalls its origins. This is the other major reason, along with mainstream ethnocentric assumptions about "successful assimilation," for the blind eye turned to the history of immigration in France. We now have enough data to be able to regard this as a general process, one repeatedly observed by scholars with genuinely close ties to the communities they studied. In her dissertation, Céline Azas observed that the refusal of people of Spanish origin in the Béziers region to collectively assert their origins had nothing to do with a loss of memory: "everyone knows that at that time, hundreds of thousands of Spaniards came here and either went home or stayed. They lived and worked, had children in the villages and the large cities of this department. But very rarely does anyone mention them" (Azas 1981, 13). In Lorraine, it was the children of Italians who had the most pronounced local accent and who marched behind the cross of Lorraine with children dressed in local folkloric garb. Similarly, anti-Belgian (and especially anti-Flemish) xenophobia in the late nineteenth century accelerated the assimilating process: "These numerous constraints affecting the condition of foreigners inflected a process of assimilation which was, on the surface, regarded as natural. That Belgian immigrants underwent a high rate of *francisation* is due to the fact that they had been coming to France for many years; a foreign colony of nearly 590,000 people in the 1880s was reduced by 80%." In this case as well, the process was accentuated in the following generation: "In Lille, Wazemmes also lost, between the two wars, the Belgian or Flemish character that so typified its settlement" (Lentacker 1973, 444, 466).

We will close this "tour de France" with an example drawn from Provence, the region that Marcel Pagnol so cherished. Philippe Joutard has noted that the Italian fishermen of Marseilles incorporated very ancient local traditions, to the point of discarding "all references to their Italian past." He attributed this "systematic loss of memory" to the fact that the city's Italian fishermen needed to construct a "foundational myth" in order to erase "the double stigmata associated with the immigrant neighborhood of Saint-Jean, a neighborhood 'reserved' for them prior to the war." What old fishermen were conveying through historical references was that "We are accused of being the newly arrived, unworthy of trust; but in reality, we were the earliest inhabitants of Marseilles, the first Christians." By incorporating a history other than their own, the old Italian fishermen of Marseilles were expressing a need to "become assimilated, to appear familiar; hence their denial of Italian memories, their adoption of the local Provençal past, the need to appear as founders" (Joutard 1983, 91ff.). This demonstration, it seems to me, should be viewed as a paradigm. It shows how the family-based mythology of genealogical rerooting, described earlier with respect to immigrants accounts of their travels, can be collectively espoused, thereby hiding the profound rupture experienced in the real history of individuals and their group behind the "continuity" of forms of sociability and the assumptions of the *longue durée* so dear to "new historiography."

Yet this argument runs up against numerous indications that, on the contrary, an immigrant identity is sometimes claimed, or even reinforced, by the second and third generations. This point of view is commonly found today with respect to young North Africans or Portuguese immigrants (see, for example, Oriol 1979). One explanation, which offers the advantage of reconciling the two perspectives, is that historical conditions have changed. The scathing xenophobia that so deeply affected the children of the immigrants who arrived in the 1920s is no longer prevalent. Schoolteachers are not what they used to be, and school is no longer the sole venue where foreign children come into contact with the host society. The invasion of "new images" (television, film) and the creation following the Second World War of a new social category called "youth," with its norms and models largely influenced by Anglo-Saxon cosmopolitanism, would tend to provide children with foreign origins with choices unavailable a half-century earlier. Pop singer Linda de Souza, the argument goes, conveys a sense of "being Portuguese" within French society, whereas the group *Carte de Séjour*[18] represents "Algerianness."[19] This perspective might even be related to Erving Goffman's description of the stigmatized individual who, having painstakingly striven to hide his guilt, spends the remainder of his life "unlearning." Given the current state of research, the question remains an open one. In contrast to those who spontaneously tend to regard the phenomenon they discover as in essence "new," the historian's role is to "bend the stick" in the other direction, to illustrate the ways in which processes are "structural" rather than "conjunctural."

Current fieldwork on this issue suggests that this claim to a specific identity is rather illusory. Indeed, several studies have shown that, even among young people today, there is still a desire not to be different from the native French. The official report written by Jacques Berque (1985) on immigrant children in schools painted a picture that in many ways resembles the reality of the interwar period, describing the double frustration of a second generation torn between French culture and its culture of origin. More significant still is the impossibility of an organized second-generation collective identity, with its own representatives, agenda for struggle, and so on. At the political level, for example, during the 1986 legislative elections the few candidates who claimed a *Beur* identity (such as Kamel Adjira in Marseilles) had given up by the middle of the campaign, partly because of a poor turnout among individuals who were expected to "recognize" themselves in the candidate. Similar problems are encountered today by the press aimed at second-generation immigrants (for example, *Baraka*). While some artists were able to base their notoriety on "playing *Beur*" (the program *Mosaïque,* for instance, provided a unique mode of access to television), most of them refuse to act as representatives for the community. Mehdi Charef, who might have been considered an ideal representative of the second generation following the success of his 1983 novel *Le Thé au harem d'Archi Ahmed,* stated that "young people like me should begin by exorcising their past origins." Actors Farid Chopel and Smaïn, dancer Kamel Balarbi, and cartoon scriptwriter Farid Boudjellad all profess their desire to become integrated within the majority culture. Moreover, there are relatively few young North African activists of S.O.S.-Racisme (see Boubeker and Beau 1986).[20] It may not be as paradoxical as it seems at first to assert that second-generation mobilization over issues of identity is less pronounced today than it was in the period following the Second World War. For years, CADI, stressing the role played by immigrants in the Resistance and in France's reconstruction, led the struggle to obtain the genuine integration of the second generation into French society.

It is because they succeeded that gradually, the questions about their origins were generally silenced, and the inquisitorial gaze of society was directed toward newly arrived immigrants. Given that many French had an interest in such a silence due to their behavior in the 1930s and during the war, it is almost as if a tacit pact had been signed in the interest of all parties.

A second objection to the arguments developed earler emanates from those who perceive a renewal of "identity-based politics" in older immigrant communities, a renewal that, according to these authors, underscores a "resistance" to assimilation. It should be noted that these arguments are not new; they are characteristic of "phase B" of the immigration cycle, a phase that, as we have seen, is characterized by a renewed interest in the question of origins.

Yet in the 1950s, the movement of "return to the sources" involved only a minority of the immigrant community, whereas today it is a much more widespread phenomenon. It expresses itself through a variety of written and oral testimonies and in new forms of grassroots mobilization, and it is not particular to any single social category.

In the area of soccer, this concern could be found among representatives of the third Polish and Italian generations. Yannick Stopyra regretted that his father had been unwilling to teach him the Polish language: "I feel something that links me to Poland.... I would like to know more about my origins. I know that my grandparents, when they arrived in Montceau, lived among Poles in wooden barracks. But I was never able to discuss it with them. My grandmother, for example, does not speak French."[21] Axel Clévenot's television documentary on the history of Italian immigration[22] showed the differences between Michel Platini, the most famous contemporary soccer player in France, and his father, and hence between representatives of the second and third generations; the latter admitted, after several years spent in Turin, that he wasn't sure exactly where "his roots" lay.

Historical studies of immigration that have begun to emerge in France are very often the work of young scholars who belong to the third generation and who justify the choice of their topic as a personal search for origins. These studies always tend to conclude that a feeling of "Armenianness" (Hovanessian 1992), a "Spanish consciousness" (Azas 1981), a "Russian culture" (Gousseff and Saadier 1983) have survived in France. In short, as Dominique Ducellier wrote with respect to her Polish ancestors, "the third generation, ours, is in search of its origins. This is not to question our parents' assimilation; it reflects a need to find out what the differences were in our grandparents' time" (Ducellier 1981–1982).

These concerns are also reflected in a growing number of cultural manifestations and in the creation of new voluntary associations for the collective expression of rediscovered identities. Dominique Schnapper (1980) discussed the renewal of Jewish culture that was symbolically expressed by the frequent use of a capital *J* in spelling the word "Jew," whereas Emile Durkheim, for example, the son of a rabbi, used a lower-case *j*. There is also a resurgence of "Italianness." In his novel *Les Ritals,* Cavanna reversed the old stigma associated with that term by making it an object of pride, and he suggested to his readers of Italian origin that they (moderately) cultivate the same "nostalgia." As a writer, Cavanna participates in the new sociability that has formed in recent years around Italian identity. In 1983, the newly created Centre d'Etude et de Documentation de l'Emigration Italienne (CEDEI) launched an ambitious research program on Italian immigration in France, complete with colloquia and publications. In the early 1980s, the Foreign Affairs Ministry counted more than 325 Italian voluntary associations in France, two-thirds of them created since the 1970s. Half of the members of these associations were of French nationality (with a high percentage of naturalized citizens). The 258 societies whose memberships were known at the time totaled approximately 52,000 members (Campani, in Oriol and Hily 1985). The ties established nearly a century ago between the inhabitants of Casalvieri (Latium) and long-time and recent immigrants from that community have resulted in the creation of voluntary associations in which the criterion for membership is not nationality but, rather, having origins in a specific place. The many ties established between Casalvieri and the localities of Val-de-Marne illustrate, according to Maurizio Catini, the "bilateral character of references" that characterized the French with Italian origins (quoted in Oriol and Hily 1985). Armenian newspapers and voluntary associations have flourished in localities where Armenian settlement was strong (Centre de Recherche et de Documentation Arménienne, Association Audiovisuelle Arménienne in Issy-les-Moulineaux), in addition to the older village-based associations (Hovanessian 1992). The same tendency is observed in Hérault. In Bédarieux, a collective publication coauthored by teachers and students traces the history of Spanish immigration in the region: accounts of crossing the border, interviews with old immigrants, descriptions of everyday life for the first generation, music and recipes from home—nothing is spared. The book even contains a preface by the Communist mayor and Conseiller Général, Antoine Martinez, entitled "*L'Espagne au coeur,*" which says of the community: "Its cultural identity, its history carry the indelible mark" of Spanish immigration. In a second preface, the headmaster of the school, Jean-Paul Linhares, writes that the inhabitants of Bédarieux "have preserved specific customs and ways of life. In this diversity lies the originality and wealth of the city's population today" (ODACH n.d.).

Many other illustrations could be given of this process. The problem for the scholar is to determine the exact nature of this cultural continuity. Public proclamations notwithstanding, the few statistics that we have at our disposal all point to a decline of identity-based claims between the second and third generations. The in-depth CNRS survey conducted by Bensimon and Pergola (1984) observes the decline of religious practice among French Jews and of the cultural elements associated with religious practice. In his thesis on Poles in France over three generations, Jan Gruszynski (1977), despite his desire to demonstrate the survival of "Polishness" in France, noted a decline in the use of the Polish language, which, by the third generation, was spoken by fewer than 10% and written by fewer than 7% of those surveyed. Holdert (1977) argued that the third generation had been totally integrated. Polish cultural associations and artistic activities should be interpreted, according to him, as an expression of originality rather than as a genuine assertion of Polish identity. Of his father's twenty-two grandchildren and great-grandchildren, not a single one speaks a word of Polish.

To explain this contradiction, it may be useful to look at the U.S. example, which is more similar to the French—at least in this respect—than is often believed. In his pioneering study, which has often been erroneously interpreted as a statement of the "new ethnic identity," Herbert Gans (1982) showed that the native culture of Italian Americans in Boston had seriously declined by the second generation: Whereas language was fairly well preserved, Italian names were gradually made to sound more American, and the furniture and spatial organization of apartments reflected the rapid Americanization of this working-class community. By the third generation, acculturation (which does not necessarily mean assimilation) was total; the grandparents' language was no longer learned at all.

Joshua Fishman's survey (1966) of language loyalty in the United States revealed a stark decline in the transmission of language between the second and third generations. Of third-generation Italian-Americans, 75% married outside their community of origin. According to Stephen Steinberg, all of this indicates that the "ethnic myth" was perpetrated by intellectuals during the 1960s: "It is clear that the state, through educational institutions, dealt a devastating blow to ethnic pluralism by refusing to organize schools on a pluralist basis" (Steinberg 1981).[23] This quote also illustrates the myth of "American pluralism" in matters of immigration and underscores the importance of studying the French and U.S. cases side by side.

In the United States, the issue of ethnicity owes its success to the arrival on the intellectual "labor market" of the third generation in the 1960s. Marcus Hansen (1952) has given an explanation of this phenomenon that also applies to the French case, given the two-decade time difference in the migratory process (immigration reached its height in the United States around 1910; in France, around 1930): The third generation, whose national identity (U.S. or French) was well established, could make a claim to origins that their parents had done their utmost to put behind them. In light of Halbwachs's work on "collective memory," it is understandable that the "need for history" and the willingness to preserve the memory of the group of origin should arise at the very moment when the lived experience of an "immigrant memory" disappears (at least for the waves of the interwar period). Social mobility between the second and third generations is also undoubtedly a factor. Whereas in most cases, parents and grandparents had been deprived of a say due to their working-class condition, the promotion of many grandchildren to the intellectual professions provided the first opportunity to reveal this "hidden facet" of French history.[24] It should also be kept in mind that this "search for origins" often serves very specific interests. Nathan Glazer has shown that in the United States, this issue has involved very high political stakes since the 1964 Civil Rights Act and the 1965 Immigration Act. Each "community" had a vested interest in claiming an "identity," high membership figures, and so on. This process produced a change in the 1980 census, which classified Americans into groups defined by "ancestry." We have not gone that far in France, but it would seem that the very same peoples who had been inclined to seek assimilation in the second generation (through naturalizations or mixed marriages, for example) now openly proclaim their difference. Italian voluntary associations in the Paris region are led by the children of those who, in the 1950s, displayed record rates of mixed marriages. In Mantes, Algerian shopkeepers are the most active members of the local friendship society due to their reliance on customers and on labor power from that country (Bekouchi 1984). Similarly, the small entrepreneur in the garment or building trades whose wealth rests on the employment of illegal aliens from his own community has a vested interest in promoting the "mythology of origins," in other words, a belief in the reality of the "ethnic" principle and in the futility of class struggle. In other social environments, foreign origin is purposely fostered as a principle of distinction. Naturalization statistics indicate that very few British became naturalized in the early part of the century. As Jan Gruszynski has noted, "the descendants of the Poniatowski family traditionally marry in the polish church of Paris, located on rue Saint-Honoré. In 1975, Nathalie Poniatowski (seventh generation born outside of Poland) was married to a Frenchman in the Polish parish. President Valéry Giscard d'Estaing and Michel Poniatowski attended the ceremony" (Gruszynski 1977, 350).

The tendency among scholars with foreign origins to overestimate the "resistance" of immigrant communities to the norms of the dominant society illustrates the inherent risk in any research endeavor whose implicit goal is to rehabilitate one's own group. By acting as the representatives of the symbolic interests of a community of origin, scholars promote a "substantialist" view of social groups, a problem discussed in the preceding chapter with respect to the sociology of immigration. The group to which these scholars claim to belong is isolated from other groups and presented, according to the period, as the most "resistant" to acculturation or, alternatively, as the most "dominated." The result is a "hierarchization" of identities, which places the group under study in a position of "exteriority." As Hannah Arendt rightly argued, there are more than just scientific risks involved in such an approach.[25]

These remarks are not intended to invalidate the discussion of the cultural specificities that are linked to differences in origins, which would play into the still-dominant myth of the national uniformity of French society since the Revolution. Indeed, historians are in no position to discredit the very commemorative practices in which they often participate, by glorifying, for example, the "roots of the French people" or the "heroes of 1789."

Five

Three Crises

Will we always be able to impose our customs, our civilization, in a word our label, on the invaders? Will assimilation go smoothly? Unmistakable symptoms seem to indicate that we are reaching a point of saturation. . . . Our customs are becoming exotic, our language is being overcome by foreign terms, even our security is threatened by dangerous elements who are attracted by our wealth and whom our leniant laws do not frighten. G. Dallier, 1914

Today, while compact hordes of foreigners are settling on our territory and while in certain districts younger elements of these beggars are more numerous than autochthonous youths, the problem takes on a whole new dimension and may expose us to the emergence in our country of ethnic minorities.

L. Naudeau, 1931

Will we still be French in thirty years?

Le Figaro-Magazine, 26 October 1985

The reappearance of xenophobic and racist discourses and practices places two essential questions before those of us who claim to defend "human rights": First, how can we explain the resurgence of "old demons"? And second, is the disquieting progression of intolerance a premonitory symptom of social and political evolution comparable to the one experienced by Europe fifty years ago? Political responses to these questions now appear insufficient. "Human rights" defenders, on the one hand, always tend to cry wolf and invoke the specter of fascism whenever they detect the slightest hint of a xenophobic discourse; this is a reaction that runs a substantial risk of rendering the term "fascist" so commonplace that the consequences may backfire against their ideal. On the other hand, there is sometimes a tendency to minimize these aggressions out of political short-sightedness, thereby contributing to their legitimation.

Contrary to a tradition that holds that the social sciences should not intervene in debates whose terms originated outside academia, I believe that these are unavoidable questions for historians. Rather than accompanying political discourse by attempting to reinforce one side or by identifying "culprits," however, scholarly courage consists of preferring autonomous, dispassionate analyses to the defense of established schools of thought, at the risk of offending the proponents of those schools; this is the only way of getting closer to the truth.

From an epistemological perspective, this is a perfect opportunity to practice that alternative approach to temporality available to historians: comparativism. Indeed, to truly understand what is happening in French society today, we must compare three moments in modern history in which the "hatred of foreigners" reached paroxysmal heights: the 1880s, which culminated in the Dreyfus affair; the 1930s, which preceded the Vichy regime; and the 1980s. While these are clearly also periods of intense economic crisis and social change, locating the similarities among them is only a first step in the research process. Though xenophobia against immigrants is like a mirror held before French society, the comparative approach must clearly identify three distinct moments in the evolution of the social structure. This is a very difficult task, and the ambition of this chapter is much more modest. If what follows succeeds in making questions out of preconceived answers and in generating new research, my goal will have been largely attained.

Three Moments of Stabilization

From the perspective of immigration history, one of the major paradoxes of conjunctural crises is that they provoke the stabilization of foreign populations exactly at a time when the host society is overcome by fundamental structural change. We will see that this observation is not unrelated to xenophobic impulses. First, however, we must begin by tracing this process in the data provided by census figures.

"Inventing" Immigration: The Crisis of the 1880s

It is not possible here to examine in detail the effects on immigration of the first major crisis experienced by modern France, precisely because the elaboration of the necessary statistical tools was among the results of this crisis. Yet the first census that was specifically directed at foreigners, which was taken in 1891, provides several indications that economic depression encouraged the permanent settlement of foreigners. Several points of comparison are provided with preceding censuses, regarding the total population by nationality and the proportion of men to women. Following a steady increase under the Second Empire and in the 1870s, the foreign population stagnated at a level of about one million in the late nineteenth century. The change in the proportion of men is even more significant: Whereas in 1861 there were 136 men for every 100 women, the number fell to 113 in 1891. This tendency toward an equal proportion of men and women has been an undeniable sign of the permanent settlement of foreign communities throughout the modern period. The presentation of the 1891 census reads: "The very fact that the proportion of women has risen steadily, notwithstanding the total number of immigrants present in the country, seems to indicate that these foreigners have tended to make our country their home." Even though there are no available statistics for the earlier period, the statistics on the economically active foreign population in 1891 (compared with those of 1931 or 1975) reveal signs that a process of permanent settlement was underway: a level of employment below 50% and a significant proportion of owners and employees. Furthermore, the proportion of married men to bachelors was similar among foreigners and Frenchmen.

Yet the essential revelation of this census is that a major fraction of the foreign population present on French soil was born in France. Of a total of about 1.1 million individuals, more than 420,000 were born in the host country, 350,000 of them in the very department where they were registered by the census. It is somewhat surprising that such basic figures have never caught the attention of historians: they invalidate the widely held thesis that it was "temporary migration" that was characteristic of nineteenth-century France, confirm the widespread stabilization of immigrants following the crisis of the 1880s, and provide clues to the key stakes involved in the 1889 Nationality Code (see chapter 2).

Indeed, if in 1891, 40% of the foreign population was born in France (compared with 10% in 1936 and 22.6% in 1982), it is also because the great divide between "nationals" and "foreigners" that nourished the political and juridical controversies of the period had not yet produced its effects. Unlike what occurred in subsequent periods, this ratio reflects not only the stabilization of the immigrant population over two generations but also the long-term settlement of these cores of "foreign" communities, who took advantage of the ambiguities of their national status to avoid the military draft.

The crisis of the 1880s therefore reflects another aspect of the construction of national space through the reduction of internal factors of heterogeneity, illustrated by the absorption of the first major historical wave of immigration: Belgians, who in 1881 represented 40% of the total number of foreigners in France. With the industrial recovery of the latter part of the century, Belgians were surpassed by Italians for the first time; the proportion of males, of employed and of adults all rose. It was the beginning of a new historical phase of immigration, which culminated in 1930.

One Effect of Crisis: The Urge to Conform to National Norms

An in-depth comparison of immigration during the two major crises of the 1930s and immigration today is possible, thanks to the censuses of 1931 and 1936 on the one hand, and 1975 and 1982 on the other. I will simply outline such an analysis here, underscoring what the two periods have in common (the differences will be discussed later in this chapter).

In contrast with those who attribute the current situation of immigration to the "conjuncture," a comparison between these two periods illustrates the structural impact of economic crises in industrialized societies.

The first observation, and the most obvious, is that the foreign population stagnated from the beginning of the economic recession onward. Between 1931 and 1936, official figures indicated a drop of nearly 20% in the foreign population (from 2.7 million to 2.2 million). The increase in naturalizations[1] must be taken into consideration, as must the increase in illegal immigration, which, while massive in 1930, had declined considerably by 1936. Although the exact figures of this decline are elusive, the tendency clearly contrasts with that of the more recent period: the census figures for 1975 and 1982 indicate that the number of illegal aliens in France rose by 300,000. While this difference must be explained, it does not fundamentally contradict the stabilizing effects of economic crises in comparison with periods of expansion. This is confirmed by a number of other indicators. The female population underwent as considerable an increase in the 1930s as in the recent period. In 1936, there were 72.7 women for every 100 men, compared with 63.9 in 1931, among the immigrant population. A comparable progression occurred between 1975 and 1982 (when the percentage of women in the foreign population increased from 70 to 76%). Yet the feminization of the foreign population was only one dimension of this process, along with the overall aging of immigrant communities and the increase in the number of economically inactive individuals. The phenomenon was most pronounced during the interwar period, perhaps because the so-called practice of family regrouping (which existed in the 1930s but did not have a name) has lowered the average age of immigrants in the contemporary period. Between 1931 and 1936, the proportion of boys younger than fifteen declined slightly (from 10.2% to 9.8%), as did that of girls (from 9.8% to 9.6%); it remained unchanged between 1975 and 1982. Conversely, whereas the proportion of people over sixty soared from 3.8% in 1931 to 7.9% in 1936, it declined between 1975 and 1982 (11.6% to 10.1%). The aging of the overall population in the context of economic crisis was most pronounced among adults. In 1931, the largest group was made up of individuals 20–29 years old (18.2%, compared with 11.7% for those 30–39 years old). After five years of crisis, the 30–39-year-old age bracket surpassed the 20–29 category (24.4% to 17.9%). Between 1975 and 1982, the 20–29-year-old age bracket declined from 18.1% to 15.6% of the total immigrant population; however, by 1982, the 30–39-year-old group had taken the lead with 18.3%. These changing population indicators could be illustrated in great detail with examples drawn from existing monographs as well as recent INSEE reports. The stabilizing effect of economic crises produced a substantial reduction of the turnover observed in the latter part of the nineteenth century and the interwar period (see, for example, Reardon 1977; Walter 1935; Ponty 1985).

This incipient rootedness of the foreign population in the host country was accompanied by a substantial increase in the proportion of nonproductive immigrants, which increased the cost of reproducing the labor force (see Meillassoux 1975). This structural modification of the foreign population made it more visible than before (in schools, in hospitals, and in neighborhoods), a fact that should be kept in mind when we examine the arguments of xenophobia over time. With respect to youths, the statistics inspire two remarks: First, as we saw in chapter 4, the rootedness of the foreign population slowly caused the "center of gravity" to shift from the first- to the second-generation communities. In 1936, one out of four immigrants was younger than twenty; in 1983 the proportion was one out of three. But at the same time, the stagnation observed in the proportion of children under fifteen reflected a trend that was as visible in the 1930s as it is today: the decline in the reproduction rate of foreign women, which brought them closer to French norms. Georges Mauco observed the swiftness with which foreign women adopted the demographic behavior of the host country. A half-century later, an INED study confirmed the generality of the phenomenon with respect to new waves of migrants. As a result of the extension of their stay in France, Algerian women marry four to five years later than they did two decades ago, which is one of the explanations for the reduction in the average number of children per family (Mauco 1932; Tribalat 1986).

An analysis of the change in the economically active population confirms this trend. The number declined by 22% between 1931 and 1936, and by 1.8% between 1975 and 1982,[2] underscoring the process of professional stabilization described earlier. More important, however, the observations of Jeanne Singer-Kerel with respect to the 1982 census can be generalized for the two periods of crisis: In both cases, the change in the rate of employment for foreigners tended to parallel, on a somewhat larger scale, the overall changes undergone by the economically active population. This was the case, for example, between 1931 and 1936, when unemployment ranged from 2% to 4% for the French and from 3.6% to 7.8% for foreigners. A half-century later, foreigners were even more plagued by unemployment than were their French counterparts. A similar trend appears in the breakdown by sectors. Between 1931 and 1936, the total working-class population declined from 32.9% to 30.7% of the economically active population, whereas service sector employment rose from 31.5% to 34.2%; the rate of those employed in agriculture remained proportionally stationary (35.6%).

These tendencies were amplified among the economically active foreign population. Although industrial workers remained by far the most important group among foreigners, the decline was most pronounced in their ranks: 10.4% were miners in 1931, compared with 8.3% in 1936; 48.8% worked in the transformation industry in 1931, only 39.7% in 1936. This evolution restored a balance in the structure of the foreign working population, which brought it closer to that of the French, given the progression in all the other sectors, particularly agriculture, which employed over 22% of foreign workers in 1936, but also liberal professions and services.

In 1982, immigrant workers were overrepresented in the same branches as in 1975 (the building trades and transformation industries). Yet here as well, a greater proportion among them left those sectors that were most affected by the crisis: agriculture and heavy industry. Similarly, the progression of foreign workers was steadier than that of the French in commerce and transportation. Hence, while the French remained a majority in the tertiary sector and foreigners a majority in the secondary sector, the difference between the two groups was slightly reduced (see Singer-Kerel 1986).

An analysis of the statistics by nationality shows that there were sometimes substantial contrasts between groups. In the two periods, the tendency was to reinforce the more recently arrived nationalities. Between 1931 and 1936, the four main nationalities (Italians, Poles, Belgians, and Spaniards) grew from 70.9% to 72.4% of the total number of foreigners in France. Yet, unlike the Italians and the Poles, Spanish and Belgian immigrants rapidly declined in number. This might be an indication that there were two divergent responses to crisis. In the case of Spaniards, the decline (27.8% in five years) probably reflects expulsions and spontaneous departures, possibly a characteristic of poorly integrated groups whose members come and go, voluntarily or by force, because they are not firmly enough established to be able to confront the crisis. The numerical (and hence legal) decline of the Belgian minority, on the other hand, might be explained by a swift integration process; the second or third generation was composed of French citizens, by birth or by acquisition.

The comparison between the censuses of 1975 and 1982 presents similar evolutions. The role of Belgians is filled today by Italian and Spanish immigrants, whose numbers fell from one census to the next because these communities had entered an advanced stage of the migratory process, to the point where, collectively at least, legal criteria of definition no longer had the same significance as before. Recent groups, on the other hand, tend to "take advantage" of the crisis to reinforce their hold on their new environment. The three main nationalities in this group (Algerian, Moroccan, and Portuguese) grew from 53.3% to 56.3% of the total. In addition, the changes that occurred in the economically active population reflect similar trends. For example, as in the 1930s, the most significant increase in the percentage of women in the working population occurred among the most "dynamic" immigrant communities (in particular, among the Algerians, with an increase of 233%). The study of age groups also reveals that these newly employed immigrant women tend to be young. This supports my argument about the "objective" integration of these communities into French society; in this respect, there is no fundamental difference between nationalities or between periods of immigration.[3]

Outlets

From the perspective of immigration, what these crises have in common is that they represent phases of stabilization for foreign communities, the realization that their settlement in France was irreversible. With the growth in the number of women and children, foreigners became more visible in the workplace, in the neighborhood, in schools, and in hospitals. In the professional domain, the stabilization of immigrants tended to bring them closer to French "norms." This is a key factor in explaining another constant feature of crisis periods: the exacerbated xenophobia to which foreigners are subjected.[4]

In Practice

If we examine practices before analyzing discourse, it is clear that in times of crisis foreigners typically fall victim to outbreaks of hostility. It is safe to assume, for example, that Bernard Stasi is wrong in asserting that Belgians enjoyed a "spontaneous capital of sympathy" in nineteenth-century France. The dissertations written by Judy Reardon and Firmin Lentacker provide ample evidence of widespread anti-Belgian aggression in northern France:

> From April to June 1848, manifestations of hostility against Belgian workers became a daily fact of life in the north: They were attacked during their return to Belgium, forcefully led to the border by gangs (such as the "Flemish" immigrants who had settled between Tourcoing and Halluin), or expelled as a result of pressure from coalitions, such as 18 May on the railroad construction site of Armentières or 20 May in Lille. (Lentacker 1973, 372)

Many other sources indicate that such aggression was common in other regions during the mid-nineteenth-century crisis: in western France against skilled English railroad construction workers, in Paris against German artisans, in public works projects throughout the country against Flemish, Piedmontese, and other workers (see especially Châtelain 1977; see also Vadalenc 1979; Chevalier 1978).

In the late nineteenth century, the intensity of xenophobic violence reached unprecedented heights, with Belgians again bearing the brunt. In Drocourt (Pas-de-Calais) in 1892, where Belgian workers made up 75% of the workforce in the local mines, the French population organized a full-scale mobilization to force their departure. A recent study underscores the scale of the movement and the haste with which the victims had to flee:

> Their return, which was more or less complete by 31 August, took place under very difficult conditions. The trains arrived from France crammed with large and impoverished families carrying their measly luggage. Housing was a problem they faced as soon as they arrived, and they also had to replace the furniture that had either been left behind or destroyed by French miners.

An official Belgian inquiry evaluated the losses suffered as a result of vandalism at forty to fifty francs per family (Dantoing 1974). Until the First World War, northern France was the stage for countless similar scenes. Fatal brawls and manhunts took place in Liévin and in Lens during 1901. In 1910, "a tumultuous Holy Monday caused a commotion among the Belgian colony of Montigny-en-Gohelle," who were once again threatened with collective fury (Lentacker 1973, 441). According to Firmin Lentacker, these threats and physical aggression played a very important role in the acceleration of the Belgian immigrants' process of integration, further illustrating the important role played by violence and stigmatization in the "assimilation" process.

Yet the fact that the Belgians had been present for a long time and were well established in France explains why, from the 1880s onward, the storm of xenophobia moved southward, where it targeted a new wave of immigrants: Italians. According to the sources consulted by Michelle Perrot, over twenty people were killed during the 1880s alone. "What is astonishing about these acts," she commented, "is the extent of the mobilizations they unleashed, easily generating popular movements of several thousand people" (Perrot 1960).

In this case as well, scenes of xenophobia occurred year after year until the First World War. Although they have not been comprehensively studied, such crises of intolerance are exemplified by the three great manhunts that traumatized the Italian community. The first occurred in Marseilles in 1881. Rioting shook the streets of the city for several days. "At 4:00 a.m.," wrote a reporter of the *Petit Marseillais,*

> brawls broke out between Frenchmen and Italians in several parts of the city. . . . At 5:30, as workers regrouped on the cours Belsunce for the shape-up, a group of young men began to actively chase the Italians they ran into, booing them and beating them rather seriously. Frightened Piedmontese workers fleeing in all directions were chased down the streets of rue de la Couronne and the rue de l'Echelle, as their assailants ordered them to shout "Long live the Republic!" Within days, hundreds of Italians had hastily left the city.[5]

In 1894, the assassination of President Carnot by an Italian anarchist provoked renewed rioting whose epicenter was the city of Lyons. Jean-Charles Bonnet has recorded the testimony of several people whose parents experienced these events. Their traumatic impact is evidenced by the vividness of memories, "which, as the extreme precision of these accounts testifies, were as painful as they were fresh; certain details were later confirmed by police reports." Many Italians preferred once again to flee the city; others changed their name to sound more French or altered their appearance to avoid acts of violence (J.-C. Bonnet, in Duroselle and Sera 1978).[6]

The highest point of anti-Italian hatred was reached in August 1893 in Aigues-Mortes. Following a series of riots among workers in the salt works, three hundred Frenchmen armed with sticks, shovels, and tree branches attacked their Italian counterparts. During the night, enraged bands roused the French population by drumbeat, forcing the intervention of several brigades of the gendarmerie. But a convoy of eighty Italians escorted out of the city by the police was attacked by rioters armed with rifles; many were killed outright, and the wounded were finished off with sticks. The accusation read by the prosecutor during the subsequent trial eloquently describes the scene: "Huge stones were thrown from all sides; with each step forward, one was forced to abandon defenseless victims on the ground, who were savagely beaten to death by frenzied rioters." The local population continued over the next few days to comb the neighboring countryside, vineyards, and marshlands in search of Italians who might have escaped from the massacre. Officially, there were eight dead and fifty wounded; but according to the London *Times,* the figures were closer to 50 dead and 150 wounded. Given the administrative gaps in the registration of foreign workers at the time, it is impossible to produce an accurate statistic. The ensuing international uproar forced the mayor of the town to resign. Yet the French government did everything it could to minimize the matter, as is evidenced by the verdict of the Assize Court, which acquitted the accused (see, in particular, Vertone, in Duroselle and Serra 1978). While Italians were the primary object of French violence in the late nineteenth century, few foreigners were spared. Gypsies (many of them French) were also particularly targeted.

Hatred of the Other was often expressed during the alcohol-drenched "collective festivities" that were typical of working-class sociability (such as village celebrations or Holy Monday). In Toulouse in 1895, following an incident during a popular ball, 4,000 demonstrators, encouraged by the "hurrahs" of the local population, marched on the neighborhood of Saint-Cyprien, where Bohemians had settled. Many houses were looted and burned. Two brigades of the gendarmerie worked for two long days to prevent a massacre (see Vaux de Foletier 1981).

In the interwar period, mass movements against foreigners became less frequent. Yet, as Ralph Schor has shown in his dissertation, brawling resumed with the crisis of the 1930s. In 1931, fights repeatedly broke out between French strikers and Belgian strikebreakers in the north. The former were molested and bombarded with stones and bricks, and some were even thrown into the canals. A Belgian worker died from his wounds. In Lyons in 1934, an incident between Frenchmen and Moroccans resulted in one dead and several seriously wounded. In 1938, a Polish foreman was assassinated by five striking French workers (Schor 1985, particularly 561–62). Series F7 of the National Archives and series M of the departmental archives are replete with similar cases. In 1923, brawls broke out between striking Spanish miners and French strikebreakers in the north. Meanwhile, in Valence, violence took place with the opposite motive: Confédération général du travail unifié (General Confederation of United Labor; CGTU) activists attacked unskilled Armenian workers who refused to go on strike (NA F7 13012; NA F7 13436).

There is no need to dwell at length on the recent period, which is marked by an upsurge in acts of racist violence. In 1977, the "red summer" resulted in fifteen deaths in the Algerian community in Marseilles, forcing the French government to temporarily block departures from Algeria to France.[7] No precise statistics on these incidents is available at present, but the data drawn from a reading of the press indicate that scarcely a month went by without representatives of the most recent wave of immigration falling victim to xenophobic violence. One writer counted twenty-three acts of violence perpetrated against foreigners in 1982 alone.[8]

In Discourse

Moving from actions to discourse (and they go hand in hand), we can draw up an inventory of the themes, fantasies, and cries of hatred that recur as leitmotivs from one crisis to the next; only the names of the aggressors and the victims change. Numerous sources from all social groups are available to historians for such an endeavor. As far as popular classes are concerned, the public archives have conserved countless letters to the prefect or the Interior Minister that allow one to trace the evolution of forms of "denunciation." Letters to the editor published over the past century in newspapers are also relevant sources. Stephen Wilson's study of the commentary that surrounded fund-raisers for the Henry monument following the Dreyfus affair, which was published by the main French anti-Semitic newspaper, *La Libre Parole,* is a good example of the possibilities available to historians for the study of xenophobic "popular mentalities." Most of the documents, however, are of course the work of "professionals" of discourse: journalists' articles, political proclamations, books of various kinds (from novels and plays to social science monographs), and countless essays and documents whose xenophobia is more or less subtly expressed according to their authors' cultural sophistication.

Within the limits of this study, it is not possible to give more than an overview. Ralph Schor's dissertation contains many examples from the interwar period that are relevant to the typology outlined here.

First, the pattern of latent xenophobia, which is easily discernable in the press prior to the Second World War, was confirmed in later decades by public opinion polls.[9] The advent of a crisis, however, always provoked a sudden upsurge in antiforeign writings. Ralph Schor's analysis of the daily press in the interwar period shows that in all newspapers, the frequency of articles on the "problem of immigration" was much greater during the 1930s than during the 1920s. At the same time, the way of perceiving the problem changed. When it was in the interest of the powerful to hire large numbers of immigrant laborers, the writing style tended to convey "understanding." The 18 September 1973 edition of *La Nation* noted that there was no excess of immigrants in France, that the phenomenon was nothing new, and that "in no industrialized country can it seriously be argued that immigrants compete with nationals for jobs." The same year, *Le Figaro* opened its pages to jurists such as Jacques Robert, who denounced the lack of rights for foreign immigrants. "Victims of constant humiliation, repeated harassment, and growing attacks—due to their number, their difficult adaptation, or simply their misfortune—foreigners of all classes may be justified in doubting that France is still the country of law and justice for all."[10] Today, in the same newspaper, demographers have replaced jurists, and "understanding" has given way to alarmist fantasies and to the same dramatic announcements as appeared in the press prior to the First World War: the imminent breakdown of the national community and the approaching extinction of the "native" French population.

The rise of xenophobic discourse in crisis periods brings the logic of "us versus them" to frenzied levels. This line of demarcation justifies the rejection of immigrants in all areas and magically explains the misfortunes of the moment. Of course, the central themes of this discourse draw from the economic effects of the crisis. At this level, the archetype of the argument is "They come here to take our jobs."

This is the concern that is most often raised in letters written to the authorities by unemployed workers. To cite one example drawn from the archives of Meurthe-et-Moselle:

> You don't want the French to rebel, but they cannot but see what we see here, while we French die of hunger, our women, our children, we ask for work, and right nearby foreigners are working thirteen or fourteen hours a day, women have work, and us, nothing. I'm go-

> ing to write to the Minister of Labor, that's right, because what you want here is for a revolution to happen. . . . At the sawmill that's how they do it, no work for us French jerks, but for the others yes, from 5 a.m. to 8 p.m. (Quoted in Noiriel 1982, clx)

This illustrates the role of national norms as a key element in the legitimation of one's social position or one's struggle against the loss of social standing. It is a theme that emerged in the late nineteenth century and that has constantly been referred to since. Popular French uprisings against foreigners are often accompanied by the exhibition of national symbols like the tricolor flag or the national anthem. In the interwar period, virtually every xenophobic text made some mention of the French sacrifice during the First World War. Today, this tradition is best exemplified by parties of the far right: numerous blue, white, and red banners, speeches extolling "our soldiers," parades in military uniform (with a fondness for parachutists' costumes), commemoration of the Jeanne d'Arc holiday. From the time of Maurice Barrès to that of Jean-Marie Le Pen, each crisis period has provided a new opportunity to denounce the "foreign" invasion. This goes for all foreigners, regardless of their nationality (Sternhell 1983, 1985). Such denunciation is always misplaced, given that, as we have seen, periods of crisis are characterized by a pause in the recruitment, and often the expulsion, of immigrants; hence the frequent manipulation of statistics and, in particular, the constantly reiterated theme of "conspiracy," of "cunning" or "invisible" infiltration. The very fact that there is no evidence of these things is seen as the best possible proof that they occur. Such arguments can influence common sense insofar as the foreign population, however diminished or stagnant, is more visible. In periods of economic crisis, issues of welfare assistance and of social aid take on a dramatic dimension. The fact that immigrants also line up for unemployment benefits or welfare checks is viewed as "tangible" evidence of the "invasion."

In the logic that consists of decrying the burden that foreigners place on welfare costs, the issue of hospitals often comes to the fore. Indeed, hospitals lend themselves to two xenophobic arguments: that foreigners take up space at the expense of nationals and that they represent a public health hazard. This argument appeared prior to 1914 when Central European Jews were accused of transmitting "trachoma" (granular conjunctivitis) to the French population; it reached a high point in the interwar period, largely supported, as we will see, by

Doctors Jeanselme and Burnier, who argued that foreigners contributed significantly to the maintenance and spread of syphilis in France (cited in Schor 1985, 419). Another argument used to justify the denigration of immigrants was the notion of foreign delinquency. The proof rested mainly on statistical "evidence," which was easy to provide since numbers can be made to say almost anything. This line of argument was present in the work of such eminent professors of the Collège de France as Gabriel Tarde; it was intensified in the interwar period, became an obligatory part of all works on immigration, and is still used today by those who are afraid of foreigners. The press played an important role in this process. As early as the pre–First World War period, the newspaper *L'Est républicain* ran a regular column on the "crimes of the Briey basin," which featured Italians and their knives. In the late 1920s, the "news items" columns of newspapers in general thrived on the episodes of the affair of the Polish bandits. Nowadays, the newspaper coverage of foreign "criminality" is generally more subtle, but as Colette Guillaumin has noted, the simple fact of mentioning the nationality of a delinquent (which is not done if the culprit is French) implies something (Guillaumin 1972). Fiction, such as the novel and film, also spreads the stereotype of the immigrant as a good-for-nothing wrongdoer. The inspiration of Georges Simenon's novel *Pietr le Letton,* for example, was the affair of the Polish bandits (see Ponty 1985). Recent studies of the images of North Africans in French cinema show a tendency among scriptwriters to give them guttersnipe roles (Iberraken 1981).

The denunciation of the "risks" that immigrants present for the nation's mental and physical well-being is but one aspect of a process that aims at stigmatizing foreigners' appearance and actions. The sources that best illustrate this process are the novels on immigrants written by French authors (from Louis Bertrand to Paul Morand, the Académie Française has been well represented in this respect) and the newspaper articles that present themselves as journalistic "inquiries."

That novelists made the figure of the foreigner into an object of exoticism is not surprising. They merely adapted procedures that had been elaborated by colonial literature. Frantz Fanon showed, for example, that "the language used by the colonist to describe the colonized is that of a zoologist. References are made to the creeping movements of Asians, to the emanations of the indigenous city, to hordes, to stench, to swarming, to gesticulations" (Fanon 1982). These zoological figures have been abundantly used by such successful authors as Pierre Loti. His novel *Le Roman d'un spahi,* for example, is full of analogies, metaphors, and comparisons identifying blacks with animals (mainly monkeys).[11] Informed by such second-rate literature, xenophobic journalists reproduce its methods in their writing on immigration. Josephine Baker's review in Paris was explicitly described by the Countess Riguidi as the copulation of animals: "Black, sweating, and enraged, apocalyptic beings bustle about, rubbing up against each other and jigging up and down in a hideous semblance of rutting."[12] Even as "innocent" a series as *La Semaine de Suzette,* intended for children, portrays a Hindi traitor, whose demeanor is that of a serpent, and whose "long and cold hand, flexible and tenacious, gave her [the heroine] a strange sensation of aversion."[13] The recurrence of this zoological lexicon merits a study in and of itself. As early as the 1880s, Eugilvic opposed naturalizations on the grounds that foreigners "phylloxerized" France's rural areas. A century later, Jean-Marie Le Pen referred to the "marabunta" of immigrants.[14] Although they are not explicitly or consciously borrowed from previous generations, the same terms—"horde," "mob," "refuse dump," "swarming," and so on—appear over and over again.

Zoological language can play a role in the process of physically stigmatizing foreigners, but it draws from a much broader repertory that seeks to make the reader interiorize the equation immigrant = exoticism = danger. This is how Ludovic Naudeau described the population of Marseilles in 1930, in a series of articles that were published by *L'Illustration* and that were reprinted in a best-selling book: "Negroes, all sorts of negroes, fat negroes and thin negroes; sidelong-glancing Chinese dancing diligently; Annamites take on distinguished attitudes, all sorts of colored men with unknown origins act before Victor Gelu as if they were at home (Naudeau 1931, 146). A journalist writing for the far-right journal *Militant* evoked similar biological references when describing the "Afro-Asianization" of contemporary France: "The current presence on French soil of some three million natives of Africa and Asia is enough to fundamentally modify the biological specificity of our people, in an irreversable manner."[15]

As Max Weber (1968) showed in his analysis of racism, however, physical criteria are not always the determining factor in efforts to discredit the Other, for horror is always socially conditioned. In the interwar period, rampant anti-German racism was most frequently directed against the Jews of Central Europe. In this case, it was their accent that was generally stigmatized, and their surnames were treated with irony. In an article entitled "Clean the Backside First" published in *Je suis partout,* the historian Pierre Gaxotte attacked individuals whose names ended in "*ski,* in *vitch,* in *o,* in *of,* and in *ez*" (quoted in J.-C. Bonnet 1974, 224).[16]

Another technique often employed to exoticize foreigners consisted of describing daily life in immigrant ghettos. This "literary genre" appeared in the popular press toward the end of the nineteenth century, when a booming newspaper industry avidly sought sensational stories. In Lorraine, the local press spoke of

> filthy old ladies with wrinkled skin and scarce hair . . . who fried bizarre foodstuffs in chipped pans. . . . Such diabolical cooking still thrives under the blue skies of Italy and is part of the "local color" of the impoverished districts of Rome and Naples. But the situation is entirely different in Lorraine, where the chronic filth and deplorable way of life of Italians expose the native population to considerable risks of contamination.[17]

Here xenophobia reached its epitome, with immigrants being blamed for living conditions that were largely the responsibility of French society. Such descriptions were frequent, particularly in Marseilles: "There Whites, and poor Spaniards in particular, are reduced to the state of savages; makeshift homes become shanties; shanties are unspeakably filthy; the filth comes to life, producing pediculous pullulations" (Naudeau 1931, 164). After the Second World War, while such "exoticized" descriptions appeared less frequently in the press, they nonetheless remained in numerous descriptions of such districts as the Goutte d'Or in Paris or the Porte-d'Aix in Marseilles. A recent analysis of the way that *France-Soir* spoke of the "Chinese" of the thirteenth arrondissement is significant. The forty-five articles on this community published between November 1978 and July 1985 can be divided into two distinct periods. From 1978 to 1980, the dominant theme was that of the "martyrdom" of "boat people." The emphasis then shifted to "*Chinatown-sur-Seine*" (17 May 1980). The image of the refugee gave way to the "Chinese" immigrant who, it was held, lived in such isolation that "even the beans he ate" were Chinese. Other articles spoke of the "Chinese connection," of hiring undocumented workers, and the "yellow drug triangle of Paris" (Hassoun and Tan 1986).

Xenophobia also expressed itself through another, purportedly more distinguished style of writing that flourishes in times of crisis: the political-literary pamphlet, an often grandiloquent statement aimed at "making French people aware of the risks" that immigration represents for the country. Maurice Barrès was without a doubt the founder of this type of discourse, in particular his 1893 electoralist manifesto entitled "*Contre les etrangers!*" (Against foreigners!). It is ironic, as the epigraphs to this chapter make clear, that present-day xenophobic discourse should repeat, almost word-for-word thirty or forty years later, the apocalyptic predictions made by earlier generations with respect to Italians, Poles, Jews, Armenians, and so on. Such assertions reflect a high degree of ignorance, on these authors' part, about the history of the nation they claim to defend; they also reflect a poor understanding of real social processes. It is true that such pamphlets often conceal a narrowly political agenda rather than a scholarly concern for the truth. As we saw in chapter 2, however, the exacerbated expression of xenophobia during periods of crisis is reflected politically in the retaliatory measures taken against immigrants, which are intended to satisfy not only the interests of social groups represented in parliament but also their fantasies.[18]

Elements of Explanation

How are we to explain this consistency in xenophobic attitudes over time? Without reviewing all of the theories successively advanced to explain racism or anti-Semitism, and leaving aside psychological or psychoanalytical interpretations, I will concentrate here on the social analysis of three major sets of factors.

First, we must consider the loss of social status incurred during crisis periods. In contrast to the traditional populist notion of "misery" (which sees misery as an abstract category defined in absolute terms, when in fact misery is always relative to a given society), to view this question in terms of the loss of social status underscores both its conjunctural dimension (that is, the uniqueness of every crisis) and its structural dimension (that is, the link to the conflict between the aspirations or representations of the future elaborated in times of prosperity and the everyday reality of the crisis). The other advantage of looking at crisis periods from this angle is that it is pertinent to all social groups, from workers to the upper classes. It allows a better understanding of the ways in which xenophobia can become generalized.

In the lower social sectors, losing one's job is the primary factor leading to the decline of social status; it tends to call into question the entire raison d'être of one's professional universe and provokes the loss of even the most elementary economic status, with the concomitant humiliation of having to "beg" for charity, welfare, or social benefits, depending on the period under consideration. Quite often, in countries with a high rate of immigration, one way of escaping unemployment is to accept low-status jobs that, during periods of prosperity, are reserved for immigrants. This logic was clearly at work in the late nineteenth century. During the period of abundance under the Second Empire and the early years of the First Republic, two parallel labor markets emerged. With the advent of economic crisis, French workers fell back on unskilled public works or mining jobs. By then, however, immigrants had in many cases become established in these sectors, and they had acquired certain skills (as in the case of Belgians working in northern mines or Italians working in construction and public works). Entrepreneurs were therefore inclined to keep them, rather than to obey considerations of "national preference" that ran counter to company interests; hence the vigor of French populist struggles and the frequent denunciations of the role of owners in promoting the "invasion of foreigners." In rural areas, the crisis could provoke a "telescoping" of interests between workers of different nationalities. Abel Châtelain showed how the reconstruction of the wine industry in Languedoc following the phylloxera crisis provoked a parallel restructuring of the labor force. Spanish workers were given priority over French migrants from the mountains, who were more demanding in terms of wages and working conditions. This created a confrontational atmosphere that the owners could not dispel, since the capitalist reconstitution of the vineyards and the investments it required forced them to reduce labor costs by taking advantage of competition in the labor market (Châtelian 1977; see also Gavignaud 1983). A similar logic may have been behind the deadly onslaught of Aigues-Mortes in 1893. Many French workers found the situation unbearable; the presence of immigrants forced them to fight for the same low-status jobs they had held in contempt a few years earlier. This is clear in the case of the iron mines in Lorraine during the interwar period. Because the victims of massive layoffs tended to be single foreign men, the crisis accelerated the *francisation* of many immigrant workers. French workers, who had suffered a loss of social status and were often regarded as less qualified than immigrants for such jobs, in some ways resembled the "poor white trash" of the southern United States described by Max Weber (1968); deprived of ownership, they became the standard bearers of racial antipathy, and their "social honor" directly depended on the symbolic social denigration of blacks (or in the French case, of foreigners).

Xenophobia is generally stronger among the middle classes, in particular shopkeepers and craftsmen. This pattern can be explained by two distinct manifestations of the loss of social identity: first, the structural decline of these social groups, which have been under constant pressure from larger competitors from the late nineteenth century onward. During periods of crisis, this tendency was combined with the conjunctural loss of social status. Countless small artisans and shopkeepers, who had often escaped the condition of wage earners during the period of expansion, were faced with bankruptcy. Not infrequently, they were directly confronted with foreign workers who, in their own efforts to survive, sought refuge in small commerce and odd jobs. This evolution was particularly clear in the 1930s: Statistics show that a growing number of foreign workers were becoming independent "*chefs d'établissement.*" French workers had difficulty facing this competition. Immigrant workers, on the other hand, were accustomed from birth to very difficult, almost subsistence-level, living conditions. They could therefore put up with hardships and working conditions that the French could no longer sustain. Furthermore, immigration facilitates the mobilization of an illegal, clandestine, and therefore inexpensive labor force, particularly in the absence of social costs. During the 1930s, chambers of commerce in all regions of France sought to intervene on these issues, most notably by creating special I.D.'s for craftsmen and foreign shopkeepers.

Xenophobic tendencies were also found in governing-class circles, with varying intensity according to the period. From the scholars's perspective, this is important because it is at that level that the discourse and the images are produced for consumption by the popular classes. As we will see in the remainder of this chapter, direct competition between French and foreign was one of the reasons for the xenophobia of the upper classes. Most often, however, what was original about the relationship of these sectors to immigration was that they used the issue as a strategic card in purely internal conflicts. In the political arena, since the late nineteenth century, criticizing foreigners has been a "magical" means of improving one's image as a "left-winger with a heart" or as an "adamant defender of human rights," a sure way to win support from voters who shared these values. Conversely, the threatening, hard-line discourse of "safety-oriented" ideology helps politicians rally the votes of the fearful in society.

At another level, as the Dreyfus affair illustrated, xenophobia sometimes became a weapon in struggles between various intellectual circles, serving as the headsman's block for victims of academic overcrowding, for scholars unable to satisfy their ambitions in the labor market.

The second type of explanation for the persistence of xenophobia has to do with the difficult question of "belonging." In periods of uncertainty, foreigners are often perceived as a threat by more firmly established groups. Xenophobia tends to be more virulent in border regions. The example of the southern cities of Nice and Marseilles, which for the past century have been notorious bastions of intolerance, contradicts the widely held notion that "cultural proximity" enourages "peaceful coexistance." In the case of the Provençal dialect and the Italian language, Arnold Van Gennep showed that both linguistic groups might perceive the coexistence of two related idioms as a threat. The author added that "it is nonsense to speak of the unity between Latin peoples simply because they all speak Romance languages" (Van Gennep 1921, 81). With the stabilization of foreign communities in times of crisis, the "established" group perceives the threat of "outsiders" even more vividly. Other explanations are to be found within immigrant society itself. Those who had striven so hard to erase the slightest signs of difference between themselves and the native French met with hostility a new wave of immigrants (with whom they ran the risk of being identified). An Italian study of the events that occurred in Marseilles in 1881 concluded that recently acculturated Italians, identifying themselves as French, often led the bands of rioters who chased newly arrived Italians through the streets of the city (Arnaudo 1881).

Similar difficulties, for comparable reasons, were experienced by the Jewish community during the interwar period (Hyman 1979). The same can be said of Italians in Lorraine during the 1950s. Those of the northern and central regions of France, who had arrived one generation earlier, kept the newcomers (who came from southern Italy) at a distance (S. Bonnet 1965).

One other factor must be taken into consideration. Crises are moments of rupture and redefinition of social rules for the host society in general. Xenophobia is often a way of expressing the identity crisis that overcomes social groups in such circumstances. Immigrants epitomized these profound changes. They were summoned during periods of expansion, in other words, in times of technological innovation, urban development, and deepening divisions of labor. The social effects of these transformations became apparent over the course of ensuing decades, as the immigrants experienced the process of stabilization in the context of a fundamentally changing society. This is one evolution that all three crises share, although its manifestations varied in intensity. In the late nineteenth century, it is clear that the hatred of foreigners that Maurice Barrès felt was linked to the tremendous industrial changes that were occurring in his homeland, Lorraine; not only did this process upset traditional economic balances, but it also altered the very makeup of the population. This feeling of anguish in the face of "disappearing landscapes," so vividly expressed by Vidal de La Blache, must be taken seriously. It is eminently respectable and was an important aspect of the formation of "regionalist" currents in the late nineteenth century in such diverse regions as Lorraine, Provence, or the north. Social change (in which immigrants unwittingly found themselves entangled and for which common sense held them responsible) affected not only geographic communities, but also professional environments. In France as in the United States, the rationalization of work produced deep changes in the composition of the working class linked to immigration. In the glassworks, technological progress caused the breakdown of communities in which the "foreigner" had been excluded from the group of "*gens de métier.*" Their professional autonomy shattered, the glassworkers were integrated into a labor market increasingly regulated by national patterns. Machines made their empirical qualification irrelevant (Scott 1974). In the interwar period and in recent times, practically all industrial sectors underwent a similar transformation, and French workers whose skills had become obsolete were often ousted in favor of immigrant labor.

A third explanation, which should naturally be articulated with the preceding ones, has to do with the conditions that "produce" xenophobia in contemporary societies. Historians of ideas often refer to notions of "propaganda" or "indoctrination" to explain the development of xenophobia in given historical periods. Such arguments essentially focus on the content of discourses and on their means of communication (political parties, the press, and so on). While this is an important issue, social history is more concerned with symbolic aspects, in other words, with the techniques that produce collective mobilizations. Briefly, what follows are a few illustrations of this approach. The propaganda of far-right parties, which seldom resorts to factual demonstrations and argumentative logic, is often deemed "irrational." This is a genuine dilemma that might lead sincere democratic thinkers, in a cynical mood, to doubt human nature itself. In fact, the force of this political strategy is precisely that it does not appeal to reason but, instead, addresses the "subconscious" that rests in each of us. As we saw earlier, xenophobic discourse plays on fantasies such as fear and exoticism. What matters here is not so much its content as its form. By constantly hammering on the same subjects, xenophobic discourse seeks to create associations of ideas and, especially, of images that can lead to the stereotypical thinking that usually underlie racist statements. By integrating the foreigner within the sphere of tastes and, especially, of distaste, such strategies undermine democratic efforts, insofar as tastes and colors are things that cannot be questioned. But, as the following quote from Drieu La Rochelle (taken from his *Discours au Français sur les étrangers*) demonstrates, in order to mobilize individuals against immigrants, distaste must also be linked to the experience of everyday life: "Despite the famed aversion of the French for geography and traveling, not one of these people, by hearing, smell, or touch, by struggle or by endearment, by hatred or by curiosity, is unaware of what a foreigner is." The author proceeded to pinpoint individuals "on the street corner, figures that we hadn't seen since the medieval invasions" (quoted in J.-C. Bonnet 1974, 19). A precise comparative study of xenophobic discourses would demonstrate that since the late nineteenth century, whatever the period under consideration, the same strategy has been applied over and over again. In the 1890s, Barrès justified his hatred of foreigners by invoking the "thousand small facts that come to mind" (1893). The efficiency of these political devices should not be underestimated. Are not immigrants, because they are unable to fill out the money order form to send money back to their families, responsible for delaying the line waiting at the post office? And do they not tend to remain seated on the spare foldback seats during rush hour in the subway? It is through such everyday signs that the difference between "us" and "them" becomes crystallized. They lend efficiency to any political discourse capable of capitalizing on them.

This points to a key problem that exclusively discourse-based analyses are unable to comprehend. For a given message to be efficient, it must take root (I would say "be experimented with") in everyday life, endowing even the most abstract memories with a concrete meaning. This is why far-right politicians are so eager to appear "familiar" and sensitive to people's concerns. Here again, language is a key factor. It is no accident that for at least a century, politicians have designated the abstract concept of "nation" by extensively borrowing from the lexicon of the family.

Three Symptoms of French Society

The primary role of the historian is to remind people who think they have discerned something new in current events that it is usually nothing but a repetition of old historical problems. By seeking to inscribe the present in a drawn-out *longue durée,* however, one runs the risk of producing an artificial continuity through a simple shopping list of arbitrarily chosen quotations. An in-depth analysis of the history of nationalist xenophobia should therefore also seek to determine what it is that differentiates each of the crises under study. If we accept that the "hatred of foreigners" in its collective forms of expression is but a symptom of the crisis of a given social formation, it is pertinent, from a scholar's perspective, to focus the analysis on strategically decisive areas in the evolution of a crisis, either because these are places where the lexicon and the thematic of xenophobia are elaborated (for example, nineteenth-century parliamentary circles, or the liberal professions in the 1930s), or because they crystallize social discomfort in general (for example, schools in the 1980s).

The Construction of the "National"

The Dreyfus affair is a culminating point of the xenophobic movement that emerged in the early 1880s. Numerous studies have shown that anti-Semitism found an echo among all groups affected by the Great Depression and by the restructuring of society that it provoked. Rather than review these well-known books in detail, I find it more useful here to describe this conjuncture as a "foundational" moment in the history of parliamentary democracy and political xenophobia.

Until the 1880s, the perception of the Other was not generally based on a definition of the "national." Numerous studies have shown that in the middle of the nineteenth century, a "foreigner" was still regarded as someone who did not belong to the local community: a Belgian (or usually a Flemish) citizen in northern France, a Piedmontese in the southeast, a native of Auvergne in Paris, or even a "*blanc*" (as the mountain dwellers of the Massif Central who worked as temporary laborers in the factories of the valley were designated) in Saint-Etienne (Chevalier 1978; Châtelain 1977; Burdy 1989).

Several factors facilitate our understanding of how the transition from the local group to the national group was carried out in the final decades of the century. There again, lived experiences are essential. The multitude of brawls that pitted workers against other workers during periods of crisis gave the French a concrete idea of what was actually at stake in the foreign peril so frequently decried in parliament. As Michelle Perrot has noted, "incidents with foreign workers created favorable and particularly concrete conditions for the crystallization of nationalism. Through the everyday rivalry with immigrants, workers became conscious of the very existence of foreigners" (Perrot 1960). Moreover, the vicissitudes of "international relations" were the direct cause of hatred in this period. In 1881, the "Marseilles affair" originated when members of the city's Club Nazional Italiano whistled at French soldiers of the Vincendon brigade returning from Tunisia (where Italy and France had conflicting colonial claims). In 1894, the assassination of President Carnot by an Italian anarchist generated riots in Lyons and in several other French cities. These assaults on foreigners were often carried out to the tune of the French national anthem, "La Marseillaise," and accompanied by the waving of the tricolor flag. What must therefore be explained here is the relation between traditional popular violence and the novel definition of it provided by new powers of universalization (such as the press or parliament).

The example of *Le Petit Marseillais* shows that until the end of the Second Empire, the local press displayed little interest in "foreigners." Because of their small size and limited circulation, their impact on public opinion was limited anyway. This situation was completely transformed in the 1880s by laws liberalizing the press, by improved standards of living, and by technical progress in the publishing industry. Given the fierce competition between daily newspapers, the only way to succeed was to attract the readers' interest. Very soon, however, it became apparent that the miscellaneous news items conceived as "the drama that could someday happen to you" were successful in this respect. For each morning edition, reporters had to find something to fill the column. Brawls between foreign workers came to be looked upon as a godsend. Jean Vidalenc has noted that under the July Monarchy, xenophobic movements against English workers, which filled countless police reports, went almost unnoticed in the press of Normandy. In 1881, the events taking place in Marseilles took on national dimensions. Not only did they make the headlines of *Le Petit Marseillais* for several days, but other newspapers, both national and regional, feasted on them. Even as respectable a newspaper as *Le Temps*, which was cautious on the issue of foreigners because of its ties to the industrialists involved in labor recruitment, devoted an increasing number of articles to the issue of immigration after 1885.[19]

Parliament, that other mainstay of the modern democratic system, is the second major player in the emergence of a national definition of xenophobia in the late nineteenth century. This question is important and deserves close attention. As Michel Offerlé (1985) has shown, this was the period in which the principle of universal male suffrage was genuinely implemented. It is too often forgotten that what has now become a routine voting procedure only gradually emerged as a "natural" fact of political life. To delegate one's voice and small parcel of power to representatives, who are elected to speak in the name of voters, did not seem natural at first; an army of "professionals" pooled extraordinary resources of imagination to generate mass support for their programs. Furthermore, universal suffrage revealed its limits once all obstacles to it had been lifted. Not only did it fail to produce miracle solutions to society's problems, but it soon became apparent that "educating" citizens did not necessarily lead them to make "reasonable" use of the democratic vote. This is made evident in the popular success enjoyed by someone like General Georges Boulanger, whose "American-style" campaign raised electoral participation in Paris by 10%. Perhaps the general should be thanked for having been the first to demonstrate in practice that the "pedagogical arguments" (appeal to "reason" and to "class interests") so dear to republicans are not sufficient, in a system of parliamentary democracy, to generate mass participation. Because the system rests on the dispossession of the majority, it tends to encourage the techniques of manipulation described earlier: playing on fantasies, on "experience," on things familiar. To put it differently, we might say that the great discovery of the late nineteenth century was the key role played by "feelings of belonging" in the expression of political choices. If the nation is to be perceived as something else than an abstract entity governed by a small circle of specialists, it must be articulated by notions that are more familiar to the masses. It is true that the legal transformations undertaken at the time, which were discussed in chapter 2, played an important role in this process. To be a "national" now meant to have specific rights and interests, which became stakes in everyday life. But the political operation that consisted of making the national abstraction more concrete required other means. Until then, people from popular sectors of society had identified for the most part with their local environment, defined as a space of mutual familiarity (*interconnaissances*). The passage to the national echelon required a process of delocalization of feelings of belonging, in order to make an unmeasurable and unfamiliar space more palpable to ordinary citizens. Political strategies were adopted in discourse as well as in practice to produce mediations and interconnections between the family space (the home), the regional (local) space, and the national space. Studies of this period all show that localism and regionalism are not incompatible with national identity but, rather, should be seen as its incarnation.

Since national propaganda must be translated into practice in order to be efficient, the visibility of foreigners must be fostered. As Jacques Néré noted, the inaugural act in this respect was undoubtedly the famed Pradon Report submitted to the Chamber of Deputies in February 1888. Pradon innovated by outlining the motives that identified foreigners and Germans as a threat to national security. His report was also an impassioned plea for the genuine statistical registration of the foreign population in France, which led soon after to the August 1888 decree. "The simple act of taking a census of foreigners," wrote Jacques Néré, "and the publicity that surrounded it served only to further attract the public's attention to this issue, in a sense to officially state the problem, but without providing a solution or even claiming to do so" (Néré 1959, 90). This key moment in the process of officializing the problem of foreigners was welcomed in republican circles. In the region of Toulon, for example, "the Republican Circle of Mourillon warmly congratulated the president of the Conseil for the decree concerning foreigners, a measure aimed at preserving the interests of the country while offering broad hospitality to honest workers of all nationalities" (NA F7 12585).

That an increasing number of legislative proposals were directed against foreigners following the publication of the 1888 decree demonstrates that the "machine" was sufficiently well-greased to function by itself. The issue of foreigners became a political problem in the sense that politicians had integrated it into their power agenda. First, a bill to curb the rights of foreigners was a practical way to show voters that they were being taken care of. An examination of candidates' preelection statements shows that proposals to protect the labor market against foreigners, particularly those made by working-class parties, spread swiftly among voters (Barodet 1880–1914). The political use of miscellaneous news items involving immigrants was a means of using "reality" to influence parliamentary debates. The events of Aigues-Mortes were cited to announce the gravest catastrophies to deputies who were not inclined to vote in favor of a given anti-immigrant bill. Congressmen would read out loud, if possible with a trembling voice, a pathetic appeal from a French worker deprived of work by foreign competition. These new techniques rapidly became routines of parliamentary life. Yet it must be emphasized that the political agitation surrounding these questions was not simply the "translation" or the "reflection" of the interests or aspirations of voters. Despite sporadic outbreaks of xenophobic violence and the endless polemics surrounding this issue, it is not clear that the question of foreigners was a central concern among workers during this period. A study published shortly before the outbreak of the First World War estimated that foreign competition was in fact a problem only in a few border zones and in marginal sectors of the labor market (essentially the building trades and public works) and that it was more of a preoccupation among elected officials than among workers (Gemähling 1910). The examination of the files containing responses to the 1884 survey on the economic crisis, some of which were directly written by workers, supports this argument. Even in border regions such as the north, although some answers displayed hostility to immigrants, most were either surprisingly moderate or outright indifferent. Clearly, however, the problematic was imposed on those surveyed by the formulation of the question itself. Whereas an identical survey conducted in 1848 made no reference to foreign workers, the 1884 questionnaire explicitly evoked the problem of immigrants' "responsibility" in the crisis (see in particular NA C 3336; NA C 3367; NA C 3371).

The gradual development of parliamentary political techniques and the role played by programs that attacked foreigners are key characteristics of the crisis of the 1880s. The fact that nationalist xenophobia contributed to the elaboration of "solutions" to the crisis should, however, not be underestimated. The conclusion of the Dreyfus affair also ended the anarchy surrounding the political positions taken by the right and the left, particularly regarding the national question. From that moment onward, there was a right-wing and a left-wing approach to the "problem of foreigners," each with their distinct vocabularies and proposals. A tradition was born that would influence later generations' responses to crisis periods. Moreover, mobilization against foreigners played a key role in the construction of the national space, whose broad contours were defined in parliament during this period. As we saw in chapter 2, the entire policy of the welfare state was organized around the principle of an internal border separating the French from the non-French. Criteria of national belonging became fundamental in the process of "splitting up" the labor market into areas that were either off-limits, accessible to, or strongly suggested for those who were not members of the "club." Notions of "national sovereignty" and "government administration," which are extensive and easy to manipulate, emerged as the most widespread means of legitimation. Foreigners had already been deprived of access to administrative jobs, which were reserved for French citizens; but the same tendency now gained ground in the sphere of liberal professions as well. Lawyers invoked an 1810 decree to exclude aspiring foreigners from their trade. In 1892, following a strong mobilization of the medical establishment, doctors succeeded in having their colleagues who had not earned French degrees declared unfit to practice; the system of equivalences was eliminated; dentists and midwives won the same advantages. Working-class positions in government-run trades were increasingly reserved for French citizens in the name of "national security." This problem appeared most clearly in the railway industry. In 1888, the director of the Compagnie d'Orléans demanded that his workers prove their French nationality. Those who were not yet French were required to become naturalized or to leave. While this critical sector of the economy obtained a series of advantages (job security, retirement pension funds), at the same time most of the companies involved purged foreigners from their staffs (Bernard de Jardin 1899).

Did You Say "Liberal" Professions?

The crisis of the 1930s was by no means a founding moment in the invention of political arguments against foreigners. On the contrary, the polemics, the lexicon, and the techniques of mobilization used simply drew from the arsenal of the previous crisis period; the difference was that the party system was now in place and the parliamentary machine was well in gear.

To illustrate the specificity of this particular crisis, let us examine the role played by two liberal professions, those of jurists and physicians, in xenophobic mobilizations. During this period, these two social groups made virulent attacks on foreigners, and they were at the center of a shift in public opinion that culminated in the Vichy regime. Once again, the problem here is not to judge their behavior but to try to understand the social mechanisms that led them astray. Hopefully these professions, which now pride themselves in leading the struggle for human rights throughout the world, will have the courage to analyze this recent past themselves.

In this case as in others, the main cause of intolerance was the excess of people graduating with degrees, due to the difference in economic conditions between the educational and the professional stages of their careers (the former in times of economic expansion, the latter in times of crisis). This made it extremely difficult for newcomers to the liberal professions to establish their own practice. In addition, refugees with intellectual backgrounds sought to recover the social positions they had enjoyed before their exile. The elite suddenly found itself confronted with foreign competition, which prior to that time had affected only the popular classes. The reaction of lawyers exemplifies the typical forms of mobilization that characterized this social group. There was no need to go on strike or to resort to violence against intruders. The "bureau of relations" was sufficient, and its efficiency was guaranteed. On 19 June 1934, to block access to the trade for three hundred young German refugees who finished their studies that year, the Union of Young Lawyers backed legislation that would revise the 1927 Nationality Code. Debated in parliament only a few weeks later, the bill was passed (with even the Socialist vote) and the law promulgated one month later, on 19 July!

For lawyers, the problem was not to keep foreigners out; they had been using the 1810 decree for years to that end. What was at stake here was the exclusion of naturalized citizens. That is why the main provision of the 1934 law was to impose on all naturalized citizens wishing to obtain public service jobs a ten-year internship from the moment of naturalization. Lawyers (as well as notaries), who were well-represented in parliament and who had a monopoly on legal expertise, could make and unmake the law as it suited them. Accordingly, they did not leave it at that. The entire jurisprudence that followed the July 1934 law served only to extend its exclusionary power. The Council of State even resolved to exclude naturalized citizens who had performed their military service in France. What is more, the Council of the Order of Lawyers, dominated by the Parisian bar, rejected the applications of citizens naturalized prior to 1934, hence producing a retroactive interpretation of the law that went against the entire French legal tradition and yet was confirmed by the Court of Appeal in Paris. Today, statements published in the press by this body often begin with this ritual phrase: "The Council of the Order of Lawyers at the Court of Appeal in Paris, in keeping with its mission of defending human rights . . ."[20] Evidently, this loyalty was not exempt from exceptions. To keep refugees and well-to-do youths from colonized countries[21] out of the legal professions, jurists were the first group in France to flout the human rights of naturalized French citizens.

This attitude was not specific to the legal realm. "In almost all professions, graduates without a practice or without work tended to league together, using the most fallacious pretexts, to prevent naturalized foreigners from collecting the fruits of their work and of their education," wrote one journalist in 1935.[22] Doctors, for example, behaved similarly as a group. In their case, however, the techniques of mobilization were different. They could not act with the same discretion by directly manipulating legislation, even though physicians were also well-represented in parliament. Their stategy was the opposite of that adopted by lawyers: They used their profession's prestige to mobilize public opinion. Their key argument consisted of invoking "the interests of the public." Was not the health of the French people at stake due to the invasion of the field by incompetent aliens? Lobbying groups, foremost among them the Academy of Medicine, campaigned for several years through petitions, press communiqués, solemn appeals, and the like. Yet the data indicate that the percentage of foreign physicians was negligible. According to figures published at the time, the total number of physicians in France rose by two-thirds from 1901 to 1930 (from 15,900 to 26,200), illustrating the congestion of the crisis years. In 1930, however, the number of foreign doctors did not surpass 750 (of whom, to be sure, 530 were established in the department of Seine). Clearly, the "invasion" argument was simply a pretext. Foreign students enrolled in medical schools, however, were much more numerous: from 960 in 1909, their total number rose to 3,780 in 1930 (most of them of Romanian, Russian, or Polish origin).[23] In Nancy, foreigners represented over half of the total student body; they represented 39% in Strasbourg and 32% in Paris. Most, however, returned to their native countries after graduation, and the government has always sought to attract foreign students as a means of displaying to the world the prestige of "French science."

The medical field essentially protested the government's prerogative of granting deserving foreign doctors the right to practice in France. The issue was raised in each period of crisis. French physicians had attempted to change the situation as early as the July Monarchy. The Ambruster Law, passed in 1933, was a step in their direction. Foreign citizens were henceforth prohibited from practicing anywhere within French national territory. Students were still not satisfied, however, and in 1935 massive strikes occurred, during the course of which a Jewish student was lynched. With active support from the nationalist political group Action française, young French physicians demanded the same "advantages" as lawyers. Since the notion of "public service" was stretchable to anyone's liking, they wanted their profession to be included within its framework. A new law was passed, requiring naturalized citizens who wished to practice medicine in France to go through military service and imposing a five-year waiting period before they could apply for a public service medical job (Schor 1985; Ayoub 1937; Gervais de Lafond 1934).

Beyond the purely corporatist aspect linked to the nationalist closing off the medical and legal professions, the xenophobic campaigns led by these liberal professions were especially important because of the strategic social role they played, especially at that time. It is safe to hypothesize that they contributed substantially to the hateful vision of foreigners that spread to the society as a whole. Physicians—some of whom would defend the most racist theories, such as Berillon's "ethno-chemistry" in 1920 or René Martial's "anthropo-biology" in 1942—used the prestige of their science to present immigrants as plague-stricken, as responsible for epidemics, as overcrowding hospital beds to the detriment of French patients; all of this with the Academy of Medicine's blessing. Similarly, to defend their corporatist interests, lawyers went as far as to violate the traditional principles of French law, paving the way for the anti-immigrant policies of the Vichy government. Indeed, the same men and the same social groups turned out to be the most adamant supporters of the regime. Laws on denaturalization and the persecution of Jews capped ten years of campaigning for privileged access to available positions.

Immigrants in School

Recalling this rather unglorious past "relativizes" (to the extent that such a word is even appropriate) present-day xenophobia. Perhaps because we now know (whichever side we happen to be on) where such a logic of hatred of others can lead, perhaps also because the outcome of previous periods (with various corporatisms excluding foreigners from the most lucrative positions) has not been questioned; and, finally, perhaps because the most recent waves of immigrants (Vietnamese boat people or Tamils, for example) present little threat to doctors or lawyers, the most explicitly xenophobic discourses are limited to marginal sectors of public opinion. Foreigners have always been widely used as convenient scapegoats for expressing grievances, among the poor or among individuals having suffered a loss of social status as a result of the crisis; and for ambitious people with few scruples about methods, political careers can be forged on this pernicious terrain. Clearly, however, to broad sectors of public opinion in the 1930s, many of the opinions articulated by the present-day far right seemed obvious.

To explain the radical transformation of French lawmakers' attitudes toward immigration from the 1950s onward would require a detailed, in-depth analysis. Today, the role of the Council of State often consists of restraining the government's zeal, rather than the other way around. In November 1977, it disavowed in a single decision no fewer than seven ministerial memoranda considered unfair to immigrants. A year later, the council blocked key measures of the government's family regouping policy. In 1980, the Constitutional Council rejected the administrative internment procedure on the grounds that it violated the principles of the Fifth Republic.[24] Whereas in 1934 the procedure to revise the 1927 Nationality Code took less than ten minutes, with a quasi-unanimity of votes in favor (and despite the gravity of new dispositions taken against foreigners), current reform projects meet with such resistance that defending them is often detrimental to the very political interests of their authors.[25]

Physicians have also radically changed their attitude toward foreigners. An official report on the health of immigrants, written by an eminent professor, perfectly illustrates this change of tone. Authoritarian policies and forms of coercive control are rejected as useless and dangerous to human dignity (Gentilini et al. 1986). Moreover, it is safe to say that television has contributed to forging a new image of immigrants. In a brief research stint in the archives of the National Audiovisual Institute, I examined the content of television programs dealing with immigration (not including explicitly political topics). I found the producers quite sincere. Many of these documentaries are shown in the afternoon and therefore reach a large audience of women from the popular classes. Two themes prevail in these shows: the desire to present the diversity of "cultures" characterizing immigrant populations (with a predilection for those from Africa) and an expressed interest in "social problems," particularly those experienced by the second generation.[26]

This insistence on the issue of the children of immigrants reflects a dominant tendency in the discourse on immigration produced by the current crisis. Because the place where this discourse originated and became established remains the schoolroom, the issue deserves particular attention.

The massive presence of foreign students in French schools is nothing new. In the late nineteenth century, there were as many as 200,000 immigrant children under the age of fifteen, and nearly 300,000 under twenty; most of them were concentrated in the border departments of northern and southeastern France. Under the Second Empire, the flow of Belgian immigrants into Roubaix led the mayor to push for new schools and more teachers to greet their children (Reardon 1977). In the interwar period, there were an estimated 300,000 foreign-born children from six to thirteen years old in the primary school system,

260,000 of whom were enrolled in public schools (or 7% of the total, compared with 9% in 1980). The concentration that we see today in the eight most important academies[27] already existed in the 1950s. Foreigners made up more than one-third of the children enrolled in primary schools in Alpes-Maritimes, one-fourth in Bouches-du-Rhone or Herault, and 10% to 20% in northern and eastern parts of the country.[28] At that time, however, even people who expressed their concern about the "future of France" were not particularly concerned about schools. On the contrary, with respect to primary schools optimism reigned. A simple list of quotes asserting (without proof) that French public schools successfully performed their assimilating role would fill an entire volume. Moreover, the children of immigrants received boundless praise for their intelligence. Prior to the First World War, the theme was already familiar:

> Our study of children of Frenchmen and those of foreigners with similar economic and social backgrounds indicates that the latter are of superior intelligence.... Schoolteachers with whom we talked were remarkably unanimous, despite the distance separating the three cities under study and their distinct conditions, in their view that young Italians, for example, were brighter than their French counterparts, more attentive and more respectful. (E. Blanchard 1913, 290)

Studies from the interwar period quote reports by the inspector general of schools that come to the same conclusions (Marcel-Rémond 1928; Mauco 1932). In the earliest studies published by INED, young Algerians in school were still discussed in these terms: "For the most part, they do good work. Many of them are the best in their class. In general, teachers find them studious, attentive, and conscientious." The same judgment was applied to schools in the mining community of Ronchamp (Haute-Saone), where 60% of the students were foreigners (many North Africans) and where the success rate for the *certificat d'études* was 85% (INED 1954, 133–34; Riché 1964).

Beyond the praise itself, what this says is that schooling for the children of immigrant workers had not yet become an issue. Statistics show that in 1930 absenteeism among the children of foreigners averaged 8%, with some percentages as high as 20% for Corsica and 14% for Haute-Garonne. In any case, as the 1939 survey by Mauco and Demangeon indicates, these children's future was all mapped out regardless of schooling. They would become workers or peasants like their fathers. As long as they did not represent a threat to native French youths, demagogy had a free hand and amateur or professional pedagogues could go into ecstasies over their intelligence.

As soon as the children reached the level of secondary education, the situation was not quite the same. In the 1920s, the influx of foreign students in high schools caused the ire of teachers and parents alike. "Concerned by the growing number of these new schoolfellows, individual parents or parental associations have often protested vehemently," one teacher wrote. "They emphasize what they see as the disadvantages linked to the influx of young people whose age or whose level of knowledge often makes the selection classes difficult. Furthermore, their grievances soon found an echo in the most discrete complaints voiced by teachers themselves (Rocher 1928). Series F17 of the National Archives reveals that in 1927, the inspector general devoted a survey to this issue, interrogating the headmasters of Parisian high schools. The percentage of foreign students in the Michelet high school in Vanves was 30%; at the school for young ladies in Saint-Germain-en-Laye, it reached a full two-thirds of the student body due to the many Czechoslovak refugees. "It is clear," wrote the headmistress, that

> the presence of these students in the school's classrooms delays the progress of their French comrades. The level of education at the Saint-Germain-en-Laye high school is perceptibly lower than that of the provincial schools with which we, the teachers and I, are familiar. The result is serious discontent among French families of Saint-Germain-en-Laye and its environs.

In Vanves, according to one school principal, "this considerable influx of foreigners has had many consequences and raises questions with respect to discipline and studying that must be resolved. They are serious, very serious, and urgent."

Yet these high percentages of foreign students were exceptions. While statistics of the education ministry show that in the late 1930s, the Parisian high school academy had the highest rate of foreign students in France, that number was as low as 3.5%. In 1927, there were 7.7% foreigners in the Louis-le-Grand school; 11% in Janson-de-Sailly; 15% in Hoche (Versailles). In these establishments, headmasters' views on foreigners were much more favorable. In Versailles, the high school needed their money to balance the budget. Elsewhere, very often it was their school performance that won them esteem, with foreign students sometimes winning all the first prizes. The true reason for the opposition of parents (among them, many lawyers and doctors) was provided by the headmaster of Janson high school: "Like everyone else, I have heard the complaints of French families about the high number of foreigners. But most of the time, what upsets them is not so much the burden of this presence on the classroom as the competition their own children have to face, particularly in language courses" (NA F17 13954).

During the interwar period, the problem of foreign schoolchildren was inversely proportional to their number. To understand this paradox, we must recall that at the time, for the dominant classes, reproducing privilege only became an issue at the level of secondary education and beyond. Therefore the issue of primary school was never really central to polemics on immigration. Today, the situation is very different. As the sociology of education has shown, the entire school system has become the fulcrum of strategies of social mobility. In 1930, there were a total of 5 million schoolchildren, compared to 14 million today. Whereas before, most lower-class kids expected to gain little from attending school other than a *certificat d'études* leading to a working-class apprenticeship or an office job, today schools generate as many high expectations as deep disappointments. Given that many attribute high dropout rates to the high percentages of foreign students, those wishing to "save their child" from unemployment or the working-class condition seek to flee zones that are densely populated by immigrants. The study by Alain Léger and Maryse Tripier of schools in the Grésillons district of Gennevilliers illustrates both parents' strategies to have their children attend schools of a "higher standing" and discreet requests by teachers to be sent to "easier" areas (Léger and Tripier 1986).[29] Those who could not afford the luxury of choice found themselves increasingly ghettoized by these massive departures, fueling resentment against a system that gave them no opportunities; that such feelings were taken out on immigrants is not surprising. But that the issue of schools has become a central problem in the current crisis is also due to the fact that, unlike in earlier periods, it now affects an ever expanding spectrum of professional categories. Today psychologists, sociologists, and advisors of all sorts contribute (not as individuals but as institutions) to the process of relegating the children of immigrants to the most subaltern sectors of the labor market, a process that in the past had occurred "by itself" because of the impervious barriers separating different groups in society. Most members of these professions are quite aware of the contradictory aspects of their social function. Perhaps it is a feeling of guilt that motivates the often sordidly realistic tone they use to describe the "problems of the second generation": high dropout rates, the fact that they are torn between two cultures, and so on. Yet the most serious statistical studies available on the subject tend to contradict these statements. Immigrant children and native French children of the same socioprofessional category perform equally well in school, unless (and this is becoming increasingly rare) they arrived in France too late to get a perfect grip on the spoken language (INED 1982; Fradet and Boulot, in *Les Temps Modernes*, 1984). The problem with treating the children of immigrants as special cases is that it contributes to a form of categorization (typical of "substantialist" rather than "relational" approaches to immigration) that can have very harmful social effects. The key merit of the INED study on this issue is that it reveals the absence of fundamental differences between the success rates of French and foreign students, founded on strictly national criteria. At the same time, the very fact of taking seriously the category "children of immigrants," particularly in the questionnaire submitted to teachers, on which the survey was based, is a means of constructing difference. By asking participants to discover a "reality" that until then did not exist as an objective category, the study invents a problem. Clearly, many teachers seemed puzzled over how to define the second generation. Should harkis, the children of French immigrants, and those of overseas territories be included? What about the "semi-foreigners" who have no idea what their nationality is? This might, many scholars have argued, be interpreted as "proof" that the statistics are erroneous and that categories should be changed or revised to fit closer to the sociological reality. A century after the "invention" of immigration, ideal conditions exist for the "invention" of the second generation.

Six

The Reconstruction of France

Of the "non-us" in the "us," of the nonindigenous *in the* indigenous, *of the non-national in the national.*

Abdelmayek Sayad, 1983.

And yet are we justified in speaking of the French *on the threshold of a so-called history of "France," and in continuing to discuss them throughout this history? Shouldn't we ask ourselves who, in each period, these "Frenchmen" were—and specify whom we call* French *at a given time, whom we exclude from France and how the excluded, the separated French, felt about these issues?*

Lucien Febvre, 1953

We must therefore disavow Yves-Marie Laulan and the Club de l'Horloge,[1] and all those who believe that "today still, to be French is to live on the national territory where one was in all likelihood born, and where one's parents and grand-parents were born" (Club de l'Horlage 1985, 38). Assuming that the expression "to be French" has any meaning at all, it would have to be phrased in much more subtle terms than simply having one's roots in the native soil, having served in the military, or having participated in elections. The contemporary "French being," so to speak, is the outcome of an extended process of upheaval that, for over a century, has gradually transformed the very foundations of rural society under the ancien régime and produced a national, industrial society in its place. It is a question not simply of the emergence of new forms of production or even of new social groups but also of decisive alterations in the "making" of individuals. Immigration was only one component of this massive assimilation process, characteristic of modern industrial societies, which created a "new person."

Immigration: A Solution to the Impossible Industrialization of the Country

The few historical studies that have sought to understand why immigration has been such a long-standing and persistent phenomenon in France generally state the same thing: that foreigners came to "fill in the gaps" created by a population that was declining, either because of early Malthusian behavior or as a consequence of the Great War, which cost over one and a half million lives. Two questions remain unanswered here: What were the causes of France's precociousness in the area of family planning? And if the First World War is to explain all, how do we account for the fact that French industry resorted in an organized and massive fashion to immigrant labor prior to 1914? In earlier research, I attempted to show that the fundamental cause of this French specificity should be sought in the widespread popular reaction against an industrialization process that radically challenged their way of life and raison d'être (Noiriel 1991b). Without reiterating the argument in detail, it is nonetheless important to recall how immigration partook in the painful "birth" of industrial society.

The work of Max Weber, Karl Marx, or Karl Polanyi emphasized that the fundamental problem of all "industrial revolutions" was the wholesale transformation of the economic logic and the value system upon which rural societies rested. The rise of capitalism and the "self-regulated market," Polanyi wrote in 1944, meant that land, currency, and work had to become forms of merchandise, to be exchanged on the market at prices that fluctuated according to supply and demand. From the perspective of social history, this implied the massive expropriation of more or less independent peasants and their transformation into industrial workers who sold their labor for a wage. In this respect, however, recent economic studies have shown that nineteenth-century France did not conform to the "British model" (see, in particular, O'Brien and Keyder 1979), for until the latter part of the century, far from disappearing altogether, the peasantry consolidated its entrenchment in French society. Following Marc Bloch, the famed medievalist, I would argue that some of these specificities can be explained from the perspective of *longue durée*. Indeed, according to Bloch, the earliest signs of differentiation between French seigniories and English manors can be traced to the twelfth- and thirteenth-century feudal rights and, therefore, the power exerted over peasant communities. From the medieval age onward, French rural communities were less amenable to the lord, in particular because it was in the interest of the royal authorities to protect them. In the seventeenth century, the triumph of the court society of Versailles exacerbated the nobility's absenteeism from the land, which was an additional factor extending small peasant property, a widespread form of land ownership long before the Revolution (Bloch 1960; Elias 1982). In the years following 1789, this process underwent legislative consolidation (with, for example, the abolition of feudal rights and the sale of national property), whereas in Great Britain the large manor was already firmly established. Furthermore, the large-scale extension of rural industry in the early nineteenth century provided peasants with a supplementary source of income, which allowed them, even with a minuscule plot of land, to survive and to avoid being uprooted. Until 1850, French society was therefore characterized by the numeric domination of small landowners who participated in industrial activity (mainly textiles) within the framework of isolated local or regional markets. The traditional urban–rural division remained an important reality. The center of the "factory," where the commercialization of products took place alongside more delicate operations such as finishing or decorating, as well as alongside more mechanized tasks, was in the city. Spinning, for example, was centered in the mechanical trades of Roubaix and Mulhouse. Yet cities remained dominated by the world of craftsmen and its long-standing corporative tradition of refined artisanal production for local elites and international trade. Paris, as a result of the centralization process that also began prior to the Revolution, was both the political capital of the country and, because of the existence of a tremendous consumer market, the main point of concentration of craft workers.

These particularities of the French situation explain the political instability that reigned in the government. Struggles between advocates of the ancien régime and representatives of the middle class sought to mobilize this mass of workers, whose revolutionary traditions dated back to the eighteenth century and who, in a single riot, could topple a regime; hence the precociousness of universal suffrage, in which all those who were haunted by this "French habit" of making revolutions saw a means of pacifying society. The ancestral force of the small landholding peasantry also prevented the possibility of exerting "economic violence" against them. The first phase of the "French model" of industrialization witnessed the spread of industrial work throughout the countryside and the entrenchment of craft workers (particularly in mining and metallurgy) in the rural areas. Temporary migration, particularly in the building industry, in which activity was subjected to a high degree of fluctuation, added to this logic. This economic "flexibility" was an important element of French industrial expansion in the nineteenth century. Immigrants were full-fledged participants in this process. They were widely active as seasonal laborers and as workers on the building sites as well as in the new factories, where they were *already* massively employed in the most mechanized jobs (as Reardon has shown in the case of the Roubaix textile mills) or in the least salubrious jobs (like the Sardinians in the Marseilles soap factories described by Frédéric Le Play) (Rearden 1977; Le Play 1859). By that time, immigrant workers were also present in the urban economy. Paris was a necessary point of departure for European artisans seeking to improve their skills through the *tour de France*. Immigrants were also massively present in the most highly skilled jobs created during the first industrial revolution. Prior to the Second Empire, an estimated 20,000 British "technicians" helped the French metallurgical and mechanical industries get off the ground. Napoleon III's popularity at the beginning of the Second Empire can undoubtedly be attributed to the fact that he encouraged a form of industrial development that implied no quantitative extension of the working class. The construction of railroads, the development of public works, and the expansion of the metal-working industry raised the possibility of supplementary income for millions of peasant-workers and contributed to an improved standard of living. Moreover, the places of production and the forms of labor that were not part of this still largely peasant-oriented logic were increasingly reserved for a foreign workforce. For this reason, the Second Empire witnessed an extraordinary increase in the foreign-born population, which doubled in less than twenty years.

Yet the very factors that had stimulated the economy during this period, free trade and railroad development, contributed to the economic crisis at the beginning of the Third Republic. The unification of the market gradually ended earlier patterns of isolation, while at the same time increasing the threat of competition from foreign products manufactured at a lesser cost and unhindered by protectionist obstacles. Furthermore, the weakness of the internal market (due, in particular, to a low level of urbanization, which was in turn engendered by the persistence of the peasant mode) made the French economy extremely dependent on international fluctuations, particularly with respect to the luxury goods that were the specialty of French artisans. In short, as a number of recent monographs have shown, a whole series of factors merged to transform the crisis of the 1880s into a watershed in contemporary French history. It marked the end not only of an economic logic but also of an entire universe centered on the multiplicity of activities and rural entrenchment. While it is true that the French peasantry would continue to be a major social force until after the Second World War, the true driving forces behind industrial expansion from the 1880s onward, those that allowed France to maintain itself more or less in the company of the most advanced nations, were no longer bound to the rural or artisanal spheres. It was toward the end of the nineteenth century that companies acquired juridical status (Ewald 1985) and emerged as units of production in their own right. The rationalization of work, which from that point on would never cease, and the triumph of science and of technology illustrate the extent of this break with the past.

Industrialists, who until then had drawn heavily on the complementarity between agriculture and industry as a source of factory labor, found themselves faced with a mind-boggling dilemma: How could a working class rooted in the world of the factory be "made" and adapted to the necessities of the second industrial revolution on which the economic renewal of the country depended?

In the former textile regions, the stabilization of immigrants that was linked to the economic crisis worked in favor of the settlement of the labor force. Furthermore, the bankruptcy of the traditional system based on multiple activities accelerated exodus from the countryside. It appeared that a process similar to that undergone by Great Britain three-quarters of a century earlier—in which no less than the formation of the industrial proletariat was at stake—had "finally" begun. Yet from the beginning, numerous signs indicated that given the degree of popular mobilization, traditional obstacles would once again steal the show. First, the labor supply was limited by the Malthusianism that had been observed by early-twentieth-century demographers but that had spread to the working class in large industry during the final decades of the nineteenth century, ruining efforts by paternalistic owners to encourage the reproduction of their labor force (Reid 1985; Ducellier 1981–1982; Burdy 1989). Without entering into the debate among experts on the reasons for this behavior, which for a long time was specific to France (Dupâquier and Dupâquier 1985), it is clear that it was also an illustration of collective resistance to proletarianization and displacement. Numerous testimonies and surveys recorded at the time indicate that by controlling birthrates, workers were providing their children with a better chance at social promotion—for example, by handing them a full-fledged patrimony or by encouraging them to acquire educational "capital" (that is, access to skilled or office jobs). As M. Lévy-Leboyer and F. Bourguignon (1986) have noted, between 1872 and 1891 the increase in the number of workers employed in the service sector alone absorbed the numerical equivalent of the entire rural exodus of the period, at a time when everyone complained of the "plethora" of administrational officials and other pen-pushers. At the same time, simply by consulting the company archives of large firms at the peak of innovation, the extent to which the labor shortage question haunted executives becomes clear. From the very beginning of the century, the Pont-à-Mousson company repeatedly attempted to "import" miners, first from other regions of France and later from countries such as Romania or Poland; it even considered, early on, calling upon Kabyles employed in the phosphate mines of North Africa. As the correspondence between factory directors indicates, some very touching efforts were made to understand the "psychology" of these new recruits, to offer them "pleasant" surroundings, to protect them from the jeers and mockery of the good people of Lorraine. Unfortunately, the scenario was always the same: After a few weeks or months, the precious worker chose to flee. Slavery and serfdom having disappeared, other solutions had to be found (Archives of the Pont-à-Mousson Society d. 6795, d. 18715, d. 25655, d. 18202; see also Moine 1987).

The saturation was particularly serious in heavy industry (mines, metallurgy, chemistry, electrochemistry of the Alpine valleys, and so on). Arduous tasks that worker-peasants had been willing to perform in order to remain peasants were now turned down because they represented the bottom of the ladder in the industrial world. Furthermore, these industrial zones were often isolated from urban centers, not only for geographic reasons (the location of sources of energy and primary materials) but also for historical reasons. The very concessions that the owners had made by allowing the labor force to retain a rural base became a major source of inconvenience when the logic of the "modern" (that is, the industrial and urban) world triumphed. As a result, not only were mining or metallurgical companies unable to secure adequate labor power, but what is more, the skilled workers that they had gone through so much trouble to train deserted the closed universe of their childhood in massive numbers, seeking work in companies that belonged to the other pole of the new phase of industrialization: mechanical construction. Not only was work in these industries less arduous and more skilled, but they were also better located (in the suburbs of large cities, particularly Paris). Although the First World War lifted the labor shortage to a desperate level, depriving French industry of roughly 10% of its prewar labor force, it was not the structural cause of the unbalanced French labor market.

To understand how, despite these handicaps, immigration played an outstanding role in French industrial achievements, the issue must be placed within a broader context. As Karl Polanyi argued, all European nations were confronted with the ruthless constraints of the "great transformations" that, in the space of a few decades, thoroughly upset conventional equilibria. Each country (or, rather, the ruling class of each national state) had to invent, according to its own specific history, the means with which to give birth to the new world. In the British case, the formation of the working class preceded the establishment of parliamentary democracy, confining the victims to such collective forms of expression as group organization, demonstrations, and strikes (Thompson 1975). In France, the weakness of the political system born out of the Revolution led to the early adoption of universal male suffrage. As Alessandro Pizzorno has noted, parliamentary democracy can be understood as a solution to a problem of social discipline by channeling previously disorderly and unpredictable opposition into codified, established forms of expression. While this avoided social chaos, the new rules of the game also forced leaders to accept a compromise with those whom their mission was to represent. As Polanyi (1944) cogently argued, then, as long as the right to vote was confined to small circles of society, state intervention remained limited. With the advent of universal suffrage, however, the interests of political representatives themselves were at stake, creating a constant need for reforms (Pizzorno, in Birnbaum and Leca, 1990). Following the well-known analyses of Albert Hirschman (1970), several studies have emphasized the possible relation between the displacement of populations (in Hirschman's words, "exit") and universal suffrage ("voice"). In Germany, for example, the lack of political democracy left the discontented with only one option: emigration, in other words, "voting with their feet." The desertion of skilled workers was a handicap for the German economy, to such an extent that Bismarck established the welfare state in 1883 not only to counter the expansion of the Socialist Party but also as a concession aimed at retaining skilled labor. This concession was quite successful, since trans-Atlantic migration diminished sharply over the next few years (Kunhle 1981).

In the French case, new forms of political expression did not have as much effect on emigration as on immigration. "Voting with one's feet" took on the aspect of a "strike of the stomach," that is, of demographic Malthusianism. At the political level, the originality of the French case was that parliamentary democracy was established prior to the great industrial upheavals. This is one of the main reasons behind the famed "bottlenecks" of the Third Republic. Despite the labor needs of large industry, elected republican officials had to make numerous concessions in order to give the new regime a solid foundation. First, the Méline laws stopped the massive rural exodus that had shaken the previous decades. Second, and more important, the legitimacy of the Republic depended more than ever on the true expression of the fiction of social equality; hence the key role of the educational system in the social "promotion" of the "sons of the people." To this day, no one has adequately explained by what stream of social magic a majority of peasants were able to remain on their lands while the middle class grew considerably, in the midst of demographic stagnation and without hampering the operation of large factories.

This is where immigration came into play. As the labor market became unified, traditional divisions (between regional markets, between city and country, and so on) gave way to new segmentations that are incomprehensible unless viewed in light of the new parliamentary logic that produced them. In an earlier chapter, we saw that xenophobia in the 1880s and 1890s was essentially an expression of the need to "protect the national labor market." Republican legislation, the work of citizens defending the interests of citizens, quite "naturally" excluded foreigners from the privileges granted by the welfare state and reserved even more areas of employment for nationals (public administration, liberal professions, workers in the public sector). Administrative measures of control over immigrants were added to this important legal procedure for channeling immigrant workers toward sectors in which there was a labor shortage. This is a good example of how the reality of legal, sociological, and economic processes are closely intertwined, in a way that is totally incomprehensible from a Braudelian or Labroussean perspective of the "economic and social" world.

I argued in chapter 2 that the earliest political program on immigration was presented by Adolphe Landry in 1915 and implemented following the First World War. The essential fact is that legislation on identification cards and on administrative and police control were key components of the strategy implemented by the state and large industrialists to direct immigrant labor to precisely those areas where workers were needed. The greatest financial, material, and political recruitment operation undertaken following the war was orchestrated in heavy industry by the Ironworks Committee and the Central Committee of the Coal Mines. Increasingly strict legislation concerning identification cards, corruption, and breaches of contract was intended to prevent this labor force from fleeing these repulsive zones. The 1920s were therefore characterized by a sizable segmentation of the industrial labor market. The least valued jobs were found not only in heavy industry but also in agriculture (as a result of the break with the earlier economic logic, the number of French agricultural laborers diminished sharply), as well as in construction and public works, areas that were also affected by the constant decline of seasonal activities. Some immigrants managed to overcome the obstacles and move from these sectors, for which they were initially recruited, into other areas. The booming transformation industry, for example, benefited both from the transfer of skilled immigrants from the old centers of the first industrial revolution and from the flight of unskilled foreign laborers, who had been recruited at high cost by heavy industry. The fact that these peak industries were often located in cities also allowed them to incorporate traditional artisanal know-how by developing a multiplicity of small subcontracting firms, which left the descendants of craftsmen from the earlier period with an illusion of independence. The legal or customary reservation of some types of activities for French workers established other divisions. This was the case, for example, in the universe of small firms, where a closed-shop policy allowed a "trade" to survive, such as the book trade, the tanneries of Annonay, and many other small sectors of activity located in small provincial towns. Workers in the service sector (in the railways and dockyards, for example) enjoyed the same type of protection. The final "isolate" worthy of mention is the textile industry, which was divided between the world of traditional worker-peasants (as in the Vosges) and the now stabilized universe of mass immigration from a previous period (as in the northern region, where the Belgian second generation was a key component of the skilled labor force).

The crisis of the 1930s in turn provoked a massive settlement of unstable workers in the basins of heavy industry and in the suburbs of the mechanical industry. From the Popular Front onward, the hegemony of "state" workers, who were also French, was challenged by the second generation of workers in large industry, dominated by the new elite of the Parisian-region metallurgical workers. The second generation of immigrants played a role in this trend toward the homogenization of the working class, which was also a movement toward integration.

Therefore, with the coming of what might be called the "third industrial revolution" in the 1960s, characterized by the automation of work, new immigrants were once again channeled, often with the same administrative and police methods, toward the least valued sectors of activity. These were, as always, unskilled tasks (agricultural labor, construction work, insalubrious activities), but they also included the most repetitious tasks, tasks that were introduced on a massive scale by the standardization of production (notably assembly line work in the automobile industry).

This very cursory presentation is sufficient to underscore one essential point: The number of immigrant workers present in a country at a given time does not in itself prove their economic importance. If the electoral logic of numbers is not confused with the logic of scientific explanation, what counts is the level of production at which they are situated. There is, in this respect, an obvious contrast with the U.S. example. In the United States, an extraordinary wave of immigration occurred at the beginning of the twentieth century, which submerged the different components of industrial work. Then, in the early 1920s, once the demand for labor had been satisfied, restrictive laws reduced the number of arrivals to a level that was proportionally very low. In the French case, by contrast, from the Second Empire to the present day the labor market consistently absorbed an immigrant labor force evaluated at roughly 10% to 15% of the working class. However, for political reasons unimaginable in the United States, where "freedom of enterprise" was taken to its most literal extreme, in France state intervention regularly directed immigrants toward the most strategic points, which, in any given period, conditioned economic development as a whole (the mechanized textile industry in the nineteenth century, heavy industry in the early twentieth century, standardized production today). In those sectors, foreign workers, although they were often statistically underestimated,[2] always made up a considerable percentage of the workforce. Furthermore, their importance must be evaluated over two generations, since corporate strategies for introducing foreign workers were also (until recently, at least) strategies of reproduction, as workers passed from deskilled to skilled levels of the workforce.

Immigration is not, of course, the only factor that must be considered in explaining the "French path" of modern industrialization. The important role played by small subcontracting firms, the economic importance of the luxury industries (such as high fashion), and the important reliance, until recently, on worker–peasant labor (transported by bus and train) must also be taken into account, as must the technological investments that, in any given sector, helped overcome the shortage of labor. Yet it is important to stress the role of immigration here, because whereas in the United States the phenomenon is taken for granted, in France it is absent from the literature on economic history. We find the same historiographical contrast with respect to the question of social mobility. Though U.S. historians may disagree on the role it played, few would question the reality of immigration as a key factor in the forms of upward or downward social mobility that developed in the United States. In France, however, the intellectual production on this issue is close to zero. Consequently, it is difficult to speak in terms of a "French model." Yet several observations deserve consideration. Mass immigration undeniably served the interests of the French people. Studies have shown that in areas where population renewal was strong, the local "nucleus" established prior to immigration took advantage of this evolution by occupying the elite positions and becoming traders or land and real estate owners.[3]

Furthermore, although this is difficult to measure statistically, immigration undoubtedly led to a process of substitution "from below," with the most recent arrivals occupying lower rungs on the ladder and the older immigrants or Frenchmen moving onto the higher ones. Available sources clearly illustrate the replacement, from the 1880s onward, of French seasonal laborers (essentially highlanders from the Alps and the Massif Central) by unskilled foreigners in agriculture and public works (Burdy 1989; Châtelain 1977; Gavignaud 1983; Bélanger 1958).

Each subsequent industrial transformation provoked a reorganization of the hierarchy of valued–devalued jobs and led to a flight by French workers that was compensated for by immigrant labor.[4]

On the whole, it can therefore be said that the reliance on immigration helped allay the shock of industrialization, so much so that the French example may be a case of Karl Polanyi's ideal gradual transformation, smooth and without entailing a traumatic break with the past. The main problem, of course, is that the two "Frances" have always coexisted. For the "French," peasant-based countryside, the exodus toward the cities (which was an extended process, as studies on the late nineteenth century, the interwar period, and the post–Second World War period have shown) often produced upward social mobility in the form of a direct transfer from the primary to the tertiary sector (Ariès 1971; INED 1964, 1981). The entire political and juridical establishment discussed earlier must be kept in mind when we discuss, often with the complacency of representatives of this group, the "sons of the people who made up the elite." In the model of upward mobility over three generations that is part of the republican mythology as well as of its reality (the brilliant student of the *grandes écoles* whose grandfather was a peasant and whose father was a railway worker, schoolteacher, or post office worker), the most important passage may be the one from peasant to public sector employee, an initial opportunity that immigrants were automatically denied.

On the other hand, however, it should be noted that the weight of legal criteria in defining individuals made naturalized workers full-scale players in the republican game. It is true that all the forms of labor market segmentation we have mentioned and the corporate strategies for reproducing the immigrant labor force prevented Frenchmen of foreign origin from reaching full equality by the second generation, particularly in areas located far from major urban centers. Nonetheless, they were never penalized by any legal form of exclusion outside the economic realm (except under the Vichy government). Furthermore, as in the United States, each new wave of immigrants pushed the preceding wave forward in the social hierarchy. The factorial analyses illustrated in Figure 3.2 reflect this point for the first generations. It is true that upward social mobility was greater for those who became French. I found this to be true in the north of Lorraine, where northern and central Italians, the most long-standing components of the foreign labor force, took advantage of the arrival of Poles, Algerians, and Portuguese to gain access to skilled jobs in the intermediate sectors of the craft industry, commerce, and so on. Another example is the Aveyron coal basin, where early Spanish immigrants, despite the fact that they originated in the mining areas of the Asturias, took advantage of the massive influx of Poles in the 1920s to abandon the mines. "They preferred to work in factories, or to set up as artisans and small shopkeepers" (Garcia 1959). It should be noted that immigrants, in their search for social mobility, benefited from the delay suffered by French industrialization. In sectors such as the building trades, for example, low levels of urbanization and the key role played by temporary workers (such as the masons of Creuse) impeded the development of a solid, structured working-class environment. Here as well, the end of rural migration as an important component of industrial activity accentuated the shortage of labor. Belgians in the north or Italians in the southeast were able to benefit from this rupture in the process of social reproduction by gaining access to an upwardly mobile path in which the bottom level was the job of mason and which often culminated in access to a position of ownership in small or medium-sized businesses.

It should also be mentioned that the "gift" of immigrants to French peasants (who escaped rural exodus thanks to the influx of foreigners) was in many ways a two-edged sword. Indeed, everything seems to indicate that the royal path to upward social mobility over several generations depended on gaining access to the urban market. By delaying the crucial moment of exile to the city, millions of French peasants did a disservice to their children, who today find themselves swelling the ranks of specialized workers, particularly in the western part of the country where factories came to them, so to speak, in search of the "rural labor source" that France possessed in the 1960s—one of the few European countries to do so. This delayed access to modernity, which illustrates all the contradictions of "popular resistance," explains why in the iron and steel factories of Lorraine, second-generation Italians exerted hegemony over the labor movement (and not only in the factories). Rural workers brought in by bus from the countryside of Meuse are often employed in the least-skilled jobs and excluded from local working-class culture (S. Bonnet 1965).

France Made Richer

"Work That the French Refuse to Perform"

We may now begin to answer the questions raised in the introduction regarding the immigrants' contribution to French society, not only with "benevolent feelings" but with arguments grounded in fact. Everything that has been said up to here confirms that in France's case, the issue of immigration is inseparable from the process of industrialization. It is this process that allowed the country to preserve its rank on the international scene, whereas many observers in the late nineteenth century had predicted its irremediable decline.[5] Some day, this reality will have to find its way into history textbooks. It is estimated that immigrants recruited since the Second World War have built the equivalent of one out of every two homes, 90% of the country's highways, and one out of every seven machines (Mauco 1977). Their contribution in earlier periods has never been evaluated, particularly in the 1920s when France was one of the foremost producers of iron ore in the world, with a labor force made up almost entirely of foreign workers. How many billions of kilowatt hours, how many hundreds of millions of tons of charcoal, steel, and laminated products were produced? Prior to 1914, in the mechanized textile mills, how many tons of cotton and wool were machine produced? In thinking about immigrants' "contributions," however, one cannot approach the problem in exclusively numerical terms. Immigration restored the flexibility that the French economy had enjoyed in the period of "multiple activities" and that it had subsequently lost as a result of the rigidity of the rationalization of work. Whereas the economically active French population, in particular due to its political power, was characterized by its sedentary ways and its obstinate attachment to the tertiary sector, the foreign labor force, which was deprived of political as well as professional rights, was capable of adapting to all conjunctures and to all labor markets. In addition to what has been said, I would add, along with Michael Piore (1979), that these immigrant "birds of passage" were a godsend for all those who profited from the secondary labor market, in which work was fluctuating and machines were worn down. We know that it is through the underground economy, which frequently characterizes this type of market, that the clothing industry, for example, was able to maintain its international standing. France, which had previously imported caps, began exporting them late in the nineteenth century, thanks to Jewish workers from Central Europe (Green 1985). The instability of foreign workers even worked to the advantage of large companies. In order to lower the cost of reproducing the labor force in the mines, management relied on the family composition of their workers, most notably through housing. For example, in the mines of Languedoc, as elsewhere, owners sought to stabilize Spanish or Italian miners by housing them in projects with their families, for, along with the miner-peasants of the surrounding villages, they represented skilled or potentially qualified personnel. Kabyle "bachelors," on the other hand, were parked in barracks because their primary role was to remain "available" for intermittent work assignments according to demand (Santucci 1977).

Another undeniable advantage of foreign labor from the point of view of French capitalism was that it kept production costs low. Because they could not express opposition other than by fleeing, this part of the working class was always restricted to those sectors where wages were lowest and working conditions most difficult. The success of textile industrialists in the north (for example, the Motte family) was in part due to the availability of an abundant and docile Belgian labor force (Lentacker 1973). In a similar vein, it is impossible to speak of the legendary power of the ironworks committee without mentioning the easy profits made at the expense of immigrants, particularly in the iron mines, where not the slightest effort at mechanization or improvement in the quality of life was undertaken until the Second World War. The studies carried out by economists for the recent period indicate that the industries where profits are the highest are also those that employ the greatest proportion of immigrant laborers. A number of spectacular success stories in the building industry attest to the truth of this observation (Beaugé, in Talha 1983).

To this we might add the savings, in terms of labor reproduction costs, achieved by the host country. French economists have long emphasized the profits that national industry gained from the massive employment of a ready-made adult labor force, which would return home with the first signs of aging (Didion 1911; Oualid 1929). Recent studies have also shown that, contrary to xenophobic claims, social security, retirement pension funds, and so on actually benefited from the presence of foreign workers (Cordeiro and Verhaeren 1977). Until the latest crisis, not only did the expulsion or "spontaneous return" of hundreds of millions of foreign workers ease the burden on welfare funds and assistance bureaus, but it also helped France avoid a social crisis as deep as the one that Germany experienced (Mauco 1932).[6] Conversely, in periods of strong expansion, when economic necessities required the immediate concentration of thousands of workers in a given area, importing "bachelors" and housing them in lodgings (or even, as during the 1920s, in barracks) represented considerable savings over the cost of decent housing for French workers and their families.

All of these points, of course, require more in-depth research. It might also be argued, as Georges Dupeux (1980) has done, that the massive reliance on foreign laborers was a handicap for French industry because it slowed the process of innovation and technological investment. This thesis is illustrated by the example of Pont-à-Mousson. Because of the advantage its low wages gave it over its main European competitors, the company there did everything to hinder the major innovation represented by the centrifugal machine, for replacing humans with machines would weaken its position in the market. There were other inconveniences as well: Because of cash transfers, a significant portion of wages paid in France were not reinjected into the national economy, thereby accentuating the narrowness of the consumer market represented by the foreign population. Another problem, observed by Claude Meillassoux (1975), was the brutal increase in reproduction costs in the phase when immigration was stabilized. Whereas in periods of expansion, costs were extremely low due to instability and the abundance of bachelors, at the very moment when a crisis began, stabilization transformed the composition of the immigrant population by displacing its center of gravity toward nonproductive individuals (women, children, and the elderly).

It must be stressed that industry was not the only beneficiary of immigration. Agriculture itself, in many regions, survived only thanks to foreigners. Abel Châtelain estimated that by the end of the nineteenth century, the cultivation of flowers and the gathering of olives or lavender in Provence could no longer do without Italian seasonal laborers and sedentary agricultural workers. The same was true of beet cultivation in the north, the vineyards of the Languedoc, and other agricultural areas. According to studies carried out during the interwar period, desertification itself was avoided in many regions only thanks to the arrival of agricultural workers from neighboring countries. The myth of the deep-rooted French peasant with a strong attachment to his land should not hide the fact that some regions, such as Gascony, were completely depopulated following the First World War. The abandoned lands were gradually becoming fallow. In this climate of abandonment, the peasants who had remained suffered from lack of motivation and innovative spirit. Everyone recognized that the arrival of Italian settlers breathed new life into the agriculture of the southwest: Village populations increased, lands were brought under cultivation, innovative cultivation techniques were introduced, and French peasants were stimulated as a result; the region regained its prosperity. Why is this never mentioned when the foremost agricultural department of France, Gers, is lauded for its performance (Marcel-Rémond 1928)? The agricultural survey conducted by Mauco and Demangeon suggests that the southwest was not alone in this case. The correspondent from the north spoke of the Belgians in these terms: "The numerous immigrants display neither the routine nor the preconceptions of peasants who have lived in the community for a long time. As a result, they readily adopt new means of improving the soil and operate the latest machines. They make good use of fertilizer, and their fences are made of reinforced concrete." In another village, "over the past fifteen years, they have transformed the land into pastures. They purchase livestock and raise it in fields that are transformed into prairies. The acreage of prairies has doubled on foreign-owned lands." In many villages of the Var, it was Italians who introduced irrigation. They innovated by focusing on milk production in stock farming, and they reintroduced sheep farming. Thanks to them, forestation was maintained (Mauco and Demangeon 1939, 432, 545). The example of Provence deserves particular attention, given the tendency of the mythological Provençal to distort historical reality. In Gardanne, "over a period of a hundred years, a population of pure Provençal race has become a cosmopolitan mixture based on Italo-Provençal cross-breeding." Of an inventory of surnames made in the 1950s, 30% of the surnames were French, 49% were of Italian origin, 10% were Armenian, and 9% were Spanish (Sabran 1973, 100). Even in rural Provence, Bernard

Kayser's analysis of the village of Valbonne reveals that from 1872 onward, the French population dropped irremediably, but that this decline was overshadowed by a continuous flow of immigrants from Italy. The study of surnames indicates that "the census of 1702 counted seventy-three patronymics for 1,059 people. Twenty-one of these remain (in 1946), but they represent only 108 people." According to the author, the fact that the structure of the village had undergone little change concealed the extent of the demographic transformation. Its form and activities remained the same, and its social groups continued to be divided up between large landowners, cultivators, and day laborers. Only by the study of migration, the author argues, can "a better assessment be made of the degree of contemporary transformation undergone by a village whose external appearance (use of the soil, population total...) makes it seem traditional and immobile" (Kayser 1954).

This example illustrates the fact that immigration's contribution to society was first and foremost a question of numbers. Behind the word "French," a genuine substitution of individuals occurred, an extraordinary transformation of lineages and genealogies that, in France more than elsewhere, renders such slogans as "*La France aux Français*" (France for Frenchmen) ridiculous. A survey directed by the Dupâquiers of families whose surname begins with "Tra" shows that as early as the turn of the century, 2,000 of the 3,000 families identified in 1803 had ceased to exist, from a patronymic point of view. All the available records illustrate the obsession of demographers and intellectuals from all spectrums with the decline of the French population prior to the Second World War, due to the limitation of births that no political measure seemed to affect. This decline was compensated for not only by the influx of first-generation immigrants but also by the fact that whatever the period, foreign populations initially displayed a fecundity that was the opposite of the Malthusian French birthrate. From the late nineteenth century to the Second World War, there were years in which the increase in French population was exclusively due to foreign births. Even before the last major wave of immigration in the 1960s, "true" Frenchmen had become a rarity. Without immigration, the French population would not have surpassed 35 million ten years ago (Mauco 1977).

Immigrant workers were called in to compensate for population deficits and to make up for the historic failings of the French economy.

Immigrant workers largely fulfilled their "contract." The preceding pages have shown that their achievements far surpassed the expectations of those who had lured them. Yet it is a mistake to reduce this "contribution" solely to its economic aspect, as is often done. Indeed, the entire spectrum of French cultural history over the past century has been enriched by immigration.

Illustrious Men and Women

We could begin by naming just a few of the foreign-born persons who left their mark on the history of France. In politics, the nineteenth century is the most interesting in this respect, perhaps because the political "marketplace" had not yet been structured along rigid nationalist principles. William Henry Waddington, naturalized at the age of twenty-three, eventually became president of the Conseil and minister of foreign affairs. Marie-Edme Mac-Mahon was of Irish origin. Baron Georges-Eugène Haussmann was born of a German family from the electorate of Cologne. The early part of the Third Republic were marked in particular by such "Italians" as Léon-Michel Gambetta, the son of a Genoese merchant, and René Viviani. In the military sphere, there was General Maxime Weygand, a Belgian who became naturalized after his passage through the academy of Saint-Cyr.

The academic world was represented in particular by Jules von Mohl, born in Stuttgart, a professor in the Collège de France, and a member *de l'Institut*; Georges Cuvier, of Swiss origin, whose brother Frédéric was also a member of the Institute as well as the perpetual secretary of the Academy of Sciences; the chemist Matthieu Orfila, who was dean of the Faculty of Medicine of Paris and an influential political figure under Louis-Philippe; he arrived in France on a scholarship from the Spanish government. We might also mention Zénobe Théophile Gramme, one of the discoverers of electricity, a Belgian artisan who had migrated to Paris; and of course the Polish-born Marie Curie, Nobel Prize winner for her discoveries on radioactivity. We also know what French colonialism owed the naturalized explorer Pierre Savorgnan de Brazza, son of an Italian earl.

Many other foreign-born intellectuals left their marks on French thought. The philosophers Henri Bergson, Emile Meyerson, and Jankélévitch were of Polish origin. The historian Funck-Brentano, who was director of the Arsenal library, was a native of Luxemburg. André Castellot, famous for his books on the queens of France (which contributed significantly to the popular mythology of French history), is a Flemish Belgian naturalized French.

Many writers also came from abroad. Paul Verlaine was of Belgian lineage; Guillaume Apollinaire came from Poland; José Maria de Heredia was a native of Cuba. The Comtesse de Ségur was the daughter of the governor general of Moscow. Emile Zola was the son of an Italian engineer. More recently, French literature has produced quality works by Romain Gary, Joseph Kessel, Emmanuel Bove, Henry Troyat, Georges Pérec, and many others. François Nourrissier once wrote, "Metchnikoff, Diaghilev, Chagall, Stravinsky are in a sense the honor of France," to illustrate the extent to which a country could be culturally enriched by practicing an open refugee policy (Nourrissier 1950, 78).There was also a close relationship between different artistic revolutions, particularly in painting, and artists of foreign origin: Camille Pissarro, born in the Danish Antilles, for impressionism; or Pablo Picasso, of Spanish origin, for cubism.

French musical tradition owes much to Jacques Offenbach, a naturalized Frenchman of German origin; to Ignaz Joseph Pleyel, also of German origin; and to Arthur Honegger and to Maurice Ravel, whose parents were Swiss.

The world of show business largely reflected this diversity. In the circus in particular, which was marked by the Bouglione family, who arrived from Italy in 1834; but also in contemporary cinema and theater. Ariane Mnouchkine was born of a Russian father and a British mother. Sarah Bernhardt was of Dutch origin. Jean-Pierre Mocky had Polish parents. Actors such as Michel Piccoli, Yves Montand, and Serge Reggiani were of Italian origin. Charles Aznavour, Alice Sapritch, and filmmaker Henri Verneuil represent the Armenian second generation, and Isabelle Adjani represents the Algerian second generation. Numerous pop artists have foreign backgrounds. Serge Gainsbourg was the son of a Russian émigré; the comedian Coluche had roots in Italy.

Finally, before ending this brief and very incomplete overview, some mention should be made of the world of sports, which was largely enriched by Italian immigration, whether it be in rugby (Spanghero), auto racing (Pironi), tennis (Noah, a native of Cameroon), or, especially, soccer. This last example, which represents a genuine form of popular chauvinism, deserves closer attention. In a series of articles published by *L'Equipe*, Didier Braun estimated that of 660 players who have made the French national team, nearly one-third were either foreigners or came from French overseas territories. In 1935, for the first time, two naturalized Poles bore the Gaul rooster on their uniforms. In 1950, a survey showed that the Poles represented one-half of the registered players in the Nord–Pas-de-Calais region, and 10% of professional soccer players. The popularity of soccer epitomized the culture of second-generation miners, drawing elements from their national origins as well as from their working-class condition. It represented their only hope to "make it" socially, to become integrated within the French community, and to satisfy a desire for social revenge.

Thirty years ago, nearly one-third of professional players playing for first-division teams came from the northern basins of heavy industry and from the eastern and central regions of France; the fatal crisis that these regions have suffered today has lowered the percentage to 16%. In the mining community of Colonne-Ricouart (Pas-de-Calais) for example, Wizsniewski, Budzinski, and Synakowski were all born on the same street. The three of them were selected no less than a total of fifty-seven times to play on the French national team. In central France, tiny mining villages such as La Combelle in the basin of Brassac (population: 200) produced many professional players, with "Italians" contributing as many as the "Poles." Such prestigious figures as Piantoni, Masnaghetti, and Piumi came from the iron mines of Lorraine. Di Lorto, Di Nallo, Repellini, and many others reflect the contribution of Italian immigration to sporting activities in southeastern France. Indeed, the French national team today genuinely reflects the "melting pot" of the French working class. After Raymond Kopa (whose real name was Kopascewski and who came from the second generation of Polish miners in the north), Michel Platini, who symbolized the "French game" (supposedly shrewder and more intelligent than the purely "physical" German game), became captain of the French team. Among his grandparents, one finds the immigrant from Novare in the Piedmont. The same is true of Battiston, Bellone, Ferreri (Italian parents); Giresse (whose Spanish mother immigrated to southwestern France prior to the civil war); Manuel Amoros (the son of a Spanish laborer in Languedoc); Luis Fernandez (a native Spaniard, naturalized French, from the suburban neighborhood of Lyons known as Les Minguettes); Tigana and Touré (both natives of Mali). Including players from French overseas territories, this adds up to two-thirds of the present-day French team. In a game against "true" native French players, the odds would be easy to predict![7]

To list names in this fashion is meaningful only if we show how the foreign origins of such illustrious figures influenced contemporary French civilization. Yet these examples are often used to illustrate the opposite thesis: the "mystery of the transplant" evoked by Maurice Barrès, in other words, the time-worn thesis of the "French nation's capacity for assimilation."[8] The thrust of this argument is that the framework established since the French Revolution has enabled immigrants to merge into the French crucible without altering the fixed nature of French identity. Sociologists such as S. N. Eisenstadt argue, on the other hand, that societies characterized by massive immigration display a pluralist cultural model (Eisenstadt 1954). Which of these hypotheses actually fits the French case?

Pluralisms

Let us begin with the easiest aspects. In many cases, intellectuals of foreign origin brought with them elements of their native culture, which they integrated into their work, thereby contributing to the making of French culture. Notwithstanding stereotypes regarding the "Slavic spirit," music and literature of Polish origin can be described as consistent with this scenario.[9] French jazz also owes a lot to the exile of African-Americans in the 1920s, and the "culture of tango" is a typical product of the Argentine exile community in Paris. As far as film is concerned, what we regard as the contemporary "French touch" owes a lot to the somewhat forgotten figure of Lotte Eisner, a German refugee in the 1930s who played a key role in founding, along with Henri Langlois, the *Cinémathèque française*. It was thanks to her that the French public was exposed to the wealth of German expressionism (Palmier, in Badia 1982).

This cultural exposure is, to be sure, more a characteristic of Paris than of France in general. Paris has always prided itself, almost to the point of snobbery, on its intellectual and artistic cosmopolitanism. At a less exalted though perhaps more meaningful level, such a popular sport as soccer was, as we have seen, enriched by foreign immigration. As Braun wrote in the series of articles mentioned earlier, "French soccer should thank this century's immigration a thousand times. Just as soccer in all countries is the expression of the cultures from which they were formed, its roots were nourished by the Latin,

Slavic, and Afro-Antillean game."[10] We will see later how these remarks can be articulated with Marcel Mauss's thinking on the "techniques of the body" as well as on the nation. In all of the industrial regions that were heavily marked by immigration, even in cases where the flow has stopped, "traces" clearly survive. "Still today," wrote Danièle Ducellier, "scores of tiny details in the basin of Blanzy point to a Polish presence that, while nowadays quite discrete, was clearly once important" (Ducellier, 1981–1982). A study by Jan Gruszynski in northern France, confirmed the observations made twenty years ago by Raymond Boudon's team about the influence of Polish models on the French population in places where the latter was a minority. "By interacting with Poles, the French adopted some of their ways, good or bad: their celebrations, their hospitality, their way of drinking alcohol, cursing, an interest in gardening, evening dances, and social life" (Gruszynski 1977, 405; Boudon 1963). Similarly, my own research on Lorraine shows that there was an "Italian way" of being a steelworker and a member of the French Communist Party. As we saw in chapter 4, this was a key aspect of the resurgence of voluntary associations.

It would therefore seem that the so-called framework of France, into which foreigners were simply expected to become integrated, was less rigid than is often assumed. It is true that the French language has long been institutionalized, and the linguistic contributions of recent immigrant communities are weak. Yet we would have to include within this heritage the contribution of foreign surnames, which has reduced the number of the French named "Dupont." Also, according to some scholars, foreign ways of speaking influenced regional dialects or patois. One physician in the 1920s wrote that massive Italian immigration to Provence had produced a "mixture (that) can even be felt in local patois, which is very different from the Mistralian tongue" (Imbert 1926). This is yet another topic of study that would certainly rejuvenate the field.[11]

It is clear that immigration exerted its influence even upon such codified and traditional realms as religion. As we will see, just as in politics, the outcome was contradictory. On the one hand, immigration produced a clash with tradition that led to a decline in religious practices. On the other hand, however, as Gérard Cholvy has observed, immigrants sometimes contributed to a religious awakening among Italians. In the mid-nineteenth century, many of them peddled rosaries, statuettes, and the like. There are many indications that the "culture of saints was influenced by immigrants" (Cholvy 1982).

Moreover, the "crisis of religious vocation" that accompanied the dechristianization of French society was partially solved by the arrival of immigrants. Many young Poles and Italians entered Catholic seminaries during the interwar period. Accordingly, the bishop of Paris was a self-defined "Pole from the *butte Montmartre.*" The same is true for the Jews, who also felt the effects of republican secularity in the late nineteenth century. In this case, the arrival of Central European and North African immigrants partially compensated for the decline of religious practice (Hyman 1979).

Fundamentally, then, the role of the history of immigration in the formation of the present-day "French identity" suggests that the framework of the nation proved less rigid than is often assumed. The delay in industrialization explains why all of the new structures associated with it (forms of labor, spaces, institutions) were not established prior to mass immigration to France. This point is illustrated by the question of urbanization. At the national level, the second industrial revolution took place within a specific space. Industrialists' need to forge a working class (which did not exist in the nineteenth century) explains the exceptional durability in France of the spatial organization associated with paternalism: the small mono-industrial town, made up of typical industrial working-class houses with small back yards. This intermediary space between the city and the village was a concession to the hundreds of thousands of rural immigrants who accepted settlement only on that condition. Conversely, however, as many studies show, paternalism—which in the late nineteenth century had been completely discredited by an extraordinarily combative labor movement—got a fresh start thanks to foreign immigrants who in many ways resembled the uprooted French peasants of the second part of the preceding century. The world of working-class housing projects, which as a result of the crisis in large industry is disappearing before our eyes, typifies the spatial organization of interwar immigration; this explains why in France, unlike in the United States, immigration and urbanization cannot be superimposed. Where there was a clear relationship between the influx of foreigners and the development of major cities, we observe another element unique to France: the spatial reflection of the delayed history of industrialization. Marseilles is, in this regard, a good example.

The large size of the population should not obscure an essential fact: In the 1920s, the city was not a city but, rather, a juxtaposition of poorly articulated "villages." Certain downtown streets did not even have names. Today, the urban space has been filled; it took shape with successive waves of immigration that augmented and transformed the original population (Peraldi 1986). In the case of the Paris region, building plots took on great importance between 1900 and 1930. There again, suburban urbanization coincided with the period of massive immigration. It might be argued that this peculiar situation contributed to the integration of immigrant communities, who (to some extent) were free to organize their living space as they pleased, with all the symbolic effects discussed in the preceding chapter. This situation undoubtedly favored the development of single-family homes and contributed to the low proportion of large buildings. It is partially for this reason that Marseilles never became Chicago. For a "street corner society" (Whyte 1943) to emerge, there at least have to be streets and corners.[12]

Even if he had limited his study to the rural world, such a lover of material traces as Fernand Braudel might have noticed the impact of the foreign presence. It is to be hoped that some day, an expert in rural archaeology will study the form of villages rebuilt by Friulian settlers of the southwest or by the Piedmontese in Provence. Such a study might start from the collective survey directed by Mauco and Demangeon. In Périgord, for example, the Italian farmer "modified the local barn-stable, which he found difficult to use and poorly ventilated. Rather than placing the livestock face to face in two rows from one end to the other of the stable, he preferred to have them stand back-to-back, head against the wall, facing mangers made up of wooden feeding-troughs fixed against the wall or on the ground. In this way, a barn-stable may hold one-third more heads and be easily ventilated by the main corridor without endangering the animals" (Mauco and Demangeon 1939, 634).

To conclude this portion, we now turn to the ways in which contemporary French political life has been transformed by mass immigration. I will not reiterate here my earlier analyses of this problem (Noiriel 1986, 1991b). Nor can I, for lack of space, tackle the question of the influence on French parliamentary traditions of the native cultures of politicians whose parents were foreigners. Some scholars, for example, argue that the parliamentary rhetoric of the Third Republic was enriched by the "typically Italian" volatility of someone like Gambetta or, especially, Viviani, who greatly impressed their contemporaries (Nourrissier 1953). Benjamin Crémieux argued instead that Italian refugees under the July Monarchy who assidiously attended parliamentary debates, such as Cavour, were strongly influenced by French political culture, so much so that "one witnessed, during the first legislatures of the Italian parliament, the same gravity of intonation, the seasoned irony that remain a trademark of eloquence under Louis-Philippe" (Crémieux 1936). This points to another problem for historical research, which is to measure the effects that immigrants' temporary residence in France had on the culture of their country of origin.

Getting back to France, it is doubtful that the political commitment of certain foreign-born activists was motivated by the internal problems of French society alone. For example, it was said that one of the causes of Gambetta's vehement opposition to Napoleon III was that he had descended "from a long line of Genoese partisans" with a "hereditary hatred for the Corsican," a hatred that he, in a sense, projected onto the emperor's nephew (Coulon 1911). Two fundamental issues are important here: (1) the relationship between political activity and loyalty to one's origins; and (2) the relationship between "political tradition" and mass immigration.

The first point is worthy of special attention. Paradoxically, Sartre's analyses in *Anti-Semite and Jew* (1948) and traditional American theories of "assimilation" (Gordon 1964) converge in suggesting that there is but one means of being loyal to one's past: that is, to maintain the culture of the group of origin and its values, by claiming either the "authenticity" (in Sartrian terms) or the "ethnicity" (in the vocabulary of American sociology) of that group. As we have seen, what defines above all the immigrant experience (for the first as well as the second generation) is a social relation, a "conflict" in Simmel's sense of the term, between a subaltern culture of origin and a dominant host culture. The important thing, however, is the socializing role of conflict, the lasting mark it leaves on the individual personality. There are, then, a number of ways to be "authentic." One might, of course, unconditionally defend one's community of origin, but it is also possible to reinvest the "meaning of rebellion" produced by stigmatization in other causes that pit oppressors against oppressed.

The latter definition of loyalty to one's origins provides a way to understand the specific contribution that French citizens with an immigrant background have made to political life and beyond. Sartre contended, for example, that French Jewish intellectuals had always expressed a passion for the Universal, "to fight the particularist conceptions that set them apart. Of all things in the world, reason is the most widely shared; it belongs to everybody and to nobody; it is the same for all. If reason exists, then there is no French truth or German truth" (Sartre 1948, 111). What this analysis tells us is that the inclination of many French Jews for intellectual activities is not always a consequence of cultural "traditions" linked to their origins; rather, it should be seen as a response to xenophobia. Defensive strategies with respect to stigmata can, Sartre believed, be much more complex. Bergson's anti-intellectualism, for example, which invalidates demonstration, is seen as a form of debaptized rationality. It illustrates the "supreme defense of the persecuted: to attack in order to defend oneself, to conquer the irrationalism of the adversary on its own ground—that is, to render it harmless and assimilate it to constructive reason" (Sartre 1948, 116–17). Given that for Sartre, an "inauthentic" Jew abhores violence and dreams of a community founded on the Social Contract, this analysis can be applied to Durkheim as well. As we saw in chapter 1, Durkheim's paradigm of the institution and the "instituted" can be understood as a gigantic effort to integrate Maurice Barrès's theory of "heredity" into a conceptual logic that does not exclude anyone on the grounds that they cannot claim a genealogy deeply embedded in the land.

It is not the purpose of this book to question the legitimacy of this argument. Yet it points in a possible direction for research seeking to establish what French culture owes to the diversity of its origins, even within a logic of denial. What is being discussed here is not really "Jews" but stigmatized individuals in general. While those individuals may often have been Jews, in most cases, particularly in France, they were foreigners. In the literature produced by writers with foreign origins, one can find (often anticipated) illustrations of Sartre's analyses. In a novel by Henry Troyat (1958), a second-generation Russian character chooses to undertake scientific studies precisely because the language of mathematics knows no boundaries; one and one add up to two in all countries of the world. This attitude among intellectuals, which consists of fleeing literary disciplines (in particular history) to avoid facing national subjectivities, is quite similar to that of Southeast Asian refugees who choose to live in the towers of the thirteenth arrondissement because the buildings are not overburdened by history.

It is not difficult to make the link to politics. If Jews do indeed seek universalism and dream of a Social Contract, it is not surprising that they should be uncompromisingly loyal to the French Republic. Can this reasoning be applied to immigrants in general? The answer may be yes. Rather than seeing Zola's attitude during the Dreyfus affair as a kind of particularly successful "strategic coup" (Charle 1977), would it not be more appropriate to discuss his Italian origins, which were also questioned during the period of intense xenophobia in the 1880s? This may suggest another way of being "authentically inauthentic" (or vice versa): remaining loyal to one's origins by combating not just overt anti-Semitism but xenophobia against foreigners in general, including against Italians, all of this by loyalty to the memory of the father.

The same basic principles would help explain the frequent involvement of second-generation representatives in causes that defend the stigmatized rather than an "ethnic" or "national" community: the political struggle within the labor movement of course, but also the struggle for "human rights," the struggle to defend drug addicts, the handicapped, and so on. It would not be difficult to demonstrate that "French generosity" owes a lot to people whose origins were outside of France.

Until now, we have limited our survey to the role of individual. What about social groups? For Peter Berger and Thomas Luckmann (1971) the stigmatization of children, for example, is a phenomenon that affects individuals but that has no structural consequences for society; the social base that would facilitate the transformation of a personal problem into a collective issue, capable of producing new institutional forms, does not exist. Again, while it is true that in the French case, immigrants were never able to mobilize collectively around principles of "ethnic" or national identity, in many instances stigmatization functioned as a "principle that generates practices" (Bourdieu 1990), contributing, for example, to the renewal of the French labor movement. Of course, very often industrialists took advantage of massive arrivals of immigrants to fan existing rivalries within the labor movement. In all periods, the image of the immigrant as a strikebreaker was partially justified. As I have indicated elsewhere, demographic change, the rationalization of work, and massive immigration were the three fundamental causes for the profound demobilization and transformation of working-class traditions that occurred in the 1920s. Given that this evolution was in some ways similar to what the U.S. working class had undergone twenty years earlier (Montgomery 1979), we might compare the French case to analyses that show that during the stabilization period of the 1930s, the values of immigrant workers in the United States changed rapidly. Aware of the fact that they would never return home, many sought integration within their new world, which led them to adopt significantly more combative stances on labor issues. In France in the 1880s, Italians were the most active participants in the strikes that shook the French building trades. Similarly, Belgian activists, taking advantage of the experience of an earlier labor movement, established class-based trade unionism in the regions of the north. In Lorraine and in Marseilles, Italians, as a result of their massive mobilizations in the mines and on the docks, became known as "*gréviculteurs*" (harvesters of strikes). During the interwar period, foreigners were responsible for the development of the French Communist Party in several regions. In recent years, immigrants have played an active role in strikes among skilled workers. All of this is a reflection of the stabilization process I described earlier (Perrot 1960; Reardon 1977; S. Bonnet and Humbert 1982; Kergoat 1978; Le Conte 1908). But the "French" tradition also involves systematic repression (at least up to the 1960s) of foreign labor activists. Since they have always been deprived of voting rights, most of them were reduced to silence; to avoid being expelled or turned back, they had to suppress the violence they felt as a result of xenophobia, injustice, humiliation, and difficult working conditions. Yet because of the forms of reproduction of the working class implemented by the industrialists, the children of these immigrants tended to share their parents' same world; they were skilled workers, but they were now fully French, with the right to vote and to strike. This, in my opinion, explains why political opinions were so often transmitted from the first to the second generation. The loyalty to one's origins is expressed here by the violence of practices of collective struggle and by a massive vote in favor of those parties that appeared, locally and depending on the period, to be the most "radical." Naturalized and second-generation Belgians formed most of the social base of Jules Guesde and the Parti Ouvrier Français in Roubaix as of the 1880s.

From the 1930s onward, and particularly during the 1950s, many localities that elected Communist officials, often following decades of right-wing government, had been completely transformed by immigration. The communities of the Briey basin in Lorraine may be an extreme case of this; but in the sixteenth industrial arrondissement of Marseilles, in Chalette at the periphery of Montargis, or in Sallaumines in the north, the same correlation can be observed between massive immigration in the 1920s and steadfast loyalty to the French Communist Party following the Second World War (Barou 1987; Bachelard 1978; Dubar et al. 1982). Often, although this was never explicitly admitted (in accordance with the logic of denial), elected officials often had immigrant origins themselves. The Communist Party in northern Lorraine was dominated until recently by politicians of the Italian second generation. In Marseilles, recent studies have shown that the "management" of "ethnic support" was an important aspect of municipal policy until the decades following the Second World War. In 1935, a representative of the Italian second generation, a son of a day laborer from Salerno, became mayor of the city. The "Italianization" of Marseilles went hand in hand with a move of the majority of the electorate from the right to the Socialist left (Sportiello 1981). In La Seyne-sur-Mer, even though his name was Merle, the Communist mayor elected in 1947 was also the son of an Italian immigrant. For the majority-Italian electorate, this schoolteacher, who was continually reelected until 1969, was a genuine symbol of working-class revenge (Martinencq 1982). When discussing the shift of southern voters from the right to the left, we must also consider the changes (often dissimulated by the term "Provençal") that occurred in the profile of the population. The same applies to the Savoy region, where several studies have underscored the relation between Italian immigration and the shift of the working-class vote in favor of the Communist Party (Hugonnier 1954). Halluin-la-Rouge, a bastion of northern communism from the 1920s onward, is another case in point. In its leftist period following the war, the French Communist Party issued its local newspaper both in local patois and in Flemish. It used the popular carnival festivities (strongly imbued with Flemish culture) to launch a massive class-based campaign against the barons of the local texile industry. The violence that characterized this working-class culture is due to the fact that "for a long time, the sons and grandsons of these immigrants reacted like uprooted individuals: defense of tradition, allegiance to popular rites and beliefs, and the ghetto complex." The French Communist Party participated in a collective effort to produce a mythology of origins, grounded in an imagined genealogy that claimed rootedness in the land (Hastings 1986). In exchange, the party won the widespread confidence of the population, which *recognized itself* in this discourse for reasons that had nothing to do with the preaching of electoral programs.[13]

Although everything seems to indicate—and xenophobic zealots of all times have made no mistake of this—that there is an important relationship between voting for the left and having foreign origins, it is nonetheless impossible to speak of an "Italian," a "Polish," or a "Jewish" vote, as is often done in the United States. We need more empirical studies to clarify this question. Apparently, immigrants most deeply transformed political traditions in those areas where changes in population and in the organization of space and of work were the most far-reaching; which seems to confirm the analyses put forth by Maurice Halbwachs. When there were enough members of the older group—usually occupying the most influential positions—political continuity was maintained. This favored the Socialist Party in Noyelles-sous-Lens, for example, but also traditional land-owning notables in the villages of Hérault (Dubar et al. 1982; Azas 1981). Furthermore, the desire to conform with local norms in some cases led representatives of the second generation to adopt dominant forms of political behavior. This is another factor explaining some of the "continuities" sometimes observed on electoral maps. More than a solution, however, this raises a problem, for if we look more closely, we can see many of the "stitches" reflecting the patchwork that French "identity" has become.

The French Model

The Power of Democratic National Law

With respect to immigration, France represents a second great model, which can be compared with the better-known U.S. one. Drawing from the main arguments contained in this book, I will now attempt to construct an "ideal-type" of French immigration over an extended period of time. The main difference between France and the United States, and this explains why the phenomenon has eluded historians for so long, is that the French social formation paradoxically combines a full-fledged nation (rooted in history, with a homogeneous population and a rigid political framework) with a history of self-induced massive immigration that fundamentally transformed the initial makeup of its population.

We need not insist here on the fact that the formation of France has deep historical roots. This theme has always fascinated historians. Political centralization was well underway during the Middle Ages. Official deeds were written in French throughout the kingdom from the time of François I. The early creation of the civil status registers upon which the legal identity of citizens (and hence their larger identity) is based, the early unification and standardization of the language, the acceptance of models of court society by the entire provincial elite, all prove that by 1789 the "nation" was indeed a reality. As Maurice Aghulon (1989) has shown, the conquest of peripheral regions was already well underway by that time. When the Republic established its political framework (a centralized state, administrative division by departments, and so on) and its instruments for "interpreting" the social world, whether it be at the linguistic, the statistic, or the archival level, there was no language problem comparable to the opposition between Walloon and Flemish in Belgium, nor was there an "ethnic" problem comparable to the Native American or the black problem in the United States (see chapter 1). To this we might add the solidity of peasant communities: Their ancestral rootedness in the land contributed to the formation of those French "*pays*" so admired by the likes of Siegfried and Vidal de La Blache. The analyses of such authors (for example, the famous "regional temperaments") were derived from such realities and hence were sociologically founded *for their time, placed within the context of a disappearing era*. The very fact that the old society was in crisis allowed them to perceive the originality of the French case at the time, compared to those of Britain or Germany.

The French Revolution, however, added two essential elements for understanding the French model: a passion for politics and the defense of "human rights." As we know, from the nineteenth century to the Second World War, France has been the country that has welcomed the largest number of refugees. In the mid-1970s, France hosted

1 immigrant for every 1,000 inhabitants, a figure comparable to that of the United States. In 1975 the Federal Republic of Germany counted only 0.05 immigrants per 1,000, and Great Britain and Sweden 0.03 per 1,000 each.[14]

The other side of the coin is that the French state has always rapidly moved to impose its laws upon those it has welcomed. As early as the beginning of the July Monarchy, Polish immigrants who had expected so much of the "fatherland of human rights" suffered a setback: They were subjected to meddlesome police controls, and the French state sought to disperse them individually throughout small provincial towns where they knew no one, transforming exile into torture (Sokolniecki 1910). As we have seen, the same tendencies have still been visible in recent years, with the administration striving (with little success) to spread Asian refugees throughout the provinces. This reflects the contradiction inherent in republican ideology and practice: Although it claims to respect the tradition of generosity toward individuals, it seeks to prevent them from becoming political actors outside of the rules established by the nation. Groups defined according to criteria of "ethnic" or national origin have never been tolerated in France. This explains the tenacious denial, which persists to this day, of voting rights to immigrants even for local elections. It also accounts for the obstacles placed in the way of naturalization. That in 1930 only 11% of the foreign population living in France had been naturalized (compared with 55% in the United States) is in part due to the different timing between waves of mass immigration in the two countries, but the main reason was that the French government was only willing to admit fully "assimilated" individuals—in other words, those who ran no risk of upsetting the rules of the national game through their vote—into the "French club." It is striking to note that during the debate on the 1972 Nationality Code, French Minister of Justice René Pleven still used this type of argument to justify the "internship" imposed upon naturalized citizens before they could be allowed to vote.

It is this unrelenting logic that explains why all the advantages associated with citizenship fell upon the second generation, in other words, upon individuals whom the land and institutions of France had supposedly fully transformed into French citizens. Clearly, the republican approach is thoroughly opposed to the "ethnic" or "racial" theories that assume the continuity of the effects of origins over several generations, notwithstanding the effects of assimilating institutions. The hypertrophy of the political in the French case also explains why the government has constantly sought to define a distinct status for refugees, more favorable than that reserved for "economic" immigrants, as if political persecution was the only "excuse" native Frenchmen could accept for immigration. This is one reason for both the high number of refugees present in the country and the imbalance observed in research on the history of immigration. Céline Azas's remark (1981) that of all the Spanish immigrants in Hérault, only refugees have attracted the least bit of interest among scholars—despite the fact that they represent only a small percentage of the total—is true for many other cases as well. Italians are perceived as interesting only if they were "antifascists," and Armenians only insofar as they were involved in the Manouchian affair. Those who could not be included in this category were disregarded altogether. Not only does such disinformation leave out the largest part of the immigrant population, but what is more, it warps political analysis by reproducing preconceived schematizations in the partisan controversies that these events still provoke in present-day France.

The other major issue that must be taken into consideration if we are to understand the uniqueness of French immigration history is the power of the legal system within which it is framed. This power draws its roots from the ancien régime and the interests of a social group that wields considerable power in France: the legal profession. Its natural tendency, as Tocqueville rightly observed, has always been to complicate the law out of professional interest.[15] This characteristic, combined with republican ideology, explains why France is one of the countries in which racial predjudice has been the least pronounced. The enthusiasm of African-American soldiers who visited France during the First World War, discovering a society without racial segregation, is notorious. Many writers have testified, in their own way, to this reality. Stefan Zweig, recalling his stay in France, noted that "in Paris, the Revolutionary heritage remained in the blood." He added: "Who (here) was concerned about our hangups which later became so threatening, race, class and origins?" (Zweig 1943).

If these remarks are true, one might wonder about the exact nature of the historical anti-Semitism in France. Two main lines of argument have prevailed: The first, and the most long-standing, claimed, along with Durkheim, that French anti-Semitism was "superficial" rather than "structural," a simple passing strike of fever. This is more or less identical to Hannah Arendt's approach in her writings on the subject (1951). Recent studies, however, have revealed a country that is viscerally anti-Semitic and that may even have "invented" anti-Semitism as a political technique.[16] These studies, which place too much emphasis on the history of ideas, make the mistake of confusing two aspects of a single problem, which must be fully distinguished in order to understand the national specificities of racism. It is in France, Arendt argued, that the distinction between "Jew" and "foreigner" was the most pronounced. In other words, anti-Semitism was only able to mobilize collective support once it had been legitimated by the hatred of foreigners. In their book on Vichy, Marrus and Paxton (1981) give numerous illustrations of this process. From the German point of view, the French did not understand a thing about the race question (there had even been a black minister in the Vichy government). "The French possess neither racial instincts nor racial consciousness," Ernst Robert Curtius wrote in his *Essai sur la France* in 1932. The majority of Jews who were deported had foreign origins. Even such an anti-Semite as Xavier Vallat firmly resisted German pressure to include French Jews in the extermination program. This is not to say, of course, that they were spared persecution, nor do I mean to minimize the scope of the atrocities committed. Nonetheless, to introduce an analytical distinction between "ethnic" and "national" criteria allows a better understanding of how, in the specific context of each country, barbarism could gain acceptance among so many people. In France, ever since the days of Drumont, Jews had been represented with foreigners' traits (in this case German ones, such as rudeness and a disregard for the French language). The same tendencies resurfaced during the interwar period. To be credible, racism had to draw from the French legal tradition, which individuals had to interiorize through laws, statistical categories, political polemics, and "miscellaneous news items" in the popular press; a tradition that, using the national argument, legitimated the essential divide between "us" and "them."

Immigration in France: An Avant-garde Model?

These past few pages are sufficient to illustrate the contrast between the French and U.S. models of immigration. In the United States, immigration is a contemporary phenomenon of national formation. It has left its mark not only on the mythology of origins but also on the

Constitution[17] and on statistical categories. Indeed, U.S. classifications established a fundamental distinction between "black" and "white" that would last well beyond the Second World War. National origins were identified in decennial censuses by the nationality of one's parents.

"Ethnic" quotas, which the French Republic has always refused to adopt, have therefore been at the center of U.S. immigration policy. In the 1920s, as prestigious an institution as Harvard University implemented an official segregation policy to limit the number of Jewish students (Steinberg 1981). To this day, however, the national identification card and all measures designed to limit individual liberties are unheard of. The Czech refugee Antonin Liehm, editor of the magazine *La Lettre Internationale,* who lived for several years in France and a total of thirteen years in the United States, accurately described the difference between the two models: In the United States, he was never asked about his nationality: "It interested nobody. At the university no one ever asked me what passport I held. This is a great thing for a country and for an exile." On the other hand, he did run up against the logic of "ethnic" society. The Jewish ghetto turned its back on him once it learned that he was not a Jew; refusing to become part of the Czech ghetto, he preferred to return to the Continent.[18]

All of this lends credence to Tocqueville's view that a nation remains forever marked by the conditions of its formation. It would, however, be a mistake to see the French model of immigration as a simple application of the principles defined under the Revolution. Instead, what this book has shown is the scope of the transformation the country underwent during the 1880s. Political leaders borrowed freely from the "republican tradition" to invent immigration in the modern sense of the word, at the price of abandoning some of the principles that were most important to the Revolution's successors: unlimited individual freedom, universalism identifying the individual with the citizen. This may be one of the main factors explaining the difference between the French and the U.S. models, which in the current state of research can only be stated as a hypothesis: The U.S. model may be seen as reflecting a traditional, "archaic" immigration process characteristic of the newer countries, which welcomed immigrants to settle vast and "deserted" lands, to cultivate idle soils, and to operate brand-new factories. France, on the other hand, can be viewed as representing the first case ever of a "modern" form of immigration: One destined not to populate the land but, rather, to satisfy the needs of an industrial system that for political reasons (that is, the existence of a system of parliamentary democracy) could not be sustained by the citizen-producers of the nation alone.

Some may find it surprising that it was André Siegfried (1946) who first articulated such a hypothesis, by defining U.S. immigration as characteristic of a young nation and French immigration, in contrast, as that of an older country. We will discuss later Siegfried's conclusions about the process of assimilation.

More recently, Anglo-Saxon research—particularly the landmark study by Gary Cross (1983)—has taken up this idea of France as a model of the European "melting pot," one-half century ahead of the immigration policies that have now become general throughout the industrialized world. Criticizing explanations framed in exclusively demographic terms, Cross focused on this central idea that France underwent an important process of political and social reorganization in the late nineteenth century, rendered necessary by changes in the system of production and by the problems raised by resistance from the popular classes. Along the same lines, Don Dignan (1981) has argued that the spread of the egalitarian and democratic values of 1789, facilitated by Parisian centralism, generated a "passion for equality," a desire for upward social mobility even in the lowest ranks of society. Demographic restriction, "republican promotion," and massive immigration, he suggested, were three facets of the same issue. For those who like to think in terms of the "advanced" or "delayed" nature of social processes, this would indicate that the political advancement of France explains the delay in its economic revolution, which in turn explains its advancement in terms of immigration. Indeed, the other industrialized European countries underwent a comparable evolution some thirty years later: the spread of democratic values, declining birthrates, and an appeal for massive inflows of immigrant labor when a new industrial revolution undermined the existing establishment. And while the discourse of "human rights" flourished, legal and administrative measures were taken on a broad scale to regulate clandestine immigration, to channel migratory flows, to "terrorize the terrorists," and so on. Nowadays, one finds U.S. experts participating in colloquia to study "French technologies" of immigration control.

If this analysis is justified, we cannot agree with Nathan Glazer's assertion that France, just like other European countries, discovered immigration issues in the 1960s or his call for the "old continent" to turn to the United States for experience. Perhaps representatives of the "new world" would be better advised to examine the French experience more closely. Is not the fact that many French experts themselves remain blind to the diversity of their country's origins sufficient proof of the political efficiency of the French "melting pot"?

Conclusion

Toward a Sociohistory of National Assimilation

The process of integration described in this book brings us to the broader historical question—which historians have yet to truly address—of the "nationalization" of French society over the past two centuries. How can we account for the success of dominant, national cultural norms in supplanting those local and immigrant cultures that were the wealth and diversity of French society? If past responses to this question have not proven satisfactory, it is because historians have held too closely to paradigms and challenges borrowed from the realm of politics. For a long time, they adopted the perspective of Third Republic administrators by boasting of the merits of an authoritarian policy of national assimilation.

Beginning in the 1960s, however, a new generation of social scientists, having experienced the turmoil of decolonization, began denouncing what its predecessors had gone to such great lengths to praise. In doing so, however, they adopted the very presuppositions upon which earlier assimilationist arguments had rested. The process of national assimilation was viewed from a strictly political angle, and the fact that millions of immigrants had blended into the French population was presented as proof that integration had been "forced" upon them. The Jacobin centralization of powers, the confusion of the cultural and the political, were listed as key factors explaining why foreign communities were never able to maintain their "identity" beyond the first generation. In contrast, the United States was described as a decentralized model that respects the autonomy of local groups, facilitating the consolidation of "community-based" or "ethnic" cultures (I myself defended this perspective in earlier publications). Yet as we saw in chapter 4, recent U.S. scholarship has questioned this "ethnic myth" and has shown that it was largely constructed by intellectuals in search of new modes of distinction, whereas all the tangible expressions of the preservation of cultural specificity (such as language, religion, marriage within the community) had clearly declined by the second or third generation (Steinberg 1981). As far as France is concerned, the aforementioned work by André Siegfried (1946) would tend to confirm these analyses. It may seem surprising, given Siegfried's intellectual breadth—no one was better qualified to compare U.S. and French society—that not a single scholar in the ensuing decades found his statements worthy of consideration (or even of criticism). For Siegfried, as far as assimilation is concerned, there is no fundamental difference between the history of the United States and the history of France. In the United States, it took three generations to transform an immigrant into a genuine American. The first generation generally remained foreign. The second was apparently assimilated, in the sense that its representatives "learned English, rapidly became used to no longer speaking other languages, and held their parents in contempt." Yet to the extent that they remained influenced by their origins, their assimilation was incomplete. Only with the third generation was the process fully accomplished. Describing immigration in Languedoc, Siegfried went on to note: "It is interesting to note that the French experience of assimilation was roughly the same. . . . We may conclude that in America as in France, adaptation occurred at the same pace and according to the same laws." Assimilation might even have been more difficult in France, he argued, because it was an old, rigid, "completed" nation, whereas the United States was a young country, by definition more capable of absorbing "foreign elements" (Siegfried 1946). The problem here is not to judge the value of Siegfried's theses or of contending interpretations but, rather, to determine the presuppositions upon which they rest.

By drawing contrasts between the French and U.S. models, this line of argument rests on the assumption that "assimilation" is fundamentally dependant on *policy,* that is, on more or less voluntaristic government measures. Being already successful, assimilation is viewed as unproblematic. This assumption is shared by both defenders and critics of republicanism. According to the former, by generously spreading universalist values through the school system, the Republic "naturally" turns foreigners into Frenchmen; according to the latter, the efficiency of assimilation rests on the constraints (resulting from political centralization and police-state policies) that prevent foreigners from remaining true to themselves. As we have seen, this has been a genuine leitmotiv of French literature on the subject.

Siegfried partially rejected this view, preferring another approach, which might be termed the "ethnicity thesis." According to him, the political structures of the host country are not responsible for the similarity between assimilation processes in France and the United States (which is somewhat paradoxical for the founder of French political science); the determining factor is, instead, the nature of the group of origin to which the immigrants belong. The underlying assumption is that in modern nations, "ethnic" groups enjoy a degree of autonomy with respect to the workings of the state and its organs of power. Family, community life, and "ethnic" characteristics that are different from the dominant traits of the host society are key factors in the reproduction of these minority groups. Siegfried, quite logically, advocates a policy (also defended, as we have seen, by Charles de Gaulle) of "ethnic" selection that privileges northern over southern peoples. For assimilation to be successful, he argues, individuals must be thoroughly uprooted from their group of origin; finally, separating individual immigrants one from another is necessary to prevent the formation of communities.

These contradictory arguments represent a continuation of the debate that in the late nineteenth century pitted Durkheim against the intellectual current that viewed "origins" and "heredity" (sociological rather than biological) as the determining factors in the social world. Do the state and the nation stand outside the family, the group, and the individual, or do they thoroughly pervade them to the point of directing their transformation? This is a key question, which any discussion of "national assimilation" must address, and its implications go beyond the specific issue of immigration. Most current sociological studies (especially those dealing with culture) are faced with these questions: Does the "national" pervade social groups (be they "popular" or "bourgeois"), determining their practices and their habits? If yes, how? Given that French sociologists have complained for more than sixty years about the lack of studies on the "national" phenomenon, the consistency of their unwillingness to tackle these problems is somewhat surprising (Mauss 1969a; S. Bonnet 1972; Touraine 1981; Laacher 1987).

A social history of France can therefore only be cast as a long-term goal. We are not without tools, however, to begin undertaking the task. Although the French university system rejected Norbert Elias in 1933,[1] it is to his credit that most of his intellectual life was devoted to elucidating the mechanisms of French national construction. In his far-reaching analysis grounded in *longue durée,* which Braudel largely ignored, Elias demonstrated the value of comparativism in dealing with these kinds of issues. Having observed that only the French spontaneously understand the term "civilization" in its "universal" sense, and that Germans are unable to translate the emotive meaning associated with the term "culture," Elias sought to demonstrate, through a detailed study of the past, that such differences can be accounted for, not by "race," not by "ethnic particularity," but by history and history alone. To briefly summarize his argument, we might say that Western civilization was a process that emerged in Europe during the Renaissance. In the nineteenth century, "national characters" emerged from this shared past as an outcome of relations between the aristocracy and the middle (or bourgeois) class, which were different in each country. France came to represent the quintessential centralized state. As early as the waning years of the Middle Ages, the monopolization of taxes and public force by the central authorities allowed the pacification of society, a necessary precondition for the development of civilization. It was in court society, which reached its zenith at Versailles under Louis XIV, that codes of proper conduct, which gradually spread through French society and beyond, were elaborated. The key element in this process was the *interdependence* between increasingly long chains of individuals. The relations of necessity by which people were conflictually united, given the weight of norms and the cruelty of social judgments, forced them to control their urges, to "interiorize" good manners; consciously at first, and increasingly unconsciously from one generation to the next, through reflexes acquired in the early stages of childhood.

In the French case, the fact that court society was by nature "assimilationist" might account for the ease with which aristocratic norms became general. The aristocracy constantly incorporated bourgeois elements and adopted their values; the bourgeoisie, on the other hand, assimilated aristocratic culture, and when they had achieved political supremacy, they spread it to broader segments of the society at large. Another factor is the precocious *democratization* of French society, which was essential to the reinforcement of interdependence among individuals. That British workers still have "country gentility" manners and that the French continue to show elements of the courtier's demeanor testifies to the continued relevance of this distant past. In the German case, on the other hand, the middle classes were kept at a distance from aristocratic circles. When the intellectual bourgeoisie became dominant, its separatist, particularistic conceptions weighed heavily on definitions of the "German national character." Whereas in France, the barrier of origins had fallen by the eighteenth century, it continued to play an important role in Germany, eventually providing Hitler with a weapon to use against Jews.

If we consider the question of the assimilation or integration of immigrants sufficiently important to be analyzed with the serenity of historical perspective, we can no longer afford to ignore the work of Norbert Elias, for it places the issue of "foreigners" within a vastly broader problematic. Because it is a historical process, assimilation is a key issue facing contemporary societies, one that leaves out no social group. I quoted in an earlier chapter from a reminiscence by Eve Dessarre in which her mother, a German Jewish refugee, powdered her face before going to the prefecture in order to "look more French." In light of what has been said, it appears that this feeling of "Frenchness" was not entirely mythical; yet it cannot be explained by "national" temperament, "race," or "culture" but, rather, by the history internalized to the point of affecting one's body language. The basic concepts in Elias's work, which have been very sketchily outlined here, provide an ideal point of departure for the study of "coexistence" between the French and immigrants; a point of departure that would transcend the litanies on "cultural differences" and the ambiguities of "ethnicity."

The analyses put forth by Norbert Elias also have the merit of emphasizing that the assimilation process operates both ways. Even though the exchange is unequal given the existence of dominant and subaltern norms, the influence of the Other is always present in the result.

The issue of the second generation may also be approached from this perspective. Assimilation, Elias argues, whether it be for the uprooted foreigner or for the successfully upwardly mobile "*fils du peuple,*" is never complete in the first generation. As Durkheim noted in 1893, individuals are always torn by a contradiction between a sense of loyalty to their native environment and the attraction of the new one, which represents hope and future. "Ethnic" arguments are largely mythical, Elias continues, because "the history of a society is reflected in the internal history of each individual: each person must undergo for himself an abridged version of the civilization process experienced by society in general; for a child is not born 'civilized' " (Elias 1982). The family is the key conditioning agent in this respect, but society also imposes its norms through scores of different channels. In order to feel "normal," to be accepted by others, a child—regardless of origin, faith, or "ethnic group"—internalizes dominant rules. While these may be in conflict with the values of the family or the local community, they nonetheless prevail, often subconsciously, as for example, does the learning of the national language for the children of immigrants. Hence the absurdity of the notion that France is becoming a new Lebanon simply because the Islamic religion is practiced there.

Elias's work also demonstrates that sociological mechanisms of assimilation cannot be reduced to pedagogy. Unlike republican history, which assumes that the process of learning is exclusively a matter of transmitting conscious ideas (leading to an overemphasis on voluntarism and education), Elias emphasized the subjective and even the affective dimensions of the inculcation of norms in history. This helps understand why, despite differences in their political systems, the "efficiency" of the collective process of assimilation is essentially the same in France and the United States.

Sociology offers yet another angle for discussing issues of assimilation; although it is in some ways similar to the approach examined thus far, it emphasizes several distinct elements. In an essay that he wrote in 1920 but that remained unpublished during his lifetime, Marcel Mauss confessed to having been astonished by differences in national customs, not only in the realm of language but mainly with respect to the use of the body. During the First World War, Mauss had observed the inability of British troops to handle French spades, to the point where 8,000 spades per division had to be replaced. Based on this concrete observation, he developed an in-depth sociological analysis of the nation. If "the very way a Frenchman walks resembles less that of a British subject than an Algonquin's walk resembles that of a Californian Indian," if "methods of thought and ways of feeling of Italians are infinitely further apart from those of Spaniards than from those of primitives," it is, according to Mauss, because modern nations forge the individuals that comprise them. "Everything in a modern nation individualizes and standardizes its members"; this, he adds, reflects "a considerable sociological phenomenon whose novelty tends to be underestimated." The migrations that characterize modern society, along with the work of homogenization performed by the modern state, produce a genuine "fusion" of the former races; it is not the race that forms the nation, but the nation that produces new "races" (Mauss 1920?). Drawing from the work of Durkheim, Mauss argued that if the nation ultimately forged even the "techniques of the body,"[2] it is because two key elements were at the center of modern national formation.

The first factor was the growing institutionalization of society. Arguing against widespread notions of the state as a closed universe increasingly detached from individuals, Mauss reiterated Durkheim's fundamental thesis that, with the growth of the state and its organs of power, individuals were gradually drawn into and "traversed" by them; this was, he argued, the very foundation of modern liberty. As we saw in chapter 1, this is a decisive sociological argument against those who cultivate "ethnicity," rootedness in a family, local community, and "ancestors." Hence for Mauss, if there are so many observable differences in the way that individuals of neighboring nations use the body, it is because the national state has literally become "incorporated" in them. The army, school, and other organs of the state are the main places of inculcation. (Elias, on the other hand, emphasizes individual interactions.)

The second factor that Mauss underscored is the centralization of social life that characterizes all modern nations and that favors the "standardization" of individuals. What we would call today "mass communication" and the symbolic universe of modern political society (Mauss compares the symbol of the national flag to the totem in primitive clan-based societies) are key elements in the formation of a nation's "personality."

Had Fernand Braudel taken these analyses into account, he would not have regarded the identity of France as a virtually completed process by the late seventeenth century. In fact, he implicitly reiterated the dominant conception among historians with respect to the formation of the French nation. They tend to view the problem geometrically: Their concern is with the appearance and consolidation of borders delimiting a physical space; such studies focus on the importance of the center (the state) and of territorial divisions (departments). If the metaphor of "formation" can be used to designate a process that, beginning in the Middle Ages, produced a centered political and territorial entity called "France," then the term "reconstruction" may designate the increasingly complex and ramified structuration of that internal space. As we have seen, immigration was a key dimension of this second phase in French national history. As France's external contours were stabilized, an increasingly rigid line of demarcation established divisions within the internal social space. But this line was not simply borrowed from earlier forms of organization; it was the outcome of a full-fledged restructuration of the entire society, which provoked the thorough redefinition of the individuals in it; hence, the study of immigration is simply an extreme case of the forms taken by individualization and binding in contemporary societies. This is yet another argument that demonstrates the scientific necessity of an approach to immigration that refuses to isolate the phenomenon from the society at large.[3] Analyses framed in terms of *longue durée* by the "new school of history," which tend to isolate one element from the whole in order to historicize it, have caused many to overlook the massive restructuring that affected French society in the late nineteenth century and that was closely linked to its "nationalization"; hence the lucidity displayed by Emile Durkheim, himself a contemporary of this "revolution."

Contemporary research has, I believe, confirmed the notion that the state does not exist apart from individuals, that, rather, the latter are traversed by the former (or by its instruments). Social history should avoid playing into widespread commonsense notions about the definition of individuals according to biological criteria and focus instead on the modalities of their social construction. As we saw earlier, techniques of *bertillonage* and of legal identification played an important role in the late nineteenth century with respect to immigrants, who found themselves saddled with a mandatory I.D. card. As Carlo Ginzburg noted, however, this was an innovation that had consequences for society in general. With industrial upheavals, progress in transportation, and the increased mobility of individuals that progress implied, the question of legal identity became increasingly important. As a result, Ginzburg argued, "a prodigious extension of the notion of individuality occurred via the relationship to the state, to its bureaucratic organs, and to police" (Ginzburg 1980). After having been applied to recidivist criminals and foreigners, techniques of individual identification were extended to the population in general. As soon as owners began complying with the 1893 law requiring them to keep track of their foreign workers, it became apparent that the whole enterprise would be impossible unless French workers were also required to carry I.D.'s; how else could one unmask an imposter who claimed to be French and who looked French but was not? (See Andréani 1896.) Identity controls were rapidly extended to the workforce in general. The mining company of Courrière inaugurated the anthropometric identification of its workers in 1905, to be followed several years later by the Liévin mining company. For owners, this was a convenient way of identifying and dismissing trade unionists.

At another level, the emergence of the welfare state, with its tendency to segregate the French from the foreigners, generalized the "carding" process—social security cards, retirement cards—to all individuals and smoothed the process out by assigning a single identification number to each individual. This process, initiated before the outbreak of the First World War, was accelerated during the war itself. The government took advantage of the situation to extend new identification procedures to soldiers discharged or retired from the army, who were entitled a pension. Photographs of heirs' fingerprints were now kept in military files. The procedure was systematized in the new military I.D. papers carried by each soldier (Valdour 1919).

It is no coincidence that the government took advantage of wartime authoritarianism to generalize such procedures. We are so accustomed to living amid I.D.'s that it is hard to imagine the extent of the resistance that these innovations provoked. Yet one of the reasons why the 1910 law on worker and peasant retirement pensions failed to generate much popular enthusiasm was that the "carding" procedure generated widespread animosity (Tournerie 1971). Records in the National Archives show that such discontent continued to manifest itself following the war. In Bouches-du-Rhône, the CGT officially protested against the new fingerprinted military I.D.'s. "This measure," wrote the police commissioner in Marseilles, "caused an uproar among militants of the labor exchange," for, in their view, it likens "the citizen to a convict." An order of the day was even voted against it (NA F7 12975, Bouches-du-Rhône). But the growing differentiation of social functions, the proliferation of different statuses, of "rightful claimants," and of "unrightful claimants" made it impossible to turn back.

The contractualization of social relations, which began in the 1930s and which was developed after the war—with the growth of collective agreements and the increased codification of professional identities, of titles, and of job positions—represents the second major breakthrough in the history of modern individual identities.

To this must be added a growing interdependence among nations themselves. This, added to the pacification of society that made the slightest crime or act of violence intolerable, contributed to making "security" a political issue of prime importance. To guarantee citizens' tranquility and to allow justice to follow its course, we could no longer do without these new techniques of individualization that increasingly rested on national identity and that are constantly being upgraded by science.[4] As the minister of justice noted in 1972, the Nationality Code is of concern to all French citizens; that year, no less than 400,000 certificates of nationality were issued.[5] This codified legal identity also affected the way in which individuals viewed themselves; professional identity; identity as a political citizen, expressed by the voters' card; the identity as a social security recipient—these all combined to define modern individuals, overdetermining their relationship to others, and particularly to foreigners who are caught up in the same networks. These are the dimensions that fashionable "psychologizing" approaches to "identity" fail to analyze.

In his *Division du travail social,* Emile Durkheim raised a second major issue for anyone who sets out to write the social history of assimilation and the national phenomenon: the process of abstraction. As mechanical solidarity gives way to organic solidarity, society, he argues, loses its concrete "substance." Given that the spatial and human framework is much larger than before, words can no longer have the same meaning for everyone; they themselves become more abstract.[6] In the late nineteenth century, this problem was visible at many levels. For example, with respect to the nationalization of political life, all social groups (including the popular classes) were asked to share an understanding of such abstract republican concepts as "nation" and "universal suffrage." The expansion of the legal system, by which individuals were required to accept the existence of universal rules founded on distant and anonymous norms, provoked similar processes. A system of judiciary identification was created that (even for recidivist criminals) no longer defined identity by a mark on the body, an outstanding physical trait or knowledge of the group to which a person belonged; instead, a series of symbols were placed on file, which is a good illustration of the transition to "abstract society." It is also a key factor in the distancing of individuals, which accentuates anonymity. The extraordinary advances made by science, and their growing accessibility, also contribute to this evolution. As Ernst Cassirer (1953–1957) argued, the scientific creation of concepts is accompanied by a new use of the sign, which is now liberated from restrictions based on sensate conditions; "dematerialized," the sign escapes from the sphere of things. Although individuals continue to live in a concrete environment, their everyday life is increasingly reliant on faraway people and events, people and events that they cannot see and over which they have little control.

This may be one of the causes behind the "crisis of civilization" that characterized the end of the last century. It is interesting to note that the antirepublican arguments of such thinkers as Taine, Barrès, and Le Play constantly warned against universalist, abstract political discourse, which was far from people's true concerns. As we saw earlier, Boulangiste anti-Semitic propaganda was the first to appeal to the affectivity and subconscious of the public, using vivid imagery and a language of familiarity. In order to impose national reality on French society in general, the Third Republic was faced early on with the problem of making new political realities tangible. Again, it was not a question of discourse and of pedagogy. Norbert Elias emphasized the enormous difficulties a political regime might face if it tried to mobilize the masses against an enemy who cannot be *seen*; hence the importance of symbols and of all devices that substitute for direct visual contact. They must, of course, become familiar to everyone and appeal strongly to affectivity. Arnold Van Gennep (1921) noted that those who brandished such "national symbols" as the flag and tricolor cockade in 1913 felt a little ridiculous; only after the First World War, after French society at large had experienced the horrors of war, did these symbols truly acquire a meaning for everyone. In the same book, Van Gennep showed that the role of schools in promoting "nationalism" was not limited to simply spreading the patriotic "message"; symbolic mediation was essential. For a child who lived far from a border zone and who had never been abroad, the image of the geography map on the blackboard was most significant. "What makes the vitality and the force of this particular symbolism, is the relative importance of the border with respect to the territories it defined, and the various nuances which the cartographers had to use." By drawing the map himself, the child feels that he is "contributing to the differentiation between his own country and the others" (Van Gennep 1921, 200). This same logic explains the efficiency of the school system as a vehicle of assimilation for the children of foreigners. "We recall very well," wrote the mayor of Villerupt, of Italian origin, "our school obsessions such as errors in spelling or syntax; and the chilling comments of the schoolteacher, written in red ink in the margin of the composition, by which I thought, although wrongly perhaps, he was hinting at something: 'not French,' 'poor French' " (quoted in Salque et al. 1982, 161).

This brings us to the understudied problem of the mediation of national consciousness, the relays it encounters in the concrete reality of individuals. We have seen that in the late nineteenth century, the presence in France of more than a million foreigners gave a tangible meaning to the notion of "national foreigners" that spread through France after 1870, and played in favor of nationalist mobilization. But the relays of national consciousness are not simply obstacles to the integration of foreigners. On the contrary, belonging to a local community or group is the fundamental stepping-stone toward integration; it is a way for these groups to assert their own way of "being French," which immigrants or their children seek to assimilate. Among the popular classes, the world of work often played this intermediary role; for some it was sports. When, in the 1950s, young Poles were achieving soccer fame, "people no longer said Tempowski but Tempo, and replaced Mankowski with Manko. Sembicki has been Stanis, and Jedresak, Maresh, for a long time. The suppression of so many *w*'s, *k*'s, and *z*'s was not meaningless. It meant adoption."[7] It is significant that what would have been interpreted as an insult had it been done by a police officer, the mutilation of surnames, in this case had positive overtones. It was the symbolic gesture by which the native group signified that it had accepted the Poles as their own. In this context, Renan's "wanting to live together" becomes more than a catchphrase. As Max Weber and Maurice Halbwachs argued, the feeling of sharing something with others is not at all univocal; it can draw from many different sources. The exceptional and dramatic circumstances of war notwithstanding, grandiose principles and good feelings about the Fatherland and the "soul" of the nation are not what inspire most individuals' attachment to the society in which they live. The real social bond lies elsewhere: in the possibilities that a society offers its members to participate, fulfill their goals, and be recognized. It is at this level that the specific problems faced by the present-day second generation (and working-class youths in general) may be encountered. The "intermediary groups" that Durkheim perceived as new places of settlement and integration adapted to the modern world—that is, the professional sphere and the labor movement—were indeed, in ways they did not foresee, the main relays of assimilation for preceding waves of immigrants in France. Given the current crisis in the world of work and its organizations, rampant unemployment and job precariousness, and the bureaucracy of political organizations, perhaps the challenge may be to invent new forms of "organic solidarity" that will give the children of immigrants, as well as the others, reasons for hope.

This analysis demonstrates that the "national assimilation" of immigrants is not solely, nor is it even essentially, the outcome of government policies aimed at forcibly imposing cultural values. On the contrary, if national norms are so easily adopted by immigrants, it is because the appropriation of such norms supports their day-to-day interests. It is clear that without a basic knowledge of the French language, no immigrant can hope to work his or her way up the social ladder. In order for the cultural practices of immigrant communities in France to have been transmitted over several generations, they would have had to offer comparable advantages; in other words, the languages, customs, and practices of these groups would have to have been officially recognized by the authorities and would have to have received institutional support. In modern societies, for a given culture to survive from one generation to the next, it must be fixed in writing, codified by laws, and defended by an administration. In matters of language, the national governments of both the United States and France have consistently refused to follow the path of diversity. While this may be regrettable, other equally legitimate claims must be taken into consideration. In any social community, however cohesive, powerful assimilationist pressures are exerted upon individuals to abandon aspects of their culture and submit to dominant norms of behavior. Those who denounce the insensitivity of the French government's policy of assimilation with respect to "*culture maghrébine,*" for example, fail to realize that such an argument has an assimilationist logic of its own. Indeed, the broad diversity of cultural practices among immigrant laborers from North African countries is associated with an abstract geopolitical entity (the Maghrib), one that is no more (and is often less) familiar to them than is French culture. Furthermore, cultural forms, even when they are institutionalized, are constantly changing under pressure from assimilationist forces that are larger than the state itself. By focusing too narrowly on political issues, social scientists have tended to completely underestimate the role of economic factors (such as the internationalization of capitalism) in the assimilation process. The present-day "national identity" of the French is undoubtedly more influenced by images borrowed from the United States (McDonald's hamburgers, Michael Jackson's songs, and Hollywood films, for example) than by the traditional symbols of the Republic; and the reorganization of native cultures among immigrants is likewise inspired by such popular North American references. If they are to approach the question of assimilation as an object of research rather than simply as a topic of political controversy, scholars must give serious thought to all of these different factors.

Notes

Foreword

1. Representative recent books include John Bodnar, *The Transplanted: A History of Immigrants in Urban America* (Bloomington: Indiana University Press, 1985), George J. Borjas, *International Differences in the Labor Market Performance of Immigrants* (Kalamazoo, Mich.: W. E. Upjohn Institute for Employment Research, 1988), Lucie Cheng and Edna Bonacich, eds., *Labor Immigration under Capitalism: Asian Workers in the United States before World War II* (Berkeley: University of California Press, 1984), Donna R. Gabaccia, *Militants and Migrants: Rural Sicilians Become American Workers* (New Brunswick, N.J.: Rutgers University Press, 1988), Ivan Light and Edna Bonacich, *Immigrant Entrepreneurs: Koreans in Los Angeles, 1965–1982* (Berkeley: University of California Press, 1988), Ewa Morawska, *Insecure Prosperity: Jews in Small-Town America* (Princeton: Princeton University Press, 1994), Alejandro Portes and Rubén Rumbaut, *Immigrant America: A Portrait* (Berkeley: University of California Press, 1990), Roger D. Waldinger, *Through the Eye of the Needle: Immigrants and Enterprise in New York's Garment Trades* (New York: New York University Press, 1986), and Virginia Yans-McLaughlin, ed., *Immigration Reconsidered: History, Sociology, and Politics* (New York: Oxford University Press, 1990).

Preface to the English-Language Edition

1. The apparent indifference with which Foucault treated the reception of his work (at least in his structuralist phase) in part explains why he was so poorly understood by French historians. On this issue, see Noiriel 1994.

2. The term "sociohistory" designates a field of historical research that is intimately linked to sociology. I find it more explicit than the general term "social history," which has become too vague to adequately define the domain of my own investigation.

3. A number of publications have addressed these issues in recent years; see in particular Wihtol de Wenden 1988; Weil 1991; Schnapper 1991.

4. Preserving the autonomy of historical research does not prevent the historian from taking part in the debates surrounding memory by translating the outcome of re-

search into a language accessible to the larger public. This is what I tried to do, for example, by participating in various ministerial commissions on the relationship between immigration and the teaching of history and by collaborating on several dozen television documentaries on the history of immigration.

5. See, for example, the works of Pierre Bourdieu and his followers.

6. On the role played by intellectuals in the formation of national memory, see Lebovics 1991.

7. My emphasis on specific aspects of immigration history led me to gloss over certain issues that would have been essential to a history of migration in general, such as, for example, the study of migratory networks and of factors leading to emigration from home countries.

8. To perceive the nation as nothing more than a system of "representations" leads scholarship in a dangerously idealist direction. The preface to the recent French reprint of Renan's conference entitled "What Is a Nation?" is a case in point. In the preface, the title of Anderson's book *Imagined Communities* is translated in French as "*Imaginary*" (*imaginaires*) rather than "*Imagined*" (*imaginées*) *Communities,* which takes us from the realm of representations to that of fiction! See Renan 1992, 28.

9. While it is easy to translate the term "*étatisation*" into German (*Verstaatlichung*), it is difficult to find an equivalent term in English. The often used notion "state control" seems dangerous, since "control" always implies that the state is outside society, whereas the point here is that society gradually *becomes* the state and vice versa. In order to avoid such a confusion, I think it preferable to employ, even in English, the French term "*étatisation,*" despite the fact that it is a neologism.

10. I recognize that this definition can only apply to the historical study of nation-states such as France. I believe, however, that social scientists should abandon the project of producing a definition of the "nation" that would account for all problems ordinarily defined as "national." Historically, the term "nation" has been used to designate extremely diverse groups. It is still used today to designate groups that share certain common characteristics (such as language or religion) and that make a claim—through those who speak in their name—for political independence, either on the grounds of these characteristics or as a means of bringing culturally diverse groups under the authority of a nation-state. To use the same term to define such contrasting communities of individuals seems to hinder historical understanding of the problem. The only way to establish a common definition would be to erase the diversity and emphasize only the similarities, and that at a very general level so as to apply it to as many groups as possible. This seems to have occurred, for example, with certain usages of the term "imagined communities."

11. This is an important aspect of male domination over women; the Napoleonic Code forced women to adopt their husbands' surnames, hence depriving them of part of their identity. For a more detailed analysis of these issues, see Noiriel 1993a.

12. From the very beginning, there was a close relationship between the emergence of this bond of national interdependence and the construction of collective national representations. The institutionalization of surnames, which reinforced the bond between individuals and the state, played an important role in the symbolic process through which individuals came to see themselves as members of a national community. On the sociopolitical importance of surnames, see, for example, Bering 1992.

13. Because the process of *étatisation* took on a variety of different forms in different national contexts, classes were designated differently and do not always encompass the same professional activities.

14. The distinction between citizen and national was also a consequence of colonization. At that time, Algerians had French nationality but were not considered French citizens. This book does not go into detail regarding the relationship between colonization and immigration, which is the object of my current research.

15. On the importance of this question, see Noiriel 1991a.

16. Indeed, we never communicate with abstract entities, such as the state, but with individuals. For example, a law becomes effective only in an over-the-counter relationship between public functionaries and entitled beneficiaries.

17. See Green 1991. The best available comparative study of these questions is Brubaker 1992.

18. In the speeches in memory of French prime minister Pierre Bérégovoy, who committed suicide in 1993, his working-class roots were often mentioned, but, significantly, the fact that he was the son of a Ukrainian immigrant was not (except by foreigners such as the Canadian prime minister).

19. According to 1990 census, 30% of twenty-two-year-old immigrant youths are unemployed; see Tribalat 1993.

20. This should not blind us to the positive aspects of the omnipresent welfare state in France. As Loïc Wacquant has shown in his comparison of neighborhoods in French and U.S. cities, the underdevelopment of public services is responsible for the much more dramatic poverty in the United States; see Wacquant 1994.

Introduction

1. The president stated: "We are part Roman, part German, part Jewish, part Italian, part Spanish, and increasingly Portuguese," and he added, "I wonder if we have not already become a bit Arabic" ("La France et le pluralisme des cultures" [15 May 1987], quoted in *Le Monde,* May 20, 1987).

2. Throughout the book, the word "ethnic" will be used in quotation marks, as Max Weber did to underscore the ambiguity of term. Following Weber, an "ethnic" group is defined here as a group of human beings that is not grounded in kinship ties but that, on the basis of shared customs and memories, encourages the subjective belief in a community of origin; see Weber 1968.

3. Bachir, quoted by A. Zehraoui, *Le Monde,* special issue, "Les Immigrés en France," October 1984.

4. This estimate reaches back three generations. Despite repeated efforts, I was unable to obtain viable statistics on this question from the Interior Ministry, from the Direction de la Population et des Migrations, or from the Institut National d'Etudes Démographiques (INED). The Interior Ministry survey that establishes the figure at one-third of the total population is often quoted but impossible to find. The most reliable source available is the survey conducted by Alain Girard (1971), which establishes that in 1971, 20% *of French adults* were of "foreign" descent. Fifteen years later, if we add the immigrant population and youths under the age of twenty (and take into account "denials" or refusals to answer this question, which some consider indiscrete), the estimate of one-third of the population is plausible.

5. A reference to Weber 1976.

One. The Denial of Memory

1. This index remains, however, of limited use to researchers. It excludes some titles, such as medical dissertations, which led me to discard the medical field altogether

despite its numerous contributions to the study of immigration. Moreover, the affiliation of authors is not always specified, causing difficult problems of interpretation (to determine, for example, whether a dissertation is in sociology or psychology). Finally, studies of immigration that omit the term from their title are not included in the listing. Overall, therefore, the index simply provides indicators, which then require verification.

2. Dissertations listed as being in "education sciences" are counted here as sociology. To do otherwise would have accentuated the predominance of psychology.

3. Quoted in *Le Monde,* 24 October 1986.

4. A category made up of French citizens born abroad, naturalized French citizens, and foreigners. I thank Philip Bourgois for his help in analyzing the American statistics.

5. This survey only took into account the *adult* population; had children been surveyed, the proportion would have been even greater.

6. See Foucault 1971. The classicism of language, with its sharply defined categories, make it impossible, for example, to translate into French the title of Eugen Weber's book *Peasants into Frenchmen* (1976).

7. In a book on foreigners in Paris under the July Monarchy, the author invoked this taboo against origins to justify the impossibility of evaluating their number (see Desnoyers 1844).

8. In the French sense of "*nationalité,*" which, as we will see, is somewhat distinct in meaning from the Engligh word "citizenship."

9. We will see later on why this apology is important.

10. Excerpts of these studies can be found in Brun 1980.

11. It is from this perspective that the text by Mauss on the nation should be read; see Mauss 1969a.

12. The recent controversies surrounding the Nationality Code demonstrated the virulence of the opposing trend.

13. Minority trends within sociology, such as those represented by Gabriel Tarde or *la réforme sociale,* were more sensitive to the issue of immigration.

14. On the day the new Sorbonne was inaugurated, in 1889, Lavisse proclaimed his "love for the soil on which I was born, my long memory of ancestors, the joy of meeting my soul in their thoughts and their actions, in their history and their legend" (quoted in Nora 1984–1986, 1:332).

15. See the issues of the journal *Population* that appeared between 1945 and 1948, and INED 1947.

16. These types of documents were, unfortunately, systematically excluded from the selection of articles from the journal *Population* recently reissued in a volume edited by Hervé Le Bras; see Le Bras 1985.

17. In his dissertation (1977), Abel Châtelain made no mention whatsoever of demo-geography.

18. The Groupe de Recherches Coordonnées (GRECO) 13, established by the CNRS to coordinate research on immigration, is currently staffed by ninety researchers.

19. Colloquia were even organized to discuss the "concept" of "maximum tolerance" (see, for example, the journal *Sociologie du Sud-Est,* July–Oct. 1975).

20. The fundamental differences between immigration policies in the two countries can be explained historically. It is because massive immigration is a recent phenomenon in West Germany that the instability of foreigners was greater during the period of expansion, and that today expulsions are simplified. This also explains why German public opinion discovered that age-old French problem, the overexploitation

of foreign workers, only recently. Walraff's *Tête de Turc* (1986) met with considerable success in Germany.

21. Marc Ferro recently recalled that Fernand Braudel had entitled a new heading in the journal *Annales* "The past in the present"; cf. Ferro 1986.

22. Lucien Febvre, who explained that the term "social" was adopted by the group because it was "misused," added: "There is no economic and social history. There is a unified thing called history, which is by definition entirely social" (Febvre 1953).

23. While this did not prevent the publication of excellent studies of social history, the directions taken by empirical research are determined in the end by the implicit or explicit definition of broad theoretical orientations. To the self-evident truths of "economic and social history," we might add those of the monographic breakdown of dissertations inspired by Vidalian sociology, with its confusion between the construction of an object and geographic divisions in physical space. The success of positivism and the influence of republican ideology were responsible for an earlier theoretical turning point in historical research: the triumph of objectivism, with its rejection of explanations in terms of "origins" (social or other)—such as those of Michelet—in favor of the analysis of "conjunctures."

24. Bloch's book *The Historian's Craft* is an extraordinary source of ideas regarding the real problems faced by historians in their work.

25. Because the conditions in which these statistics were produced is never critically analyzed, the analysis is completely blind to immigration.

26. On the "traces" of the barbarian invasions "in our blood," see also Braudel 1988–1990.

27. It is therefore illusory to expect that this survey will tell us everything or almost everything about "the social history of our compatriots" and their social mobility, as does Elisabeth Gordon (*Le Monde,* 5 August 1987).

28. Althusser 1977 produced the most thorough critique of the Braudelian conception of time, which he opposed to that defended by Marx.

Two. The Card and the Code

1. The 4 June 1814 ruling refers to the "dispositions of the Civil Code regarding foreigners and their naturalization," but the code contains no judgment on naturalization whatsoever. Domat implied that the simple fact of having been born on French soil confers French nationality. Cf. Domat 1989.

2. See Moheau 1912 (first published in 1778), particularly chapter 12, "Immigration and the Introduction of Foreigners," in which he deplores the fact that despite the existence of French neighborhoods in all the major cities of Europe, no foreign neighborhoods existed in France.

3. Demographic history is often oblivious to the fact that the documents upon which it rests are themselves the outcome of a conflictual history. Struggles to impose civil status as we know it today were still in full swing during the nineteenth century. Under the First Empire, an official noted "the frightening state of the registers, and in particular, the falsifications introduced to avoid conscription. In Lozère alone, the prefect estimated that to punish the authors of such offenses would require 20,000 legal actions. In certain departments such as Ariège, arson destroyed the copies of the records held by the prefecture" (NA F2 I 380). The 1849 edition of the *Dictionnaire de l'administration* lists the numerous restrictions that the officers of civil status had to learn to observe in order to confer upon official statements the "neutrality" that

they now display: A register is better than a loose sheet of paper, the mayor should not let days or weeks pass before signing the statements, the civil status officer should refrain from inscribing his remarks on official documents; parents and friends, if they are not witnesses, should not sign public statements, and so on.

4. For example, one naturalization decision was recorded by the *Bulletin des lois* thirty-seven years after its pronouncement; its beneficiary had died in the meantime (Folleville 1880).

5. See, for example, the *Bulletin de Paris* published by the police prefecture from 1830 to 1845, NA F7 3884; see also examples contained in NA F7 11979A, NA F7 11980B, and NA F7 12338. An in-depth analysis would require a history of this unique form of archive, the police report. Under the Restoration, such reports were handwritten, poorly structured, and filled with "literary" considerations on the weather, the stock exchange, and odd news items. The police vision of the world in general remained overdetermined by the leitmotiv of "public peace." (On 26 July 1830 the police prefect of Paris observed "no particular event worthwhile of attention"!) The July Monarchy accomplished a first step toward the regularizing of information gathering (such as beginning to keep records on hotel registers and standardizing police reports).

6. The first International Congress of Statistics to directly address the issue of nationality was held in 1872. Opinions clashed on whether a "juridical" or an "ethnic" definition of the term should be employed, as well as over the meanings of the words used. Whereas the Romance languages employ a single term to designate both one's membership in a political entity and one's "ethnic" origin, in English the terms "nationality," "race," and "people," and in German the terms "*Staatsangehörigkeit,*" "*Volkstumszugehörigkeit,*" and "*Stammeszugehörigkeit,*" are differentiated. The congress nonetheless adopted the principle according to which "the language of origin or most commonly spoken is the sole ethnographic criterion that the census may retain"; cf. ILO 1936.

7. [A qualifying exam for entrance into the corps of professors eligible to teach at the high school or university level—Trans.]

8. In the departments along the border, particularly in the north, the problem of military service for foreigners was a long-standing issue. Amendments to the existing military laws to impose conscription on young foreigners were proposed as early as the Restoration. The stubborn efforts of Maxime Lecomte, a northern deputy, explain why nationality law evolved toward a reinforcement of jus soli (consider, for example, the 1874 Rotours law). It is therefore no coincidence that allegations of an "invasion" of foreigners appeared in the northern juridical literature some twenty years before being pronounced elsewhere (see Preux 1860; Preux was assistant public prosecutor of the court of Douai).

9. *Journal Officiel,* Chambre des Députés, Documents et Débats Parlementaires, 16 March 1889; the transcription is followed by "shouts of *Very good! Very good!* emanated from the benches."

10. *Journal Officiel,* Chambres des Sénat, Document et Débats Parlementaires, 3 June 1889.

11. "Admission to domicile" was officially abolished in 1927, but it was stripped of its original meaning as early as 1889 and became simply another stage in the naturalization process.

12. See the debates in NA C 5404.

13. *Journal Officiel,* Chambre des Députés, Documents et Débats Parlementaires, Rapport Pradon, n°2364, 2/2/1888.

14. To many prefects, this simple procedure seemed unwarranted. For example, the prefect of the Hautes-Pyrénées replied that "the application of this memorandum in all the communities without distinction could present the inconvenience, given the poor culture of municipalities and the possibility that indiscretions might hinder effective surveillance, of throwing the country into a regrettable state of disorder."

15. Decree of 4 February 1912, article 8.

16. To the long-standing problem of the contradiction between labor market protection and international agreements, the hotel industry added pressure to exempt tourists from the requirement. The political influence enjoyed by representatives of large industry allowed them to turn measures that had penalized them before the war to their advantage. The new identification card for foreigners became a means of channeling the labor supply toward those sectors that had previously been lacking in labor power; furthermore, it introduced a measure of discipline between industrialists by limiting the risks of layoffs.

17. Albert Lebrun had presented such a bill in 1905, on the grounds that the 1902 legislation against smallpox was not specific enough for immigrants. The bill suggested that a "certificate of vaccination" valid for less than ten years be added to the list of required I.D. papers. On interwar legislation concerning immigrants, see Ponty 1985; Bonnet 1974; and Economic and Financial Archives (EFA) B 39914–39916.

18. *Journal Officiel,* Chambre des Députés, Documents et Débats Parlementaires, 17 July 1984.

19. Ibid., 1 May 1893.

20. *Journal Officiel,* Chambre des Députés, Documents et Débats Parlementaires, 10 October 1972.

21. Take, for example, the Polish-born miner who had lived in France since 1931, who was a contributor to the *Gazetta Polska* (the newspaper of Polish immigrants), who had volunteered in 1939, and whose wife had been deported to Auschwitz; a "denationalization" decree deprived him of his rights as a Frenchman because of his political activities. Many foreign-born activists (such as veterans of the International Brigades in Spain and Central European refugees) played an active role in the French Resistance, only to be later expelled or deported to "camps"; *Le Monde,* 3 Jan. 1953.

22. *Journal Officiel,* Chambre des Députés, Documents et Débats Parliamentaires, 10 October 1972.

23. The link to physical anthropology is illustrated by Bertillon's use of records established by the Judicial Identity Service for an in-depth study of height and eye color in the various cantons of France.

24. See the allusion to the problem in the preface to Niceforo 1907.

25. In the case of the Spaniards, see, for example, NA F7 13066.

26. All identification papers contain a simple nomenclature of data on the physical characteristics of individuals: height, weight, eye color, complexion, distinctive marks. In everyday interaction, these interiorized signs effectively designate the foreigner as such. This, to be sure, is not unrelated to the severity with which they are treated by the police, as countless sociological studies testify (see, for example, Desdevises 1977).

27. *Journal Officiel,* Chambres des Députés, Documents et Débats Parlementaires, 5 May 1882.

28. In the case of Jews as well as nomads, the police inquisition was preceded by a specific census.

29. Under the Second Empire, the prefect of Haute-Normandie had to issue several memoranda to dissuade inhabitants from giving illegitimate children women's names as a reminder of their origins; cf. Zonabend 1980.

30. Letter of the National Alliance against Depopulation to Philippe Serre, secretary of state for immigration, 22 February 1938; cited in Bonnet 1974, 166.

31. *Journal Officiel,* Chambres des Députés, Documents et Débats Parlementaires, 28 June 1972.

32. Arguments among municipalities, regional councils, and ministries broke out over the proportional distribution of the tax revenues. In the early 1930s, municipal officials agitated to have other institutions take up the administrative costs represented by foreigners. See, for example, for deliberations in Haute-Savoie, NA F2 2701; in Meuse, NA F2 2561; in Meurthe-et-Moselle, NA F2 2548.

33. Laws of 9 January 1973 on the French Nationality Code; of 17 July 1984 on the single residence and work permit, modified by the 9 September 1986 law on the conditions of entry and residence applicable to foreigners in France.

34. A 7 March 1986 decree reduced the time that the certificate of residence for new arrivals was valid from five years to one and put Algerians on the same level as other immigrant groups.

35. On the specific situation of young Algerians with respect to nationality, see J. Costa-Lascoux, "Quelle nationalité?" in *Les Temps modernes* 1984.

36. *Le Moniteur,* 15 November 1849.

37. But as F. Baille noted, "the exclusion from optional retirement plans is not an outcome of the law itself but, rather, the consequence of an administrative practice that, for financial reasons, consistently denied foreigners access to such plans" (1927, 33). Moreover, foreigners saw their pensions reduced by various penalties. A French worker who began contributing to a pension plan at the age of thirty received 494 francs at age sixty-five, compared with 153 francs for an Italian worker under the same circumstances.

38. *Le Journal des Tribunaux,* 27 March 1900; quoted in Martin 1908, 73.

39. The socialist government's laws in the early 1980s, generally favorable to foreigners, met with similar difficulties.

40. As far as rights of expression are concerned, restrictions on immigrant associations were lifted only in 1979. Foreign-born workers who spoke French earned voting and eligibility rights in professional elections only in 1972. A 1968 law reserved the function of trade union representative within companies for French workers; it was extended to foreigners in 1982, but discriminations remain for non-wage-earning workers. In the late 1980s, foreigners still could not be members of the conciliation board (*prud'hommes*) or of a jury, nor could they belong to the board of directors of certain public firms or to university boards.

41. "An emigrant is a person who leaves his country with the goal of seeking work.... An immigrant is a foreigner who arrives in a country to look for work and with the stated or presumed intention of settling permanently in that country; a foreigner who arrives with the sole intention of establishing himself temporarily is considered a simple worker" (quoted in Nguyen Van Yen 1987, 25).

42. A refugee was defined mainly as an individual who "by his race, religion, nationality, membership in a certain social group, or political opinions has reason to be persecuted" (quoted in Nguyen Van Yen 1987, 69).

43. Trade unions, however, have always been less hostile to forms of exclusion that run no risk of encroaching on the rights of French nationals. In 1898, a bill presented

by Coutant asserted the principle of equality of wages among workers but requested that foreigners be limited to 10% of the workforce on government-sponsored public works projects. Alexandre Millerand issued decrees in 1899 satisfying this trade union demand.

44. The need for a policy of assimilation was recognized as early as the 1920s. Radical political circles, encouraged by large industrialists, took the first steps; and several associations, such as the Foyer Français worked toward this goal. Their program shows that the objective was to assimilate foreigners within the French working class (see, for example, Brand 1932). The numerous books by René Martial also advocated a policy of assimilation founded on ethnic criteria, but his impact was small until the advent of the Vichy government; see Martial 1931.

45. *Journal Officiel,* ACP, Documents et Débats Parlementaire, 21 June 1945.

Three. Uprooted

1. [DP: Displaced Person—Trans.]

2. [Name of a Moroccan tribe and of its members—Trans.]

3. At least until the time of the Second World War, statistics on immigration were flawed by a high degree of nonregistration, which renders any in-depth quantitative analysis illusory. These figures should therefore be read solely as general indicators.

4. On this subject, see the colorful descriptions in Châtelain 1977.

5. These were also the sectors with the highest rate of work-related accidents. During the interwar period, the annual rate of fatal work-related accidents in the iron mines was sometimes as high as 5% (almost a world record), and almost all the underground labor force was foreign. In the 1960s, the situation had not changed. According to B. Granotier, immigrants still fell victim to twice as many work-related accidents as did French-born workers (Granotier 1979, 106).

6. Marie-Ange Schiltz aided me in the analysis of these statistics.

7. The particular position of the English is due to the substantial number of idle individuals living in resorts.

8. For the Belgian case see Lentacker 1973; for the Spanish case see Azas 1981; for the Turkish case see INED 1981.

9. For the case of Central European Jews, see Valensi and Wachtel 1991.

10. An example of written testimony is Troyat 1987.

11. During the interwar period, the old downtown districts of Grenoble and Ugine were also taken over by Italians (R. Blanchard 1936; Miège 1934). A comparable phenomenon is occurring today in the thirteenth arrondissement of Paris, with the arrival of "Chinese" immigrants (Guillon and Taboada-Leonetti 1986).

12. See, in addition to the aforementioned monographs, Ducellier 1981–1982; Walter 1935; Le Huu Khoa 1986.

13. For an analysis of "ethnic" businesses today, see Raulin 1987.

14. This question can be studied with some precision in the archives. For Armenians, see, for example, NA F7 13436; for the Chinese, NA 47 AS; for the Russians, NA 49 AS.

15. In particular, the old recruitment center of Toul.

16. Other elements confirm this. Traditionally, celebrate the birth of a child, a sugar pyramid is offered; in Lorraine, however, people had to settle for lumps of sugar. These elements of the culture of origin nonetheless help consolidate group identity within the host country. For Moroccan women of the Pays-Haut, these rituals played

the same role as did the act of eating the *cappellette* down in the mine for Italians in Saint-Eloi prior to the Second World War.

Four. Battered Roots

1. By the "first generation" of immigrants I mean those individuals who arrived in France in their teens or as adults. The "second generation" is defined neither by nationality nor by place of birth but by place of initial socialization (and primary schooling); this point will be discussed later in the chapter.

2. The study was commissioned by UNESCO and carried out with the help of schoolteachers, which somewhat distorted the responses regarding schooling.

3. The article by F. Muñoz-Perez and M. Tribalat (1984) contains a few historical elements on the subject.

4. The term "white-collar workers" designates, for 1931, the category "employees" (*employés*), and for 1975 liberal professions and management ("*cadres*").

5. With the exception of the British, who display a modest rate of naturalization due to the fact that if they are to retain their titles they must maintain their nationality.

6. [Messengers—Trans.]

7. This alludes to Jean Leca's 1985 assertions in the journal *Esprit.*

8. Sayad in Laacher 1987. This did become an issue, however, for immigrants from nations, Germany and Italy in particular, that had fought against France.

9. In a survey conducted in the Pays-Haut, I asked one of my "privileged informers" to keep a detailed journal of her daily life. The resulting text revealed the importance of cooking habits in the transmission of knowledge from mother to daughter, in particular the baking of traditional Moroccan cookies "in the form of intertwined strips, flavored with orange blossom water, soaked in honey and spiced with sesame seeds." See Noiriel 1993b, 114–30.

10. Franco-Armenian pop singer Charles Aznavour recalled: "We were constantly warned: be careful, children, we have come here as foreigners; we have been well received, we make no trouble, let's behave well" (*Le Monde,* 11–12 June 1984).

11. [Disparaging term for Arab immigrants—Trans.]

12. Quoted by Rouch, in Milza 1987, 716. See also Noiriel 1984.

13. Letters addressed to A.-M. Blanc, the author of a novel on Italian immigration in Lorraine (1978).

14. Malewska-Peyre, in *Les Temps Modernes,* 1985.

15. This can be explained by the fact that in mono-industrial regions, the model with which immigrant workers identified (until the 1950s) was the skilled worker or foreman in Lorraine.

16. D. Braun, *L'Equipe,* 28 January 1986.

17. His study was based on research conducted in 1958–1959. The second-generation Italians surveyed were between thirty and forty years old. By that time, differences between Sicilians and other Italians had disappeared. Of 128 individuals between twenty and sixty-five years old, 18% were unskilled workers, 39% were specialized workers, 30% were skilled workers, 14% were employees, and 1% were professionals.

18. ["*Carte de séjour*" means "residency permit"—Trans.]

19. *Carte de Séjour*'s main hit, "Douce France"—an ironic take on a song by Charles Trenet—indeed reflects the critical distance taken by second-generation youths with respect to national norms.

20. [S.O.S.-Racisme is an antiracist movement founded in the mid-1980s by young

Beur activists to protest against the rise of the far-right National Front party and violence against minority groups—Trans.]

21. In *L'Equipe,* 29 January 1986.

22. The film was canceled twice on French public television after the legislative elections of March 1986 and was finally shown on 11 November 1987.

23. In 1960, 2.3 million Italian-Americans still spoke Italian, compared with only 147,000 among the third generation. Between the second and third generations of Polish-Americans, the number of Polish speakers dropped from 1.5 million to 37,000; and from 422,000 to 39,000 from the second to the third generations of Yiddish speakers.

24. There are, of course, no reliable statistics on this matter. Jan Gruszynski (1977) has argued that upward social mobility was higher among third-generation Poles than among the native French.

25. A sociology of immigrant literature would be of interest here. Two major genres coexist: the novel and the testimony. In many cases, the novel appears to permit a certain "inauthenticity" that does not imply a denial of origins. The characters and situations are illustrative of immigrants' reality, but using fiction allows the authors to avoid confronting the dominant society, which is always quick to "catalogue" such works as "Russian," "North African," or "Jewish" novels, when in fact they tell the "true story" of French history. Writing one's testimony is far more pathetic. It is usually an exercise in which the author, out of dedication to the memory of loved ones, forces him- or herself to overcome years of conscious denial by recounting previously "forgotten" traumatic events. Such documents far from resembling ghost-written "false testimonies," form an aspect of new marketing strategies aimed at popular sectors of society. This is best exemplified by popular singer Linda de Souza's "image": that of a young Portuguese maid who became a star.

Five. Three Crises

1. From 1931 to 1935, there were approximately 210,000 naturalizations, counting children (according to Depoid 1942).

2. For the sake of accuracy, these differences should be understood against the backdrop of the overall economically active population, which also declined substantially between 1931 and 1936 but which increased slightly between 1975 and 1982.

3. Another sign that foreign women are increasingly integrated is that they display a growing tendency to marry French men. According to the INSEE, between 1971 and 1981 the total number of women to do so rose from 7,114 to 8,257. Whereas the number of Italian women who married French men decreased (from 1,528 in 1971 to 718 ten years later); among Algerians the number grew from 201 to 1,002.

4. I use these terms here without entering into the debates surrounding the definition of the terms "xenophobia" and "racism."

5. *Le Petit Marseillais,* 19 June 1881; see also Milza 1981.

6. Contemporary observers of these riots believed that they contributed to the disappearance of Italian "*petits métiers*" (odd trades) from major French cities.

7. *Le Monde,* 22 November 1977.

8. V. Borgogno in the journal *Peuples-Méditerranée* 1985.

9. In 1970, before the crisis, 71% of French workers believed there were too many North Africans in France. According to the authors of this study, "the dominant characteristic of these figures is that racial and xenophobic prejudice tends to

transcend the internal differentiation of the working class, which seems unified only in its refusal of foreigners" (Adam et al. 1970).

10. *Le Figaro,* 27 September 1973.

11. My source is an unpublished study of Pierre Loti's novels by Bernard Magné.

12. *L'Oeuvre,* 5 November 1925.

13. 25 June 1925; these two quotes are taken from Schor 1985, 360, 431.

14. "Marabunta" refers to the march of giant ants.

15. *Militant,* November 1983, quoted by Taguieff, in *L'Identité française* 1985, 101.

16. In his *Histoire des Français* (1972), Pierre Gaxotte was as silent on this matter as he had been loquacious forty years earlier.

17. *L'Etoile de l'Est,* 24 July 1905, quoted in S. Bonnet 1972, 190.

18. Bonnet (1974) showed that during the crisis of the interwar period, all the political parties tailored their position on immigration to satisfy their electoral constituencies. Under the Popular Front, as in the period following 1981, foreigners were disappointed by the failure of the left to keep its promises. It is true, however, that the "social gains" of the working class in 1936 also benefited immigrant workers.

19. See the research on the "*Tables du Temps*" carried out by the *Institut Français de la Presse* (1974–1982).

20. *Le Monde,* 21 June 1979.

21. Charles Ayoub (1937) evoked the incomprehension of Arab youths in the face of this law, which he regarded as the "farewell gift of barrister Saint-Auban" to his young colleagues.

22. *Le Temps,* 8 February 1935.

23. The high number of Romanian students was a tradition that dated back to the Second Empire (see NA F17 4513).

24. See *Le Monde,* 12 January 1980; *Le Nouvel Observateur,* 12 May 1980.

25. That such anti-immigrant projects today encounter greater legal obstacles does not mean that they necessarily fail. The present-day tendency is characterized by the use of euphemisms to bypass the law. When an automobile construction firm refuses to hire foreigners, it no longer states in its job announcements: "reserved for French citizens"; now it states: "strictly for OI"; *Le Monde,* 7 August 1987.

26. The thirty-odd television programs on immigration seen in France between 1980 and 1985 illustrate present-day stereotypes on the subject. Each nationality was represented by a given topic. "Problems facing the second generation" almost always referred to young North Africans (for example in "Islam 86," *l'Ennemi intime,* 23 June 1986, channel 2; "Aujourd'hui la vie," *Les Enfants d'Ali,* 20 March 1984; *Les Loubards et leurs victimes,* 8 April 1983, channel 2; "Féminin présent," *Une jeunesse à vif,* 22 February 1983, channel 1. Turks were presented as typical undocumented workers (5 October 1985, channel 3; 23 April 1985, channel 1). Blacks and Asians were used to illustrate the "richness of cultures" (the inevitable Senegalese "griot": 30 March 1983, channel 1; the music of Mali, 14 December 1981, channel 2). Jews were represented in the "historical" programs: *Histoire du peuple juif,* 13 June 1983; *Les Révolutionnaires du Yiddishland,* 3 November 1984, channel 2; *Mémoires juives,* 25 September 1980, channel 1.

27. [An administrative unit comprising the schools of a given city or group of cities and their environs—Trans.]

28. See the statistics published by the Ministry of Agriculture in 1929 and Mauco 1937.

29. Identical attitudes in the Lyons region are described by Grillo 1985.

Six. The Reconstruction of France

1. [The Club de l'Horloge is a far-right think tank that produced several of the National Front's ideologues; it is credited with "reinventing" the ideology of the neofascist right to make it more "modern" than its prewar predecessors—Trans.]

2. According to the personal study carried out by Mauco (1932), in a significant number of companies, the percentage of immigrant workers was slightly higher than census figures would indicate.

3. For Grenoble, see Blache 1931; for Lorraine, see Noiriel 1984.

4. For the 1920s, see Oualid 1929; for the period following the Second World War, see Granotier 1979. Whatever the period, the simple arrival of immigrant workers in a company represented a factor of depreciation from the perspective of French workers (see, for example, Condevaux 1928; Bachelard 1978). A segmentation of the labor force often occurred at the level of each industrial site, which labeled French workers as "peasant-workers" and immigrants as "pure" workers. In Savoy in 1950, 80% of workers living in industrial localities were of foreign origin (Bélanger 1958).

5. In the late nineteenth century, France slipped in a matter of years from the second to the fourth industrial rank in the world. Its renewal subsequently proved most spectacular in sectors that employed numerous immigrants.

6. Hiring a large number of border dwellers also helped in this respect. In each period of crisis, the supplying country had a duty to assist the unemployed. For the Belgian case, see Vannestre 1964.

7. This information is taken from Didier Braun's study in *L'Equipe,* 29, 30, and 31 January 1986.

8. See, for example, Argoutine 1953 and Léon Noël's preface to his essay.

9. This process has even influenced children's literature. Anne Chatel Babouchka, the granddaughter of a Russian émigré who as a child listened to her grandmother's memories from Russia, later made them her main source of inspiration (see *La Fée de l'étang,* Dargaud 1987).

10. D. Braun, *L'Equipe,* 28 January 1986.

11. In the interwar period, Spanish immigrants in the Minervois spoke patois. According to Gérard Cholvy, "the importance of immigration contributed to delaying *francisation* in Languedoc and even more in Roussillon" (1982).

12. Regarding Seyne-sur-Mer, one study states that "foreigners, who are naturalized French and who have been adopted by the city after decades of immigration, make the city as they work in large numbers in the shipyards; simply passing through, they remained. With time, every sector, every neighborhood of the city received something from the character of its inhabitants" (Martinencq 1982, 155).

13. Hence the following prediction by a Norwegian sociologist who studied Lorraine in the 1920s: "Once the population has been stabilized and foreigners more or less assimilated, industrialists will be confronted with a mass of much more class-conscious workers than has been the case until now. Foreign workers will never quite forget their origins, and what remains of their former nationality will reinforce their socialist spirit" (Sömme, quoted in Gani 1972).

14. *L'Express,* 30 June 1975.

15. "Civil laws are familiar only to jurists, that is, to those who have a direct interest in maintaining them as they are, good or bad, simply because they know" (Tocqueville, *Democracy in America*).

16. See, in particular, Sternhell 1983 or the more nuanced study in Marrus 1971; and Hyman 1979.

17. "Immigrant" is an American term. It appeared the same year in which the Constitution was drafted (Brun 1980).

18. A. Liehm, *Le Migrant,* 1986.

Conclusion. Toward a Sociohistory of National Assimilation

1. Elias referred to his relationship with France as "a unilateral love affair." "When Hitler came to power in 1933," he wrote, "I initially sought refuge in France. But the French university system was unwilling to accept me. In Great Britain, I was more fortunate and British libraries introduced me to the treasures of the French Middle Ages" (1982, 446–47). For those who believe the historical well-foundedness of the discourse of French "generosity" against historical reality, this is yet another incident that they would do well to consider!

2. This is the title to Mauss's most famous article, published in 1934. That the source of this study was a discussion of the nation, however, has often gone unnoticed. It is true that all references to the national phenomenon were dropped from the definitive version. Curiously, Mauss reproduced in 1935 the same confusions for which he (and Durkheim) had attacked Comte in 1913. To illustrate his argument that the techniques of the body were a "total social phenomenon," he borrowed examples indiscriminately from primitive and contemporary societies. He constantly reiterated the vague concept of "civilization," which twenty years earlier he had called inadequate to understand the specificity of contemporary societies (Mauss and Durkheim 1913).

3. For some theoretical arguments supporting this point, see Balibar, in *Les Temps Modernes* 1984.

4. Recent advances in molecular biology make it possible to identify individuals through "genetic prints." We can safely predict a bright future for this discovery.

5. *Journal Officiel,* Chambre des Députés, Documents et Débats Parlementaire, 10 October 1972.

6. Tocqueville (in "L'Ancien Régime") observed that the ideological and legal evolution of the second half of the eighteenth century had provoked the emergence of new and abstract words in everyday language.

7. D. Braun, *L'Equipe,* 29 January 1986.

Bibliography

Primary Sources

Between most sociologists' reluctance to explore the archives and traditional historians' attribution of unrelenting explanatory power to archival sources, I have chosen a third path. The files listed here were those appropriate to the topics under discussion and were consulted to fill the gaps existing in the literature or printed sources. Consequently, what follows is not an exhaustive catalogue of archives on the subject; such a catalogue would in any case be impossible to establish, given the current dispersal of sources.

National Archives

Series AS

47 AS: Catalogue of archives kept at the Center of Research and Documentation on Contemporary China (1981)

49 AS: Association of former officers of the S.M. *Maria Feodorovna* battleship regiment (1892–1970)

Series BB

BB 12: Name changes (1815–1830)

BB 18: Assassinations of Italian political refugees (1837–1838)

Series C

C 943; 947; 960; 963: Labor survey, departments of Seine, Bouches-du-Rhône, Moselle, and Bas-Rhin (1848)

C 3336; 3365; 3367; 3371: Parliamentary survey of labor, departments of Bouches-du-Rhône, Meurthe-et-Moselle, Nord, and Pas-de-Calais (1884)

C 3325; 5404; 5486; 5594; 7323; 7725: Chamber of Deputies, legislative bills on immigration and foreigners (1880–1918)

Series F

F1 A 3345–3346, 3364: Jewish and foreign affairs (1944–1947)
F1 C III Bouches-du-Rhône 7 and 13: Prefecture reports (1848–1870)
F2 I, 380, 441: Civil status (Year XI [1827]) and naturalizations of foreigners
F2 I 1694–1696: Census instructions (1866–1891)
F2 106 34: Foreigners; administrative precedents (Year V [1825])
F2 I 448: Problems regarding national borders
F2 2701; 2548; 2549; 2560–2561; 2623: Municipal council deliberations concerning foreigners Haute-Savoie, Meurthe-et-Moselle, Meuse, and Pas-de-Calais (1932)
F7 3884–3893: Paris Bulletin (1830–1845)
F7 3942; 4104–4106: Police reports (1828–1845)
F7 11925–11980: Movement of foreigners (1814–1837)
F7 12076–12078; 12112–12119: Spanish and Portuguese refugees (1831–1832)
F7 12251–12594: Surveillance of foreigners
F7 12641–12646: Espionage, border surveillance
F7 12975–76, 13012: Monthly prefecture reports, Bouches-du-Rhône and Pas-de-Calais (1919–1925)
F7 13066–67: Spanish anarchists (1908–1909)
F7 13436; 13437; 13438; 13487–13490; 13466: Activities of Armenians, Belgians, Chinese, Russians, and Italians (1918–1931)
F7 13518–13519: Foreign labor force
F14 12352: Foreign workers employed in public works by the government (1917)
F17 2451–2452: Distribution by nationality of academic ranks (1892–1903)
F17 4513: Authorization for foreigners to practice medicine (1836–1864)
F17 9255, 9270 A: Situation of primary schools, Bouches-du-Rhône and north (1873–1885)
F17 13954: Statistics on foreign students (1927–1948)

Other Archival Collections Consulted

Economic and Financial Archives (EFA) of Fontainebleau

B 33241: Activities of foreigners in financial circles
B 39914–39916: Foreigners' identity cards (1917–1943)

Departmental archives (DA) of Meurthe-et-Moselle (MM):

4 M 136: Foreigners; circulars and instructions (1826–1916)
6 M 296: Naturalizations

Archives of the National Audiovisual Institute

Survey of programs concerning immigration aired by public television (1981–1985)

Archives of the Pont-à-Mousson Society

d. 41512: General Assembly proceedings (1915–1939)
d. 41734–41736: Congress of factory executives (1919–1939)

d. 18715; 25665: Problems related to the recruitment of the labor force

d. 18202: Immigration association of the eastern ironworks and mines; minutes of sessions (1924–1929)

Documentation Center

Center of Documentation on the press; political science library; press clippings (1945–1985)

d. 473/10: Status of foreigners; naturalizations
d. 473/11; 473/13: North African workers and other foreigners
d. 473/20: Political émigrés
d. 473/91 and 92: Refugees and stateless individuals

Secondary Sources

Abou-Saada, G., and H. Milet, eds. 1986. *Générations issues de l'immigration.* Paris: Arcantère.
Adam, G., F. Bon, J. Capdevielle, and R. Mouriaux. 1970. *L'Ouvrier français en 1970.* Paris: Colin.
Agel, L. 1889. *De la Nationalité d'origine.* Thèse de droit. Paris: Giard et Jouve.
Ageron, C.-R. 1968. *Les Algériens musulmans et la France (1871–1919).* Thesis in history. Paris: PUF.
Agulhon, M. 1980. "Conscience nationale et conscience régionale en France de 1815 à nos jours." in J. C. Boogman, ed. *Federalism: History and the Current Signification of a Form of Government.* The Hague: Nijhoff.
Albert-Birot, P. 1983. "Les Amusements naturels." In *Poésies IV (1945–1967).* Paris: Mortemart-Rougerie.
Albou, A. 1930. *Etude sur la tuberculose des travailleurs indigènes algériens dans les grandes villes (France et Algérie).* Thesis in medicine. Alger: Imprimerie Moderne.
Althusser, L. 1977. *Reading Capital.* London: NLB. (1st ed. 1966)
Amendola, G. 1983. *L'Ile.* Paris: Messinger. (1st ed. 1980)
Amiot, M. 1986. *Contre l'Etat les sociologues.* Paris: Ed. EHESS.
Amselle, J. L., ed. 1985. *Au Coeur de l'ethnie: Ethnie, tribalisme, et Etat en Afrique.* Paris: La Découverte.
Anderson, B. 1992. *Imagined Communities.* New York: Verso. (1st ed. 1983)
Anderson, R. T., and G. Anderson. 1962a. "Ukrainian Night Courting." *Anthropology Quarterly,* Jan.
———. 1962b. "Voluntary Association among Ukrainians in France." *Anthropology Quarterly,* Oct.
Andréani, A. 1896. *La Condition des étrangers en France et la législation sur la nationalité française.* Paris: Guillaumin.
Anglade, J. 1976. *La Vie quotidienne des immigrés en France de 1919 à nos jours.* Paris: Hachette.
Archdeacon, T. J. 1983. *Becoming American.* New York: Free Press.
Arendt, H. 1951. *The Origins of Totalitarianism.* New York: Harcourt-Brace.
Argoutine, L. 1953. "Les Français d'origine étrangère." Mimeo.
Ariès, P. 1971. *Histoire des populations françaises.* Paris: Seuil. (1st ed. 1948)
Arnaudo, G. B. 1881. *Gli Italiani à Marsiglia: Lettere sei.* Turin: Roux, Favale.

Arnauld, A. J. 1975. *Les Juristes face à la société du XIXème siècle à nos jours.* Paris: PUF.

Association Française d'Anthropologie (AFA). 1986. "Inventaire et bilan critique sur les communautés immigrées dans leur rapport avec la société d'accueil française." Paris. Mimeo.

Ath Messaoud, M., and A. Gillette. 1976. *L'Immigration algérienne en France.* Paris: Entente.

Audiganne, A. 1860. *Les Populations ouvrières et les industries de la France.* 2 vols. Paris: Capelle.

Aymes, J.-R. 1983. *La Déportation sous le Premier Empire: Les Espagnols en France (1808–1814).* Paris: Publications de la Sorbonne.

Ayoub, C. 1937. *La Nouvelle Législation de la naturalisation en France.* Paris: Sirey.

Azaïs, R. 1876. *De la condition juridique des étrangers en France.* Thèse de droit. Paris: Georges Chamerot.

Azas, C. 1981. "Migrants espagnols dans le Biterrois (1886–1934): Contribution à l'étude des communautés viticoles languedociennes." Thèse de 3ème cycle. University of Paris V. Mimeo.

Azzano, L. 1985. *Mes Joyeuses années au faubourg.* Paris: France Empire.

Bachelard, G. 1964. *Poetic of Space.* New York: Orion Press.

Bachelard, P. 1978. *L'Industrialisation de la région du Centre.* Paris: Gilbert Clary.

Badia, G., ed. 1982. *Exilés en France: Souvenirs d'antifascistes allemands émigrés (1933–1939).* Paris: Maspero.

Baille, F. 1927. *Les Italiens en Provence devant nos lois de prévoyance et d'assistance.* Thesis in political science and economics. Toulon: Imprimerie J. d'Arc.

Banine. 1968. *La France étrangère.* Paris: Desclées De Brouwer.

Baratier, E., ed. 1969. *Histoire de la Provence.* Toulouse: Privat.

Barbara, A. 1985. *Mariages sans frontières.* Paris: Centurion.

Bardakjian, G. 1973. "La Communauté arménienne de Décines (1925–1971)." *Bulletin du Centre d'Histoire Economique et Sociale de l'Université de Lyon II.*

Barodet. 1880–1914. *Recueil des proclamations et des programmes électoraux, 1880–1914.* 6 vols. Paris: Imprimerie Nationale.

Baroin, H. 1935. *La Main-d'oeuvre étrangère dans la région lyonnaise.* Thesis in law. Lyon: Basc et Rieu.

Barou, J. 1987. "Genèse et évolution d'un village urbain: Un groupe d'émigrés algériens dans un ensemble d'ilôts du XVIème arrondissement de Marseille." *Ethnologie Française.*

Barrès, M. 1893. *Contre les étrangers: Etude pour la protection des ouvriers français.* Paris: Grande Imprimerie Parisienne.

Barrier, A. 1898. *La Police des étrangers et la taxe de séjour.* Paris: A. Rousseau.

Basmadjian, V. 1979. *Les Arméniens: Réveil ou fin?* Paris: Entente.

Beauchesne, H., and J. Esposito. 1981. *Enfants et migrants.* Paris: PUF.

Beaud, S. 1987. "Les Démographes français et l'immigration (1918–1950): Science sociale ou science politique?." D.E.A. thesis, EHESS-ENS. Mimeo.

Begag, A. 1986. *Le Gône du Chaâba.* Paris: Seuil.

Bekouchi, M. H. 1984. *Du Bled à la ZUP et/ou la couleur de l'avenir.* Paris: CIEM-L'Harmattan.

Bélanger, M. 1958. "L'Industrialisation des grandes vallées savoyardes et ses répercussions démographiques et sociales." Thèse de géographie, University of Grenoble. Mimeo.

Beltramone, A. 1966. *La Mobilité géographique d'une population.* Paris: Gauthier-Villars.
Benfredj, C. 1990. "L'Immigration algérienne en France (1900–1962)." Thèse de doctorat, University of Paris VII. Mimeo.
Ben Jelloun, T. 1988. *La Réclusion solitaire.* London: Quartert. (1st ed. 1976)
Bennani, J. 1982. *Le Corps suspect.* Paris: Galilée.
Benoit, S. M. 1931. *Histoire et méthodologie du recensement de la population aux Etats-Unis (1787–1930).* Paris: Sirey.
Bensimon, D., and S. Della Pergola. 1984. *La Population juive en France: Socio-démographie et identité.* Paris: CNRS.
Bérard, A. 1886. *L'Invasion des étrangers et la taxe de séjour.* Lyons: Mougin-Rusand.
Berdoulay, V. 1981. *La Formation de l'école française de géographie (1870–1914).* Paris: Imprimerie Nationale.
Berger, P. L., and T. Luckmann. 1971. *The Social Construction of Reality.* London: Penguin Books. (1st ed. 1967)
Berillon, 1920. *Les Caractères nationaux: Leurs facteurs biologiques et psychologiques.* Paris: Amédée Legrand.
Bering, D. 1992. *The Stigma of Names: Antisemitism in German Daily Life, 1812–1933.* Oxford: Polity Press. (1st ed. 1987)
Berjont, J. 1903. *De l'envahissement des étrangers en France (la Provence italienne).* N.p.: Imprimerie spéciale de la Ligue.
Bernard de Jardin, R. 1899. *Des professions que les étrangers peuvent exercer en France.* Thèse de droit. Paris: A. Pedone.
Berque, J. 1985. *L'Immigration à l'école de la République.* Report to the Ministry of Education. Paris: La Documentation Française.
Bertillon, A. 1896. *Signaletic Instructions Including the Theory and Practice of Anthropometrical Identification.* Chicago: Werner. (1st ed. 1893)
Bertillon, J. 1911. *La Dépopulation de la France.* Paris: Alcan.
Bertoquy, A. 1934. "Un Type d'émigration italienne: L'Emigration bergamasque." *Revue de Géographie Alpine.*
Bes de Berc, E. 1988. *De l'expulsion des étrangers.* Thèse de droit. Paris: A. Rousseau.
Bigallet, H. 1901. "Y a-t-il lieu de protéger le travail national en France contre l'immigration étrangère?" *Composition d'Economie Politique* Agrégation de droit.
Birnbaum, P., and J. Leca. 1990. *Individualism: Theories and Methods.* Oxford: Clarendon Press. (1st ed. 1986)
Blache, J. 1931. "Compte rendu du livre de M. Jouanny: 'Les Origines de la population de l'agglomération de Grenoble.'" *Revue de Géographie Alpine.*
Blanc, A. 1901. *L'Immigration en France et le Travail national.* Thèse de sciences politiques et économiques. Paris: A. Rey.
Blanc, A.M. 1978. *Marie-Romaine.* Metz: Ed. Serpenoise.
Blanchard, E. 1913. *La Main-d'oeuvre étrangère dans l'agriculture française.* Thèse de droit. Paris: Marcel Rivière.
Blanchard, R. 1906. *La Flandre.* Thèse de géographie. Lille: Danel.
———. 1936. *Grenoble.* Paris: Didier et Richard.
Bloch, M. 1953. *The Historian's Craft.* New York: Knopf. (1st ed. 1947)
———. 1960. *Seigneurie française et manoir anglais.* Paris: A. Colin.
Bonato, J. 1960. *A la sueur de ton front.* Paris: Alsatia.

Bonn, C. 1982. "Le Roman algérien contemporain de langue française." Thèse de lettres. Bordeaux. Mimeo.

Bonnafous, S. 1991. *L'Immigration prise aux mots.* Paris: Ed. Kimé.

Bonnet, J. C. 1974. "Les Pouvoirs publics et l'immigration dans l'entre-deux-guerres." Thèse de 3ème cycle. University of Lyon II. Mimeo.

———. 1975. "Etude des petits commerçants étrangers dans l'agglomération lyonnaise (1919–1939), à partir du registre du commerce." *Bulletin du Centre d'Histoire Economique et Social.* University of Lyon II. 1.

Bonnet, S. 1965. "Les Ouvriers migrants quotidiens des usines sidérurgiques de l'agglomération de Longwy (1962–1963)." 2 vols. Thèse de sociologie, University of Paris. Mimeo.

———. 1972. *Sociologie politique et religieuse de la Lorraine.* Paris: A. Colin.

Bonnet, S., and P. Humbert. 1982. *La Ligne rouge des hauts fourneaux.* Paris: Denoël.

Bonnet, S., C. Santini, and H. Barthelemy. 1962. "Appartenance politique et attitude religieuse dans l'émigration italienne en Lorraine sidérurgique." *Archives de Sociologie des Religions,* Jan.–June.

Borkowski, J. L. 1990. "L'Insertion sociale des immigrés et leurs enfants." *Données Sociales,* 310–14. INSEE.

Boubakri, H. 1985. "Le Petit Commerce immigré du Sud tunisien à Paris." Thèse de 3ème cycle (géographie), University of Strasbourg. Mimeo.

Boubeker, A., and N. Beau. 1986. *Chroniques métissés.* Paris: A. Moreau.

Boudjera, R. 1969. *Topographie idéale pour une agression caractérisée.* Paris: Denoël.

Boudon, R. 1981. *The Logic of Social Action.* London: Routledge and Kegan Paul. (1st ed. 1979)

Boudon, R., et al. 1963. "Ostricourt: Prenquête sur l'immigration polonaise en France." Paris: Centre de Sociologie Européene. Mimeo.

Bourdieu, P. 1982. *Ce que parler veut dire.* Paris: Fayard.

———. 1990. *The Logic of Practice.* Berkeley: Stanford University Press. (1st ed. 1980)

Bouvier, J. 1968. *Histoire économique et histoire sociale.* Geneva: Droz.

Brand, M. N. 1932. *Le Foyer français: Cours élémentaire et moyen suivi d'un lexique.* Paris: Author.

Braudel, F. 1980. *On History.* Chicago: University of Chicago Press. (1st ed. 1969)

———. 1988–1990. *The Identity of France.* London: Collins. (1st ed. 1986)

Brecht, B. 1966. *Poèmes 4 (1934–1941).* Paris: L'Arche.

Brisou, C., C. Maltone, and M. Rouch. 1989. *Comprar un pra: Des paysans italiens disent l'émigration (1920–1960).* Bordeaux: Ed. de la Maison des Sciences de l'Homme d'Aquitaine.

Brubaker, R. 1992. *Citizenship and Nationhood in France and Germany.* Cambridge, Mass.: Harvard University Press.

Brun, J. 1980. *America, America: Trois siècles d'émigration aux Etats-Unis (1620–1920).* Paris: Julliard/Gallimard.

Burdy, J. P. 1989. *Le Soleil noir: Formation sociale et mémoire ouvrière dans un quartier de Saint-Etienne, 1840–1940.* Lyons: Presses Universitaires de Lyons.

Bureau International du Travail (BIT). 1936. *La Statistique des étrangers.* Geneva: Etudes et Documents.

Cacérès, B. 1970. *La Solitude des autres.* Paris: Seuil.

Callovi, G. 1971. "Déracinés et intégrés." Thèse de sociologie. Paris: EHESS. Mimeo.

Carreno, J. A., A. Hayot, and F. Lesure. 1972. "Le Quartier de la Porte d'Aix à Marseille: Essai d'ethnologie d'un centre urbain." Maitrise d'ethnologie, University of Aix-Marseille. Mimeo.
Cassano, de. 1889. *Procès-verbaux sommaires du Congrès international de l'intervention des pouvoirs publics dans l'émigration et l'immigration.* Paris: Imprimerie Nationale.
Cassirer, E. 1953–1957. *The Philosophy of Symbolic Forms.* 3 vols. New Haven: Yale University Press. (1st ed. 1929)
Catani, M. 1987a. "Les *Scaldini* de Paris." *Terrain* 7.
Catani, M., ed. 1987b. "Le Rôle du mouvement associatif dans l'évolution des comunautés immigrées." Report on research carried out for the Ministry of Social Affairs. Paris. Mimeo.
Cauwes, P. L. 1869. *De la condition faite par la loi de recrutement aux enfants nés en France de parents étrangers et des modifications à y apporter.* Nancy: N. Collin.
Cavanna, F. 1978. *Les Ritals.* Paris: Belfond.
Centre National de Documentation Pédagogique (CNDP). 1985. "Répertoire des thèses universitaires sur l'immigration, soutenues en rance de 1953 à 1983." Montrouge. Mimeo.
Certeau, M. de. 1974. "L'Opération historique." In J. Le Goff and P. Norar, eds., *Faire de l'histoire,* vol. 1. Paris: Gallimard.
Chamboredon, J.-C. 1971. "La Délinquance juvénile: Essai de construction d'objet." *Revue Française de Sociologie,* July.
———. 1984. "Emile Durkheim: Le Social Objet de science." *Critique,* July.
Charle, C. 1977. "Champ littéraire et champ de pouvoir: Les Ecrivains et l'Affaire Dreyfus." *Annales ESC,* April–May.
Charrasse, D., and G. Noiriel. 1986. "Lorraine du Nord et anthropologie industrielle en France: Bilan provisoire." *Anthropologie et Sociétés,* 10.
Châtelain, A. 1946. "Influence de l'apport étranger sur les densités de population du Midi méditerranéen." *Les Etudes Rhodaniennes,* 21: 5–31.
———. 1948. "Méthodes d'enquêtes démo-géographiques: Les Recherches sur les étrangers dans la région lyonnaise." *Les Etudes Rhodaniennes,* 23: 121–26.
———. 1977. *Les Migrants temporaires en France de 1800 à 1914.* Thèse d'Etat (géographie). Lille: Atelier de reproduction des thèses.
Chaunu, P. 1974. "L'Economie, dépassement et prospective." In J. Le Goff and P. Nora, eds., *Faire de l'histoire,* vol. 2. Paris: Gallimard.
———. 1982. *La France.* Paris: Laffont.
Chevalier, L. 1962. Preface to C. Roland, *Du ghetto à l'occident: Deux générations yiddiches en France.* Paris: Minuit.
———. 1978. *Laboring Classes and Dangerous Classes in the First Half of the 19th Century.* New York: H. Fertig. (1st ed. 1958)
———. 1978. *Classes laborieuses et classes dangeureuses.* Paris: Librairie Générale Française. (1st ed. 1958)
Cholvy, G. 1982. "Déracinement et vie religieuse: Italiens, Espagnols, et Tisganes dans le Midi depuis 1830." *Recherches Régionales.*
Cicourel, A.-V. 1974. *Cognitive Sociology: Language and Meaning in Social Interaction.* New York: Free Press.
Club de l'Horlage. 1985. *L'Identité de la France.* Paris: Albin Michel.
Cohen, A. 1986. *Solal.* Paris: Gallimard. (1st ed. 1930)
Condevaux, J. 1928. *Le Mineur du Nord-Pas-de-Calais: Sa psychologie, ses rapports avec le patronat.* Lille: Danel.

Corbes, H. 1962. "L'Immigration anglaise dans les Côtes du Nord au XIXème siècle." *Société d'Emulation des Côtes du Nord.*

Cordeiro, A., and R. Verhaeren. 1977. *Les Travailleurs immigrés et la Sécurité Sociale.* Grenoble: Presses Universitaires de Grenoble.

Cordier, M. 1887. *Les Conditions de l'étranger en France.* Caen: Henri Deslenques.

Cornette, C. 1889. *L'Etat-civil des Italiens en France: Aide-mémoire des officiers d'état-civil.* Paris: Maresq Ainé.

Couder, L. 1987. "Les Immigrés italiens dans la région parisienne pendant les années vingt." Thèse d'histoire, Institut d'Etudes Politiques. Mimeo.

Coulon, M. 1911. *Témoignages (deuxième série).* Paris: Mercure de France.

Courgeau, D. 1970. *Les Champs migratoires.* Paris: PUF.

Craig, J. 1979. "Halbwachs à Strasbourg." *Revue Française de Sociologie,* 20.

Crémieux, B. 1936. "L'Emigration politique italienne et la France sous la monarchie de Juillet." *Revue des Etudes Italiennes.*

Crespo, G., and J.-J. Jordi. 1991. *Les Espagnols dans l'Ariégeois de 1830 à 1914.* Paris: Althantrope.

Cross, G. 1983. *Immigrant Workers in Industrial France: The Making of a New Laboring Class.* Philadelphia: Temple University Press.

Dalla Volta, R. 1906. "L'Emigration italienne et son récent accroissement." *L'Economiste Français,* 10 June.

Dallier, G. 1914. *La Police des étrangers à Paris et dans le département de la Seine.* Thèse de droit. Paris: A. Rousseau.

Danguillecourt, A. 1875. *La Condition des étrangers en France.* Thèse de droit. Paris: E. Plon.

Dantoing, A. 1974. "Une Manifestation de défense contre le travail étranger dans les mines du Pas-de-Calais en 1892." *Revue d'Histoire Belge Contemporaine.*

Daulatly, J. 1933. *La Main-d'oeuvre étrangère en France et la crise économique.* Paris: Domat-Montchrestien.

Defer, P. 1932. *Les Polonais à Troyes après 1870.* Troyes: Grande Imprimerie.

Depoid, P. 1942. *Les Naturalisations en France (1870–1940).* Paris: Imprimerie Nationale.

Desdevises, M.-C. 1977. "La Délinquance étrangère: Analyse statistique." Thèse de droit, University of Rennes. Mimeo.

Desnoyers, L., ed. 1844. *Les Etrangers à Paris.* Paris: Charles Warée.

Desrois, A. 1939. *Les Etrangers dans le département de l'Ain.* Thèse de lettres. Bellegarde: Sordag.

Dessare, E. 1976. *Mon enfance d'avant le déluge.* Paris: Fayard.

Dewitte, P. 1985. *Les Mouvements nègres en France (1919–1939).* Paris: L'Harmattan.

Dictionnaire général de l'Administration française. Paris: Imprimerie P. Dupont.

Didion, M. 1911. *Les Salariés d'origine étrangère en France.* Thèse de sciences politiques et économiques. Paris: Giard et Brière.

Dignan, D. 1981. "Europe's Melting Pot: A Century of Large-Scale Immigration into France." *Ethnic and Racial Studies,* April.

Domat, J. 1989. *Les Quatre Livres du Droit Public.* Caen: Publications de l'Université de Caen. (1st ed. 1697)

Dosse, F. 1987. *L'Histoire en miettes.* Paris: La Découverte.

Drelon, R. 1982. *Le Westphalak.* Paris: France-Empire.

Dreyfus, H., and P. Rabinow. 1982. *Beyond Structuralism and Hermeneutics.* Chicago: University of Chicago Press.

Drouard, A. 1983. "Les Trois Ages de la Fondation pour l'étude des problèmes humains." *Population,* 6.

Dubar, F., G. Gayot, and J. Hédoux. 1982. "Sociabilité minière et changement social à Sallaumines et à Noyelles-sous-Lens (1900–1980)." *Revue du Nord,* April.

Dubois, J. 1963. *Vocabulaire politique et social en France 1869–1872.* Paris: Larousse.

Duby, G., ed. 1972. *Histoire de France.* 3 vols. Paris: Larousse.

Ducellier, D. 1981–1982. "L'Immigration polonaise dans le bassin de Blanzy dans l'entre-deux-guerres." *Revue Périodique de la "Physiophile."* Montceau-les-Mines, Dec.–Jan.

Duchac, R. 1974. *La Sociologie des migrations aux Etats-Unis.* Paris: Mouton.

Duguit, L. 1907. *Manuel de droit constitutionnel.* Paris: A. Fontemoing.

Dupâquier, J., and M. Dupâquier. 1985. *Histoire de la démographie.* Paris: Perrin.

Dupeux, G. 1974. "L'Immigration britannique à Bordeaux au XIXème et au XXème siècle." *Revue d'Histoire de Bordeaux.*

Dupeux, G., ed. 1980. "Les Migrations internationales de la fin du XVIIIème siècle à nos jours." Paris: CNRS. Mimeo.

Dupin, L. 1900. *L'Immigration ouvrière en France.* Thèse de droit. Lyons: A. Storck.

Durand, P. 1910. *L'Identité du point de vue judiciaire: Son histoire.* Thèse de droit. Lyons: Imprimerie de la Revue Judiciaire.

Durkheim, E. 1933. *The Division of Labor in Society.* New York: Free Press. (1st ed. 1893)

———. 1951. *Suicide: A Study in Sociology.* New York: Free Press. (1st ed. 1897)

———. 1956. *Education and Sociology.* New York: Free Press. (1st ed. 1922)

Duroselle, J.-B., and E. Serra, eds., 1978. *L'Emigrazione italiana in Francia prima del 1914.* Milano: Franco Angeli.

Echinard, P. 1973. *Grecs et Philhellènes à Marseille de la Révolution française à l'indépendance de la Grèce.* Thèse de 3ème cycle. Marseilles: A. Robert.

Eisenstadt, S. N. 1954. *The Absorption of Immigrants.* London: Routledge and Kegan Paul.

Elias, N. 1982. *The Civilizing Process.* Oxford: Blackwell. (1st ed. 1939)

———. 1983. *The Court Society.* Oxford: Blackwell. (1st ed. 1969)

———. 1978. *What Is Sociology?* London: Hutchinson. (1st ed. 1970)

———. 1991. *The Society of Individuals.* Cambridge: Cambridge University Press. (1st ed. 1987)

Esmein, A. 1896. *Eléments de droit constitutionnel.* Paris: Larose.

Espace-Temps. 1986. "Braudel dans tous ses états." No. 34/35.

Espagne, M. 1991. *Bordeaux-Baltique: La Présence culturelle allemande à Bordeaux aux XVIIème et XIXème siècles,* Paris: CNRS, 1991

Espagne, M., M. Werner, and F. Lagier. 1991. *Le Maitre de langue: Les Premiers Enseignants d'allemand en France, 1830–1850.* Paris: Albin Michel.

Esprit. 1985. "Français et immigrés." Special issue, June.

Etienne, B. 1991. *L'Islam en France: Islam, etat, et société.* Paris: CNRS.

Ewald, F. 1985. *L'Etat-Providence.* Paris: Grasset.

Fabiani, J.-L. 1988. *Des philosophes de la République.* Paris: Minuit.

Faidutti-Rudolph, A. M. 1964. *L'Immigration italienne dans le sud-est de la France.* Thèse de géographie. Gap: Louis Jean.

Fanon, F. 1982. *Les Damnés de la terre.* Paris: Maspero.

Febvre, L. 1935. "L'Economique derrière le politique." Introduction to vol. 10 of *L'Encyclopédie Française, L'Etat Moderne.* Paris.

———. 1953. *Combats pour l'histoire.* Paris: Armond Colin.
———. 1962. *Pour une histoire à part entière.* Paris: EHESS.
Ferras, R. 1986. "L'Espagnol dans les campagnes du Biterrois." In Actes de Proceedings of the round table L'Etranger dans le monde rural. Avignon. Mimeo.
Ferro, M. 1985. *L'Histoire sous surveillance.* Paris: Calmann-Lévy.
———. 1986. "Au nom du père." *Espace-Temps* 34/35: 6–10.
Fishman, J. 1966. *Language Loyalty in the United States.* La Hague: Mouton.
Fitzgerald, Z. 1973. *Accordez-moi cette valse.* Paris: Laffont. (1st ed. 1932)
Folleville, D. de. 1880. *Traité théorique et pratique de la naturalisation.* Paris: A. Maresq.
Foucault, M. 1971. *The Order of Things: An Archeology of the Human Sciences.* New York: Pantheon Books. (1st ed. 1966)
———. 1972. *Histoire de la folie à l'âge classique.* Paris: Gallimand, coll. Tel.
———. 1982. "Deux Essais sur le sujet et le pouvoir." In H. Dreyfus and P. Rainbow, eds., *Beyond Structuralism and Hermeneutics.* Chicago: University of Chicago Press.
François, E. 1985. *Immigration et société en Europe occidentale (XVIème-XXème siècles).* Paris: Ed. Recherches sur la Civilisation.
Fridenson, P., and A. Strauss, eds. 1987. *Le Capitalisme français (XIXème-XXème siècles).* Paris: Fayard.
Furet, F. 1981. *Interpreting the French Revolution.* Cambridge: Cambridge University Press. (1st ed 1979)
Gallissot, R. 1985. "Un Regard sur l'histoire: Les Générations de l'entre-deux-guerres." *Revue Européenne des Migrations Internationales,* Dec.
Gand, M. 1853. *Code des étrangers ou état-civil et politique en France des étrangers de tout rang et de toute conduite.* Paris: Author.
Gani, L., ed. 1972. *Syndicats et travailleurs immigrés.* Paris: Editions Sociales.
Gans, H. J. 1982. *The Urban Villagers: Groups and Class in the Life of the Italian-American.* New York: Free Press. (1st ed. 1962)
Garagnon, P. 1955. "La Colonie arménienne de valence sur le Rhône (résumé d'un diplôme d'études supérieures par Mme Veyret)." *Revue de Géographie Alpine.*
Garcia, A. 1959. "Le Bassin houiller de l'Aveyron." *Revue de Géographie Pyrénéenne.*
Garfinkel, H. 1967. *Studies in Ethnomethodology.* Englewood Cliffs, N.J.: Prentice Hall.
Gaspard, F., and C. Servan-Schreiber. 1985. *La Fin des immigrés.* Paris: Seuil. (1st ed. 1984)
Gavignaud, G. 1983. *Propriétaires viticulteurs en Roussillon.* Paris: Publications de la Sorbonne.
Gaxotte, P. 1972. *Histoire des Français.* Paris: Flammarion.
Gellner, E. 1983. *Nations and Nationalism.* Cambridge: Cambridge University Press.
Gemähling, P. 1910. *Travailleurs au rabais.* Paris: Bloud et Cie.
Gentilini, M., et al. 1986. *La Santé des migrants: Rapport au ministre des Affaires sociales.* Paris: La Documentation Française.
Gervais de Lafond, P. 1934. *De l'etude et de l'exercice de la médecine en France par les étrangers.* Thèse en médecine. Tours: Arrault.
Ginzburg, C. 1980. "Signes, traces, pistes: Racimes d'un paradigm de l'indice." *Le Débat.*
———. 1989. *Clues, Myths, and the Historical Method.* Baltimore: Johns Hopkins University Press. (1st ed. 1986)

Girard, A. 1971. "Attitude des Français à l'égard de l'immigration étrangère: Enquête d'opinion publique." *Population,* Sept.–Oct.
Giresse, J.-L. 1867. *Essai sur la population.* Paris: Guillaumin.
Glasberg, Abbé. 1946. *A la Recherche d'une patrie: La France devant l'immigration.* Paris: Réalité.
Glazer, N., and D. P. Moynihan. 1963. *Beyond the Melting Pot.* Cambridge, Mass.: Harvard University Press.
Goffman, E. 1961. *Asylums.* New York: Anchor Books.
Gomar, N. 1931. *L'Emigration algérienne en France.* Paris: Les Presses Modernes.
Gordon, M. M. 1964. *Assimilation in American Life.* New York: Oxford University Press.
Gossiaux, J.-F. 1984. "L'Immigration polonaise à Nampcel." In M. Segalen et al., *Diversité des formes de la famille et évolution: Approches locales.* Paris: Centre d'Ethnologie Française.
Gousseff, C., and N. Saadier. 1983. "L'Immigration russe en France, 1920–1930." Maitrise, University of Paris I. Mimeo.
Grandjonc, J. 1974. *Marx et les communistes allemands à Paris: Vorwärts 1844.* Paris: Maspero.
Grando, R., J. Queralt, and X. Febrès. 1981. *Vous avez la mémoire courte. 1939: 500,000 républicains venus du Sud "indésirables" en Roussillon.* Perpignan: Chiendent.
Granotier, B. 1979. *Les Travailleurs immigrés en France.* Paris: Maspero. (1st ed. 1970)
Green, N. 1985. *Les Travailleurs immigrés juifs à la Belle Epoque.* Paris: Fayard.
———. 1986. *The Pletzl of Paris: Jewish Workers in the Belle Epoque.* New York: Holmes and Meier.
———. 1991. "L'Immigration en France et aux Etats-Unis: Historiographie comparée." *Vingtième Siècle,* 29 (Jan.–Mar.).
Grillo, R. D. 1985. *Ideologies and Institutions in Urban France: The Representation of Immigrants.* Cambridge: Cambridge University Press.
Gruszynski, J. 1977. "La Communauté polonaise en France de 1919 à 1975: Problèmes de l'intégration de trois générations. Thèse de 3ème cycle de sociologie. University of Paris V. Mimeo.
Guillaume, P., ed. 1990. *Etrangers en Aquitaine.* Bordeaux: Maison des Sciences de l'Homme d'Aquitaine.
Guillaumin, C. 1972. *L'Idéologie raciste: Genèse et langage actuel.* Paris: Mouton.
Guillon, M., and I. Taboada-Leonetti. 1986. *Le Triangle de Choisy.* Paris: CIEMM-L'Harmattan.
Guiomar, P. 1984. "Le Tableau géographique de la France." In P. Nora, *Les Lieux de mémoire,* vol. 1. Paris: Gallimard, 1984–1986.
Halbwachs, M. 1932. "Chicago expérience ethnique." *Annales d'Histoire Economique et Sociale,* Jan.
———. 1935. "L'Espèce humaine et les faits de population." In *L'Encyclopédie française,* vol. 7, *Peuples ou races.* Paris: Encyclopédie français.
———. 1992. *On Collective Memory.* Chicago: University of Chicago Press. (1st ed. 1964)
Handlin, O. 1959. *Immigration as a Factor of American History.* Englewood Cliffs, N.J.: Prentice Hall.
———. 1972. *A Pictorial History of Immigration.* New York: Crown Publishers.
Hansen, M. C. 1952. "The Third Generation in America." *Commentary.*

Harbulot, M.-C. 1977. "Bouligny: Ses mines, ses cités." Maitrise, University of Nancy II. Mimeo.

Hassoun, J.-P., and Y.-P. Tan. 1986. "Les Réfugiés de l'Asie du Sud-Est de langue chinoise." Research report of the Mission du Patrimoine Ethnologique, Paris. Mimeo.

Hastings, M. 1986. "Communisme et folklore: Etude d'un carnaval rouge." *Ethnologie Française*. April.

Hauser, C. 1978. "La Population italienne dans les vallées intra-alpines de Savoie du rattachement à la deuxième guerre mondiale (1860–1939)." Thèse de 3ème cycle (géographie). University of Paris I. Mimeo.

Hemingway, E. 1964. *A Moveable Feast*. New York: Scribner.

Hepp, E. 1862. *De la note d'infamie en droit romain: De la condition légale des étrangers en France*. Thèse de droit. Nancy: Berger-Levrault.

Higham, J. 1975. *Send These to Me: Jews and Other Immigrants in Urban America*. New York: Atheneum.

Hirschman, A. 1970. *Exit, Voice, and Loyalty*. Cambridge, Mass.: Harvard University Press.

———. 1982. *Shifting Involvements: Private Interest and Public Action*. Princeton: Princeton University Press.

Holdert, J. 1977. *En toi France, mes racines meurtries*. Paris: La Pensée Universelle.

Hollande, M. 1912. *La Défense ouvrière contre le travail étranger*. Thèse de droit. Paris: Blond et Cie.

L'Homme. 1980. *Formes de nomination en Europe*. Special issue, Oct–Dec.

L'Homme et la Société. 1985. *Racisme, antiracisme: Etranges etrangers*. Special issue, July–Dec.

Horowitz, D. 1992. "Immigration and Group Relations in France and America." In D. Horowitz and G. Noiriel, eds., *Immigrants in Two Democracies: French and American Experience*. New York: New York University Press.

Horowitz, D., and G. Noiriel, eds. 1992. *Immigrants in Two Democracies: French and American Experience*. New York: New York University Press.

Houzé de L'Aulnoit, A. 1885. *Les Ouvriers belges à Lille: Etude sur les conditions d'admissibilité des indigents étrangers aux secours publics*. Lille: Danel.

Hovanessian, M. 1992. *Le Lien communautaire: Trois générations d'Arméniens*. Paris: A. Colin.

Hugonnier, S. 1954. "Tempéraments politiques et géographie électorale dans deux grandes vallées intra-alpines des Alpes du Nord: Maurienne et Tarentaise." *Revue de Géographie Alpine*.

Hyman, P. 1979. *From Dreyfus to Vichy: The Remaking of French Jewry 1906–1939*. New York: Columbia University Press.

Iberraken, M. 1981. "Cinemas et télévisions face à l'immigration maghrébine en Europe: Analyse de la production filmique (1961–1979)." Thèse de 3ème cycle, University of Paris IV. Mimeo.

L'Identité française. 1985. Proceedings of Colloquium, March. Paris: Tierce.

Ikor, R. 1963. *Les Eaux mêlées*. 1st ed. 1955. Paris: UGE.

Imbert, L. 1926. "Les Malades étrangers dans les hôpitaux de Marseille." *Bulletin de l'Académie de Médecine*.

Ingouff, J. 1881. *De la naturalisation des étrangers en France: ses règles, ses formalités: qui est et qui devient français*. Paris: Maresq.

Inspection Générale des Etudes de la Seine. 1967. *L'Immigration des Espagnols dans le département de la Seine*. 4 vols. Paris: AUREG.

Institut d'Histoire du Temps Présent (IHTP). 1986. *"Réfugiés et immigrés d'Europe centrale dans le mouvement antifacsiste et la Résistance en France (1933–1945)*. 2 vols. Colloquium organized by the University of Paris VIII. Mimeo.
Institut National d'Etudes Démographiques (INED). 1940. *Français et immigrés: Nouveaux documents sur l'adaptation. Travaux et documents no. 20.* Paris: PUF.
———. 1947. *Documents sur l'immigration.* Paris: PUF.
———. 1953. *Français et immigrés: L'Attitude française, l'adaptation des Italiens et des Polonais,* ed. A. Girard and J. Stoetzel. Paris: PUF.
———. 1954. *Français et immigrés: Nouveaux documents sur l'adaptation. Travaux et documents n°1ç.* Ed. A. Girard and J. Stoetzel. Paris: PUF.
———. 1955. *Les Algériens en France.* Paris: PUF.
———. 1964. *Le Peuplement de Paris: Origine régionale, composition sociale, attitudes, et motivations.* Paris: PUF.
———. 1975. *L'Immigration étrangère en France, 1946–1973.* Paris: PUF.
———. 1981. *L'Argent des immigrés,* ed. J.-P. Garson and G. Tapinos. Paris: PUF.
———. 1982. *Les Enfants d'immigrés et l'enseignement du français.* Paris: PUF.
———. 1991. *Cent ans d'immigration: Etrangers d'hier, Français d'aujourd'hui.* Paris: PUF.
Institut National de la Statistique et des Etudes Economiques (INSEE). 1954–1982. *Recensements de la population.* Paris: Imprimerie Nationale.
———. 1977. *Pour une histoire de la statistique.* Paris: Imprimerie Nationale.
———. 1983. *Les Etrangers en France.* Paris: Imprimerie Nationale.
International Labor Organization (ILO). 1936. "La Statistique des étrangers." Etudes et Documents. Geneva: ILO.
Jacque, A. 1985. *Les Déracinés: Réfugiés et migrants dans le monde.* Paris: La Découverte.
Joas, H.-J. 1984. "Durkheim et le pragmatisme." *Revue Français de Sociologie* Oct.–Dec.
Journal Officiel, Chambre des Députés et Sénat. 1880–1914, 1945–1947, 1972–1973, and 1984. *Documents et Débats Parlementaires.* Paris: Imprimerie Nationale.
Joutard, P. 1983. *Ces voix qui nous viennent du passé.* Paris: Hachette.
Juret, A. 1947. "La Francisation des noms de personnes." *Population,* July–Sept.
Karady, V. 1982. "Le Problème de la légitimation dans l'organisation historique de l'ethnologie française." *Revue Française de Sociologie* Jan.–March.
Kayser, B. 1954. "Conséquences sociales et politiques des transformations démographiques dans un village des Alpes-Martimes." *Revue de Géographie Alpine.*
———. 1960. *Campagnes et villes de la Côte d'Azur.* Thèse de géographie. Monaco: Ed. du Rocher.
Kergoat, D. 1978. *Les Pratiques revendicatives ouvrières (processus revendicatifs et dynamiques collectives).* Paris: CNRS.
Keuroghlian, A. 1977. "Les Arméniens dans la région Rhöne-Alpes." Thèse de 3ème cycle, University of Lyons, II. Mimeo.
Khatibi, A. 1987. *Figures de l'étranger dans la littérature française.* Paris: Denoël.
Koestler, A. 1941. *Scum of the Earth.* New York: Macmillan.
Köll, L. 1981. *Auboué en Lorraine du fer.* Paris: Karthala.
Kowalski, E. 1945. "Les Immigrés au service de la France: Rapport présenté au Congrès national des immigrés le 25 janvier 1945 à Paris." Paris: CADI. Mimeo.
Kronowski, A. de. 1837–1838. *Almanac historique en souvenir de l'émigration polonaise.* Paris: Bourgogne et Martinet.

Kunhle, S. 1981. "Emigration, Democratization, and the Rise of the European Welfare States." In Per Torsik, ed., *Mobilization, Center-Periphery Structure, and Nation-Building.* Bergen: Universitätforlaget.
Laacher, S., ed. 1987. *Questions de nationalité.* Paris: CIEMM-L'Harmattan.
Labov, W. 1972. *Sociolinguistic Patterns.* Philadelphia: University of Pennsylvania Press.
Labrousse, E., ed. 1967. *Histoire sociale, sources et méthodes.* Paris: PUF.
Lacombe, P. 1894. *De l'histoire considérée comme une science.* Paris: Hachette.
Lambert, C. 1928. *La France et les Etrangers.* Paris: Delagrave.
Langlois, C., and C. Seignobos. 1898. *Introduction aux études historique.* Paris: Hachette.
Lannes, X. 1953. *L'Immigration en France depuis 1945.* The Hague: Nijhoff.
Lebovics, H. 1991. *True France.* Ithaca, N.Y.: Cornell University Press.
Le Bras, H., ed. 1985. *Population.* Paris: UGE.
———. 1986. *Les Trois France.* Paris: Odile Jacob/Seuil.
Le Bras, H., and E. Todd. 1981. *L'Invention de la France.* Paris: UGE.
Le Conte, R. 1908. *Etude sur l'émigration italienne.* Thèse de droit. Paris: Michalon.
Lefebvre, G. 1929. *Hommes-Travail.* Paris: Baudinière.
Le Febvre, Y. 1901. *L'Ouvrier étranger et la protection du travail national.* Paris: C. Jacques.
Legat, N.-J. 1832. *Code des étrangers.* Paris: Béchet Ainé.
Léger, A. and M. Tripier. 1986. *Fuir ou construire l'école populaire?* Paris: L'Harmattan.
Le Goff, J. 1986. "Le Changement dans la continuité." *Espace-Temps,* 34/35:20–22.
Lehmann, L. 1861. *De la condition civile des étrangers en France.* Thèse de droit. Paris: De Moquet.
Le Huu Khoa. 1986. "L'Immigration du Sud-Est asiatique: Les stratégies socio-professionnelles et la typologie de l'insertion. Report of an investigation made for MIRE, Paris.
Lejeune, P. 1980. *Je est un autre.* Paris: Seuil.
Lentacker, F. 1973. "La Frontière franco-belge: Etude sur les effets d'une frontière internationale sur la vie des relations." Thèse d'Etat (géographie), University of Lille III. Mimeo.
Lépidis, C. 1973. *L'Arménien.* Paris: Seuil.
Le Play, F., ed. 1856. "Tailleurs d'habit." *Ouvriers des Deux Mondes.*
———. 1859. "Paysan et savonnier de Marseille." *Ouvriers des Deux Mondes.*
Lequin, Y. 1977. *Les Ouvriers de la région lyonnaise (1848–1914).* 2 vols. Lyons: Presses Universitaires de Lyons.
———. 1988. *La Mosaïque France: Histoire des étrangers et de l'immigration.* Paris: Larousse.
Le Roy, E. 1955. "La Colonie russe dans les Alpes-Maritimes des origines à 1939." Ph.D. diss., Aix-Marseille. Mimeo.
Le Sueur, L., and E. Dreyfus. 1890. *La Nationalité: Commentaire de la loi du 26 juin 1889.* Paris: G. Pédone-Lamiel.
Levasseur, E. 1889. *La Population française.* 3 vols. Paris: A. Rousseau.
Lévi-Strauss, C. 1952. *Race and History.* Paris: UNESCO.
Lévy-Leboyer, M., and F. Bourguignon. 1986. *L'Economie française au XIXème siècle.* Paris: Economica.
Linhart, R. 1981. *The Assembly Line.* Amherst: University of Massachusetts Press. (1st ed. 1977)
Lochak, D. 1985. *Etranger de quel droit?* Paris: PUF.

Mairet, G. 1974. *Le Discours et l'historique.* Paris: Mame.
Malewska-Peyre, H., ed. 1981. "Crise d'identité et problème de déviance chez les jeunes immigrés." Centre de recherche sur l'éducation surveillée, Vaucresson. Mimeo.
Mangin, J. 1952–1953. "Réfugiés polonais dans les Hautes-Pyrénées." *Bulletin de la Société Académique des Hautes-Pyrénées.*
Marangé, J., and A. Lebon. 1980. *Démographie, immigration, naturalisation: Rapport remis au ministère du travail.* Paris: La Documentation Française.
———. 1981. *L'Insertion des jeunes d'origine étrangère dans la société française: Rapport au ministre du Travail.* Paris: La Documentation Française.
Marcel-Rémond, G. 1928. *L'Immigration italienne dans le sud-ouest de la France.* Thesis in law. Paris: Dalloz.
Marchal-Lafontaine, G. 1886. *L'Invasion pacifique de la France par les étrangers.* Paris: Dentu.
Margossian, K. 1975. *Odyssée d'un enfant arménien.* Paris: La Pensée Universelle.
Marié, M., et al. 1977. *La Fonction miroir.* Paris: Galilée.
Marrus, M.-R. 1971. *The Politics of Assimilation: The French Jewish Community at the Time of the Dreyfus Affair.* Oxford: Clarendon Press.
———. 1985. *The Unwanted: European Refugees in the 20th Century.* New York: Oxford University Press.
Marrus, M.-R., and R. Paxton, 1981. *Vichy France and the Jews.* New York: Basic Books.
Martial, R. 1931. *Traité de l'immigration et de la greffe interraciale.* Paris: Larose; Mons: Imprimerie Fédérale.
———. 1942. *Français qui es-tu?* Paris: Mercure de France.
Martin, J. 1908. *De la situation des ouvriers étrangers en France au point de vue des assurances ouvrières.* Châlons-sur-Marne: Martin.
Martinencq, J. 1982. "Ouvriers des chantiers navals et mode de vie: La Seyne-sur-Mer et son marché de l'emploi (1830–1981)." Thèse de sciences économiques. Paris: EHESS. Mimeo.
Mathorez, J. 1919–1921. *Les Etrangers en France sous l'Ancien Régime.* 2 vols. Paris: Champion.
Mauco, G. 1932. *Les Etrangers en France.* Thèse de géographie. Paris: Colin.
———. 1937. "Mémoire sur l'assimilation des étrangers en France." Paris: Institut international de coopération intellectuelle. Mimeo.
———. 1977. *Les Etrangers en France et le problème du racisme.* Paris: La Pensée Universelle.
Mauco, G., and A. Demangeon. 1939. *Documents pour servir à l'étude des étrangers dans l'agriculture française.* Paris: Herman.
Mauss, M. 1934. "Les Techniques du corps." Reprinted in C. Lévy-Strauss, ed., *Sociologie et anthropologie.* Paris: PUF, 1950.
———. 1920 (?). "Nation, nationalité, internationalisme." In vol. 3 of *Oeuvres.* Paris: Minuit, 1969.
———. 1927. "Divisions et proportions des divisions de la sociologie." In vol. 3 of *Oeuvres.* Paris: Minuit, 1969.
Mauss, M. and E. Durkheim. 1913. "Note sur la notion de civilisation." In vol. 2 of *Oeuvres.* Paris: Minuit, 1969.
Médecin, P. 1909. *Etude sur l'administration des étrangers en France. Thèse de droit.* Paris: Sirey.
Medzadourian, G. 1975. *Les Exilés de la paix.* Paris: Entente.

Meillassoux, C. 1975. *Femmes, greniers, et capitaux*. Paris: Maspero.
Michel, A. 1955. *Les Travailleurs algériens en France*. Paris: CNRS.
Miège, J. 1934. "Le Développement d'Ugine (Savoie) 1901–1933." *Revue de Géographie Alpine.*
Le Migrant. 1986. Colloque d'Aurillac. Aurillac: Gerbert.
Milza, P. 1981. *Français et Italiens à la fin du XIXème siècle*. Rome: Ecole Française de Rome.
———. 1983. "Le Fascisme italien à Paris." *Revue d'Histoire Moderne et Contemporaine,* July–Sept.
Milza, P., ed. 1987. *Les Italiens en France de 1914 à 1940*. Rome: Ecole Française de Rome.
Milza, P., and M. Amar. 1990. *L'Immigration en France au XXème siècle*. Paris: A. Colin.
Ministère de l'Agriculture. 1929. *Enquête sur les étrangers*. Paris: Imprimerie Nationale.
Ministère du Travail, Direction de la population et des migrations. 1977. "Répertoire des études en cours de réalisation sur les migrations internationales." Paris. Mimeo.
Miroz, J. 1979. "L'Immigration polonaise en Bourgogne au XXème siècle: Textes et documents." Association Culturelle Franco-Polonaise Warzawa, Dijon. Mimeo.
Moheau. 1912. *Recherches et considérations sur la population de la France*. Paris: P. Geuthner. (1st ed. 1778)
Moine, J.-M. 1987. "Les Maitres de forge en Lorraine du milieu du XIXème siècle aux années trente." Thèse de doctorat (histoire), University of Nancy II.
Montgomery, D. 1979. *Workers' Control in America*. Cambridge: Cambridge University Press.
Morazé, C. 1942. "La leçon d'un échec: Essai sur la méthode de François Simiand." *Mélanges d'Histoire Sociale,* 1.
Moulier Boutang, Y., J.-P. Garson, and R. Silberman. 1986. *Economie politique des migrations clandestines de main-d'oeuvre*. Paris: Publisud.
Muñoz-Perez, F., and M. Tribalat. 1984. "Mariages d'étrangers et mariages mixtes en France: Evolution depuis la première Guerre Mondiale." *Population,* May–June.
Muraciolle, L. 1950. *L'Emigration algérienne: Aspects économiques, sociaux et juridiques*. Alger: Ferraris.
Nadaud, M. 1976. *Léonard, maçon de la Creuse*. Paris: Maspero. (1st ed. 1895)
Naudeau, L. 1931. *La France se regarde*. Paris: Hachette.
Néré, J. 1959. "La Crise industrielle de 1882 et le mouvement boulangiste." Thèse d'Etat (histoire), University of Paris–Sorbonne. Mimeo.
Nguyen Van Yen, C. 1987. *Droit de l'immigration*. Paris: PUF.
Niceforo, A. 1907. *La Police et l'enquête judiciaire scientifique*. Paris: n.p.
Nicolay, T. 1987. "Quelques aspects démographiques et sociologiques de l'immigration d'étrangers dans le bassin houiller de Lorraine. Nancy: CREDES. Mimeo.
Nicolet, C. 1982. *L'Idée républicaine en France*. Paris: Gallimard.
Noiriel, G. 1982. "Les Ouvriers sidérurgistes et les mineurs de fer dans le bassin de Longwy (1919–1939)." Thèse de 3ème cycle, University of Paris VIII. Mimeo.
———. 1984. *Longwy: Immigrés et prolétaires (1880–1989)*. Paris: PUF.
———. 1989. "L'Histoire de l'immigration dans l'enseignement supérieur et dans la recherche aujourd'hui." In P. Vieille, ed., *L'Immigration à l'université et dans la*

Recherche: Rapport au ministre de l'Education nationale, special issue of *Babylone,* 6–7 (May).

———. 1991a. *La Tyrannie du national: Le droit d'asile en Europe, 1793–1993,* Paris: Calmann-Lévy.

———. 1991b. *Workers in French Society in the 19th and 20th Centuries.* Oxford: Berg. (1st ed. 1986)

———. 1993a. "L'Identification des citoyens: Naissance de l'état civil républicain." *Genèses* 13, Sept.

———. 1993b. "Le Journal indigène comme matériau d'enquête: Traces et indices de la vie quotidienne d'une famille immigrée." *Genèse,* 12 (May): 114–30.

———. 1994. "Foucault and History: The Lessons of a Disillusion. *Journal of Modern History,* Sept. 1994

———. 1995. *Sur la "crise" de l'histoire.* Paris: Belin.

Nora, P. 1984–1986. *Les Lieux de mémoire.* 4 vols. Vol. 1: *La République*; vol. 2: *La Nation.* Paris: Gallimard.

Nord, P. 1981. "Le Mouvement des petits commerçants et la politique en France, 1888–1914." *Le Mouvement Social,* Jan.

Nourrissier, F. 1950. *L'Homme humilié.* Paris: Spes.

Nourrissier, F., and A. Pillepich. 1951. *Enracinement des immigrés.* Paris: Bloud et Gay.

O'Brien, P., and C. Keyder. 1979. "Les Voies de passage vers la société industrielle en Grande-Bretagne et en France." *Annales ESC,* Sept.–Oct.

Offerlé, M. 1985. "Mobilisation électorale et invention du citoyen: L'Exemple du milieu urbain français à la fin du XIXème siècle." In P. Gaxie, ed., *Explications du vote.* Paris: Presses de la Fondation Nationale des Sciences Politiques.

Office Départemental d'Action Culturelle de l'Hérault (ODACH). n.d. *Paroles: Histoire d'une migration: Des Espagnols racontent....* Montpellier: ODACH.

Ollier, C. 1981. *Nébules.* Paris: Flammarion.

Oriol, M. 1979. "Identité produite, identité instituée, identité exprimée: Confusion des théories de l'identité nationale et culturelle." *Cahiers Internationaux de Sociologie* 16.

———. 1981. "Bilan des études sur les aspects culturels et humains des migrations internationales (1918–1979)." Strasbourg: Fondation Européenne pour la Science. Mimeo.

Oriol, M., and M. C. Hily, eds. 1985. "Les Réseaux associatifs des immigrés en Europe occidentale." Nice: IDERIC. Mimeo.

Oualid, W. 1929. "Les Travailleurs étrangers en France: Leur répartition professionnelle et sociale." *Revue Internationale du Travail,* Aug.

Paczkowski, A. 1978. "La Presse des émigrés polonais en France (1920–1940)." *Revue du Nord,* Jan.–March.

Pairault, A. 1926. *L'Immigration organisée et l'emploi de la main-d'oeuvre étrangère en France.* Thèse de sciences économiques et politiques. Paris: PUF.

Paon, M. 1926. *L'Immigration en France.* Paris: Payot.

Papault, A. 1933. *Le Rôle de l'immigration agricole étrangère dans l'économie française.* Thèse de droit. Paris: Marcel Giard.

Pasquet, L. 1927. *Immigration et main-d'oeuvre étrangère en France.* Paris: Rieder.

Paulucci di Calboni, M. de. 1895. *L'Italie vagabonde.* Paris: Davy.

Péguy, C.-P. 1986. "L'Universe géographique de Fernand Braudel." *Espace Temps* 34/35: 77–82.

Peraldi, M. 1986. "La Frontière mobile: Destins migrants et réseaux politiques locaux à Marseille." Intermediate report of research done for MIRE, Marseilles. Mimeo.

Perrin, J. 1925. *La Main-d'oeuvre étrangère dans les établissements du bâtiment et des travaux publics en France.* Paris: PUF.
Perrot, M. 1960. "Les Rapports entre ouvriers français et étrangers (1871–1893)." *Bulletin de la Société d'Histoire Moderne,* 1.
———. 1987. *Workers on Strike: France 1871–1890.* Oxford: Berg. (1st ed. 1974)
Petonnet, C. 1985. *On est tous dans le brouillard.* Paris: Galilée.
Piore, M. 1979. *Birds of Passage and Promised Lands: Long-Distance Migrants and Industrial Societies.* Cambridge: Cambridge University Press.
Polanyi, K. 1944. *The Great Transformation.* New York: Columbia University Press.
Pomian, K. 1986. *L'Ordre du temps.* Paris: Gallimard.
Ponty, J. 1981. "Des Polonaises parlent." *Revue du Nord,* July–Sept.
———. 1985. "Les Travailleurs polonais en France." 3 vols. Thèse d'Etat (histoire), University of Paris I. Mimeo.
Portemer, J. 1959. "L'Etranger dans le droit de la Révolution française." In *L'Etranger.* Brussels: Recueil de la Société Jean Bodin.
Portes, A., and R. G. Rumbaut. 1990. *Immigrant America: A Portrait.* Berkeley: University of California Press.
Portet, J. 1882. *De la condition juridique des étrangers en France et de la naturalisation.* Evreux: Charles Hérissey.
Poszwa, L. 1930. *L'Emigration polonaise agricole en France.* Paris: Gebethner et Wolff.
Preux, A. 1860. *De la Naturalisation.* Douai: J. Six.
Projet. 1983. "Ces etrangers qui ont fait la France." Special issue. Jan.–Feb.
Raulin, A. 1987. "Mises en scène des commerces maghrébins parisiens." *Terrain,* 7.
Ray, J. 1937. *Les Marocains en France.* Paris: Lavergne.
Reardon, J. A. 1977. "Belgian Workers in Roubaix, France, in the 19th Century." Ph.D. diss., University of Maryland. Mimeo.
Rébérioux, M. 1984. *The Third Republic from Its Origin to the Great War (1871–1914).* Cambridge: Cambridge University Press. (1st ed. 1975)
Reid, D. 1985. "The Limits of Paternalism: Immigrant Coal Miner's Communities in France, 1919–1945." *European History Quarterly.*
Renan, E. 1992. *Qu'est-ce qu'une nation?* Introduction by J. Roman. Paris: Presses Pocket. (1st ed. 1882)
Repiton, I. 1986. "L'Opinion française et les émigrés russes à travers la littérature française de l'entre-deux-guerres. D.E.A. thesis, Institut d'Etudes Politiques. Mimeo.
Reybaud, L. 1863. *Le Coton.* Paris: Michel Levy.
Richard-Jalabert, E. 1974. "Les Réfugiés carlistes à Marseille pendant la Monarchie de Juillet." *Provence Historique,* April–June.
Riché, J. 1964. *L'Evolution sociale des mineurs de Ronchamp aux XIXème et XXème siècles.* Besançon: Jacques et Démontrond.
Ricklin, A. 1965. "Note sur l'évolution sociale des colonies d'ouvriers italiens." In *Artisans et ouvriers d'Alsace.* Strasbourg: Librairie Istra.
Robinson, M. 1978. *Les Canards majuscules.* Paris: Laffont.
Roche, D. 1986. "Les Historiens aujourd'hui: Remarques pour un débat." *Vingtième Siècle,* Oct.–Dec.
Rocher, L. 1928. "Les Élèves étrangers dans l'enseignement secondaire et dans l'enseignement primaire." *L'Enseignement Public.*
Roland, C. 1962. *Du ghetto à l'occident: Deux générations yiddiches en France.* Paris: Minuit.

Sabel, C. 1982. *Work and Politics.* Cambridge: Cambridge University Press.
Sabran, J. 1973. *Non! Aux villes tentaculaires.* Grenoble: Presses Universitaires de Grenoble.
Safran, W. 1989. "The French State and Ethnic Minority Cultures: Policy Dimensions and Problems." In Joseph A. Rudolph Jr., and Robert J. Thompson, eds., *Ethnoterritorial Politics: Policy and the Western World.* Boulder, Colo.: Lynne Rienner.
Sahlins, P. 1989. *Boundaries: The Making of France and Spain in the Pyrenees.* Berkeley: University of California Press.
Salah, A. 1973. *La Communauté algérienne dans les départements du Nord.* Lille: Presses Universitaires de Lille.
Salmon-Ricci, C. 1929. *La Naturalisation des étrangers en France: Etude critique de la loi du 10.8.1927.* Paris: Goddé.
Salque, J. et al. 1982. *L'Anniversaire de Thomas.* Villerupt: Studio 16.
Santucci, M.-R. 1977. "La Main-d'oeuvre étrangère dans les mines de La Grand'Combe jusqu'en 1940." Colloquium on Mines and Miners in Languedoc-Roussillon. Montpellier: Dehan.
Sapey, C.-A. 1843. *Les Etrangers en France sous l'ancien et le nouveau droit.* Paris: Joubert.
Sarraute, R. 1953. *Etude sur la situation juridique des immigrés en France.* Paris: Imprimerie Centrale Commerciale.
Sartre, J.-P. 1948. *Anti-Semite and Jew.* Trans. George J. Becker. New York: Schoken Books. (1st ed. 1945)
Sauvy, A. 1927. "La Population étrangère en France et les naturalisations." *Journal de la Société Statistique de Paris.*
Sayad, A. 1975. "El Ghorba: Le Mécanisme de reproduction de l'émigration." *Actes de la Recherche en Sciences Sociales,* March.
———. 1977. "Les Trois 'Âges' de l'émigration algérienne." *Actes de la recherche en Sciences Sociales,* June.
———. 1979. "Qu'est-ce qu'un immigré?" *Peuples-Méditerranée,* April–June.
———. 1991. *L'Immigration ou les paradoxes de l'altérité.* Brussels: De Boeck-Wesmael.
Schirmacher, M. 1908. *La Spécialisation du travail par nationalité à Paris.* Paris: A. Rousseau.
Schnapper, D. 1974. "Centralisme et fédéralisme culturels: Les Emigrés italiens en France et aux Etats-Unis." *Annales ESC,* Sept.–Oct.
———. 1980. *Juifs et Israélites.* Paris: Gallimard.
———. 1991. *La France de l'intégration: Sociologie de la nation en 1990.* Paris: Gallimard.
Schor, R. 1985. *L'Opinion française et les étrangers, 1919–1939.* Thèse d'Etat (histoire). Paris: Publications de la Sorbonne.
———. 1986. *L'Immigration en France, 1919–1939, sources imprimées en langue française et filmographie.* Nice: Université de Nice, Centre de la Méditerranée Moderne et Contemporaine.
Schramm, H., and B. Vormeier. 1979. *Vivre à Gurs: Un Camp de concentration français, 1940–1941.* Paris: Maspero.
Schütz, A. 1964. "The Stranger: An Essay in Social Psychology." In *Collected Papers II.* The Hague: Nijhoff. (1st ed. 1944)
Scott, J. W. 1974. *The Glassworkers of Carmaux: French Craftsmen and Political Action in a Nineteenth-Century City.* Cambridge, Mass.: Harvard University Press.

Seignobos, C. 1901. *La Méthode historique appliquée aux sciences sociales.* Paris: Alcan.
Serre, M. 1952. "Problèmes démographiques d'hier et d'aujourd'hui: Note sur l'immigration italienne à Toulon et dans le Var." *Revue de Géographie Alpine.*
Siegfried, A. 1946. "La France et les problèmes de l'immigration et de l'émigration." *Les Cahiers du Musée Social,* 2, no. 3.
Signoret, S. 1985. *Adieu Volodia.* Paris: Fayard.
Simiand, F. 1903. "Méthode historique et science sociale." *Revue de Synthèse Historique,* 6.
———. 1906. "La Causalité en histoire." *Bulletin de la Société Française de Philosophie,* May.
———. 1932. *Le Salaire, l'évolution sociale, et la monnaie.* 3 vols. Paris: Alcan.
Simon, P. J. 1981. *Rapatriés d'Indochine: Un Village franco-indochinois en Bourbonnais.* Paris: L'Harmattan.
Singer-Kerel, J. 1986. "La Population active étrangère au recensement de 1982." Paris: GRAMI, working paper no. 16, Oct. Mimeo.
Sociologie du Sud-Est. 1975. "Le Seuil de tolérance aux étrangers." Special issue. July–Oct.
Sokolniecki, M. 1910. *Les Origines de l'émigration polonaise en France (1831–1832).* Paris: Alcan.
Souza, L. de. 1984. *La Valise en carton.* Paris: Editions 13.
Sportiello, A. 1981. *Les Pêcheurs du Vieux Port: Fêtes et traditions.* Marseille: Jeanne Laffite.
Stasi, B. 1984. *L'Immigration: Une Chance pour la France.* Paris: Laffont.
Statistique Générale de la France (SGF) 1851–1936. *Recensements de population.* Paris: Imprimerie Nationale.
Stein, L. 1979. *Beyond Death and Exile: The Spanish Republic in France 1939–1955.* Cambridge, Mass.: Harvard University Press.
Steinberg, S. 1981. *The Ethnic Myth: Race, Ethnicity, and Class in America.* New York: Atheneum.
Sternhell, Z. 1978. *La Droite révolutionnaire.* Paris: Seuil.
———. 1983. *Ni droite ni gauche: L'Idélogie fasciste en France.* Paris: Seuil.
———. 1985. *Maurice Barrès et le nationalisme français.* Brussels: Complexe. (1st ed. 1972)
Stora, B. 1983. "Les Travailleurs indochinois en France pendant la deuxième guerre mondiale." *Les Cahiers du CERMTRI,* April. Mimeo.
Sudre, P. 1903. *Le Droit au nom.* Paris: Larose.
Taboada-Leonetti, I., and F. Levy. 1978. *Femmes et immigrées.* Paris: La Documentation Française.
Tahla, L., ed. 1983. *Maghrébins en France: Emigrés ou immigrés?* Paris: CNRS.
Taravella, L. 1983. "*Histoire sociale des habitants de Rocca di Ferriere émigrés dans la région parisienne à travers les récits biographiques.* Maitrise de sociologie, University of Paris VII. Mimeo.
Tarde, G. 1886. *La Criminalité comparée.* Paris: Alcan.
Tchernoff, J. 1938. *Dans le creuset des civilisations.* 4 vols. Paris: Rieder.
Temime, E., ed. 1990–1991. *Migrance.* 4 vols. Marseille: Edisud.
Les Temps Modernes. 1984. "L'Immigration maghrébine en France: Les faits et les mythes." Special issue. March–April.
Ternois, Y. 1967. *Zola et ses amis italiens.* Dijon: Presses Universitaires.
Ternon, Y. 1983. *La Cause arménienne.* Paris: Seuil.

Thelot, C. 1982. *Tel père, tel fils.* Paris: Dunod.
Thomas, W. I., and F. Znaniecki. 1958. *The Polish Peasant in Europe and America.* New York: Dover. (1st ed. 1918)
Thompson, E. P. 1975. *The Making of the English Working Class.* London: Penguin Books. (1st ed. 1963)
Tocqueville, A. de. 1952. *L'Ancien régime.* Oxford: Blackwell. (1st ed. 1856)
———. 1835–1840. Democracy in America. London: Saunders and Otley.
Tomasi, J. 1975. "Le Migrant dans l'entreprise." *Recherches Régionales.*
Toujas-Pinède, C. 1990. *L'Immigration étrangère en Quercy.* Toulouse: Privat.
Toulemonde, J. 1966. *Naissance d'une métropole.* Tourcoing: Georges Frère.
Touraine, A. 1981. *Le Retour de l'acteur.* Paris: Fayard.
Tournerie, J.-A. 1971. *Le Ministère du Travail.* Paris: Cujas.
Trempé, R. 1971. "La Main-d'oeuvre étrangère aux mines de Carmaux entre les deux guerres." *Revue du Tarn,* Dec.
Tribalat, M. 1986, "Natalité et fécondité des étrangères: Tendance à la baisse." *Population et Avenir,* July–Sept.
———. 1993. "Les Immigrés et les populations liées à leur installation en France au recensement de 1990." *Population,* 6.
Triolet, E. 1955. *Le Rendez-vous des étrangers.* Paris: Gallimard.
Troyat, H. 1958. *Strangers on Earth.* New York: Crowell. (1st ed. 1950)
———. 1987. *Un si long chemin.* Paris: Stock. (1st ed. 1977)
Turabian, A. 1928. *Trente Ans en France: Ma vie.* Marseilles: L'Aiguillon.
U.S. Bureau of the Census 1975. *Historical Statistics of the US: Colonial Period to 1970, Part I.* Washington, D.C.: GPO.
———. 1983. *1980 Census of Population.* Washington, D.C.: GPO.
———. 1986. *Statistical Abstracts of the US: 1985.* Washington, D.C.: GPO.
Vacher de Lapouge, G. 1909. *Race et milieu social.* Paris: Marcel Rivière.
Valdour, J. 1919. *Les Mineurs.* Paris: Giard et Rousseau.
———. 1929. *Sous la Griffe de Moscou.* Paris: Flammarion.
Valensi, L., and N. Wachtel. 1991. *Jewish Memories.* Berkeley: University of California Press. (1st ed. 1987)
Van Gennep, A. 1921. *Traité comparatif des nationalités.* Vol. 1, *Les Eléments extérieurs de la nationalité.* Paris: Payot.
Vannestre, O., ed. 1964. *Les Frontaliers de la Flandre occidentale dans le nord de la France.* Brussels: H. M. Schauman.
Vaux de Foletier, F. de. 1981. *Les Bohémiens en France au XIXème siècle.* Paris: Lattès.
Vejarano, F. 1985. "Les Naturalisés et leur destin." Thèse de 3ème cycle (démographie historique). Paris: EHESS. Mimeo.
Verneuil, H. 1985. *Mayrig.* Paris: Laffont.
Viargues, R. 1982. "Formes et contenu de la motivation des actes administratifs: L'Exemple des décisions d'expulsions des ressortissants étrangers." *Revue de Droit Public.*
Vidalenc, J. 1979. "Les Etrangers en Seine-Inférieure jusqu'au milieu du XIXème siècle." *Etudes Normandes.*
Videlier, P., and B. Bouet. 1983. *Vénissieux de A à V.* Lyons: Presses Universitaires de Lyons.
Vingtième Siècle. 1985. "Etrangers, immigrés, Français." Special issue.
Wacquant, L. 1994. "The Comparative Structure and Experience of Social Exclusion: 'Race,' Class, and Space in Chicago and Paris." In R. Lawson, C. McFate, and W.

J. Wilson, eds. *Urban Marginality and Social Polity in America and Western Europe*. Newbury Park, Calif.: Sage Publications.
Walraff, G. 1986. *Tête de Turc*. Paris: La Découverte. (1st ed. 1984)
Walter, G. 1935. *Le Problème de la main-d'oeuvre en Lorraine désannexée*. Mâcon: J. Buguet-Comptour.
Weber, E. 1976. *Peasants into Frenchmen*. Stanford, Calif.: Stanford University Press.
Weber, M. 1949. *On the Methodology of the Social Sciences*. Glencoe, Ill.: Free Press.
———. 1968. *Economy and Society*. New York: Badminster Press. (1st ed. 1919)
Weil, P. 1991. *La France et ses étrangers: L'Aventure d'une politique d'immigration, 1938–1991*. Paris: Calmann-Lévy.
Whyte, W. F. 1943. *Street Corner Society*. Chicago: Universitiy of Chicago Press.
Wihtol de Wenden, C. 1988. *Les Immigrés et la politique*. Paris: Presses de la Fondation Nationale des Sciences Politiques.
Wilson, S. 1977. "Le Monument Henry: La Structure de l'antisémitisme en France. *Annales ESC*.
Winock, M. 1982. *Edouard Drumont et Cie*. Paris: Seuil.
———. 1986. *La Fièvre hexagonale*. Paris: Calmann-Lévy.
Wirth, L. 1928. *The Ghetto*. Chicago: University of Chicago Press.
Wlocevski, S. 1935. *Les Mineurs polonais en France*. Lens: Imprimerie Druck.
Zehraoui, A. 1971. *Les Travailleurs algériens en France: Etude sociologique de quelques aspects de la vie familiale*. Paris: Maspero.
Zweig, S. 1943. *The World of Yesterday*. New York: Viking Press.
Zonabend, F. 1980. "Le Nom de la personne." *L'Homme*, Oct.–Dec.

Index

Compiled by Eileen Quam and Theresa Wolner

Gérard Noiriel was born in 1950 in Nancy (France), and after obtaining his *agrégation* in history in 1975, he graduated with a Ph.D. from the University of Paris VIII in 1982. From 1983 to 1985, he was a lecturer in modern history at the University of Paris VII, and from 1985 to 1994 a lecturer in social history at the Ecole Normale Supérieure (ENS) in Paris. Currently, he is both director of research at the Ecole des Hautes Etudes en Sciences Sociales (EHESS) in Paris, and director of the joint graduate program in social sciences at the EHESS and ENS. In addition to *The French Melting Pot,* he has published *Longwy, immigrés et prolétaires (1880–1980)* (1984); *Workers in French Society in the 19th and 20th Centuries* (1990); *La Tyrannie du national: Le Droit d'asile en Europe (1793–1993)* (1991); and *Population, immigration et identité nationale en France (19e–20e siècles)* (1992), as well as numerous articles on historical methodology and the comparative history of immigration in France and the United States. He is also an editor of the interdisciplinary social science journal *Genèses.*

Geoffroy de Laforcade graduated with a Ph.D. in history from Yale University in 1995, specializing in the social and labor history of migration and port cities. His current research focuses on Buenos Aires and Marseilles. He is the coordinator of the international research network (History of Nationalism, Racism, and Migration in Europe [HINARME]), which has 175 members in thirteen countries. He has translated into French *True France: The Wars over Cultural Identity, 1900–1945,* by Herman Lebovics (1995), and *Boundaries: The Making of France and Spain in the Pyrenees,* by Peter Sahlins (1995), and has translated into English numerous articles and conferences by Gérard Noiriel, in particular "Foucault and History: The Lessons of a Disillusion" (1994).

Charles Tilly is University Distinguished Professor at the New School for Social Research, New York City, where he directs the Center for Studies of Social Change. His recent books deal with popular struggles in Europe, European cities and states, and revolutions. His *European Revolutions, 1492–1992* won the 1995 Amalfi Prize.